Nature in Grace

National Association of Baptist Professors of Religion

JOURNAL

Perspectives in Religious Studies
Editor: Watson Mills
Mercer University

SERIES

Special Studies Series
Editor: Watson Mills
Mercer University

Dissertation Series
Editor: Charles Talbert
Wake Forest University

Bibliographic Series
Editor: E. Glenn Hinson
Southern Baptist Theological Seminary

NATURE IN GRACE

A Study in the Theology of Nature

NABPR Dissertation Series, Number 3

by
Claude Y. Stewart, Jr.

MERCER UNIVERSITY PRESS, Macon, Georgia 31207

ISBN 0-86554-068-3

BT
695.5
.S73
1983

All books published by Mercer University Press are produced
on acid-free paper that exceeds the minimum standards set by
the National Historical Publications and Records Commission.

Library of Congress Cataloging in Publication Data

Stewart, Claude Y., 1940-
    Nature in Grace.

    (NABPR dissertation series ; no. 3)
    Bibliography: p. 301.
    Includes index.
    1. Nature—Religious aspects—Christianity.
I. Title. II. Series.
BT695.5.S73   1983   261.8'362   83-8196
ISBN 0-86554-068-3 (pbk.)

TABLE OF CONTENTS

PREFACE   ix

PREFACE TO THE NABPR EDITION   xiii

NOTE ON LINGUISTIC PRACTICE   xv

ACKNOWLEDGMENTS   xvii

CHAPTER 1
Introduction:
The Theology of Nature: Whence, Whither—and Why?   1
  A. The Theology of Nature and the Doctrine of Creation   6
  B. The Theology of Nature and Ecological Ethics   15
  C. Medieval Precursors of a Contemporary Theology
     of Nature   15
  D. Recent Pioneers of a New Theology of Nature   23
  E. Issues in the Theology of Nature   34

PART ONE
Charting the Landscape:
  Three Contemporary Approaches
    to the Theology of Nature   37

CHAPTER 2
A Neo-Reformation Theology of Nature:
  The Approach of H. Paul Santmire   39
  A. Humankind's Dilemma before Nature   40
    1. The Modern Bifurcation of Experience   41
    2. Nature as a Problem in the Modern Church   45
  B. The Nature of the Theology of Nature   50
  C. Beyond the Dilemma: The Theology of Co-Citizenry   56
    1. The Kingdom of God as Creative Rule
      and Created Realm   60
    2. The Relationship between Humankind and Nature   73

D. Towards an Ethic of Ecological Renewal: Responsibility
   and Ecstasy   79
E. Conclusion   82

CHAPTER 3
A Whiteheadian Theology of Nature: The Approach of
   of John B. Cobb, Jr.   89
   A. Foundations: The Major Foci of
      Cobb's Theological Concerns   91
      1. Structures of Existence   91
      2. Vision of Reality   97
   B. Critical Analysis: "The Need for a New Vision"   102
   C. Methodological Interlude: A Christian Natural Theology and a
      and a Christian Theology of Nature   108
   D. Reconstruction: "The New Vision We Need"   115
      1. A "New" Vision of Reality   116
         a. Foundation of an Ecological Attitude   116
         b. God as Creative-Responsive Love   125
         c. Nature as Historical   133
         d. A Process Theodicy   136
      2. A "New" Christian Existence   141
         a. The Creative Transformation of Christian Existence   141
         b. Of Vision and Venture   148
   E. Conclusion   151

CHAPTER 4
A Neo-Catholic Theology of Nature:
   The Approach of Pierre Teilhard de Chardin   161
   A. Teilhard as Theologian of Nature   162
   B. The Teilhardian Vision: Foundations   168
      1. The Vision of the Past: From Cosmogenesis
         to Anthropogenesis   168
      2. The Vision of the Future: From Anthropogenesis
         to the Omega Point   175
   C. The Theology of Nature as Christological Problem   182
      1. "Christogenesis": Incarnation and Eucharistic
         Transformation   185
         a. The Incarnation as Historical Event   186
         b. The Incarnation as Personal Center of Creation   188
         c. The Incarnation as Physical Center of Creation   190
         d. The Incarnation as Continuing Historical-Organic
            Event   191
      2. Christ: Redeemer and "Evolver"   193
         a. Original Sin Reconsidered   194
         b. Redemption of a World in Evolution   199

3. "Christogenesis": Creation and "Pleromization"   209
   a. Building the Earth: The Sanctification of Endeavor   210
   b. Alpha and Omega: Creation as Creative Union   215
   c. Creation and Incarnation: The Fulfillment   221
D. Conclusion   222

PART TWO
Surveying the Horizons: Towards an Alternative Approach
  to the Theology of Nature   235

CHAPTER 5
The Three Approaches: A Retrospective Synopsis   237
  A. Conclusions Foundational and Methodologial   237
  B. Conclusions Metaphysical and Theological   238
    1. The Nature of "Nature"   238
    2. Nature as Complexifying Temporal Process   239
    3. Humankind's Place in Nature   243
    4. God and Nature   244
    5. Christ and the Cosmos   250
  C. Conclusions Axiological and Ethical   252

CHAPTER 6
"Metatheology" and the Theology of Nature   255
  A. Metaphors, Models, and Paradigms   256
  B. Major Models of God and the God-World Relationship   258
    1. The Deistic Model   259
    2. The Dialogic Model   259
    3. The Monarchical Model   261
    4. The Processive-Organic Model   263
    5. The Agential Model   268
  C. Complementarity and Synthesis in Theological Models   276

CHAPTER 7
Conclusion
Nature and Divine Intentionality   283
  A. The Nature of "Nature" Reconsidered   283
  B. Process and Action   286
  C. Nature in Grace   290

APPENDIX
The Christian Paradigm: Its Distinctive Character   293

BIBLIOGRAPHY   301
INDEX   317

PREFACE

It was said that the seventies would be the decade of ecology. That prediction has proven to be but partially accurate at best. Many saw the first "Earth Day" (April 22, 1970) as marking the opening of a new era of ecological concern. In some quarters interest in the quality of the environment is deep-rooted and flourishing. But in most sectors of our local, national, and international communities, business (the term is used advisedly) goes on in fairly traditional patterns—patterns that are qualified here and there only by energy shortages, higher prices on goods and services, and somewhat stricter governmental regulations. Like other interests, vital concern for environmental quality proved to be ephemeral among most of those in whom concern was ever awakened at all. The result was that already by the mid-seventies there occurred a marked decline outside of the circle of professional ecologists in the number of significant publications dealing with ecological issues. That decline was dramatically apparent in the field of theology. Almost all the important attempts at constructing a new "ecological theology" or "theology of nature" had been issued in print well before 1975; and one important contributor to those efforts reported, as the seventies drew to a close, that publishers were reluctant to issue additional works in the field since the widespread interest in ecology had already waned.[1] Although a few articles and an occasional book of merit still made their way through the presses, the seventies did not quite prove to be the decade of ecology it was predicted they would be. It would be more correct to say that the early seventies constituted a half-decade given to vital ecological concern.[2]

In another sense also the prediction has proven to be but a half-truth. The environmental disruptions of this planet and the attitudinal patterns that have contributed to them are far too complex to be altered signifi-

---

[1]John B. Cobb, Jr. in conversation, 30 September 1977, at Harvard Divinity School.

[2]We are currently witnessing some renewal of interest in "ecology," both popular and scholarly, as "Earthday X" (22 April 1980) approaches and as the awareness becomes more general that environmental problems simply will not go away.

cantly in a mere decade. In a century, we may hope, new directions may be clearly in evidence—*if* grand enough efforts, both practical and theoretical, are sustained in the next several decades. But even if the efforts of the final quarter of this century do prove adequate to the challenge of setting in motion developments that lead to the averting of ecological catastrophe, we wanderers in the wilderness of environmental degradation, we searchers for the promised new land—and sky and sea—of our dreams will never enter into the heritage we seek; yet we may hope that our grandchildren, or perhaps our great grandchildren, will begin to inhabit the new land. However, if we fail, our generation and that of our children will almost certainly realize the inadequacy of our efforts; and succeeding generations (if there be any) will likely find the prospect of crossing over into a desirable new earthly habitation receding into the distant ages of the future, if not lost forever.

It is fitting, therefore, at the conclusion of the seventies—that purported "decade of ecology"—that we review how far we have come in order better to measure the distance that remains to be traveled and that we take stock of the provisions we have for our journey toward the "new land." The issues and decisions are complex and multi-dimensional, and cartographers of many kinds are needed. Some can chart our progress, and lack of it, in practical affairs. Others can and are updating the rapidly increasing information in the young science of ecology.[3] My own efforts in this study are directed at reviewing and evaluating some of the major paths that have been explored during the twentieth century by Christian theologians who have become concerned about the renewal of philosophical and religious attitudes towards nature. Only by clarifying where we have come from and where we are today can we hope to ascertain with some assurance and adequacy the theological directions in which we need to move next—as we seek to fashion a new "theology of nature" and its correlative "ecological ethic" as part of the contribution of the theological-ethical community to the search for a "new land" or, in grander religious imagery, "a new heavens and a new earth."

This, then, is a work of cartography—and exploration. And many persons have, in a variety of ways, contributed to it. To each of them I owe a unique debt and have an especial sense of gratitude. I cannot, regrettably, mention all who have shared in and assisted with this study. But I want to register my gratitude to several.

---

[3]For the background of ecological thinking as well as an assessment of its present status, see Donald Worster, *Nature's Economy: The Roots of Ecology* (San Francisco: Sierra Club Books, 1977).

To my parents. They have stood with me during years of study, graciously encouraging my interests and projects and providing assistance in multiple ways.

To my children, Carlyle and Loren, who have been eager for me to complete my writing about nature so that we could resume hiking, camping, and canoeing.

To my wife, Chris, above all. She has been a companion to me in all the joys and struggles of the years of study culminating in this thesis. Typing is but the most evident of her contributions. My indebtedness to her is boundless, as is my gratitude. To Chris, this study is affectionately, and appreciatively, dedicated.

To my companions in the wilderness—Dr. Lewis E. Rhodes, Professor. W. Gale Rhodes, Professor David P. Young, and my brother, Robert—with whom I have shared many happy hours on trails in the Great Smoky Mountains, as well as in other, more prosaic, settings. These have helped nurture my interests and insights into the themes treated in this work. We are scattered now, but the memories bind us—and the common concerns.

To colleagues in two institutions. During my years at Maryville College, Dean Carolyn L. Blair, Professors David R. Cartlidge, Arthur S. Bushing, as well as Rhodes, Young, and others, provided support that has meant much. During two years at Southeastern Baptist Theological Seminary, I have had the generous assistance and encouragement of many friends and colleagues, especially President W. Randall Lolley, Dean Albert L. Meiburg, Professors John W. Eddins, Jr., G. Thomas Halbrooks, Glenn T. Miller, and James E. Tull. The invitation to give the Fall Faculty Lecture at Southeastern Seminary in 1978 provided the occasion for the sharpening of some of the ideas which have found expression in this study.

To students at Maryville College and Southeastern Seminary who have joined me in consideration of issues that lie at the interface of science and religion.

To Professor Sam H. Franklin, Jr., formerly of Tokyo Union Theological Seminary, and Dr. Victor F. Scalise, Jr., our pastor at The United Parish in Brookline, Massachusetts, for friendship and support extending over many years.

To Mr. Donald Dills of Dyersburg, Tennessee, who was with me in some of my youthful explorations of nature and who has now, after twenty years, rejoined me with assistance that has been vital to the completion of the explorations of nature recorded in this essay.

To Ms. Maria Cedargren of Harvard for patient assistance in attending to the many details associated with the presentation of a doctoral thesis.

To my teachers, Professors Gordon D. Kaufman, Richard R. Niebuhr, and Arthur C. McGill of Harvard Divinity School, Professor Herbert W. Richardson, formerly at Harvard and now at St. Michael's College in the University of Toronto, and Professor John B. Cobb, Jr. of the School of Theology at Claremont. I am especially grateful to Professors Niebuhr and Kaufman who have, in a variety of courses and ways, encouraged me over several years to dream new dreams and explore fresh horizons. My indebtedness to both—for superior teaching, for new insights, for openness and acceptance, for the vigorous challenges that result in new breakthroughs—is great. I am grateful, in particular, to Professor Kaufman for his guidance during the writing of this Th.D. dissertation. He has—through both encouragement and criticism—proven an excellent facilitator of this project. Moreover, through his writings, and in conversation, he has contributed greatly to the formation of my thinking on the subject matter of the thesis. My indebtedness to him is evident in the text and the notes, but it extends beyond what is recorded there.

Claude Y. Stewart, Jr.
Palm Sunday, 1980

PREFACE TO THE NABPR EDITION

My indebtedness grows. In addition to those mentioned in the original preface, I owe large, new, and very pleasant, debts of gratitude to several persons who have helped make possible the issuance of this study as part of the Dissertation Series sponsored by the National Association of Baptist Professors of Religion.

To Dr. Charles Talbert of Wake Forest University, Editor of the NABPR Dissertation Series, Dr. Watson E. Mills, Director of Mercer University Press, and Mr. Edd Rowell, Editor in Chief. They have enabled this publication in the most gracious, and competent, manner.

To Professor Gordon Kaufman and the faculty of Harvard Divinity School for recommending the dissertation for publication.

To Dean Morris Ashcraft and Southeastern Baptist Theological Seminary for making available the assistance necessary for the preparation of the manuscript.

To Ms. Carolyn Bailey and Ms. Nancy Howell for help with the correspondence, the indexing, and other details involved in readying the manuscript for publication.

To Ms. Diane Stewart for her efficient and competent work of typing an encoded text for usage in the automated typesetting process employed by Mercer Press.

To readers, both colleagues and students, who have made helpful suggestions and shared valuable insights.

Through their interaction and my own growth, I have been reminded of the limitations of this study. There are several points that I would develop differently were I writing now; in addition, I would carry further the process of trying to find alternatives to sexist linguistic conventions. I have, however, refrained from making significant alterations in the text. Since the volume is being issued as part of a dissertation series, I have limited revisions to minor editorial matters. My hope is that, its limitations notwithstanding, this study can contribute in some measure to the renewal of our perception of creation as the theater of the divine glory and to the enhancement of our capacity, as Christians, to value rightly *all* God's creatures, humankind and otherkind alike.

The publication of this study has for me the character of a conclusion and a prospectus. It brings to a certain close several years of effort. In so doing, it opens up the possibility of engaging in fresh explorations of some of the issues dealt with in the study, and of some that lie beyond it. If I am able to follow through in subsequent essays on some of those "explorations," I hope that those future efforts will show the influence of the many persons—family, friends, colleagues, and students—who have so generously encouraged me and entered into conversation with me about the reflections contained in this volume. That would be my best expression of gratitude.

Claude Y. Stewart, Jr.
19 October 1982

NOTE ON
LINGUISTIC PRACTICE

Since no generally accepted alternative to the generic usage of masculine pronominal forms has yet emerged, I have, with considerable discomfiture, followed traditional usage in this study (using "he" instead of "he/she" and the like). Usage of the nominal forms varies. Frequently, the traditional terms ("man," "mankind") are employed in a generic sense, especially in those cases in which this is the usage of the author under discussion. My usual wont, however, is to employ the more acceptable (but still not fully satisfactory) generic language of "humankind" and the like; and whenever I have been able to make such substitutions without undue awkwardness or distortion of the authors discussed, I have tended to do so. Although I have experimented with new forms in other contexts, no attempt has been made in this writing consistently to employ circumlocutions that would allow my talk about God to be free of masculine connotations. Again, in this essay, traditional usage is retained; but the need for new linguistic conventions—rooted in a renewed vision of the divine reality—is appreciated.

In referring to the "extra-human" dimension of creation, the terms "subhuman," "prehuman," and "otherkind" are generally used interchangeably—although at times the context dictates the employment of one term rather than another. The meaning of "nature" and its cognates is investigated in the text.

ACKNOWLEDGMENTS

Permission to quote excerpts from the following copyrighted publications is gratefully acknowledged.

Brother Earth: Nature, God and Ecology in Time of Crisis by H. Paul Santmire. Copyright © 1970 by H. Paul Santmire. Reprinted by permission of Thomas Nelson Publishers, Nashville.

Christ and Culture by H. Richard Niebuhr. Copyright 1951 by Harper & Row, Publishers, Inc. Reprinted by permission of Harper & Row, Publishers, Inc.

Christianity and Evolution by Pierre Teilhard de Chardin, translated by René Hague. Copyright © 1969 by Editions du Sevil, Paris; English translation copyright © 1971 by William Collins Sons & Co. Ltd, London and Harcourt Brace Jovanovich, Inc., New York. Reprinted by permission of Harcourt Brace Jovanovich, Inc.

A Christian Natural Theology: Based on the Thought of Alfred North Whitehead by John B. Cobb, Jr. Copyright © 1965 by W. L. Jenkins. Reprinted by permission of Westminster Press, Philadelphia.

The Divine Milieu by Pierre Teilhard de Chardin, translated by Bernard Wall. English translation copyright © 1960 by William Collins Sons & Co., Ltd., London and Harper & Row, Publishers, Inc., New York. Reprinted by permission of Harper & Row, Publishers, Inc.

Ecological Renewal by H. Paul Santmire and Paul E. Lutz. Copyright © 1972 by Fortress Press, Philadelphia. Reprinted by permission of Fortress Press.

Essays on Nature and Grace by Joseph A. Sittler. Copyright © 1972 by Fortress Press, Philadelphia. Reprinted by permission of Fortress Press.

"Five Ways of Reading Teilhard" by Ian G. Barbour. Published in *Soundings* 51:2 (Summer 1968):115-145. Copyright © 1968 by The Society for Religion in Higher Education. Reprinted by permission of *Soundings.*

The Future of Man by Pierre Teilhard de Chardin, translated by Norman Denny. English copyright © 1964 by William Collins Sons & Co., Ltd., London and Harper & Row, Publishers, Inc., New York. Reprinted by permission of Harper & Row, Publishers, Inc.

Review of Frederick Elder, *Crisis in Eden: A Religious Study of Man and Environment* by Claude Y. Stewart, Jr. Published in *Foundations* 14:2 (April-June 1971):189-192. Copyright © 1971 by the American Baptist Historical Society. Reprinted by permission of *Foundations*.

Saint Francis: Nature Mystic by Edward A. Armstrong. Copyright © 1973 by The Regents of the University of California. Reprinted by permission of the University of California Press.

Science and Christ by Pierre Teilhard de Chardin, translated by René Hague. Copyright © 1965 by Editions du Seuil, Paris; English translation copyright © 1968 by William Collins Sons & Co., Ltd, London and Harper & Row, Publishers, Inc., New York. Reprinted by permission of Georges Borchardt, Inc.

"Science and God's Action in Nature" by John J. Compton. Published in *Earth Might Be Fair*, edited by Ian G. Barbour. Copyright © 1972 by Prentice-Hall, Inc., Englewood Cliffs NJ. Reprinted by permission of Prentice-Hall, Inc.

The Self as Agent by John Macmurray. Copyright 1957 and 1969 by Faber and Faber, Ltd., London. (Humanities, Press, Inc., United States.) Reprinted by permission of Faber and Faber, Ltd.

The Structure of Christian Existence by John B. Cobb, Jr. Copyright © 1967 by The Westminster Press, Philadelphia. Reprinted by permission of John B. Cobb, Jr.

Teilhard de Chardin and the Mystery of Christ by Christopher F. Mooney. Copyright © 1964, 1965, 1966 by Christopher F. Mooney. Published by Harper & Row, Publishers, Inc., New York. Reprinted by permission of the author.

"Teilhard's Process Metaphysics" by Ian G. Barbour. Published in *The Journal of Religion* 49 (1969):136-159; copyright © 1969 by The University of Chicago Press. Reissued in *Process Theology: Basic Writings*, edited by Ewert H. Cousins. Copyright © 1971 by The Missionary Society of St Paul the Apostle in the State of New York. Reprinted by permission of the author and *The Journal of Religion*.

A Theology of Things by Conrad Bonifazi (J. B. Lippincott Company). Copyright © 1967 by Conrad Bonifazi. Reprinted by permission of Harper & Row, Publishers, Inc.

Toward the Future by Pierre Teilhard de Chardin, translated by René Hague. Copyright © 1973 by Editions du Sevil, Paris; English translation copyright © 1975 by William Collins Sons & Co. Ltd., London and Harcourt Brace Jovanovich, Inc., New York. Reprinted by permission of Harcourt Brace Jovanovich, Inc.

Writings in Time of War by Pierre Teilhard de Chardin, translated by Renë Hague. Copyright © 1965 by Editions Bernard Grasset. English

CHAPTER 1

INTRODUCTION: THE THEOLOGY OF NATURE: WHENCE, WHITHER —AND WHY?

"The heavens are telling the glory of God; and the firmament proclaims his handiwork" (Psalm 19:1).

"Holy, holy, holy is the Lord of hosts; the whole earth is full of his glory" (Isaiah 6:3).

The world is "the theater of God's glory." With this phrase John Calvin echoes the words of the psalmist and the prophet. With the ancient seers the reformer affirms that the splendor and majesty of God are manifested in the things that God has made. The world is the theater of God's glory. Calvin might just as well have said that the world is the theater of divine grace. For all of God's majestic dealings with the world have, in the view of the great reformer, the character of grace: creation is grace, providence is grace, redemption is grace, the final fulfillment is grace. The world as the theater of the divine glory is a world in which divine grace is manifested in God's dealing with, and his enjoyment of, that which he has made.

For John Calvin nature was a significant part of the worldly theater of the divine glory and grace. The emphasis in Calvin's thinking is upon God and humankind, but nature is not ignored. Humankind is of especial concern to God, but the prehuman dimensions of creation are valued by the Creator as well.

Calvin's view is typical—typical of the pre-modern understanding of the world, including nature, in its relationship to God. For Catholic and Protestant alike, the world of nature has been thought to reflect the glory and the grace of God. It is appropriately considered a theater of the divine splendor.

In recent times, however, a new attitude toward the natural world has come to dominance. Some of Calvin's own followers contributed to the emergence and triumph of the new view. It is appropriately denominated "the modern view."[1] In the modern view, nature is understood in ways that do not fit very well with the understanding of nature as a theater within which the divine glory and grace are manifested.

For many moderns nature has the character of a machine. The mechanical "model" has a long history. It dates back at least to the time of Galileo (1564-1642) and was promoted by Descartes, Newton, and Kant. In spite of the fact that contemporary physics has rendered it obsolete, it still controls the thinking of vast numbers of modern men and women, including many professional scientists and religionists.

Whenever nature and the humanity-nature relationship are understood in terms of the image of the machine, the character and value of nature and the character and value of humanity are radically distinguished. Galileo identified nature with that which is objective, unchanging (that is, given to conformity to "fixed laws"), and mathematical. He connected that which is subjective, changing, and sensible with humanity. Hence, nature is identified with that which is measurable (the "primary qualities"), while more elusive qualities (the "secondary") such as color, beauty, love, happiness, *et cetera.* belong to a sphere outside, or beyond, nature. With various kinds of refinements, this dichotomous pattern of thinking has persisted through centuries and is widespread today.

Viewed in terms of the mechanical metaphor, nature is something that can run by itself. God is not needed. He has no place within the mechanistic imagery, so he is either pushed back from the world (deism) or simply

---

[1] R. G. Collingwood labels this "the Renaissance view of nature" and reserves the appellation "modern" for very recent (post-Hegelian) understandings of nature. See *The Idea of Nature* (New York: Oxford University Press, 1960. First published, 1945). Since the view which achieved dominance at the time of the Renaissance has functioned, and continues to function, as one of the chief ideological foundations of "modernity," we shall denominate it "the modern view" and distinguish newly emergent (e.g., Bergsonian, Whiteheadian, Heisenbergian) understandings from it.

My brief characterization of the chief images for nature involved in the "modern view" is informed by several sources. In addition to Collingwood, the following, in particular, should be noted: E. A. Burtt, *The Metaphysical Foundations of Modern Science* (Garden City NY: Doubleday Author Books, 1954); Leo Marx, *The Machine in the Garden* (New York: Oxford University Press, 1964); Lewis Mumford, *Technics and Civilization* (New York: Harcourt, Brace and Company, 1943); Max Weber, *The Protestant Ethic and the Spirit of Capitalism*, trans. Talcott Parsons (New York: Charles Scribner's Sons, 1958); and various works by H. Paul Santmire (see chapter 2).

denied in theory or practice, or both (secularism). Humankind's relation to nature is of more significance than God's. Like God, humanity is excluded from nature; but the value of nature becomes dependent upon humanity. Because nature is lifeless and valueless in itself, its meaning and value become altogether dependent upon that for which humankind employs it.

This suggests the second image of nature that is widely presupposed in the modern world: nature is a tool and/or resource. This utilitarian metaphor for understanding nature and the humanity-nature relationship is primarily the product of the economic community. The mechanical view of nature and the utilitarian view are closely related; a machine is, after all, a tool. But the two metaphors suggest somewhat different things. The image of the machine indicates something about the structure and characteristics of the tool, whereas the images of tool and resource suggest something about the availability of the tool/resource for human manipulation and even exploitation.

The emergence of the utilitarian imagery was furthered by the development of what Max Weber called "the Protestant ethic." The true end of man, according to Calvinism, is to serve the glory of God. Moreover, the world exists for the glorification of God and for that purpose alone. Humanity becomes the agent for the glorifying of God by actualizing the ancient admonition to "subdue" the earth and "exercise dominion." Furthermore, Weber points out that this motif of glorifying God by worldly activity was coupled with the attempt to demonstrate one's election by worldly success. Work became within the Calvinist/Puritan ethos the way of contributing simultaneously to the greater glory of God and to one's own sense of security about the reality of one's election to salvation. To summarize, then, the world, or nature, exists to glorify God; humanity exists to glorify God and does so, in part at least, by "ruling" nature; believers confirm their election by worldly success. The result of this complex of attitudes was to make of nature resource and tool for human manipulation.

Weber contends that, from its inception on, the Calvinist ethos was intimately interwoven with "the spirit of capitalism." The capitalist entrepreneur, like the Calvinist faithful, believed that nature was basically resource and tool; however, the new breed of businessman considered the manipulation of nature to be the means of their own aggrandizement and the enhancement of their own wealth rather than the means of the glorifying of God and the furthering of God's cause. In any case, both Calvinist and capitalist—and consistently or not, they have tended historically to coalesce—adopted an attitude toward nature and humankind's relationship to the natural world that emphasizes the utilitarian character of nature. On this view, nature is depicted, above all, as a realm defined by its openness to manipulation and exploitation.

The third major image for nature that is widely used, or at least presupposed, by "modernity" is that of the stage. Understood as a stage nature is the impersonal setting of the human drama. The stage, be it noted, is not the entirety of the theater; and the stage can be understood over against both its maker and those who play upon it. As stage, nature has purely instrumental significance. Again, the sole sphere of (intrinsic) meaning and value is the human sphere; and the chief character and the sole worth of nature is its role as the setting or stage of the drama of personal existence. Even God is thought to have little or no interest in the setting he has provided for the human drama; rather, God cares only for the personal and historical dimensions of the drama itself. Nature has no purpose apart from humanity.

All three of the "models" or images that are characteristic of modern thinking about nature accent the dualism between humanity and nature, and they do so in such a way as to make humanity the source and center of the meaning of nature.[2] The mechanical, the utilitarian, and the instrumental views of nature—resting on the metaphors of nature as a machine, a resource, and a stage respectively—are all alike anthropocentric: they put man at the heart of things in such a way as to make the significance of that which is other than man depend solely upon him. He and he alone is, as it were, the final end of nature.

Now, I suggest that all of this is disgraceful! Or, better perhaps, disgracing. It is disgrace*ful* and disgrac*ing* to regard nature as a mere machine, mere resource, mere stage.[3] It is significantly disgraceful to regard God with respect to nature only as the creator of a world-machine, only as the provider of "resources," only as a shaper of the stage and scenery for human life. This is *dis*-gracing in at least two major ways. First, this is not a grace-*ful* view of nature because God has been pushed back, or excluded, from nature in such a way and to such an extent as to make it very difficult to make sense out of claims that God acts in the world of nature. When nature is understood as a machine, resource, and stage, God is understood as positing nature and then letting it go its merry way. The continuing operations of grace in nature are denied by all these

---

[2]The meaning of the terms "model," "metaphor," and the like is examined in Chapter 6.

[3]It must be allowed, even emphasized, that all these images are helpful and have a certain propriety so long as they are not developed in a reductionistic and exclusivistic fashion.

images. This is the metaphysical problem—and the first way in which nature is disgraced in the modern period. Secondly, the modern view is not a graceful view of nature because in it the value of nature is reduced to utilitarian or instrumental considerations alone. Nature as machine, resource, and stage is valuable only as it serves human purposes; it is not valuable in itself. It does not enjoy itself, nor is it enjoyed apart from its utility. Neither God nor humanity takes delight in nature for its own sake. This is the axiological problem, the problem of value. And in these two major ways nature is disgraced in the modern period: God is excluded from nature, and nature itself is devalued.

The problem is that have consequences. Disgraceful ideas lead to disgraceful results. The problematical, limited, modern understanding of nature affects our lives at every turn; and what is most pressing, the environmental crisis results from it. Since nature is mere thing—machine, resource, stage—we can do with it as we wish; and we proceed to exploit nature to the hilt. Our graceless understanding of nature leads us to treat nature disgracefully. Our question then is this: How can we come to see nature again as the arena of divine glory and grace? How can we recover for our day the vision of the psalmist, the prophet, and the reformer? What kind of theological understanding of nature will carry us beyond our modern difficulties with nature?

"Today we need a theology of nature as well as [a theology] of human existence," says scientist-theologian Ian Barbour.[4] The need for a theology of nature has become really clear only during recent decades—as the difficulties inherent in the "modern" but now obsolete view of nature have become manifest. Thus, the project of searching out, and developing, a viable theology of nature represents a significant new theological frontier.

New frontiers require explorers. Every frontier has its pioneers: those pathfinders and trailblazers who enter an uncharted territory and explore the horizons. The frontiers of the mind are like that. Theological frontiers are like that. And one of the theological frontiers of our time has to do with nature and the value of nature. Several hearty souls have taken up the challenge of exploring the uncharted territory of a twentieth century theology of nature. As a result, a number of paths have been opened up before us. Three in particular invite our exploration.

Frontiers require mapmakers as well as pathfinders and trailblazers. The two roles are not entirely separable, but they can be distinguished. The mapmaker follows the tracks of the pathfinders and charts the

---

[4]Ian G. Barbour, *Myths, Models and Paradigms* (New York: Harper & Row, 1974), 158.

landscape. So in this study we shall adopt the role of cartographer and retrace (in Part One) the steps of three contemporary theological pathfinders. Paul Santmire opens before us a Neo-Reformation path; John Cobb introduces us to a Neo-Naturalistic, Whiteheadian approach to the theology of nature; and Teilhard de Chardin leads us into a Neo-Catholic path. We shall retrace the steps of these pioneering pathfinders and sketch, as we go, a map of some of the outstanding features of the landscape that they have seen and have opened up to the rest of us. Then, after doing that, we shall try to add to our role of mapmaker that of pathfinder and attempt to suggest (in Part Two) where a further promising path may lie.

Before we proceed with the main part of our explorations, however, we need to get our bearings. Hence, Chapter One is given to orientation.

THE THEOLOGY OF NATURE AND THE DOCTRINE OF CREATION

We need to inquire, first, and in a preliminary fashion, about the relationship between the theology of nature and the classical Christian doctrine of creation. We have described the theology of nature as a new theological frontier, and it is that; but the novelty is relative and not absolute. For—as our introductory comments about John Calvin suggest and as this study in its entirety will substantiate—the theology of nature represents a refocusing, a continuation, an enlargement, and, at the same time, a restriction of the kinds of theological reflections that have traditionally been carried on under the rubrics of the doctrines of creation (especially) and providence.

If we could describe the new interest manifested in recent times in the "theology of culture" and of history as an elaboration (motivated in part at least by the emergence of modern historiography) of themes traditionally subsumed under the rubrics of creation and providence, then we might consider the newly emergent interest in the "theology of nature" as a parallel elaboration (occasioned in part at least by the impact of the natural sciences and environmental perturbations) of another set of themes ingredient to the classical doctrines. From this perspective, the theology of culture and the theology of nature are taken to be sister disciplines, "new" theological enterprises born of a common parentage. Both represent the offspring of the classical doctrines of creation and providence or, in slightly altered imagery, the "coming to age" within the contemporary context of interests ingredient to Christian thinking in all ages.[5] If this is the case, it is worthwhile at the beginning of this study (charting recent attempts to do the theology of nature) to review the function and character of the doctrine of creation, the traditional enterprise most closely related to the "new" theology of nature.[6]

Basically, the Christian doctrine of creation makes an affirmation about the relationship between God and the world. It specifies the status of God, both ontological and axiological, with respect to everything which is not God; and it specifies the ontological and axiological status of everything else, humankind and otherkind alike, with respect to God. These doctrinal affirmations are rooted in the reformulated creation myth(s) found in a variety of biblical writings: Genesis, Second Isaiah, certain Psalms, the Johannine works, Ephesians, and Colossians.

Critical examination of these various expressions of the biblical myth of origins reveals something important about the origin of the myth itself: it is derived from the Hebrew-Christian vision of God as the Lord of history, the "God who acts" to deliver his people from their various forms of bondage and to bring them (and thus the historical process which shapes them and which they help shape) to an appropriate fulfillment. This is the case in both the Old and the New Testaments. God is perceived first of all as the Redeemer who works in history for the historical and, for some biblical authors, the trans-historical transformation and completion of his people. The perception of God as the Creator and the vision of the world as creation are correlative implications of what is disclosed about God in his mighty acts of redemption. The doctrine of creation thus has its ultimate roots in an inference drawn from the nature of God as that is revealed in his acts of deliverance: preeminently, in the Old Testament, the Exodus from Egypt and, in the New Testament, the life, death, and resurrection of Jesus Messiah. The One who acts to restore and fulfill is

---

[5]This perspective involves an important corollary. Since the theology of nature is related by origin and common concern to the theology of history/culture, the two can be distinguished but never fully separated. The theologian of nature has his own particular interests; but he will be involved, ineluctably, at every turn with the conclusions of thinkers whose special province is human history and culture.

[6]My summary characterization of the doctrine of creation is informed by several sources, among them Langdon Gilkey's *Maker of Heaven and Earth* (Garden City NY: Doubleday & Company, 1959). All references are to the Anchor Books edition, 1965. Gilkey's book represents one of the best recent attempts to state the meaning of this unique Christian construction. Written from a Neo-Orthodox perspective, it is, however, like other Neo-Orthodox treatments of creation and providence, vitiated by a tension between the author's claim that the meaning of the doctrine is independent of the deliverances of the natural sciences and scientifically informed philosophies and a curious dependency upon those deliverances.

(inferred to be) the One who created his people, their companions, and the context in which their historical vocation is being actualized. The "Father all-governing," as the creed formulates it, is "the Maker of heaven and earth."

As this brief discussion indicates, consideration of the biblical myth of creation reveals that historical and soteriological considerations were controlling in the development of Hebrew and Christian reflection about "origins." Neither "old" nor "new" Israel engaged in abstract speculations about the question of ultimate origination for its intrinsic interest alone. Both were governed in their religious postulations and theological musings about creation by the need to discover what must be affirmed in order to make sense of their conviction that God is presently acting to effect the creative transformation of his people. Thus is suggested a second point of crucial consensus in Hebrew and Christian belief: the identity of the Redeemer and the Creator. The Redeemer is the Creator and the Creator is the Redeemer. This, says Langdon Gilkey, is "the most fundamental affirmation of the Old and the New Testaments," "the heart of the theological battles of the early church," "the dominant concern of the whole Christological controversy of the fifth century." "The identity of God the Creator and God the Redeemer, of the almighty power of existence with the love of Christ, is the theological axis of the Gospel. . . ."[7] Religiously, this identification means that salvation is to be understood as the restoration and/or completion of creation, rather than as an escape from the conditions and context of creatureliness.

Now, the doctrine of creation makes a number of highly significant affirmations. Schematically, we can treat them, in summary fashion, as affirmations about God, the world, and human existence; but it should be remembered that the three kinds of affirmations are interdependent throughout.

---

[7]Gilkey, *Maker of Heaven and Earth*, p. 250. It should be noted that in the New Testament the identity of the Redeemer and the Creator is interpreted in a christological fashion. Picking up certain Old Testament passages in which God is said to create through his word (Gen. 1, Ps. 3:6, 9) and his wisdom (Prov. 8:27, 29f.; Wisdom 7:22, 9:1, 9), some New Testament authors treat Christ, the chief agent of redemption, as the agent of creation (1 Cor. 8:6, Col. 1:16, Heb. 1:2, Jn. 1:3). The basic meaning of this identification appears to consist of the conviction that in the Messiah is manifest the meaning of the divine plan which began to unfold in the act of creation itself (Eph. 1:9f., Col. 1:16). History from beginning to completion is governed by the purpose of God—a purpose disclosed in Christ Jesus. Moreover, this is a purpose that cannot be actualized apart from God's action in Christ. Only in him, the Redeemer, is the divine purpose for humankind—and through human agency, the divine purpose for otherkind—completed; thus, precisely as Redeemer, he is also the agent of creation.

About God the classical doctrine maintains such things as the following: (a) God is the sovereign and transcendent source of all that is; (b) he is free and purposeful, hence personal; and (c) God is good. The affirmation of the divine sovereignty implies that the idea of God's lordship and his status as Creator are related. God's status with respect to creation is established by the doctrine of creation. He alone is unconditioned, self-sufficient, and independent of all else for his being; he alone, in the classical jargon, is *a se*. This means that God is transcendent. The doctrine of creation affirms God's otherness or distinctness from what he has made: he is "beyond," "above," and "before" the world. Various images (spatial, temporal, personal, and otherwise) are employed to suggest the mode of the divine otherness. Some of the ways of depicting the distinction of God and the world turn the distinction into a separation; others maintain the distinction while affirming also that "in him we live and move and have our being." In any case, the doctrine of creation denies an ultimate ontological dualism but affirms an ontological distinction between the created and the Creator. Forged historically over against both dualism and monism (or pantheism), the doctrine of creation has affirmed God to be the source of all else; and, for the most part, it has made this affirmation in such a fashion as to deny that God created out of pre-existent stuff (dualism) or out of the divine substance (monism, pantheism). He is said, rather, to have created "out of nothing"—by his word or will alone. This view of the divine originating agency protects, among other things, both God's sovereignty and his transcendence.

It also protects his freedom, (an aspect, to be sure, of his sovereignty) and suggests that creation is rooted, ultimately, in the divine purposing. Although the freedom and purposefulness of the Creator can be maintained apart from the *ex nihilo* doctrine, the latter makes clear the unconditioned character of the divine creative activity. God does not create because he has to by virtue of some external compulsion. He freely chooses to create; but his uncoerced decision and his creative action are in accord with what, or who, he is. Thus, the doctrine of creation eloquently denies that the divine reality is merely an impersonal structure or an automatic process, or a victim of powers within the world; and it affirms that God is, rather, a personal agent, free and purposeful in what he does.

This means that the doctrine of creation asserts the motive of creation to be nothing less than the goodness, that is, the love, of God. God creates because he is a lover, and it is of the essence of love to express itself (freely). God creates because he is good, and it is of the nature of goodness to communicate itself. Said Calvin: "There was no other cause why He should make all things, neither can He be moved by any other reason to conserve them, than for His only goodness."[8] Said Augustine: There is "this good and simple explanation of the creation of the world, namely, that it is the nature of a good God to create good things. . . ."[9]

About the world the classical doctrine of creation maintains such things as the following: (a) the world is dependent and real, and marked by a certain creaturely freedom; (b) it is orderly and, hence, intelligible; and (c) it is good. God's status with respect to creation is established by the doctrine of creation; correlatively, the status of everything else is established with respect to God. God is *a se*; the world is derived and dependent. Contingent, the world did not come into being of itself; but it has been posited or originated. The world depends upon another for its being and, in part at least, for its character. The doctrine of creation asserts the ontological dependency of the world upon God. Moreover, and this is related, the doctrine of creation affirms that what God has made, and is making, is in fact fully real in the whole and in all parts. Over against the tendencies of monistic philosophies to suggest that creaturely existence is less than fully real or is even altogether illusory—due to its distance from the divine originating center and/or to perspectival limitations—the doctrine of creation maintains that rocks, trees, and women are genuinely real. Finite existence, and the individuality characteristic of it, are not illusions to be overcome. Nor is the relative independence and freedom of finite entities illusory. Creaturely existents are derived and ultimately dependent, but they have been posited as relatively independent and self-shaping actualities. The world, including finite individual existents possessed of the various properties of finite existence, is fully real. Beyond the affirmation that the world is dependent and real are others: the world is orderly and intelligible. God has given shape to his world. There is a pattern to spatial relationships; we can draw maps. There is a pattern to time; our clocks and calendars reflect it. So God has created an orderly world, a world marked by relationships. And its orderliness is the basis of its intelligibility. Because the world is orderly, we can know it. If creation were a chaotic welter of events, science, and even ordinary life and knowledge, would be impossible. But because God has created a relational, orderly world we can know it.

Moreover, the world is essentially good. Since everything is the product of the creative agency of the good God, no finite entity can be intrinsically evil. "It is," said Augustine, "the nature of a good God to

---

[8]John Calvin, *Commentary on the Epistle of St. Paul to the Romans* (Edinburgh, Calvin Translation Society, 1844), p. 28. Cited by Gilkey, ibid., 79.

[9]St. Augustine, *The City of God*, ed. Vernon J. Bourke (Garden City NY: Doubleday & Company; Image Books, 1958), XI. 23 (p. 230).

create good things." Of everything in the Genesis story it is said, "And God saw that it was good." Included in the classical doctrine which is based on the ancient Hebraic insight is a positive valuation of matter, a respect for the value as well as the reality of finite individuality (human and subhuman), and a recognition that history is charged with significance. The world which results from, and is everlastingly rooted in, the divine purpose is congruent: it accords with the divine will and is thus, in the whole and all parts, essentially "good." The ancient story concludes with the claim that God surveyed the variegated results of his creative workings and pronounced them "very good." Implied in this pronouncement is a point which is voiced more clearly in recent formulations of the doctrine of creation than in the classical: that which is good is perfectible. That is, that which is good "in the beginning" can and will be good "in the end"—as the potentialities of creation are actualized, along however tortured a path.

About human existence the classical doctrine of creation maintains such things as the following: (a) human beings are creatures, thus dependent, real, relational, and good; (b) they are constituted *imago Dei* in their vocation and in the equipping for their vocation; (c) humankind has chosen an alien vocation and thereby disrupted the divine project of creation; and (d) the human vocation is being restored, and the project is being completed. The major affirmations about the character of the world ingredient to the doctrine of creation apply to the character of human existence also: humankind is ontologically dependent, "really real" in its finite individuality, relational, and essentially good. That is, human existence is creaturely existence; the general prerogatives of creaturehood humankind shares with all "kind."

But humankind, in biblical and classical Christian perspective, has its unique prerogatives. Humankind has a vocation that is relevant to, but not shared in, by otherkind. That vocation—the human vocation—and the equipping for it is given in the predicate applied to Adam and Eve by the Priestly writer(s): *imago Dei.*

> So God created man in his own image, in the image of God he created him; male and female he created them. And God blessed them, and God said to them, "Be fruitful and multiply, and fill the earth and subdue it; and have dominion over the fish of the sea and over the birds of the air and over every living thing that moves upon the earth."[10]

---

[10]Genesis 1:27-28. All biblical quotations are, unless otherwise specified, from the Revised Standard Version. The Hebrew term translated by "image" is *tezelem* (figure, form, statue) and is used, in Gen. 1:26a, in conjunction with *demuth* (likeness). The reformers maintained that the attempt, from Irenaeus onwards, to draw a sharp distinc-

The human vocation indicated by this ancient and economical phrase "in the image of God" is the noblest creaturely career conceivable. The human vocation consists of adopting the divine project of promoting creaturely good as the human project, and that in a twofold fashion. Humankind ("Adam") is to join with God in his creative workings by exercising "dominion" over otherkind—on God's behalf. Adam's call is at once a call to kingship and to stewardship. His is to be a lordship of servanthood.[11] As the "last" or noblest of God's creatures Adam is to rule creation on God's behalf, doing within and for the created realm what can be done by creaturely agency alone.[12] This is the first aspect of the human vocation. The second is related. Adam is called to fulfill the potentials of creation, not only by tending and furthering the welfare of otherkind, but by promoting the growth of community among his own kind. "God created man in his own image . . .; male and female he created them." Human existence, created *imago Dei*, is communal existence.[13] The divine creative project includes the actualization of the "male and female" character of "man." The second aspect of the unique human vocation consists of the creation of a universal family ("Be fruitful and multiply, and fill the earth . . .") of royal stewards united both biologically and in a common devotion to the Creator and his grand project—and thus to one another.

This, then, is the twofold human vocation given in that ancient predicate: *imago Dei*. Adam and Eve are "called" to further creation by caring for otherkind and building community among humankind. Yet more is given. Implicitly, the notion of being made in the image of God carries an affirmation of the divine equipping of humanity for the realiza-

---

tion between the two terms represents tortured exegesis. Most contemporary scholars appear to agree.

[11]This is not, of course, the usual or traditional reading of the dominion motif. If it were, the need for the kind of investigation this study represents might have been obviated.

[12]The older Yahwistic account of creation (Gen. 2:4ff.) depicts Adam as actualizing this aspect of his vocation in the function of naming "every living creature."

This Hebraic-Christian perspective on the human vocation as stewardly lordship stands in sharp contrast to the perception of the human status and task found in other ancient near Eastern myths of creation. For example, in the Babylonian account "the blackheaded ones" are the slaves of the gods, destined to attend to menial chores. In Israel's perception, Adam and his family have a royal calling.

[13]This is the deepest meaning of the Yahwistic account of the creation of woman from a rib of Adam: Eve is made out of the very stuff of "man," human stuff. The biological oneness of Adam and Eve is affirmed and completed in their sexual-social union. In becoming "one flesh" they actualize their communal nature and, at the same time, become the agents of the extension of the human community.

tion of its unique vocation. Being constituted *imago Dei* means being equipped or empowered for the vocation of world-ruling/tending and community-building. In addition to an appropriate biological structure, human existence is marked by rationality, freedom, responsibility, the capacity to love, and all the other prerequisites of a successful actualization of the divinely willed creaturely-fulfilling human vocation.[14]

But the creation story is not complete, nor is the doctrine based upon it, apart from Genesis 3 and all that follows in Scripture. The burden of the third chapter of the Book of Beginnings is that humankind has rejected its noble twofold calling in favor of another vocation and that, thereby, the divine project of creation has been disrupted. Faced with the challenge of being human, confronted by the call to actualize the human vocation and thereby to find the joy of the fulfillment appropriate to human existence, Adam and Eve have chosen—inexplicably—an alien vocation; in so doing, they have become heir to its correlative destiny, frustration and futility. Instead of promoting the divine project of creation by exercising a royal stewardship, humankind has eaten the forbidden fruit of defilement of creation. Instead of promoting the divine project of creation by building human community, humankind has partaken of the unlawful diet of befoulment of community. The twofold vocation of world-ruling and community-building—and the fulfillment ingredient to it—has been rejected in favor of an alien vocation of world-defiance and community-disruption. And, in rejecting his authentic summons, "humankind" (the term now applies only very loosely) has rejected his Creator. By turning against the divine project, humankind has turned against the Creator and broken the relation basic to, and inclusive of, all others. And this condition, freely chosen, is one that cannot be reversed by a simple decision.

---

[14]The biblical writers remained notoriously reticent about specifying in what human structure or structures the image of God consists; and later authors have exploited this reticence by multiplying words in attempts to locate the divine image in our rationality, our freedom, our sense of responsibility, and the like. But, in the last analysis, the most adequate perspective seems to be that of G. Ernest Wright; the phrase "in the image of God" suggests that "the total being of man bears a likeness to the total being of God" (G. Ernest Wright and Reginald H. Fuller *The Book of the Acts of God*, [Garden City NY: Doubleday & Company; Anchor Books, 1969], p. 54). Beyond this, about all that can be said with confidence is what I have maintained: being in the image of God means that we have been (a) summoned and (b) adequately equipped for what we have been called to do, and be. (My identification of the *imago Dei* with human vocation and equipping for vocation echos Gordon Kaufman's treatment of the image in terms of human historicity. See his *Systematic Theology: A Historicist Perspective* [New York: Charles Scribner's Sons, 1968], esp. ch. 23.)

For the plight of the sons and daughters of Adam is that they—we—have ceased to be human. We have become "inhuman." In rejecting our human vocation we rejected our humanness. And this we cannot restore by simply willing it, although it cannot be restored apart from our willing it. Thus the doctrine of creation "ends" in the doctrine of redemption, the reality of redemption being the means by which the reality of creation is being continued, restored, and completed. The doctrine of redemption maintains that the Creator has not given up on his project of creation, although his purposes for creation have met with frustration. Rather, the doctrine of redemption involves the affirmation that God has acted, and is acting, in history, and particularly in the history of one people and one human, to reconstitute the human as a universal possibility and, ultimately, the reigning reality. The Creator is our Redeemer: he who established the conditions and the possibility of human existence—rejected to a greater or lesser extent by all those called to actualize the human possibility—has done and is doing that which must be done to bring us (humans *in potentia*) to our authentic, our human, vocation and destiny. This too, then, the doctrine of creations affirms: the human vocation is being restored and thereby, in part, the Creator's project is being completed.

Now, the theology of nature assumes and develops further these kinds of insights, insights contained in and borne by the doctrine of creation. But in doing so, it is governed by certain especial interests. The theology of nature involves a more direct affirmation of the ecological motif than has been the case in Christian reflection on creation historically. This new emphasis and interest is occasioned both by the rise of "ecological thinking," which emphasizes interdependencies, and by the occurrence of environmental perturbations for which the Judeo-Christian vision of the world as creation may bear some responsibility. Secondly, as these remarks already suggest, the theology of nature is shaped, both methodologically and substantively, by concern about the relationship pertaining between "science and religion." The theology of nature represents the particular sensitivity of the theological community to the deliverances of the special natural sciences; it involves explicit inquiry into the proper way of appropriating, or otherwise responding, to those deliverances. This implies that at the heart of the theology of nature, as at the heart of the classical doctrines of creation and providence, lies the issue of how God acts in the world. The theology of nature is especially concerned with the issue of how God acts in the "world" of "nature." Thirdly, the theology of nature is governed in part by an attempt to clarify further the nature and significance of the subhuman creatures and the character of their relationship with humankind and with the divine reality. These things the theology of nature shares with the classical doctrine of creation; but the theology of nature represents a refocusing, an enlargement, and a concomitant delimiting of the kinds of theological interests and reflections that have traditionally been pursued under the older rubric.

THE THEOLOGY OF NATURE AND ECOLOGICAL ETHICS

We have spoken of the relationship between the theology of nature and ecological ethics as a correlative one. A theology of nature and an environmental ethic cannot be separated, but they can be distinguished. The two interact all along the way: the ecological failure of traditional ethics—which is tied in with historic modes of perceiving nature, some of which are theological and philosophical —give rise to the need for a new vision of nature with happier eco-ethical implications and consequences. In short, we can say that it is a practical and an ethical crisis that most dramatically indicates the need for a new theology of nature; the new theology of nature in turn can and must function as part of the theoretical foundation of a new ecological ethic. Hence, throughout this study we shall be compelled to labor on two fronts at once: the theological and the ethical, the theoretical and the practical.[15] We shall find several of our various authors beginning with cultural and ethical analysis, moving through theological reconstruction, and concluding with ethical reconstruction. Thus, while the focus of this study is the *theology* of nature, we shall inescapably be caught up in the enterprise of doing ecological ethics, in both its analytical and constructive modes. The theology of nature and an ecological ethic, while distinguishable, are inextricably related.

MEDIEVAL PRECURSORS OF
A CONTEMPORARY THEOLOGY OF NATURE

In recent years a debate has flourished about the best way for modern men and women to respond to the ecological crisis. This modern contro-

---

[15]This is a schematic characterization; it is not intended to deny that there is such an enterprise as "practical theology," on the one hand, or "theoretical ethics," on the other. In fact, we shall be engaged throughout in criticizing and constructing a "theoretical" ethic. We shall not, however, much attend to the more practical considerations that have come to be thought of as falling under the rubric of "ecotactics." The current study has some important implications for the more practical enterprise, but the development of a programmatic ecotactic is not the intent of this study itself. In that connection see such

versy has centered around the names of two prominent saints within the medieval Western Catholic tradition: Francis of Assisi (1182-1226) and Benedict of Nursia (480-543). Contemporary champion of the Franciscan response to the created order is Lynn White, Jr. in his now famous essay "The Historical Roots of Our Ecologic Crisis."[16] A chief proponent of, what is from the standpoint of technological intervention in nature, the milder Benedictine approach, is René Dubos who pits "Franciscan conservation" against "Benedictine stewardship."[17]

The view, which was the academic fashion during the sixties, that the blame for the desecration of nature in the West is to be attributed to the Judeo-Christian tradition, appears to have been promulgated around 1950 by the Zen Buddhist scholar Daisetz Susuki.[18] But it was Lynn White's article which gave the thesis notariety.

White reminds us that the marriage of science and technology, which led not only to many enormous creative accomplishments in recent times but also to dramatic environmental deterioration, is of quite recent origin. It is in fact little more than a hundred years old. And White argues that for several centuries preceding the final union of theory and practice, both science and technology were nourished in the West in a manner without parallel elsewhere.

White points out that the ancient Oriental and Greco-Roman religions maintained a perspective in which plants, animals, mountains, and rivers had a spiritual significance akin to that of humankind's and were considered to be deserving of respect and even reverence. In contrast, the Judeo-Christian religions set humankind apart from nature. The Hebrews developed a monotheistic vision in which God was interpreted in strictly anthropomorphic terms. Christians furthered this trend by elaborately emphasizing the uniqueness and superiority of humankind

---

works as *Ecotactics: The Sierra Club Handbook for Environmental Activists*, ed. John G. Mitchell with Constance L. Stallings (New York: Simon and Schuster, 1970); "Christian Ecotactics," the epilogue of Eric Rust's *Nature—Garden or Desert?* (Waco TX: Word Books, 1971); and John Cobb's essay "The Local Church and the Environmental Crisis," in *The Christian Ministry* 4 (September 1973): 3-7 and *Foundations* 17 (April-June 1974): 164-72.

[16]First published in *Science* 155 (10 March 1967): 1203-1207, and since reissued several times, as in *The Subversive Science: Essays Toward an Ecology of Man*, ed. Paul Shepherd and Daniel McKinley (Boston: Houghton Mifflin Company, 1969), 341-51. Page references are to the original printing in *Science*.

[17]See especially "Franciscan Conversation Versus Benedictine Stewardship," ch. 8 in Dubos's book, *A God Within* (New York: Charles Scribner's Sons, 1972), 153-174.

[18]Clarence J. Glacken, *Traces on the Rhodian Shore* (Richmond CA: University of California Press, 1967), 494. Cf. Dubos, ibid., 157.

within the created order. Christianity, "the most anthropocentric religion the world has seen,"[19] interpreted all non-human creaturely entities as having been posited to serve human ends. Animistic inhibitions to the abusive exploitation of nature gave way before the dominion of the one creature created *imago Dei.* The Creator was depicted as radically transcending that which he had made, and "man," made in the image of God, reflected and partook of the divine transcendence of extra-human creation. Thus, Western Christianity "not only established a dualism of man and nature but also insisted that it is God's will that man exploit nature for his proper ends."[20] It is this attitude which has engendered the current ecologic crisis; therefore, indicts White, "Christianity bears a huge burden of guilt."[21]

White denies that the cure for our ecological ills lies in more and better science and technology; for, although science and technology have been weaned from their Judeo-Christian parentage, they remain deeply infused with and shaped by the ideals of the traditions making their maturation possible. Even "post-Christian" practitioners and beneficiaries of science and technology are infected by the traditional Christian understanding of the man-nature relationship; thus they perpetuate, ineluctably, the abusive treatment of nature. Not "until we reject the Christian axiom that nature has no reason for existence save to serve man"[22]— and thus "not until we find a new religion, or rethink our old one"[23]—will a cure be possible.

Since the roots of the ecological crisis are largely religious, the remedy must itself be preeminently religious, says White. Accordingly, he seeks "an alternative Christian view"; and this he finds within the Western tradition itself. White proposes that—as the needed corrective to the excessively anthropocentric outlook of Western attitudes toward the man-nature complex—the tradition of theology and piety associated with the name of Francis of Assisi be given renewed attention. As is now well known, White goes so far as to propose that this "greatest radical in

---

[19]White, "The Historical Roots of Our Ecologic Crisis," 1205.

[20]Ibid. White notes that Christianity took different forms historically, with varying ecological results. In the Eastern forms the saintly ideal which emerged centered in the more passive attitudes of prayer and contemplation, whereas in the Western sector of the Church the saintly ideal focused on effective action. It was the latter tradition which led not only to greater scientific-technological accomplishments but to deleterious environmental consequences.

[21]Ibid., 1206.

[22]Ibid., 1207.

[23]Ibid., 1206.

Christian history since Christ" be made the patron saint for ecologists.[24]

Francis's significance lies in the fact that he extended the virtue of humility from a personal to a generic, or perhaps a "specific," good: "The key to an understanding of Francis is his belief in the virtue of humility—not merely for the individual but for man as a species."[25] White suggests that man, especially Western man, needs to (re)acquire the humility whereby an anthropocentric perspective can be exchanged for an ecologic or universalistic orientation. Such a reorientation will involve the substitution of a Franciscan democratic view of the relations and value of all God's creatures for the traditionally Western monarchical view of the man-centered relationship:

> Francis tried to depose man from his monarchy over creation and set up a democracy of all God's creatures . . . . The greatest spiritual revolutionary in Western history, Saint Francis, proposed what he thought was an alternative Christian view of nature and man's relation to it: he tried to substitute the idea of *the equality* of all creatures, including man, for the idea of man's limitless rule of creation. He failed.[26]

Although success eluded Francis in his time, White considers it imperative that the essentials of the Franciscan vision be recovered and cultivated in ours; for, if the triumph of his vision continues to elude his heirs and successors, the prospects for the future are bleak.

Saint Francis was indeed the first Western Christian thinker to provide a powerful statement of an ecologically promising alternative to the traditional Western view of the value of extra-human nature and the character of the man-nature relationship.[27] The fact that we find contemporary theologians doing in suggestive fashion for our time what Francis willed to do for his does not gainsay the significance of his vision—even if we need not, and cannot, simply return to a Franciscan orientation as White seems almost to recommend. Francis has in fact pointed up directions that remain valuable. These can be seen, for example, in the theocentric character of his vision of all creatures, in the attendant

---

[24]Ibid., 1207.

[25]Ibid., 1206.

[26]Ibid., 1206-1207. Emphasis added.

[27]In spite of a plethora of books about Francis, the only extant study dealing with the nature motif in the Franciscan legend that is both thorough and critical is a recent work by Edward A. Armstrong, *Saint Francis: Nature Mystic* (Berkeley: University of California Press. 1973). Another valuable critical study dealing with a different but related aspect of the Franciscan legacy is Ray C. Petry's volume, *Francis of Assisi: Apostle of Poverty* (Durham: Duke University Press, 1941). The early Franciscan literature is now available in a convenient collection entitled *St. Francis of Assisi: Writings and Early Biographies*, ed. Marion A. Habig (Chicago: Franciscan Herald Press, 1973).

reverence for all being(s), and in the humility that makes his vision possible. Moreover, Francis's orientation is in salient respects more sensitively informed by the biblical witness to the character of nature, man, and God than are the perspectives of many of those who shaped the dominant strands of thought in the history of Western Christianity.

Francis's sensitivity to scriptural motifs is reflected in his adoption and employment of the socio-political metaphor of the family as the organ through which he sought to give voice to his vision. He evidently took seriously the analogy by which God is called "Father." In his exploration of the logic of this metaphor he was able—without apparently the severe struggle of a Luther—to appreciate the tender implications of familial iconography and to downplay the sterner elements so often associated with fatherhood. The image of the father universalized (he clothes the lilies of the field in splendor and notes the fall of even a lowly sparrow; compare Francis's Sermon to the Birds) and tenderized (he makes his sun to shine on the just and unjust; compare the legend of the Wolf of Gubbio) became again an apt image for deity. Moreover, this recovery of Jesus' sense of the benevolent and universal character of the fatherhood of God was accompanied by a universalizing of the New Testament motif of *koinonia* or brotherhood. The Franciscan legends are constituted to a significant extent by graphic portrayals of Francis's wondrous capacity to relate to his fellow creatures, human and extra-human. Collectively, the effect of the legends is to suggest a genuinely universal "brotherhood" in which all worldly creatures of the heavenly Father have a real and worthful place. As the biblical portrayals of God the Father suggest, all creatures great and small—in modern parlance, all creatures organic and inorganic, rational and pre-rational—have a place in the "family" of God. Familial imagery is prominent in Francis's famous Hymn of Creation:

> Be praised, my Lord, with all Thy works whate'er they be,
>   Our noble Brother Sun especially,
> Whose brightness makes the light by which we see,
> And he is fair and radiant, splendid and free,
> A likeness and a type, Most High of Thee.
>
> Be praised, my Lord, for Sister Moon and every Star
>   That Thou hast formed to shine so clear from heaven afar.
> Be praised, my Lord, for Brother Wind and Air,
>   Breezes and clouds and weather foul or fair—
> To every one that breathes Thou givest a share.
>
> Be praised, my Lord, for Sister Water, sure
>   None is so useful, lowly, chaste and pure.
>
> Be praised, my Lord, for Brother Fire, whose light
>   Thou madest to illuminate the night,
> And he is fair and jolly and strong and bright.

Be praised, my Lord, for Sister Earth, our Mother,
   Who nourishes and gives us food and fodder,
   And the green grass and flowers of every colour.[28]

Although the familial imagery dominates Francis's approach to the understanding and valuation of the natural world as well as the human dimension, the sources testify that his perspective included elements of other metaphors and modes of thought as well. There is, most notably, a trace of a unique sort of panpsychism akin to that developed characteristically by some of the process thinkers who represent the second contemporary approach to be examined in this study. Moreover, there is in Francis a general if tacit acknowledgment of the sacramental character of all creation—a mark of the third contemporary approach to be examined in this study. But notwithstanding traces of panpsychic and sacramental elements in his theology and the legends associated with him, Francis is significant to the theology of nature chiefly for his development of an approach to the created order that centers in the elaboration of sociopolitical imagery. And notwithstanding certain political overtones to his imagery, Francis's vision centers in a uniquely powerful development of a metaphor which can only be identified as the familial. The more explicitly political metaphor of the Kingdom of God is present in Francis, to be sure; but Kingdom imagery is decisively subordinated to the familial. One suspects that the Kingdom of God is too monarchical an image for Francis's fraternal and even egalitarian sensibilities. In his view the various fellow creatures of man that collectively constitute the dimension of creation that Westerners have come to denominate as "nature" are members of a vastly extended family. This genuinely universal family consists of "Brother Sun," "Sister Moon," and "Mother Earth," as well as of Adam and Eve (humankind). The head of the family of all creatures is more aptly characterized as God the loving Father than as God the reigning Monarch. And, as the Franciscan legends dramatically illustrate, in this universal family the egalitarian principles of mutual respect, care, sharing, and affection take priority over the hierarchical principles of privilege and authority.

Thus in Francis egalitarianism is expanded to the limits. This great saint of the late twelfth and early thirteenth centuries has provided the rudiments of a theology of nature with its attendant ecological ethic that is characterized by several significant accomplishments. Francis's "theology of nature" (1) is biblically informed in a sensitive fashion, (2) centers

----

[28]These selections from Francis's Canticle are from the translation by F. C. Burkitt, *The Song of Brother Sun in English Rime* (London, 1926); cited by Armstrong, *Saint Francis*, 228.

in familial imagery, and (3) emphasizes the worth and even a certain equality of all creaturely members of the divine family, thereby (4) promoting the respect or reverence of all beings; moreover it (5) relates all family members to their divine source as the only legitimate center of "family life." Such a theocentric theology of nature, it is clear, must (6) promote the virtue of humility, as Lynn White has emphasized; in so doing it stands in sharp contrast to the dominant— prideful when made exclusive?—Western images of nature as resource, tool, and stage.

Francis's contributions to an acceptable Christian vision of nature are real and significant. One measure of his accomplishment is found in the fact that virtually all contemporary theologians of nature hark back to him. His thoroughgoing emphasis upon familial imagery remains unique and meaningful, even if somewhat quaint in his (and his associates' and successors') developments of it.[29] The chief difficulty of the Franciscan vision lies in the fact that it provides no clear principles in terms of which the relative worth of the various members of the family of God can be ascertained; in fact, the desire to make such distinctions is itself in tension with the dominant metaphor in terms of which reality is understood and valued. The emphasis upon "the equality of all creatures" (in White's descriptive phrase) characteristic of the Franciscan tradition provides a corrective to an exaggerated anthropocentrism that devaluates nature by implication. But Francis's—and White's—elevation of the prehuman dimension, however necessary it is as a corrective to the alleged ideological and ecological distortions ingredient to the type of anthropocentrism that has dominated the West, does not sufficiently guard against the inadvertent devaluation of humankind. In our examination of the development of the theology of nature in the twentieth century, we shall have to search for a way of avoiding the unfortunate consequences of what may be regarded as an exaggerated anthropocentrism without thereby committing the error of failing to appreciate the really unique, and superior, aspects of the human dimension.

Lynn White and the Franciscan tradition have received a vigorous challenge from René Dubos. Dubos proposes Benedict of Nursia ("certainly as good a Christian as Francis of Assisi"!) as "a patron saint of

---

[29]Although the Uncle Remus stories are tainted by racial stereotyping, Uncle Remus almost alone in our recent history echoes Francis's perception of the brotherhood of all God's creatures. "Brer Rabbit" and "Brer Bear" are not brothers at all in the sensibilities of most Westerners. And many smile condescendingly at the romantic sentiment of an Uncle Remus and a St. Francis.

The familial imagery does find at least implicit application and development in fantasy; see, e.g., the works of C. S. Lewis, J. R. R. Tolkien, and Ursula LeGuin.

those who believe that true conservation means not only protecting nature against human misbehavior but also developing human activities which favor a creative, harmonious relationship between man and nature."[30]

Dubos regards White's thesis that Judeo-Christian attitudes are accountable for the flowering of technology and for environmental catastrophe as "at best a historical half-truth." He finds considerable evidence to suggest that the ecologic records of the civilizations White glorifies are not as pristine as the latter suggests; in fact, Dubos argues that the respectful attitude toward nature characteristic of, say, certain Oriental traditions may have arisen (like the newly awakened interest in environment in our own civilization) "as a response to the damage done in antiquity."[31] Exploitation of the environment, accompanied by a sense of human uniqueness and even superiority, he regards as essentially universal.

> All over the globe and at all times in the past, men have pillaged nature and disturbed the ecological equilibrium, usually out of ignorance, but also because they have always been more concerned with immediate advantages than with long range goals. Moreover, they could not foresee that they were preparing for ecological disasters, nor did they have a real choice of alternatives. If men are more destructive now than they were in the past, it is because there are more of them and because they have at their command more powerful means of destruction, not because they have been influenced by the Bible. *In fact, the Judeo-Christian peoples were probably the first to develop on a large scale a pervasive concern for land management and an ethic of nature.*[32]

Pointing out that "human life implies changes in nature,"[33] and that conservation is always rooted in human value systems, he lists several reasons for conservation: all man-centered. Dubos argues that an attitude of Franciscan "reverence [towards nature] is not enough."[34] Since "man" changes the environment by his very presence, "his only options in his dealings with the environment are to be destructive or constructive."[35]

> To be creative, man must relate to nature with his senses as much as with his common sense, with his heart as much as with knowledge. He must read the book of external nature and the book of his own nature, to discern the common patterns and harmonies.[36]

---

[30]Dubos, *A God Within*, 168.

[31]Ibid., 160.

[32]Ibid., 161. Emphasis added.

[33]Ibid., 167.

[34]Ibid., 173.

[35]Ibid.

[36]Ibid.

Dubos illustrates this creative way of relating to nature—this humane way of exercising wise stewardship—by appeal to St. Benedict and the tradition he set in motion. For the Benedictine order was a model of wise land management, of creative capacity to integrate architecture with the requirements of both worship and landscape, and of "adapting rituals and work to the cosmic rhythms."

> Human life implies choices as to the best way to govern natural systems and to create new environments out of wilderness. Reverence for nature is compatible with willingness to accept responsibility for a creative steward-ship of the earth.[37]

This is well said. Benedict and Dubos surely represent a salutary corrective to the exaggerated egalitarianism of Francis and White. But they do so precisely by perpetuating the type of anthropocentric bias which suggests that the sole reason for the existence of otherkind is humankind. We shall, as we go along, have to inquire about the possibility of an alternative vision, marked by a "new anthropocentrism," which integrates the authentic insights of both Francis and Benedict, White and Dubos.

RECENT PIONEERS OF A NEW THEOLOGY OF NATURE

A widespread consensus has emerged in the twentieth century regarding the general character of Christian theological affirmations about creation. That consensus includes the conviction that the burden of the biblical myth of creation, and the ecclesiastical doctrine based upon it, is "religious" in character. The myth and the doctrine bear primarily existential and relational meanings of perennial significance; they do not bear binding cosmological meaning. Thus, after some three centuries of "warfare" a truce of sorts has emerged between science and theology. "But," as one interpreter notes,

> while *the consensus* has made possible the declaration of a truce, it *has done no more than clear the way for a development of a theology of the created order.* The working out of such a theology remains to be done. New directions in biblical, systematic and philosophical theology have stressed kerygmatic and linguistic themes. It cannot be said that the doctrine of creation has played a lively part in recent Christian thought and imagination. The doctrine has been formally expressed, in the context of a new rapprochement between science and theology, but it has not been explicitly related to the second and third articles of the creed.[38]

---

[37]Ibid., 174.

[38]Harold H. Ditmanson, "The Call for a Theology of Creation," *Dialog* 3 (August 1964): 267. Emphasis added.

Calls for a new "theology of the created order" have come from a variety of quarters. The clearest call from the camp of those who dominated the theological scene during the first half of this century was made by Paul Tillich. Noting that "the religious significance of the inorganic is immense," Tillich bemoaned that "it is rarely considered by theology." In fact, he lamented, "a 'theology of the inorganic' is lacking."[39] The situation was only relatively better, in Tillich's view, with regard to a "theology of the organic." In the third volume of his *Systematic Theology* (1963), Tillich made significant contributions to the task of supplying what he perceived as lacking.

But, early on, another took up Tillich's challenge to supply a viable theology of the inorganic. In 1967 Conrad Bonifazi set forth *A Theology of Things,* which purported to be "a study of man in his physical environment."[40] Bonifazi's book rests on the premise that "the concept of the natural must be . . . reinstated"[41] and the antitheses of previous ages— ages rethought, with respect to categories such as nature and grace, material and spiritual, things and persons. The question, he suggests, is not simply attitudinal and axiological ("What is the attitude of the Christian towards those particular, human relationships with the natural world described by the sciences, and expressed by technology?"). The question is, rather, existential and metaphysical: "What is the relation of the Christian man [*sic*] to the natural world itself?"[42]

Bonifazi's attempted answer draws upon an extraordinarily rich variety of sources: Hebraic vision and Franciscan sensitivity, Marx, Nietzsche, Bergson, Unamuno, Scheler, Levy-Bruhl, Buber, Macmurray, Teilhard de Chardin, and others. The result is suggestive and stimulating but also a bit bewildering, for the insights drawn from such a variety of sources are not very fully integrated. The shape of the new view of things which we are invited to share in does not come quite clear. Nonetheless, certain dominant themes emerge.

Bonifazi identifies the penchant for dualism as the root problem necessitating a fresh look at "things," organic as well as inorganic. The dichotomizing of body and soul, man and world, world and God implicitly distorts and devaluates one term of the polarity: the "physical." In a

---

[39]Paul Tillich, *Systematic Theology*, 3 vols. (Chicago: University of Chicago Press, 1951-1963), 3:18.

[40]Conrad Bonifazi, *A Theology of Things: A Study of Man in His Physical Environment* (Philadelphia: J. B. Lippincott Company, 1967).

[41]Ibid., 13.

[42]Ibid., 16.

variety of ways Bonifazi attempts to bring together again that which modern thinkers have put asunder.

He appeals, for example, to a number of philosophical resources in an attempt to discover "the truth of things." Against skepticism concerning the noetic accessibility and even the reality of "things-in-themselves" he employs the phenomenological perspectives of Edmund Husserl and Max Scheler to suggest that in the mutuality of "intuition" and "object" "the abyss between what appears in sensibility and the cause of its appearance" is bridged.[43] Against the tendency to strip things of all interiority he employs a vast array of thinkers (as diverse as Leibnitz, Nietzsche, Marx and Engels, Bergson, and Karl Heim) to suggest that things are properly understood only when their "inwardness" is recognized. Ostensibly rejecting panpsychism, he rightly avers that "to grant them "inwardness" is not to invest them [things] with souls."[44] But none of this is developed very fully; Bonifazi tends to supply rhetoric at precisely the points at which sustained argument is most needed.

Still, philosophic inquiry represents one line of approach to his quest for a more satisfactory view of things. An examination of the biblical understanding of "nature," man, and God, and of selected theological perceptions of the same, represents another. According to Bonifazi, the ancient Hebrews understood the world of nature "as thoroughly animated, capable of fellow feeling with man, and capable of obedience to its sustaining depth of force."[45] That is, the Hebrews understood nature "anthropomorphically." The basis for this contention lies, according to Bonifazi, in the meaning of *nephesh*—"soul," "life," "man," but always "insouled body and enfleshed soul."[46] Consciousness was seen by the ancients as a function of (in modern parlance) the whole person.

> So, because the Hebrews understood consciousness to be distributed throughout the body, it was possible to conceive of physical qualities in the natural world . . . . Therefore, *nephesh* is not peculiarly human; there is no ultimate division between human and animal *nephesh;* life and sensibility extend through the animal kingdom into the world of objects.[47]

Just as the Hebrews failed to separate soul from body, so they refused to separate spirit from matter in general. Both belong to humankind and otherkind alike.

---

[43]Ibid., 89.

[44]Ibid., 104.

[45]Ibid., 183.

[46]Ibid.

[47]Ibid., 183-84.

This perspective leads Bonifazi to the conclusion that things, the earth, indeed all facets of nature, "speak."

> . . . for the Hebrews, a thing is principally *dabhar,* a word.

> In English a *thing* means any action, speech or thought with which we are concerned; it is any object of perception or knowledge; it is both idea and event. But our sense of discontinuity between thinking and doing makes us judge of this usage as ambiguous. The Hebrews find no ambiguity here: idea, word and event are a continuous whole. Abraham's returning servant recounts "all the words he had done" (Gen. 24:66). His adventurous journey in its entirety is comprised of *words!* Things are not objects in space; they are words! Things are not inflexibly *there,* but only changeably so! For they are directly and continuously related to man. Descriptions of earth in terms of motion and energy, the skipping mountains and their trembling foundations are more than poetic images of seismic phenomena and express a lively earth related to living man. *Dabhar,* or "word," comprises all: thoughts, words, deeds and concrete objects; while nonbeing, or nothingness, is explained by *lo-dabhar:* that which is "not-word." And between these extremes, couched within that unity of word and deed represented by *dabhar,* was a sense of counterfeit language: men recognized the word which lacked the strength of accomplishment, and deemed only the effective word to be the venture of *nephesh.* But the effective word could create or destroy in accordance with its character.

> So the liveliness of *nephesh* becomes *dabhar* . . . .[48]

According to Bonifazi, all existence possesses this "word character." This is perceived in the idea of Torah as the going forth of the active divine word (in the prophetic literature) and in the divine wisdom present and active in creation (in the wisdom literature), and preeminently in the creative-redemptive Logos (attested by the Johannine literature). "The vital energy which imbued matter, the soul which spoke within and from the material world with human accents is now articulately 'full of grace and truth'."[49]

Thus, Bonifazi finds "nature" to be perfused by spirit throughout and to be marked by a nisus towards the full flowering of "nephesh" in the emergence of the personal—with the latter apparently perceived as at once included in and inclusive of the natural. Finally, then, Bonifazi presents us with a holistic and "panpsychic" perspective simultaneously mystical and philosophical, sacramental and scientific, a perspective reminiscent of the vision of Teilhard de Chardin. But suggestive as it is, Bonifazi's "theology of things" is inconclusive. It leaves us eager to see these things pursued more systematically, rigorously, and completely.

---

[48]Ibid., 186.

[49]Ibid., 190.

Another pioneering theologian of nature—indeed one of the earliest and most perceptive of them—is Joseph Sittler. Long before "ecology" became a popular term, Sittler was utilizing the concept in order to explicate the content of Christian faith. Initially he used it to demonstrate the organic interrelations pertaining amongst the various faith affirmations, and this was done with especial reference to the divine presence in nature. Out of this matrix of thought came an increasing insistence that modern man has vitiated his relationship with God by his abusive treatment of the natural, as well as the human, component of creation. Thus, Sittler began to speak and write about human responsibility for "the care of the earth"[50] and to explore the possibility of defining a new perspective on an old theme: the relationship of nature and grace. Indeed, he perceives "the most urgent theological task of our time to be a radical restatement of the relation of grace to nature."[51] More generally, reacting against both "neo-orthodoxy's almost proud repudiation of earth" and a neo-naturalistic repudiation of heaven, Sittler asserts that "the largest, most insistent, and most delicate task awaiting Christian theology is to articulate such a theology for nature as shall do justice to the vitalities of earth and hence correct a current theological naturalism which succeeds in speaking meaningfully of earth only at the cost of repudiating specifically Christian categories."[52]

Sittler's own attempt to articulate the required new theology for earth, or nature (he utilizes the terms interchangeably), is seminal and profoundly engaging; but, like the work of Bonifazi, it is not as systematically and fully worked out as are the orientations we shall examine in Part One. Nonetheless, certain themes stand out and deserve attention.

Sittler's reflections begin with the observation that contemporary man is man-engaged-with-nature. The sphere of human operations today, as always, is nature as well as history; but in recent times the engagement of man with nature—via high science and technology *and* the secular mood—has become far more pronounced than was the case in previous ages. Consequently, "an expanded Christian doctrine of grace" is an imperative, if the relevancy of the Gospel to our age is to be perceived.[53] That is, "the reality of grace must be 'relocated' in the spheres

---

[50]The title of a sermon in which Sittler explores the counterpoint between joy and usage, in Franklin H. Littel, ed., *Sermons to Intellectuals*, (New York: Macmillan Company, 1963).

[51]Untitled essay, in *Criterion* 6 (Winter 1967):21.

[52]"A Theology for Earth," *The Christian Scholar* 37:3 (September 1954):373.

[53]*Essays on Nature and Grace* (Philadelphia: Fortress Press, 1972), 81.

of creation where contemporary man's operational actuality is most clearly evidenced."

> This relocation of grace within the actuality of man's life within history and nature, and amidst the most common and formative episodes of experience, is not only a formal requirement of the interior energy of the plentitude of grace itself; it is an absolute requirement arising from the post-Enlightenment embeddedness of man's mind, self-assessment, and operational life in the world. If, therefore, the proposal of grace is not made to man in the matrix of his life-situation, the proposal is either unintelligible or uninteresting.[54]

Sittler is fully aware of how tenuously grace has been related to the vitalities of nature by post-Reformation Western theologians. The wont of such thinkers has been to demonstrate the pertinence of grace to the spiritual maladies of egocentricity and idolatry (*sola*) and to elaborate their christological doctrines accordingly. Only rarely have they extended their understandings of redemption and the Redeemer beyond the life of the soul to dimensions that reflect concern for the entirety of the created order. Lutheran theologian Joseph Sittler regards the Reformers as no longer reliable guides for our reflections on the relations of grace and nature. Instead, he urges "the recovery of catholic comprehensiveness in the doctrine of grace" and the development of a Christology, and theology of the sacraments, that accord with it.[55]

The new "place of grace," the locus of the operations of that supportive and beneficent agency which posits and completes us, must be "the webbed connectedness of man's creaturely life," in all its dimensions, historical-social and material-natural.[56] Moreover, "the sheer phenomenality of the world-as-given,"[57] the vast ecosystem of history and nature wherein human beings actually dwell, must henceforth, in its totality, be the object of the reflections of those who have experienced grace in and through the mediations of this complex system.

Sittler's theology is rooted in an "ecological ontology," suggestive of the vision of Whitehead and others, but derived by Sittler less from philosophy than from Scripture.

> . . . the question of reality is itself an ecological question! Because the question is ecological, reality itself must be spoken of ecologically. Reality is known only in relations. This statement conflicts with the very structure of a

---

[54]Ibid., 83.

[55]Ibid.

[56]Ibid., 94.

[57]Nathan A. Scott, Jr., "The Poetry and Theology of Earth: Reflections on the Testimony of Joseph Sittler and Gerard Manley Hopkins," *Journal of Religion* 54:2 (April 1974):108.

good deal of post-Enlightenment thought in the Western world. I mean by
such a statement that we must think it possible that there is no ontology of
isolated entities, or instances, of forms, of processes, whether we are reflecting about God or man or society or the cosmos. The only adequate ontological structure we may utilize for thinking things Christianly is an ontology of
community, communion, ecology— and all three words point conceptually
to thought of a common kind. "Being itself" may be a relation, not an
entitative thing.[58]

Moreover, says Sittler, creation is itself "an ecological event."[59] And
Psalm 104 is "an ecological doxology" reflecting the ecological vision
which perfuses Scripture.

> Beginning with the air, the sky, the little and then the great animals, the work
> that man does upon the earth and the delight that he takes in it, the
> doxological hymn unfolds to celebrate both the mysterious fecundity that
> evermore flows from the fountain of all livingness, up to the great coda of the
> psalm in which the phrase occurs—"These all hang upon Thee." The word
> "hang" is an English translation of a word that literally means to "depend," to
> receive existence and life from another. These all *hang together* because they
> all hang upon Thee, "You give them their life, You send forth Your breath,
> they live." Here is teaching of the divine redemption within the primal
> context of the divine Creation. Unless we fashion a relational doctrine of
> creation—which doctrine can rightly live with evolutionary theory—then we
> shall end up with a reduction, a perversion, and ultimately an irrelevance as
> regards the doctrine of redemption.[60]

In short, "the fundamental terms of the Scripture—God, man, love, sin,
hate, grace, covenant—are all relational words."[61] And any scripturally
informed ontology must, accordingly, be "ecological" in character.

It is this vision of the interconnectedness of things which warrants
Sittler's claim that nature itself is a sphere of grace. His doctrines of grace
and redemption are set forth in the context of a larger—ecological—
doctrine of creation which sees the positing, shaping, and completing of a
cosmos, and all parts thereof, to be the divine project. Thus, nature as well
as history, subhuman as well as human entities, are understood as both
the results and the vehicles of the expressions of the divine goodwill.
Nature and grace are not, therefore, mutually exclusive polarities; they
are rather, as Nathan Scott expresses it, "coordinates of one reality which
is none other than a universe, in its most essential aspect, everywhere (as

---

[58]"Ecological Commitment as Theological Responsibility," *Zygon* 5:2 (June
1970):174.

[59]Ibid., 177.

[60]Ibid., p. 178. In another reflection on this Psalm, Sittler notes that here "the trees and
birds, the grass and the cattle, the plump vine that gladdens the heart of man are *all bound
together in a bundle of grace*" ("A Theology for Earth," 372; emphasis added).

[61]"Ecological Commitment as Theological Responsibility," 174.

Hopkins says) 'charged with the grandeur of God.' "[62] Nature and grace, in a word, coinhere.

Sittler attempts to buttress his ecological vision of a universe marked by the coinherence of nature and grace by a theology of Christ and his work that asserts Christ's relevancy to the total cosmos. To do so, he returns to the Fathers of the Eastern Church, especially Irenaeus, and elaborates a Christology that affirms that the God met in the incarnation is identical with the God met in nature: the Word spoken in Jesus of Nazareth is understood as (a "recapitulation" of?) the everlasting love of God active in all the processes and events of history and nature. Sittler's concern, then, is not to set forth a natural theology but rather a theology for earth, or nature, that joins the author of Colossians in finding in Christ the one in whom all things cohere.[63]

Since Sittler's treatment of the theme of Christ as "pantocrator" has so many points of parallel with the Christology of Teilhard de Chardin, we shall not follow the Lutheran's development of it further at this point. Like Teilhard, too, Sittler sets forth a profoundly sacramental vision of creation in conjunction with his Christology; and, again, its parallels with the vision of the Jesuit paleontologist warrant our refraining from tracing the lines of its development by Sittler. But, in concluding our remarks about this pioneering Lutheran theologian of nature, we note this one prophetic affirmation regarding the sacramental coinherence of the realities of nature and grace:

> *God—man—nature! These three are meant for each other, and restlessness will stalk our hearts and ambiguity our world until their cleavage is redeemed.* What a holy depth of meaning lies waiting for our understanding in that moment portrayed on the last evening of Christ's life: "And he took bread, and when he had given thanks he broke it and gave to them, saying, 'This is my body'. . . . Likewise also the wine . . . 'this cup is the new covenant in my blood.' "
>
> *Here in one huge symbol are God and man and nature together.*[64]

The third pioneering theologian of nature who merits our attention is Frederick Elder.[65] Significantly, at the beginning of the last decade Elder published a small volume entitled *Crisis in Eden*.[66] In this "religious study

---

[62]Scott, "The Poetry and Theology of Earth," 106.

[63]Colossians 1:17.

[64]"A Theology for Earth," 373. Emphasis added.

[65]An "exhaustive" list of such "pioneers" would, of course, include many others, among them, Charles Raven, Karl Heim, and Eric Rust.

[66]*Crisis in Eden: A Religious Study of Man and Environment* (Nashville: Abingdon Press, 1970). My brief characterization of Elder's contribution consists of a slightly

of man and environment" Elder became one of the first to present in popular form an important theological analysis showing the way in which religious attitudes have fed the growing ecological crisis.

Elder's concern is (a) to promote an appreciation of the intrinsic value of nature as opposed to the merely instrumental value that dominant theological and economic attitudes encourage and (b) to argue—like Bonifazi and Sittler—for a more integrated view of the man-nature relationship than the traditional perspective allows. In making his case for this revision of Western man's view of nature and of humanity's place in nature, Elder distinguishes between "anthropocentrism" and "biocentrism." The anthropocentric attitude—"man's concentration upon himself" and his tendency to view himself "as outside the grasp of nature"—is the defining characteristic of the type of thinkers that Elder labels "exclusionist." This category includes not only Elder's contemporary illustrative figures (Pierre Teilhard de Chardin, Herbert Richardson, and Harvey Cox) but most post-Ritschlian Protestant theologians.

Elder reminds us that thinkers in the Ritschlian tradition have been concerned to delineate the dimensions of the uniquely human sphere. Thus, they have concentrated upon the problems of history, the properly human dimension of reality and the sphere in which legitimate religious concerns appear. Having sharply distinguished history from nature, they have given the latter over to natural science so exclusively that a positive and well-developed doctrine of nature is sought in vain among the pages of most post-Ritschlian Protestant theologians. Although it is important to note the intensification of the problem in theology after Kant and Ritschl, Elder himself does not dwell extensively on the modern manifestation of the man-nature dualism; rather like Lynn White, he describes it as the attitude dominant throughout Christian and Western history. In Elder's typological interpretation, Teilhard, Richardson, and Cox represent imaginative contemporary continuations of this ancient tendency to view humanity over against rather than within nature and to see nature in terms of its instrumental value to humanity.

Against the anthropocentric attitude characteristic of the exclusionists Elder sets a holistic or biocentric attitude which characterizes the other pole of his typology, namely, the "inclusionist." The inclusionists are mostly life scientists (the naturalist and anthropologist Loren Eiseley is Elder's primary example) and others, such as landscape architects, whose work brings them face to face with the negative consequences of

revised version of my review of his book, published in *Foundations* 14:2 (April-June 1971): 189-92. *Crisis in Eden* is based on a master's thesis done by Elder at Harvard Divinity School.

the traditional stance toward nature. They view nature as an interrelated unity that is intrinsically valuable.

> The inclusionists say that value pervades all life, and not just its human expression. An insect, a bird, a beast, are all important as such. Looking at their position theologically we note that Jesus said that God had regard for a sparrow. The point is that God regards the sparrow qua sparrow and not as some bird that man might see or somehow use.[67]

Elder argues that ecological and demographic pressures make imperative the widespread adoption of the inclusionist vision of man and nature. Since an integrated view of the man-nature relationship and a positive valuation of nature have always been present as minority themes in the intellectual life of the Church, Christians in particular and Westerners in general do not have to look outside their own heritage to find warrant for adoption of the inclusionist view. We have only to bring forth into a position of dominance what has heretofore been a minor theme. But that change in itself will represent a major conversion.

Reviewing the relevant biblical texts, Elder argues that the traditional exegesis has been unduly one-sided and that significant scriptural support for the inclusionist view can be uncovered. Furthermore, important inclusionist themes can be traced in the theological writings of several major Christian figures, including Francis of Assisi, Calvin, and Jonathan Edwards. Coming to more recent times, Elder contends that H. Richard Niebuhr, among others, has articulated a vision sufficiently broad to provide an adequate theological basis for adoption of the inclusionist perspective. Building primarily on themes drawn from Niebuhr and aspects of Richardson's work, Elder calls for the development of a vision of God as the unity of "the manifold systems of the world" wherein the encompassing system of relations is understood to include relationships between nature and humanity as well as among humans.

Elder's theological challenge to the prevailing attitudes toward nature and humanity's place in nature is an important contribution. It is unfortunate, however, that Elder has developed his thesis that nature has intrinsic value by castigating all anthropocentric attitudes. He identifies anthropocentrism with an attitude of exclusive concentration on man which disregards the larger nexus of relationships within which man's own life is lived. This type of concentration on man surely needs correction. But Elder's failure to distinguish forthrightly between various types of human-centered visions of the world has the effect of demeaning or, at least, of obscuring the unique position of humanity, a uniqueness agreed upon by virtually all inclusionists. Such obfuscation was far from being

---

[67]Ibid., 132-33.

Elder's intention. Elder contends, in fact, that inclusionists do not oppose human culture as such or even human dominance in the world. "However, they do stand against what they consider are the overly narrow directions of that culture, and what they see as a misunderstanding of dominance."[68] But when Elder attempts to define the uniqueness of the human dimension and the type of human dominance that is acceptable— that is, a kind of man-centered emphasis appropriate to a holistic vision of nature—he leaves much to be desired.

Elder describes the man-nature relationship as properly symbiotic or interdependent. In this biological nexus man's greater intellectual capacity defines his uniqueness and is given expression in his cultural creations. Man, allows Elder,

> can express his uniqueness in a variety of ways—music, art, poetry, philosophy, literature, worship of God, even invention and manipulation within limits—but he cannot pose as unique in the area of the biological, for he is of the earth, earthly. This is all, really, that the inclusionists are trying to say.[69]

In other words, Elder holds that humanity is intellectually unique but biologically "no more than an aspect of the whole physical reality."[70]

It would appear that Elder has fallen back into an unfortunate mind-body or history-nature dualism before fully finishing his argument on behalf of the inclusionist position whose object it is to deny or at least modify that dualism. A clue to this confusion may be found in Elder's concluding remarks in his interpretation of Loren Eiseley. "The problem," Elder says in taking up a suggestion made by Eiseley, "is that man and nature have become natural," meaning "one-dimensional."[71] This passage suggests that Elder is attributing to the terms "nature" and "natural" a variety of meanings which are not carefully distinguished or kept separate. Early in his study Elder differentiates between the dualistic view of nature understood as the environment standing over against man and culture and the holistic vision which "includes man and his works within its compass." But it is not clear that this distinction exhausts the senses in which Elder uses the term: the identification of "natural" with the "one-dimensional" seems, for example, to introduce another sense.

Furthermore, Elder's contention that the holistic vision of nature is inclusive of man and civilization seems belied by his concession that ultimately all that the inclusionists are arguing for is an appreciation of

---

[68]Ibid., 40.

[69]Ibid., 135.

[70]Ibid., 134.

[71]Ibid., 60.

man's biological kinship with the rest of nature. As a result of the shifting usage of the key term Elder can argue against a man-nature dualism (anthropocentrism) in favor of a holistic vision large enough to include man and then proceed to reaffirm, in effect, the man-nature dualism by narrowing the meaning of the term "nature" and leaving the uniqueness of "man" ill-defined.

In spite of this deficiency, Elder's concern to modify the traditional dualism between humanity and nature and to affirm the intrinsic value of non-human nature is significant. The problems that remain merely indicate that, as Elder himself recognizes, theologians are at the beginning rather than the end of the attempt to rethink the meaning of nature and humanity's place therein. And some of Elder's remarks, especially his brief development of a theocentric ground of the unity of nature, hold promise as a creative starting point for the much-needed theological reconstruction.

ISSUES IN THE THEOLOGY OF NATURE

Enough has now been said to indicate the types of issues that must be given attention if a Christian theology of nature is to be elaborated. Schematically, the issues can be divided into three kinds of considerations.

First, there are those considerations which are foundational and methodological in character. The problem of defining "the nature of 'nature' " is itself the over-riding foundational issue. What is it that theologians of "nature" are theologizing about? Exactly what kind of linguistic and cognitive status does the concept of nature have? What alternative understandings of nature are available to us, and with what understanding(s) do contemporary "theologians of nature" actually work? This issue is crucial for determining the character of the task denoted by the term "theology of nature." That is, the foundational issue of specifying the nature of "nature" bears importantly on the methodological questions of how the theology of nature is to be done and how the theology of nature is related to other theological tasks. What, in particular, is the relationship between the theology of nature and "natural theology"?

Secondly, there are those considerations that are metaphysical and theological in the substantive (rather than methodological) sense. The question of the nature of nature belongs here, too, of course; for this "foundational" issue is precisely a metaphysical problem of the first order. But in addition to the issue of how we are to understand nature, there are other large problems of religious metaphysics. How are we to understand God? Human existence? And the relations pertaining among nature, humanity, and God? What kinds of models of divine transcendence and immanence—and thus of the God-world relationship—are available to the theology of nature? How do these various models function? That is, what functions do the various models perform; and how are these functions/models related? Are some models of the divine reality and the relationship between God and the world more congenial to a theology of nature than others? If so, and if employed, do these models allow the preservation of crucial Christian insights concerning God and human existence; or do they, in their openness to the category of "nature," threaten crucial insights? What is the character of the relationship between history and nature? And what of Christ? How is Christ related to the cosmos? Is sacrament a meaningful, and even a necessary, category for specifying this relationship? What, more generally, is the proper specification of the relationship between nature and grace?

Thirdly, in addition to "considerations foundational and methodological," beyond "considerations metaphysical and theological"—but rooted in them—there are "considerations axiological and ethical." The valuational perspectives which follow from the metaphysical and theological visions must be examined. What kind of value does nature (in its totality and its parts) have? Can the various subhuman components of creation be meaningfully spoken of as possessing "intrinsic" value? What is the nature, and what are the limits, of their instrumental value? And, finally, what kinds of ethical implications follow from the various metaphysical, theological, and axiological perspectives on nature? What, that is, might be the shape of an "ecological ethic"?

These kinds of considerations we shall have before us as we do our work of cartography. These issues, and others, we must bear in mind as we explore in Part One (Chapters 2 through 4) the major new theological paths that have recently been cut for us by pioneering theologians of nature. Then in Part Two (Chapter 5) we shall summarize the results of our mapmaking and (Chapters 6 and 7) pursue our explorations a bit further.

It is only by meeting the challenge involved in the critical confrontation of these kinds of issues—only by openly examining the options we confront, their possibilities and their liabilities—that we can dare to hope that the ancient vision of creation as a theater of the divine splendor may be renewed in our time.

PART ONE

CHARTING THE LANDSCAPE: THREE CONTEMPORARY APPROACHES TO THE THEOLOGY OF NATURE

CHAPTER 2

A NEO-REFORMATION THEOLOGY OF NATURE: THE APPROACH OF H. PAUL SANTMIRE

The most explicit and fully developed contemporary attempt to do the theology of nature within a Neo-Reformation perspective is to be found in the work of H. Paul Santmire. Like the theology of John Calvin, Santmire's program centers in the imaginative elaboration of the socio-political image of the Kingdom of God. Building on the foundations laid by Reformation theologians, Santmire extends, molds, and adapts this ancient Judeo-Christian image to fit the needs of a contemporary theology of nature.

Santmire's major discussions are found in his Harvard Th.D. dissertation "Creation and Nature: A Study of the Doctrine of Nature with Special Attention to Karl Barth's Doctrine of Creation;[1] his book entitled *Brother Earth: Nature, God and Ecology in Time of Crisis* (which represents an adaptation of parts of his doctoral thesis);[2] and "Catastrophe and Ecstasy," Santmire's contribution to a volume entitled *Ecological Renewal*.[3] Santmire has also published a number of brief essays dealing with issues pertaining to the theology of nature and ecological ethics.[4] The

---

[1]Harvard University, 1966.

[2]New York: Thomas Nelson, Inc., 1970. *Brother Earth* represents the substance of Parts Two and Three of Santmire's 1966 Harvard Th.D. dissertation. Part One, "Karl Barth's Doctrine of Creation," in some respects the most penetrating aspect of Santmire's thesis, remains unpublished.

[3]Philadelphia: Fortress Press, 1972. The other contributor to *Ecological Renewal* is biologist Paul E. Lutz.

[4]A few of Santmire's shorter essays are selections from and/or adaptations of his 1966 Harvard thesis. In chronological order the relevant brief publications include the following:

present discussion attends first to Santmire's analysis of the ecological crisis and of the inadequacies of traditional theologies of nature. Secondly, the discussion explores the nature of Santmire's efforts at theological and ethical reconstruction, including his description of the program of the theology of nature.

HUMANKIND'S DILEMMA BEFORE NATURE

Like Lynn White, Paul Santmire thinks that "many of the deepest roots of America's dilemma before nature are religious."[5] This judgment can be generalized and extended beyond the American scene to include many (most?) modern cultures as well as many historical civilizations, for any culture caught up in a "dilemma before nature" is likely to have religious foundations for its difficulties. But it is in the modern technological civilizations—in the West and more particularly in the United States—that the difficulties have become most acute. Accordingly, Santmire's analysis of the roots of the ecological crisis, like White's, is broad at the foundations but narrows toward the apex (as it moves to our own time and the emergence in acute form of an environmental problem) to a consideration of Western and especially American technological man's "dilemma before nature."

"I-Thou, I-It, and I-Ens," *Journal of Religion* 48:3 (July 1968):260-73;

"A New Theology of Nature?," *Lutheran Quarterly* 20:3 (August 1968):290-308;

"Is Dogmatic Theology Dead?," *Dialog* 8 (Winter 1969):48-50;

"The Integrity of Nature," in Alfred Stefferud, ed. *Christians and the Good Earth.* (Alexandria VA: The Faith-Man-Nature Group, [1969]:128-133;

"The Struggle for an Ecological Theology: A Case in Point," *Christian Century* 87:9 (4 March 1970):275-77;

"It's His World We're Spoiling," *Resource* 11 (May 1970), 2-5;

"The Reformation Problematic and the Ecological Crisis," *Metanoia* 2 (June 1970), Special Supplement;

"Ecology and Schizophrenia: Historical Dimensions of the American Crisis," *Dialog* 9 (Summer 1970):175-92;

"On the Mission of the Church: Reflections Along the Way," *Lutheran Quarterly* 23:4 (November 1971):366-87;

"Reflections of the Alleged Ecological Bankruptcy of Western Theology," *Anglican Theological Review* 57:2 (April 1975):131-52;

"World Hunger (1): A Global 'Final Solution'?," *Dialog* 14 (Winter 1975):6-10;

"World Hunger (2): A "Confessing Church" in the U.S.?," *Dialog* 14 (Spring 1975):87-89;

"Ecology, Justice and Theology: Beyond the Preliminary Skirmishes," *Christian Century* 93:17 (12 May 1976):460-64;

"Ecology and Ethical Ecumenics," *Anglican Theological Review* 49:1 (January 1977):98-102.

[5] *Brother Earth*, 14.

The Modern Bifurcation of Experience. Santmire traces the "fundamental problem" of modern American man to the judgment that "the life of humankind and the world of nature have been bifurcated." "Properly," he contends,

> the life of man, that is "civilization," and the world of nature are *one* world. This is a theme we will return to again and again: man's very being is constituted not only by his relationship to God and to his fellow creatures but by his relationship to the whole world of nature, by his life together with *all* of God's creatures, including those "creatures" fabricated by man himself.

> It is of the essence of nature that it should offer a congenial living space, a home, to man. But civilization and nature have in fact been opposed to each other. The essential harmony of the created order has been disrupted. That is the major problem before us in this study. It is a problem which has been particularly evident in American history.[6]

Santmire's analysis of the bifurcation of experience that constitutes our dilemma before nature begins with the recognition that the dilemma of modern man has ancient roots. Utilizing a distinction set forth by Harvard historian Perry Miller in his study of early American experience, Santmire points out that the dual themes Nature versus Civilization and Civilization versus Nature are perennial and essentially universal aspects of human experience.[7] His discussion suggests that the first motif, Nature versus Civilization, can be seen in Vergil's celebration of the superior quality of the rustic life and in the wilderness elements surviving in the records of ancient Israel.[8] Moreover, the theme has found embodiment in the lives of Christian monks and ascetics who chose the virtues of the wilderness over the spiritually inferior life afforded by "civilization," including the traditions associated with the name of Saint Francis. More recently, the motif is readily seen to be prominent in the preference for nature over civilization characteristic of Henry David Thoreau, Ralph Waldo Emerson, James Fenimore Cooper, John Muir, and others. The second motif, Civilization versus Nature, is "as old as the history of man"; for humans have always found it necessary to utilize the resources of nature in order to sustain human life. But the celebrants of the "war on nature" have become both more numerous and more vocal with the rise of industrial civilization.

---

[6]Ibid., 15-16.

[7]Ibid., 16ff. See Perry Miller, *Errand Into the Wilderness* (Cambridge MA: Belknap Press, 1956) and *Nature's Nation* (Cambridge MA: Belknap Press, 1967).

[8]*Brother Earth*, p. 16. Santmire's perception of the wilderness motif in ancient Israel is informed by the illuminating study by George H. Williams, *Wilderness and Paradise in Christian Thought* (New York: Harper & Brothers, 1962).

Santmire offers an illuminating development of the two ancient motifs. With each attitudinal stance he identifies an ethic and with each ethic a cultic orientation.[9] He suggests, perhaps too schematically, that in nineteenth century America the attitude Nature versus Civilization found expression in an "ethic of adoration" and that in the twentieth century the attitude-ethic took on a compulsive form and acquired the dimensions of a religious orientation in "the cult of the simple rustic life." In similar fashion, the motif Civilization versus Nature is said to have given rise to an "ethic of exploitation" during the course of the nineteenth century and to have acquired larger, religious dimensions in the twentieth as "the cult of compulsive manipulation."[10]

The results of each ethic/cult have been mixed. Santmire appears curiously reticent about allowing the positive effects of the ethic of adoration and the so-called cult of the simple rustic life. But, rather obviously, this orientation has contributed significantly to the development of a national parks system and such conservation policies as we have. Moreover, as the expression of the Dionysian strain in American life, it provides for the development of the elements of festivity and fantasy, play, feeling, relaxation, spontaneity, even creativity.[11] Santmire

---

[9]See especially chs. 1 and 2 of *Brother Earth*.

[10]Santmire supports his analysis by a review of various developments in both intellectual and popular cultural history. Besides tracing the ethic of adoration to, among other sources, the Thoreauvian love of wilderness, Santmire locates the roots of the modern form of the ethic of exploitation in the convergence of a number of early modern events. Contrasting that which he calls "the modern anthropocentric view of nature" with "the modern telic-theocentric view of nature," Santmire identifies the former as the ideological foundation of the ethic of exploitation and the cult of compulsive manipulation. His examination of "the modern anthropocentric view of nature" results in the conclusion that it is buttressed by a number of "models," the kinds of images (machine, tool, stage) of nature which we identified in Chapter 1. Santmire sums up his discussion this way: "By the expression 'the modern anthropocentric view of nature,' then, we mean to indicate a general coalescing of the mechanical, utilitarian, and purely instrumental views of nature. Although these three views have had distinguishable origins, and although in a strict logical sense each view does not necessarily imply every other, they have grown up and lived together, as it were. Each one can be easily associated with the other—and each one has been so associated. All three considered together form a coherent, even lucid, picture; nature the useful machine posited by God for man's sake. Such is the overall shape of the modern anthropocentric view of nature" ("Creation and Nature," 21).

[11]This is a point that Santmire seems not fully to appreciate, at least not in *Brother Earth*. His later essay "Catastrophe and Ecstasy" gives evidence that it was not his intention to neglect the Dionysian strain in human life, although he does not, as far as I see, confess in straightforward fashion the more beneficial features of what he calls the ethic of adoration and the cult of the simple rustic life. In this connection the suggestive essays of Harvey Cox and Sam Keen are worth consulting: respectively, *The Feast of Fools* (Cambridge: Harvard University Press, 1969) and *Apology for Wonder* (New York: Harper & Row, 1969).

appears to deal more easily with the positive effects of the ethic of exploitation and the so-called cult of compulsive manipulation[12]— perhaps because he sees this orientation more a direct expression, albeit a distorted one, of our historicity, whereas the other orientation appears as a more direct denial of it. He points out that this more Apollonian stance (he does not call it that) has led to notable improvements in the way in which humankind deals with its ancient enemies: disease, hunger, natural disasters, poverty, injustice, and so on. Furthermore, he can describe the ethic of exploitation as egalitarian, in contrast to the conservative character of the ethic of adoration; as progressive and forward-looking, as opposed to the regressive longing for a "natural" state of affairs forever lost or rapidly disappearing; and as capable of finding deity "near at hand in the affairs of men," rather than out there on some remote wilderness mountaintop. In the purview of those who share in the ethic of exploitation, God is considered to be with human beings as they work with nature and in society. "Correspondingly, virtue and vitality [are] not located in the raw wilderness so much as in the context of challenges posed by the machine."[13]

Finally, however, the results of both ethics/cults are pernicious, notwithstanding certain beneficial features of each. In the last analysis, one failing is common to both. The problem is not simply that the ethic of exploitation and the corresponding "cult" lead to the abusive use and/or neglect of nature or that the ethic of adoration and its corresponding "cult" lead to the neglect of social concerns, although each ethical-cultic orientation does lead to the indicated result. The problem lies deeper, according to Santmire; and here his analysis reflects the finer insights of the prophetic critique of culture. Ultimately,

> Both cults have the same foundation in a rejection of authentic life in history for the sake of worldly security. Adoring nature and exploiting nature are two sides of one coin used to buy release from the challenge of historical existence.[14]

Support for this conclusion to his analysis of (a) the reasons behind the ecological crisis and (b) the need for a new theology of nature is found in Santmire's thesis that nowadays the two ethics have become the property of one person. Formerly, especially in the nineteenth century (the temporal locus of Santmire's analysis of the two ethics), "the two conflicting attitudes toward nature were characteristic of *two relatively*

---

[12]See *Brother Earth*, 31ff.

[13]Ibid., 32.

[14]Ibid., 58.

distinct groups: on the one hand, the nature philosophers and nature lovers who were fearful of the machine, and certain older aristocratic segments of society; on the other hand, the growing group of city-based entrepreneurs, an urban proletariat work force, and many hardy frontiersmen inclined to view the nature [*sic*] not as a friend but an enemy, not as a landscape but as a life-and-death challenge."[15] But today (that is, in the twentieth century—in Santmire's schematic characterization of history) the participants in the cult of the simple rustic life are chiefly suburbanites and well-to-do urbanites who are caught up in the dominant economic and academic currents of modern society. This means that the same people "are thereby priests of *both* the cult of the simple rustic life and the cult of compulsive manipulation."[16] In short, modern American man is schizophrenic; his life is compartmentalized.

Santmire supports this analysis of the bifurcated life orientation of many moderns by pointing to the lifestyle common among suburbanites and affluent urbanites. Many work in the city while dreaming of the country. They help produce noisy, polluting airplanes, but retreat to antiseptic, quiet homes in the suburbs during weekdays and to isolated hideaways on holidays.

Santmire's cultural analysis leaves him with a question: how are we to account for the fact that one and the same person has two sets of ethics? worships in two different "churches" at the same time? likes both "Bonanza" and "Mission Impossible"? If the life of technological man is unwittingly characterized by two, seemingly incompatible, foci, what is the common element holding the two together, or better, encouraging easy acceptance of the state of schizophrenia? As was suggested above, Santmire's answer is biblical:

> From a theological perspective, the American schizophrenia appears to have its deepest roots in *a failure to meet the challenge of historical existence* . . . .

> Nature thus has functioned in nineteenth and in twentieth century America, as in ancient Israel, both as an escape for those who have despaired over the society's failure to give justice to all, and as a refuge for those who have "made it" and fear further social change. The ethic of adoration and the cult of the simple rustic life have functioned as an existential rejection of history, in the full theological sense of that word.

> The other American theme, Civilization versus Nature, in both its nineteenth and twentieth century forms, has functioned in a similar way. Man's transcendence of nature was pushed to an extreme in the modern industrial West. The freedom of historical existence was employed *against* nature. Rather than accept a balanced and harmonious interrelation of nature and history,

---

[15]Ibid., 50.

[16]Ibid., 51.

those who had benefited most from the birth of a thoroughgoing historical consciousness made war on nature. Nature had been demythologized, the power of Baal undercut; but to the winner went the spoils. Nature became a mere object for exploitation and compulsive manipulation, particularly in America.[17]

In biblical perspective humankind is a historical creature. In an analysis informed by Reinhold Niebuhr,[18] Santmire points out that the Judeo-Christian understanding of human existence centers in the appreciation of our historicity. Man has been equipped (with consciousness, freedom, etc.) to be a responsible participant in the divinely initiated and shaped historical process. But historical existence has its price. and the price is high: burdensome responsibilities, insecurity before an open future, guilt associated with preventable failures, and discomforting, even incapacitating anxieties. In the face of it all the temptation, both ancient and modern, is (as Teilhard might have put it) to go on strike against our very historicity. And that is exactly what we have done and continue to do! We strike against historical existence.

Santmire's analysis of our ecological difficulties and the reasons for them comes to its crux in his identification of the ethic of adoration and the cult of the simple rustic life with a modern form of Baal worship, and the parallel identification of the ethic of exploitation and the cult of compulsive manipulation with a modern form of the worship of Mammon. As in ancient days, participation in the contemporary cults of Baal and Mammon, with their attendant ethics, becomes a way of fleeing the challenge of historical existence. This common inspiration for participation in both cults accounts, contends Santmire, for the "schizophrenia" of modern man: through both obsessive adoration and compulsive exploitation of nature man denies the demands of his divinely given mode of historical existence and destiny. This discomfiture with our historicity accompanied by our attempts to deal with it—either by losing ourselves in nature or, conversely, by waging war on nature, or both—constitutes humankind's perennial "dilemma before nature."

Nature as a Problem in the Modern Church. Before turning to Santmire's attempt to point the direction "beyond the dilemma," we should look briefly at his view of the way in which an inadequate appreciation of nature has affected the life of the Christian Church.[19] "Surprisingly," he

---

[17]Ibid., 51, 55-56.

[18]Especially *The Nature and Destiny of Man: A Christian Interpretation* (New York: Charles Scribner's Sons, 1955).

[19]This discussion focuses especially upon the following: "Nature and the Life of the

concludes, "the Church like society in general has been unwilling consist-
ently to face the challenge of historical existence."[20] Those within the
Church, like those without, have often gone after the false gods, Baal and
Mammon. The results, while varied, are uniformly pernicious.

Santmire contends that "the Church has participated in, and thereby
reinforced, the general cultural schizophrenia with regard to nature."[21]
By the terms of Santmire's analysis, the Church's inner life is vitiated
insofar as some members of the Church give allegiance to the cult of the
simple rustic life and others to the cult of compulsive manipulation. There
is within the life of the Church considerable practical support for the
flight to nature characteristic of the former cultic orientation. This is
manifest in many ways—retreat centers, Bible camps, hymnology ("I
come to the Garden alone . . . ."), et cetera—although there is little effort
given to theological articulation of the rustic motif in popular piety. In
fact, as Santmire points out, the tendency of most eccesiastical spokesmen, especially in the academic centers, is decidedly in opposition to what
is perceived to be the romanticizing tendencies of those who attend to
nature either in practice or theory. The primary reason is simple: concern
with nature is thought to deflect energy and attention from the Church's
duty of promoting social justice. And, of course, oftentimes it has; this is
the point that Santmire wishes to underscore with his talk about the cult
of the simple rustic life. But a curious thing has happened. In effect, what
Santmire's analysis suggests is that in their eagerness to oppose the
churchly followers of Baal the majority of influential theological spokesmen have lent support to the worshipers of Mammon, both within and
without the Church. By their vigorous emphasis upon humankind, by
their praiseworthy preoccupation with social concerns, by their acceptance of the dominant cultural images of nature (as machine-tool-stage),
theologians have inadvertently lent support to the cult of compulsive
manipulation.

This is readily apparent in the urban-oriented secular theology of
thinkers like Harvey Cox.[22] In *On Not Leaving It to the Snake*, Cox

---

Church," ch. 3 in *Brother Earth*, "A New Theology of Nature?," and "Creation and
Nature," xff.

[20]*Brother Earth*, 79.

[21]Ibid., 78.

[22]This is, of course, the Cox of *The Secular City* (New York: Macmillan Company,
1965) and *On Not Leaving It to the Snake* (New York: Macmillan Company, 1967). There
is evidence that Cox has taken to heart the kind of critique of his earlier orientation set
forth by theologians of nature like Santmire and Elder. In the preface to his more recent
volume *The Feast of Fools*, Cox points out that this latter work is more Dionysian in

predicts: "Future historians will record the twentieth century as that century in which the whole world became one immense city."[23] In *The Secular City* Cox explicitly warns against "the wishful thinking that hankers after Walden Pond."[24] Not only does such nostalgic longing neglect the clear and irreversible trend of the times toward greater urban and technological development, it runs directly contrary to the biblical nisus toward the "desacralization of nature." Leaning heavily on the Yahwistic creation account, Cox claims that "the Hebrew view of Creation . . . separates nature from God and distinguishes man from nature."[25] This means that

> Man becomes in effect a subject facing nature. He can still enjoy it and delight in it, perhaps even more so since its terrors have been reduced for him. But man is not a mere expression of nature and nature is not a divine entity.[26]

Cox goes on to emphasize the theme of man's dominion over nature. Since the Genesis account of creation "allows man to perceive nature itself in a matter-of-fact way,"

> The mature secular man neither reverences nor ravages nature. His task is to tend it and make use of it, to assume the responsibility assigned to The Man, Adam . . . . It is his task to subdue the earth. Nature is neither his brother nor his god . . . . For the Bible, neither man nor God is defined by his relationship to nature. This not only frees both of them for history, it also makes nature itself available for man's use.[27]

There is much in Cox's perspective that cannot properly be gainsaid. But the consequence of his position, as it is developed in his earlier essays at least, is to direct attention *away* from the natural world or toward it *only* in a utilitarian fashion. Man "can still enjoy it and delight in it," he allows: that is, nature has a kind of hedonistic and aesthetic utility.[28] Man

---

character and hence functions as a partial corrective to the more Apollonian tendencies of the former essays. A fair appraisal of Cox's ecological bearing must consider his later as well as his earlier work.

[23]*On Not Leaving It to the Snake*, 101.

[24]*The Secular City*, 174.

[25]Ibid., 22.

[26]Ibid., 24.

[27]Ibid., 23.

[28]The enjoyment of and delight in nature could become part of the basis of a sacramental theology of nature, as is the case in the theology of Joseph Sittler. But Cox's theology of the secular does not give a prominent place to the category of the sacramental, although (as H. Richard Niebuhr emphasizes) the proper correlate of the recognition of the secularization of all things is appreciation of the sanctification of all things. Thus, while Cox's interest is not in the development of the theology of nature as such, *The Feast*

can use it as the setting for his cities and as the raw stuff out of which he forges his urban environment: nature has material and economic utility. But nature has no status or significance in itself, or none that Cox attends to in his early essays. In Cox, then, all vestiges of the cult of the simple rustic life have vanished; but his theology of urban secularity and his praiseworthy expressions of social concern inadvertently lend support to the exploitative attitude toward nature that is foundational to what Santmire calls the cult of compulsive manipulation.

In most of its forms existential theology, with its stress on human transcendence of and dominion over nature, has had much the same effect as urban-oriented secular theology. With its exclusivistic emphasis upon existence in history and upon history as the locus of revelation, existentialist theology has helped deflect serious ecclesiastical attention from nature and has (inadvertently?) supported the dominant cultural utilitarian attitude toward nature. The most apt metaphor to describe the role of nature in the work of most existentialist theologians is the metaphor of the stage: nature is the setting for the human historical-personal drama.[29]

One of the far-reaching factors at work in the theology of the contemporary Church leading to the neglect of nature and the concomitant bolstering of the exploitative utilitarian attitude has been the influence of Karl Barth. Santmire devoted a significant amount of his Harvard doctoral dissertation to exploring the contours of the doctrine of nature present in Barth's doctrine of creation. Among his findings are the following. Not only does Barth vigorously emphasize the gulf separating God and man but he accents the distance between man and the remainder of the created order. Barth makes man the sole legitimate interest of theology insofar as theology is concerned with the created world. Says Barth, "In practice the doctrine of creation means anthropology—the doctrine of man."[30] Moreover, Barth denies any legitimacy to a Christian

---

of Fools can be seen as, among other things, his (post "secular city") attempt at recovery of the sacramental element in Christian piety and theologizing.

[29]There is another more positive treatment of nature among certain existentialist thinkers; Santmire himself, following leads from Martin Buber and Karl Heim, utilizes existentialist categories in his own reconstructive efforts. There is also a more negative treatment of nature to be found among existentialists, especially in the philosophy of Jean-Paul Sartre. Sartre seems to have little or no positive regard for nature; on the contrary, nature essentially becomes for Sartre an image of the diabolical and fills him with "nausea." So while the metaphor of the stage is the dominant image for nature in the writings of existentialist theologians and philosophers, it is not the only one.

[30]Karl Barth, *Church Dogmatics*, 4 vols., trans. and ed. G. W. Bromiley et al. (Edinburgh: T. & T. Clark, 1936-1969), 3:2:3.

theological interest in nature as such. Accordingly, Barth does not develop a doctrine of nature in terms of the best modern insights available. Instead, contending that the Christian theologian does not need a doctrine of nature as part of his doctrine of creation, Barth involuntarily and unwittingly incorporates the modern mechanical-utilitarian understanding of nature into his theology. The result of the coupling of Barth's strenuously anthropocentric orientation (anthropocentric as far as the created order is concerned) with his refusal to develop a doctrine of nature, and the correlative borrowing of the dominant modern doctrine, is ecologically devastating: "As the last stages of myth and ontology disappear, which they do in Barth's theology, man's freedom to master and shape, to create and explore now reaches out to the ends of the earth and beyond."[31] Barth's widely influential theology inadvertently baptizes the ethos characteristic of the cult of compulsive manipulation.

Thus, in Santmire's analysis, the life of the Church, like the life of modern technological culture in general, has become schizophrenic with regard to nature. Elements of both uncritical adoration and mindless support of the exploitation of nature are present in the life of the Church. But given the vigorous emphasis upon man and human dominion over the environment it is clear, contends Santmire, that "by default, if not by conscious intention, theology works to support the general American cultural theme, Civilization versus Nature."[32] Hence, the attitude toward nature characteristic of the cult of compulsive manipulation has achieved ascendancy in the life of the Church. The results are far-reaching.

"Subtly but relentlessly, the cult of compulsive manipulation is sapping the vitality from the internal life of the Church itself."[33] Santmire attempts to support this contention by reviewing, somewhat sketchily, modern expressions of the faith, hope, and love of the Church. Briefly his argument is as follows. The ancient *faith* that God is at work in all the vicissitudes and joys of life, including earthquakes and abundant harvests, is undetermined by the purely mechanical and utilitarian view of nature. Since God is excluded from nature when it is understood as a machine (and hence as self-operating), faith cannot trace the operation of the hand of God in natural occurrences, beneficent or otherwise. Similarly, *hope* is undercut. Calvin's sense that the daily metamorphoses within nature indicate that *natura spirat resurrectionem* is not available

---

[31]"Creation and Nature," 82.

[32]*Brother Earth*, 66.

[33]Ibid., 67-68. The concerns of this paragraph are discussed in *Brother Earth*, 67-74, and "A New Theology of Nature," 295-301.

to those whose sense of nature is shaped along mechanical-utilitarian lines.[34] The latter simply do not have, says Santmire, meaningful analogies that would make the hope of resurrection a possibility. Moreover, the inability to hope for the ultimate salvation of the corporeal (whether the body or the cosmos) vitiates our power to *love* and to act lovingly. If corporality finally does not matter, or matters little, why treat either the environment or the embodiment of a brother with care? An inadequate view of nature has disastrous practical consequences for the Christian: it destroys his capacity to "faith," hope, and love deeply and authentically.

Thus does Santmire suggest that in multiple ways the Church, like society in general, is caught up in a "dilemma before nature."

THE NATURE OF THE THEOLOGY OF NATURE

It is in Scripture that Santmire finds the inspiration and insights needed to transcend the human-American-churchly dilemma with nature. He maintains that in the biblical vision of nature, man, and God both of the perennial themes—Nature versus Civilization and Civilization versus Nature—are left behind. Acknowledging that the idea of "nature" is not readily identifiable in Scripture and that "we cannot simply turn to the Bible to read how to resolve our modern societal and ecclesiastical dilemmas with nature,"[35] Santmire is convinced nonetheless that the biblical writings contain neglected but highly suggestive pointers that can help us along the way toward the requisite new theology of nature and revised ecological ethic.

Before examining the contours of Santmire's reconstructive efforts, however, it is necessary to look at how he understands "nature" and the "theology of nature." *Like most of the new theologians of nature, Santmire nowhere attends in depth or detail to exactly what it is that he is theologizing about.* In other words, he does not engage in a critical examination of the concept of nature. Yet he does set forth the way in which he intends to employ the term "nature" and its cognates: he postulates his linguistic intentions without offering a critical investigation of the meaning of "nature."

His postulations are as follows. The term "nature" in his usage means "the physical-vital aspect of the whole creation," "the material-vital

---

[34]Cf., for example, Calvin's comments on 1 Corinthians:15 (esp. vss. 36 and 41) in the *Commentary on the Epistles of Paul the Apostle to the Corinthians*, trans. John Pringle (Edinburgh, 1849).

[35]*Brother Earth*, 80.

universe in which we live," "the whole matrix of man's organic and physical existence."[36] Santmire intends his employment of "one of the most divergently used words in the English language" to be in line with the meaning that emerged in nineteenth century German thinking about the nature-spirit distinction—especially as the meaning of both "nature" and "spirit," and the relationship between them, was given shape by the influence of Immanuel Kant. "According to this distinction," as Santmire employs it, "the whole of finite reality is natural, including man, but man is also spiritual, that is, capable of transcending the physical-vital world of which he is a part."[37]

By his definition of the term "nature" Santmire rejects any identification of this term with the entire creation, although the notion of nature is frequently employed in this more universal sense. Moreover, he is involved in rejecting any suggestion that the "natural" is something that follows the fall or that has no reality or status apart from human sin or that disappears when redemption is effected. Nature, as the physical-vital aspect of the whole creation, exists before, during, and after "the fall"; it is, therefore, present "throughout the economy of Redemption." Thirdly, Santmire's employment of the term denies any suggestion that houses, automobiles, cities, and so on are "not natural." He deals with "fabricated nature" as "nature [that is, the physical-vital aspect of creation] taken up into, or stamped by, the world of spirit."[38]

The problems of delineating the meaning of "nature" are, of course, immense; and we shall return to them repeatedly in this study. Santmire appears to recognize the limitations of his own treatment of the concept of nature, for he sets forth his definition as a "working" rather than a "normative" definition. "It has," he rightly acknowledges, "a certain lack of clarity. . . ."[39]

Santmire's specification of the nature of the theology of nature is somewhat more fully developed than his explication of the meaning of nature as such, although the failure really to clarify the latter term remains an obfuscatory element within his theological enterprise. This may, of course, be a limitation that the theology of nature cannot trans-

---

[36]See especially "A New Theology of Nature?," 291f. and *Brother Earth*, 7 and 15.

[37]"A New Theology of Nature?," 292.

[38]Ibid.

[39]Ibid. The most penetrating and thorough-going challenge to the lackadaisical attitude with which most contemporary theologians of nature approach and employ the concept of nature is to be found in Gordon Kaufman's "A Problem for Theology: The Concept of Nature," *Harvard Theological Review* 65 (1972):337-66. We shall attend to some of the issues and ideas of this essay in the present study, especially in part two.

cend at the present time, if ever. But the extent to which the "nature of 'nature' " can be properly specified remains an open issue. Be that as it may, Santmire has not yet provided a comprehensive statement of his methodological program; even his programmatic "A New Theology of Nature?" is more concerned with the need for a new theological treatment of nature than with the methodological character such an enterprise should manifest. Still, he provides certain guidelines; and we can draw conclusions from his actual performance.

Most important, Santmire's understanding of the theology of nature is informed by his acceptance, in large part, of the Neo-Orthodox critique of natural theology. Karl Barth's denial that there is any knowledge of God apart from the revelation in Christ or that there is any *Anknüpfungspunkt* in fallen man whereby reception of revelation could be rendered possible from the human side has not found universal acceptance. Yet his affirmation that God is known clearly, reliably, and accurately only through his own self-disclosure in Christ has (until fairly recently, at any rate) found widespread consensus among Protestant theologians.[40]

The methodological consequence of this epistemological conviction has also been widely influential: "natural theology" in the sense of a prolegomenon to and substructure of dogmatic theology (as in both Catholic and Protestant Scholasticism) as well as in the sense of a virtual replacement of dogmatic theology (as in Protestant Liberalism) is unnecessary and illegitimate. What is more, since it is an expression of man's propensity to fashion gods in his own image, natural theology must even be reckoned sinful. Essentially, theology is dogmatics—reflection on the faith of the Church as that faith is manifested in Scripture (especially), preaching, and sacraments. Theology arises out of and presupposes the meeting between God and man, whether that encounter is understood as totally governed from the divine side, as in Barth, or as conditioned also by the human participant, as in Brunner.

Santmire's theological program has taken shape against the Barthian background in particular and within the general ethos created by the Neo-Orthodox polemic. This means that his is a dogmatic enterprise: he reflects on the character and significance of nature and on the relationships pertaining among God, humanity, and nature from the standpoint

---

[40]Barth's broadside against natural theology is found throughout his many volumes. Of especial relevancy to the discussions of Barth in this study are his early commentary *The Epistle to the Romans*, trans. Edwyn C. Hoskyns (London: Oxford University Press, 1933), his interchange with Emil Brunner in *Natural Theology*, trans. Peter Fraenkel (London: Geoffrey Bles; Centenary Press, 1946) and various passages in his *Church Dogmatics* (the following in particular: 1:1:147f., 219, 448, 540; 1:2:123, 263ff.; 2:1:76ff., 85ff., 162ff., 215ff., 453; 4:1:79ff.; 4:2:100ff.).

of revelation and the faith that attends it. The theology of nature is not a propaedeutic to some other kind of theology, nor is it designed to create faith. Rather, it presupposes faith and arises out of it. In a brief essay entitled "Is Dogmatic Theology Dead?"—an essay which seems to reflect his attempt to reassure the validity of his theological enterprise in a changed theological climate—Santmire describes approvingly the program of Regin Prenter in words that could apply to his own work:

> Prenter sees the need for dogmatics arising here: to nourish and to guide the secret discipline of faith by reformulating the classical dogmas which gave substance to faith in the past. Dogmatic theology, then, is an intramural enterprise. It is not meant directly for ears outside the walls of the worshipping community. . . . Dogmatics interprets the confession of the worshipping congregation.[41]

There is some evidence that Santmire leaves open the question of the legitimacy of the program of natural theology as that undertaking has recently been reformulated by Schubert Ogden and John Cobb.[42] However, his understanding of the theology of nature is that it is an enterprise to be clearly and sharply differentiated from natural theology.

> The latter question arises in the context of the *dogmatic prolegomena* in relation to the concepts of revelation and reason. The question of a theology of nature or a theology of the earth arises in the context of the *positive theological exposition* itself, in particular the doctrine of creation.[43]

In Santmire's view, then, the theology of nature represents a contemporary reexamination and reformulation of (sometimes neglected) aspects of the faith of the Church. Its primary concern is with motifs that have traditionally been treated (if at all) under the rubric of the doctrine of

---

In the early sixties the theological climate began to shift dramatically with the emergence of the so-called secular and death-of-god theologies. Interestingly, these new currents represent a simultaneous repudiation and continuation of Neo-Orthodox theology. The Barthian emphasis upon human sinfulness and limits has been replaced by a celebration of the human qua human; and the Barthian emphasis upon the transcendence of God has been extended to the point that God in his transcendent dimension has disappeared. We are left in a position of waiting for God (the William Hamilton of *The New Essence of Christianity*), giving up on God entirely (the later Hamilton), or discovering that God now has being only in an immanent, this-worldly dimension (Thomas Altizer and, in a different fashion, Richard Rubenstein).

[41]"Is Dogmatic Theology Dead?," 48-49. Santmire's discussion in this brief essay focuses on Regin Prenter's *Creation and Redemption*, trans. Theodore I. Jensen (Philadelphia: Fortress Press, 1967).

[42]See, e.g., "A New Theology of Nature?," 291. This post-Barthian reformulated natural theology is examined in Chapter 3.

[43]Ibid.

creation. As such, the theology of nature is a dogmatic enterprise that is based on the confession of the Church.

As his position on natural theology suggests, Santmire tends to argue along Neo-Orthodox lines in spite of numerous divergences from Karl Barth. The dogmatic and Neo-Orthodox character of Santmire's theology is perhaps most clearly evidenced by his adoption of Christ as "*the key* to the new theological horizon" which his explorations in the field of the theology of nature are intended to open before us.[44] As we shall see, Santmire correctly perceives that Christian faith and theology must finally be theocentric rather than merely christocentric. But like Luther, Calvin, *and Barth*—Barth does appear to allow for an ecological theology or a theology of the earth, in spite of his refusal to attend to the theology of nature in the fullest sense of the word[45]—Santmire intends his theological treatment of nature to be done in the light of the Christian faith response to the revelation in Christ. Picking up motifs characteristic of Paul, Irenaeus, and Luther, Santmire interprets Christ as the "mediator" or "royal minister" who both "restores the disrupted present creation" and "represents and realizes the coming of the new creation in the midst of the present creation."[46] Accordingly, nature or the physical-vital aspect of creation (past, present, and future) can properly be understood only in the light of Christ.

To differentiate the recently renewed theological interest in nature, including his own, from that of previous ages Santmire sometimes employs the term "a *critical* theology of nature." [47] Prior to Kant, Christian interest in and theological employment of the concept of nature was essentially pre-critical in character. Appeals to nature for religious purposes were virtually ubiquitous in the writings of both Catholic and Protestant scholars. The Enlightenment employment of "natural reason" to discover and substantiate the truths of religion—as illustrated by such works as Locke's *Reasonableness of Christianity* (1693) and Butler's *Analogy of Religion* (1736)—was but one moment in the long and comfortable marriage between "nature" and "reason" that produced such fateful offspring as Thomas's five ways and Paley's evidences. Hume's *Dialogues on Natural Religion* (1779) and Kant's *Critique of Pure Reason* (1781) introduced—or better, brought to consciousness—tensions in

---

[44]See especially *Brother Earth*, ch. 8.

[45]See especially the part of Barth's doctrine of creation entitled "Man in the Cosmos," in *Church Dogmatics*, 3:2, par. 43.

[46]*Brother Earth*, 163.

[47]"A New Theology of Nature?," 306-308.

this happy marriage which have not yet, and likely will not ever, be laid to rest. Karl Barth's polemic against natural theology is in part a product of the revolutionary heightening of consciousness attributable especially to Kant.

Santmire treats rather summarily the characteristics a critical theology of nature will have;[48] and, since these features are illustrated by our examination of the shape of his theology of nature, they will be treated even more summarily here. Santmire maintains that a critical theology of nature (1) will respect the contemporary consensus concerning nature and history that has emerged in modern biblical theology: the recognition, namely, that the main theme of the biblical writings is history rather than nature as such. Moreover, the enterprise (2) must recognize man's historical transcendence of nature as such and his "special place in the greater scheme of things." As we have seen, a critical theology of nature (3) will respect the Kantian insights regarding the limits of human reason and the Barthian perception of the proper placing of a Christian theological interest in creation. With Barth, too, a critical theology of nature (4) will "affirm and defend" the reality of divine transcendence in opposition to all pantheising reductions of God to the level of nature or exaltations of nature to the status of God. It (5) will be written with an appreciation of the limits of the discipline of theology, even as it takes serious and informed cognizance of developments in the natural sciences: "Theology, if it is to be critical, cannot and should not claim that it can do without the natural sciences or that it has the right to instruct the natural sciences about the results at which they ought to arrive."[49] And the required critical theology of nature (6) will be sensitive to the social concomitants of the perspectives on nature with which it begins and in which it issues.

Finally, a word about terminology. Besides the terms "theology of nature" and "critical theology of nature," Santmire, like other authors, sometimes employs the phrases "theology of earth" and "ecological theology" to describe his project. The latter terms have the advantage of directing attention to what we are calling the ecological motif in the writings of thinkers who have relevancy to the theology of nature but have not attended to it forthrightly, including theologians like Karl Barth who have relevancy but reject the enterprise.

Santmire points out certain advantages and disadvantages of the most commonly employed terms, "theology of nature" and "ecological theol-

---

[48]See ibid.; also "Creation and Nature," xxxiiiff.

[49]"A New Theology of Nature?," 307.

ogy."[50] The phrase "ecological theology," he thinks, elicits a sense of active human participation in the physical-vital *oikos* and of interdependence between man and nature, whereas the phrase "theology of nature" may suggest a more narrow focus upon the physical-vital dimension to which man is related in an essentially passive fashion bordering on exclusion from participation. However, he considers the term "theology of nature" to be less anthropocentric than the sister phrase; accordingly, he maintains that "it allows us to emphasize the integrity of nature as well as man's proper relationship to nature."[51] Thus, we find Santmire utilizing a variety of nomenclature, but the "theology of nature" seems to be his most frequent denomination for his project.

This, then, is Santmire's understanding of his theological project. We have already examined his analysis of the need—in both its practical and theoretical dimensions—for a new theological approach to nature. We can now proceed to map the contours of his own reconstructive efforts.

BEYOND THE DILEMMA: THE THEOLOGY OF CO-CITIZENRY

Although Santmire recognizes that modern Western understandings of nature are not readily identifiable in Scripture; notes that modern biblical scholarship has not concerned itself very much with such scriptural themes as do bear upon our conceptions of nature; he observes that recent scholarship has even worked at times more to obscure than to clarify the biblical understanding of what has come to be called "nature," he thinks that Scripture can provide the needed corrective to our human-American-churchly dilemma with nature—if we will allow it to speak to

---

[50] *Brother Earth*, 201.

[51] Ibid. Notwithstanding Santmire's defense of the term "ecological theology" and my own tendency to consent to custom by using it, the phrase seems to me to be somewhat fuzzy and potentially misleading. Above all, there appears to be an occasional initial lack of clarity as to whether the interest of the person using the term is directed at the physical-vital aspect of creation or only at interrelationships between human (or human and divine) subjects. It might be possible to have an "ecological theology" that shows little or no interest in the earth or in "nature"; and there is evidence that some authors utilize the term in just this fashion. The term "ecological ethic" does not appear to me to partake of the same ambiguity, for in this phrase the adjective "ecological" is a redundancy unless it directs attention to the extra-human dimension of creation.

Other authors, of course, employ still additional terminology: for example, "a theology of (or for) the environment," "environmental theology," "eco-theology," "a theology of the inorganic," and "a theology of things." Each of these terms has its advantages and its liabilities. But they all represent a widespread contemporary interest in finding a way of reflecting theologically and ethically about "nature" without falling into the now widely recognized pitfalls of natural theology.

us in spite of all our prejudgments. Here Santmire follows the Barthian mode of theologizing: in time of crisis and human perplexity he returns to listen again to the words of Scripture in hopes of hearing anew the Word of God. The result at which he arrives, however—what he hears as the Word of God for our time of ecological crisis—is in some respects more in keeping with the theology of H. Richard Niebuhr than with the dogmatics of Barth.[52] It is the message of the Kingdom of God.

Santmire selects the scriptural motif of the Kingdom of God as the imaginative framework within which the various relevant elements of the biblical vision can be brought together and the dilemma with nature transcended. Making the socio-political image of the Kingdom the foundation of the theology of nature functions constructively in several ways. Initially, Santmire stresses two advantages.[53]

Since the Kingdom of God is a socio-political metaphor and its theological employment is generally associated with an ethical concern for human justice (as, par excellence, in the "social gospel" of Walter Rauschenbusch), the utilization of this image for a theological interpretation of nature should rule out any tendency towards the linking of religious concern for nature with social quiescence and escapism. Yet, as Santmire's analysis of the human dilemma with nature has shown, a lively interest in nature is often accompanied by social conservatism, neglect of social justice, anti-urban and even (we might add) misanthropic attitudes, a vital interest in nature nurtured within the framework provided by the image of the Kingdom of God can scarcely lead to such results. It cannot, at least, if the ethical implications of the basic imagery are properly appreciated. Thus, contemporary affirmation of the biblical and theologically classical metaphor of the Kingdom of God provides the occasion for the expression of a coequal interest in and concern for both nature and human society. This is the first of the two major reasons that Santmire gives for adopting the socio-political image of the Kingdom as the foundation of his theology of nature.

The second reason turns on Santmire's attempt to bring out some frequently neglected implications or aspects of the Kingdom imagery: the rule of the King requires a realm, and the realm has its own integrity and

---

[52]Niebuhr, of course, elaborated his own theology in conversation with Karl Barth, among others; and both thinkers trace a common theological ancestry to John Calvin, to identify only the lineage most apropos of the metaphor and orientation to be discussed in this section. Curiously, Santmire does not much mention Niebuhr in spite of the basic similarity of aspects of his theology of nature to what we are calling the ecological motif found in the theology of H. Richard Niebuhr. In some other respects, as the above paragraph suggests, Santmire's orientation is thoroughly Barthian.

[53]*Brother Earth*, 101ff.

value for the Sovereign. What Santmire is trying to do is "avoid the kind
of problematic personalism which has come to dominate contemporary
theology, at least in Protestantism."[54] By the "problematic personalism"
of Protestant theologians, Santmire intends the kind of development
found in Barth and Brunner and, in another sense, in Tillich. The so-
called "hyper-personalism" of the latter tends to obscure any recogniz-
ably personal qualities of the ultimate. The virtually exclusive concern of
the former for the divine history with humankind tends to reduce the
realm of nature to nothing but the stage and scenery for the human
drama. Santmire argues, in effect, that the biblical vision in general and
the Kingdom imagery in particular are in tension with both types of
"problematic personalism." Adopting the Kingdom of God as the
imaginative framework for the theology of nature provides a corrective.

> It allows us to conceive of a personal God who relates himself directly both to
> a personal creature (man) and to an a-personal creature (the whole of nature)
> with the same degree of intensity, if not the same kind of intimacy. This, in
> principle, will allow us to do justice to the Bible's picture of the Divine history
> with nature [contra Barth and Brunner]. At the same time, it is evident that
> the image preserves and emphasizes the personalism of the biblical vision
> [contra Tillich]: a king is fittingly thought of as one who deliberates, acts,
> enjoys, loves, punishes, and generally relates himself to both things and
> people in a personal way.[55]

Santmire wants to retain the classical emphasis upon the personal character of God, which he thinks Tillich fails to do. He wants to retain an
interest also in the extra-human dimension of creation, which he thinks
theologians like Barth and Brunner fail to do.

Santmire recognizes that the connotation of the Kingdom imagery as
understood and employed by many, both classical and contemporary, is
predominately spiritual, social, and ethical. In fact, as we have seen, that
is part of the strength of this kind of imagery for those who, in doing the
theology of nature, wish to avoid the pitting of concern with nature
against concern with social justice. The Kingdom of God has included the
ethical relations between the divine Sovereign and his people and the
ethical relations obtaining among the people themselves. Santmire traces
the tendency to limit the connotations of the image to its socio-ethical and
spiritual functions to Kant and, before him, to Augustine and a minority
of passages found in the biblical writings (such as Rev. 1:5b-6). But he
maintains that a more comprehensive understanding of this metaphor is
in evidence in the theology of Luther and Calvin and in the dominant

---

[54]Ibid., 101.

[55]Ibid., 102.

thrusts of both the Old and the New Testaments. He cites in evidence
Luther's doctrine of the Two Kingdoms, maintaining that the first Kingdom is constituted by the rule of God over the entirety of creation—
including both history and nature.[56] Calvin, too, can be interpreted as
including the whole of nature in his conception of the Kingdom of God:
the dynamic rule of God is such that "he governs all events."[57] Most
important, however, for this essentially Neo-Orthodox theology of
nature, significant aspects of Scripture evidence the comprehensive
understanding of the Kingdom.[58] Santmire points specifically to such Old
Testament passages as the prayer of David found in I Chronicles 29:11:
"Thine, O Lord, is the greatness, and the power, and the glory, and the
victory, and the majesty; for all that is in the heavens and in the earth is
thine; thine is the kingdom, O Lord, and thou art exalted as head above
all." This passage Santmire regards as suggestive of the dominant nisus of
the Old Testament attitude toward the relationship between the physical-
vital dimension of creation and the notion of the Kingdom. Moreover, he
finds this line of thought continued in the New Testament. Maintaining
that the notion of the transformation of the cosmos is included in Jesus'
proclamation of the Kingdom of God, he points out that recent studies of
the parables of growth suggest that Jesus thought of the Kingdom as
coming immediately in his own works and words and ultimately in a
dramatic consummation of the world.[59] The same broad understanding

---

[56]See ibid., 103 and 213, note 9.

[57]John Calvin, *Institutes of the Christian Religion*, 2 vols., ed. John T. McNeill
(Philadelphia: Westminster Press, 1960); see especially 1:xvi, 3, 4, and 7. In the latter
article Calvin affirms that "no wind ever arises or increases except by God's express
command."

[58]See especially *Brother Earth*, ch. 4 and 104, 208ff.; also passim. I regard Santmire's
point that the biblical understanding of the Kingdom includes the notion of realm as well
as rule to be a refinement of the biblical vision, a refinement that is essentially correct and
that has substantial scholarly support.

The literature relevant to the position Santmire is setting forth includes the following:
John Bright, *The Kingdom of God* (Nashville: Abingdon Press, 1953); Norman Perrin,
The Kingdom of God in the Teaching of Jesus (Philadelphia: Westminster Press, 1963);
and Gerhard von Rad, et al., "Basileia," *Bible Key Words*, 2nd vol., trans. and ed. J. R.
Coates and H. P. Kingdon (New York: Harper & Brothers, 1958).

[59]*Brother Earth*, 90. See N. A. Dahl, "The Parables of Growth," *Studia Theologica*,
5:2 (1951):132-66 and S. E. Johnson, "Matthew," *The Interpreter's Bible*, vol. 7 (New
York: Abingdon-Cokesbury Press, 1951) whose discussion of the term *palingenesia* (Mt.
19:28) Santmire follows.

On Santmire's sense of the character of the scriptural perspective on nature, the
following passage is particularly worthy of note:
"The *main lines* of the biblical picture of the Divine history with nature are set forth in
both Testaments, but most of the *details* of the picture come from the Old Testament. But

of this basic biblical image is reflected in other New Testament passages: "The Book of Revelation envisions the world as having become the Kingdom of God and his Christ (11:15) with the implicit idea of the creation of a new heaven and a new earth (cf. 21:1), along with the implicit idea of a more spiritual kingdom, the New Jerusalem (cf. 21:2)."[60]

Essentially, then, what Santmire does is adopt the image of the Kingdom of God as the imaginative framework for his theology of nature because it is a biblical image capable of fulfilling an important correlating function. The metaphor of the Kingdom provides a means of bringing concern for social justice into a concern for nature; in so doing, it makes possible the transcending of the one-sided and problematical interest in nature that characterizes "the ethic of adoration" and "the cult of the simple rustic life." Moreover, the Kingdom imagery provides a means of bringing an affirmation of the divine concern for and governance of nature into an affirmation of the divine concern for and governance of history. Essentially, the Kingdom metaphor becomes the foundation of Santmire's assertion of the integrity and value of nature by virtue of his employment of it to provide a corrective to a certain "problematic personalism" and to make possible the transcending of "the ethic of exploitation" and "the cult of compulsive manipulation." In the biblical vision centering in the message of the Kingdom of God, understood as both realm and rule of God, the human-American-churchly dilemma before nature is overcome—as God, man, *and* nature are brought together in the framework provided by this image.

The Kingdom of God as Creative Rule and Created Realm. Santmire's biblically based theology of nature turns on a distinction, oftentimes passed over with little or no notice, between the divine rule or "creative working" of God and the divine realm or "created works" of God. "This double connotation" of the Kingdom imagery "expresses the fundamental biblical conviction that God both *rules majestically* . . . and rules majestically throughout his *creation*."[61] Santmire strives to follow what appears to him as the lead of the biblical writers in holding in equilibrium

---

in its main lines, the New Testament is consistent with the Old, and that continuity is decisive. Of subordinate significance is the fact that many of the details concerning nature found in the Old Testament are taken for granted by the New, particularly in the teaching of Jesus. That we find most of the colors and the lesser lines of the biblical picture of nature in the Old Testament, then, should present no difficulty if we take our stand with the classical tradition of the Church and approach the *whole* Bible as Scripture." (*Brother Earth*, 81-82).

[60]Ibid., 104.

[61]Ibid.

concern with the governing activity of the divine Sovereign and concern with the sphere governed by the Sovereign. He perceives dangers in an overemphasis upon either one of these concerns accompanied by a neglect of the other. He suggests that the rule or sovereignty of God can be so emphasized as to make the creation appear as "no more than an extension of the Creator." Conversely, the realm can be so emphasized as to come to be perceived as autonomous in character. This is one of the points at which Santmire's theology of nature can be most clearly seen as continuing the kinds of functions and motifs that have traditionally been found under the rubric of the doctrine of creation: the functions, namely, of distinguishing the creation from the Creator, on the one hand, and on the other, of affirming the absolute dependency (Schleiermacher) of the creation upon the Creator. Santmire's theology of nature performs the same functions in a way not dissimilar to Calvin's theology by employing the political (as opposed to the cosmogonic) imagery of Ruler, rule, and realm. In any case, the distinction between divine rule and divine realm is one upon which much of Santmire's discussion turns, and to which we must now attend.[62]

Santmire attempts to maintain an equilibrium between concern with the governing activity of God and concern with the sphere governed by God through the elaboration of a series of parallel distinctions. The first of the three sets of distinctions has to do with the creative rule of God over nature. The second lists the corresponding characteristics of the created realm of God. And the third presents certain marks of humankind that are said to parallel the distinguishing features of God's rule and his realm.

Santmire develops his theology of the divine ruling and the divine realm from a historicized standpoint; he attempts to depict "the divine history with nature."[63] The bearing of his reflections is strongly eschatological in character, and at this point a processive or dynamic element clearly emerges in his theology. However, as with Karl Barth, the process motif is inspired by the biblical concern with history and "last things," rather than by the modern scientific interest in origins and evolution which is reflected in John Cobb's theology of nature.

The creative rule of God is dynamic. It is characterized, says Santmire, by three "simultaneous aspects" or "moments": (1) God's powerful establishing of all things, (2) his wise shaping of all things, and (3) God's joyful valuing of all things. These are "moments in process, moments on the way." That is, Santmire wants to emphasize that God's rule in all its

---

[62]See especially *Brother Earth*, chs. 6 and 7, and Nature, chs. 7-9.
[63]See *Brother Earth*, 106ff.

aspects is goal-oriented; and he wants to envision the goal-orientation of the divine ruling in terms of strictly biblical imagery. "When God establishes, shapes, and values all things, he always does so with a goal in mind, the new creation of all things, the consummation of his own creative rule."[64] Corresponding to these "moments" of the divine rule are certain characteristics of the created realm: nature is said to have its own spontaneity, continuity, and congruity.

Santmire employs a series of biblical images to suggest the eschatological terminus and consummation of the divine rule: new creation, divine sabbath rest, and Omega. The point of his discussion of each image of consummation is to suggest that a biblically informed theology *must*—if its author attends to Scripture aright—affirm the notion that God is so ruling in his creation that all aspects of it, natural as well as human, will be brought to an appropriate fulfillment. Santmire's polemic is directed at those who would give to the biblical images of hope a purely human-historical content. This includes not only thinkers like Rudolf Bultmann but Teilhard de Chardin in his employment of the idea of Omega as a symbol of consummation. As is well known, some passages in the Teilhardian corpus suggest that the sole function of the material aspect of creation is that of energizing, as it were, the emergence and the ascent of spirit toward Point Omega. In spite of his emphasis upon the inner side of things and in spite of his obvious interest in the prehuman dimension of nature, Teilhard appears at times to suggest that ultimately in the evolutionary ascent toward maximum "personalization" all pre-personal aspects of creation will fall away into nothingness. As a corrective to what Santmire perceives as a distortion of the biblical perspective at this point, he recommends that the Teilhardian symbol be modified and that we speak of "the Omega-world as the telos of the universe" in order to offset any unscriptural tendency toward devaluation of the physical-vital aspect of creation.[65] Santmire's concern is that each of the eschatological symbols be understood and employed in such a way as to affirm that the divine rule is directed at the fulfillment of natural as well as human possibilities.

Thus, the theology of nature is necessarily cast in an eschatological framework, according to Santmire; or, at least, it is to be done in

---

[64]Ibid., 107.

[65]Ibid., 108. There are significant problems with Teilhard's program. It is not clear, however, that his critics—Santmire and Elder among them—have properly understood him or done him justice at this point. An alternative interpretation of Teilhard's vision of the ultimate destiny of the material aspect of creation—and, hence, a corrective to Santmire's and Elder's reading of the priest-paleontologist—is offered in Chapter 4.

conjunction with a theology of last things. Santmire evidently recognizes the difficult circumstances he is putting himself in by his forthright affirmation of the biblical images of hope, for he says that he has moved into the language of prayer and confesses that ultimately in these matters *omnium exeunt in mysterium*. This is an important allowance. For there are major questions about the contemporary availability of biblical images of the future and of hope; and the problems may well be compounded rather than lessened if one proceeds as Santmire, and Barth, do—by reaffirming the biblical imagery in the contemporary situation and, especially, by asserting the relevancy of the biblical images for the theology of nature without really showing the links that bind the two together. For example, Santmire proceeds to affirm some of the ideas that appear to be implicit in the New Testament theme of the new creation:

> The new creation will stand in a relation of *continuity* with the first creation. The creative rule of God will not destroy the first creation and establish something entirely different. That would be no fulfillment. . . . At the same time, however, the new creation will stand in a relation of *radical transcendence* to the first (cf. 2 Peter 3:12f.). The Last Day of the Divine Rest will not be "more of the same."

> . . . the new creation will be the end of the "dark side" of the first creation. All the chaotic elements of nature will be put to rest. This seems to be the meaning of the Apocalypse's affirmation that the sea will be no more (Rev. 21:1). The natural pain and death of the first creation will thereby be overcome (Rev. 21:4). So too, aggression and conflict of the first creation will vanish in the "peaceable kingdom."[66]

Santmire affirms these things, but he does not help us see how they may be so. He even disallows the propriety of the theological employment of such scientific and philosophical notions as that of evolution to increase the contemporary intelligibility of such ancient affirmations, for the theologian "does not have the data in his primary source, the biblical witness, which would allow him to speak in any technical sense about such a process in nature."[67] The theologian of nature is compelled by the biblical witness to affirm such things as the idea that God is involved with nature, nature is fluid or processive in character, and God intends to bring the process to fruition; but the theologian is not permitted to employ the scientific vision of evolutionary process in any vital fashion to explicate the meaning of the ancient biblical affirmations.

---

[66]*Brother Earth*, 109.

[67]Ibid., 110.

There appears to emerge here an unresolved tension in Santmire's theology. As we have seen, he asserts that a critical theology of nature must take respectful cognizance of the deliverances of modern science. Moreover, he invites his readers to take note of a rapprochement between the biblical vision and the modern scientific vision: "The scientific doctrine of evolution surely complements and is complemented by the [biblically based] theological idea of cosmic epochs."[68] But he disallows the constructive employment of data, presumably important data, derived from an extra-biblical source; hence, the idea of evolution is not allowed (as it is in Cobb and Teilhard) to influence our attempt to give contemporary intelligibility to the classical biblical imagery of hope. There is evidence, however, that practice does not always follow theory in Santmire's theologizing; for it is dubious that his characterization of either nature, God, or man would have followed the course it does apart from the impact of the recently emergent scientific view of nature and mankind.

Santmire employs the phrase "God's powerful establishing of nature" to refer to the initial and continuing action whereby God gives both being and becoming to the world, and he suggests that the "spontaneity" of nature is the creaturely correlative of the divine creative activity. His intention is evidently to reaffirm that which has classically been maintained through the doctrine of creation out of nothing: the notion, that God is the ultimate and continuing source, and the sustainer, of all that is and, along with this, certain motifs that are implicit in this primary affirmation. Santmire's depiction of the first "moment" of God's creative rule is designed to affirm the reality of the divine creative action and the reality of that which is created, although he does not speak in precisely this fashion. Moreover, his discussion of the first moment of the creative rule of God posits, as has the classical doctrine of *creatio ex nihilo*, a clear distinction between Creator and created; and it maintains both the ultimate dependency of the latter upon the former and the penultimate independency of the creaturely order, since nature is marked by a certain spontaneity or freedom to go its own way.

Three elements of Santmire's discussion of the first moment of the divine rule deserve especial attention, for the three elements are bound together by a common difficulty that runs throughout much of Santmire's musings about nature. The first element concerns the problem of individuality. Santmire rightly senses the importance of relating God's creative rule to the individual within nature as well as to the whole: faith affirms that God is source, sustainer, and shaper of all things, small and

---

[68]Ibid.

great. But like other Neo-Orthodox thinkers, Santmire refuses to specu-
late about the mode of God's creative ruling. The problem here is not
unique to the theology of nature. It is found also in the theology of history
(how can God attend to the destinies of so many people?) and the
theology of piety (how can God attend to so many prayers?). Says
Santmire:

> Notwithstanding the inadequacy of our concepts, however, our confession
> must be that God *does indeed* attend to even the most insignificant of
> individuals—"But even the hairs of your head are numbered" (Mt. 10:30).
> *How* God does this is not finally within our power to say. The creative Source
> of our universe is clothed in mystery.[69]

The point at issue is not whether the Creator is shrouded in mystery.
But it is imperative in our confession of the ultimate mystery with which
we have to do that we locate it properly, neither giving up the search for
clarity of understanding prematurely or pressing it beyond the limits
appropriate to our creaturely condition. We must wonder, then, if Santmire's theology of nature is not vitiated by a premature abandonment of
the search for understanding. Is it responsible in a time in which faith
affirmations have become particularly problematical to affirm that God
creates and guides individuals within the world as well as the world as a
whole without making some attempt to specify how this can be so? Is it
not incumbent upon contemporary theologians of nature either to refrain
from such claims as those Santmire is making here or to elaborate (or
borrow) a philosophy of nature and incorporate it into our theology of
nature in order to make somewhat more intelligible such claims as these?
It would appear that Santmire's refusal of the latter alternative leaves his
affirmations about the character of the divine creative rule of individuals,
as well as of the whole, relatively powerless and unconvincing even for the
believers whom he purports to be addressing.

Santmire does make one attempt at explanation, but it is itself subject
to the same misgiving. (This is the second element.) He follows Luther
and Calvin in emphasizing the "immediacy" of God in his creative ruling
of nature and history. Rejecting the tendency of Augustine and especially
Thomas Aquinas to utilize the notion of a hierarchy of being and to
describe God's creating and governing rule as exercised through descend-
ing orders of mediating agents, Santmire, like the Reformers, affirms that
God rules his creation directly and immediately. But again, to one who
purports to be doing a *contemporary* theology of nature we must direct
the question: how can these things be? In this essentially Neo-Orthodox

---

[69]Ibid., 116-17.

theology of nature no attempt is made to render intelligible or convincing the affirmation of faith that God rules all things—immediately.

The third element is similar but has to do more particularly with the character of the created realm than with the creative rule of God. Like traditional doctrines of creation, Santmire's theology of nature affirms both the ultimate dependency of the created upon the Creator and a measure of independency of the creaturely order. The limited independency of creation is seen in what Santmire calls the "continuity" and "congruity" of nature but especially in the element of "spontaneity" characteristic of the created realm; and it is seen in the freedom of human beings. Both nature and man are, in some measure, self-shaping.

At this point in Santmire's discussion a curious thing happens. Santmire describes the openness of nature and the possibility of novel occurrences in natural events in terms that would scarcely be possible apart from the influence of the scientifically informed philosophy of nature current among Whiteheadian process thinkers:

> Every natural entity is open to new possibilities every moment of its existence. As a whole and as a constellation of individuals, nature continually actualizes new possibilities, moving toward new configurations of being and new patterns of becoming. The world of nature is characterized by a universal spontaneity.[70]

Such a perception may be compatible with Scripture, but it is difficult to see how it could be derived from the biblical materials apart from the influence of contemporary science and a processive philosophy of nature. Santmire does not attempt to conceal his admiration for some of the achievements of process philosophy or his awareness of a certain affinity between his own thought and that of process philosophers. Yet he would evidently have us think that this rather modern perception of the openness and capacity for novelty ingredient to nature is the conclusion of a biblically informed theology shaped rather independently of the deliverances of modern sciences. "That there is newness in the course of nature, the theology of nature can affirm, as well as *why*: Spontaneity is real because it is established and permitted by God as the creaturely moment of correspondence to his creative rule."[71] Santmire proceeds to maintain, correctly, that *how* and *when* the spontaneity of nature is manifested is fundamentally a problem of the natural sciences rather than of the theology of nature; that is, it is the task of the natural scientists to describe

---

[70]Ibid., 135.

[71]Ibid.

the moments of the evolutionary process, for example, and the natural agents governing evolutionary change.

The curious thing is that, wittingly or not, a philosophy of nature is employed by Santmire to clarify certain features of the nature of nature; but when he turns to the issue of how the spontaneity of nature is related to the sovereign creative rule of God—in more general terms, the issue of how the independency of creation is related to the ultimate dependency of creation upon the Creator—he refuses the assistance of philosophy and returns to the Neo-Orthodox fold, endorsing Barth's paradoxical formulation "God works the creaturely working."

> As Barth observes, the *how* of the Creator-creature togetherness cannot be specified. It seems best for us to accept a similar cognitive tension in our discussion . . . , to say simply that the creative rule of God is in, with, and under every created moment [such as the spontaneity] of the natural world, yet these are not illustory, but real moments.[72]

Again we must inquire whether *this amount* of cognitive tension is acceptable in a contemporary theology of nature, or whether—if the theology of nature is to be a meaningful enterprise—it is not imperative that an attempt be made to reduce the tension between what faith now perceives to be correlative affirmations: God is sovereign creative ruler of all that is, including the processes of nature; nature is characterized by openness and the capacity for novelty.[73] Santmire takes note of process theologian Ian Barbour's attempt to modify the cognitive tension between these two affirmations by a line of reasoning which we shall examine in the next chapter. But he repairs to Barth's position. The curiosity is that a philosophy of nature can be happily employed to render more intelligible one point of concern to a biblically based theology of nature (namely, the nature of nature) but its potential to clarify another vital point (the nature of God's relation to nature) is simply discounted. This is not to say at the present time that the Whiteheadian conceptuality affords the best promise of solving the point at issue. It is intended to suggest that a really significant contemporary theology of nature is going to have to find a way of rendering intelligible claims such as those

---

[72]Ibid., p. 134. The passages from Barth that are referred to here are found in *Church Dogmatics*, 3:3:132 and 135.

[73]Traditionally, of course, the point at issue here has been discussed in terms of the relationship between divine sovereignty and human freedom. Our newly emergent awareness of the self-creating capacities of natural events and entities adds new dimensions to the ancient problem of attempting to hold together an affirmation of divine sovereignty and creaturely freedom, but the "spontaneity" of nature does not present us with a new problem in principle.

Santmire makes in his discussion of "God's powerful establishing of nature."

Santmire's discussion of "God's wise shaping of nature" is aimed at showing that the divine creative rule results in a "concordant and beautiful structure."[74] The affirmation is that this second moment of the divine rule involves the giving of both order and beauty to creation. The corresponding moment of the created realm Santmire describes as nature's "continuity"—an affirmation that nature is a cosmos rather than a chaos, and that the ordered whole is aesthetically remarkable. Moreover, within the "concordant and beautiful whole" there appears "a constellation of concordant and beautiful individuals" which is constitutive of the whole. Here Santmire's desire to emphasize individuality as a motif indispensable to the theology of nature becomes evident again. And as should be expected, the concerns embodied in the traditional doctrine of creation find expression in this further development of the notions of the divine creative rule and the divine created realm. Classically, the doctrine of creation has functioned as a means of affirming the orderliness of creation as the foundation of its beauty (which Santmire emphasizes) and its intelligibility (which he does not).

It is in the context of this discussion of God's shaping of a concordant and beautiful whole that Santmire takes up the problem of sin, disease, suffering, and death—the discordant elements within the concordant whole. Unlike the tendency of much traditional theology to treat all these elements as intrusions into the created order—disease suffering, and death being considered as consequential to human sin—Santmire, like a growing number of post-Darwinian theologians, treats sin alone as an intrusion. The other forms of that which we experience as evil are regarded as present in nature *ab initio*. In an appendix to *Brother Earth*, Santmire examines in some detail the question as to whether the notion of a fallen cosmos is representative of the major movement of biblical thought.[75] Concluding that the notion is by and large an alien importation derived from Platonic philosophical and Persian religious sources, he maintains that in the biblical perspective the fall is largely an anthropological rather than a cosmological theme. Although there exists an intimate relationship between man and nature that results in the effects of human sin spilling over, as it were, onto nature—a motif that is symbolized biblically by the curse upon the land (Gen. 3:17; 8:21; Is. 24:5-6a)—it is man alone who is given the capacity for voluntary obedience and hence

---

[74]See *Brother Earth*, 120-26 and 136-37.

[75]Ibid., 192-200.

man alone who can "fall" into sin. Thus, nature is exonerated from guilt. It is not a sinful reality, although it manifests the disruptive consequences of human sin; of these, the ecological crisis is itself the prime example.

Such a view means that biblical motifs such as the demonic cosmic powers and the wrath of God, insofar as they affect nature, must be interpreted in the light of the effects of human sin rather than as an affirmation of the fallen character of nature as such. Moreover, disease, suffering, and death would have to be seen fundamentally from the perspective of a historicized understanding of nature. Such a perspective is indicated by both modern scientific developments and the dynamic eschatological bearing of Scripture. From the scientific vantage, nature includes as givens such elements as disease, suffering, and death. From the eschatologically oriented biblical vantage, these elements are givens too—for God created the world good, not perfect, and is working creatively still to bring the world to its appointed perfection. To be sure, some occasions of suffering, disease, and death must be recognized as resultant from human sin; but suffering, disease, and death as such are to be seen as ingredient to the creaturely condition of God's world-in-the-making.

What Santmire has done here, once again, is borrow elements from a processive view of nature without taking up those further elements that help mitigate the harsher consequences of the viewpoint he is adopting. Since the dynamic view of nature became a compulsory part of our consciousness (that is, since Hegel, Lyell, and Darwin), it has become virtually impossible to neglect the evidence that disease, suffering, and death were part and parcel of the history of life even before Adam and that they would have been part of the story of human life whatever Adam's dietary preferences. Santmire, like other moderns, recognizes this and reads Scripture in the light of what is now a given among the scientifically informed. This does not mean that Santmire's exegesis is wrong; it may well be, in fact, that his reading of the dominant scriptural intent regarding the relationship between sin and nature is largely correct, although a fairly strong case can be made for the presence of the notion of a "fallen cosmos" in certain biblical passages. The difficulty lies in the result and, for Santmire, in the question of whether he has the requisite theological conceptuality to handle the implications of the position he represents. This is implicitly to ask the larger question of whether a Neo-Reformation theology is really capable of incorporating the contemporary understanding of nature into itself *without being transformed*, willy-nilly, into a quite different kind of theological orientation. Santmire has refused the traditional theological options of blaming disease, suffering, and death on sin and the devil, and has made these elements givens of the creation as it comes from the hands of the Creator. Evil, then, is made ingredient to finitude; and God is, accordingly, culpable. Santmire's employment of the eschatological motif to blunt the harshness of this consequence is not successful because he evidently maintains a traditional view of the sovereignty of God and refuses to go the next theological step of reinterpreting the doctrine of God in any significant fashion. The process theologians have, of course, gone this next step, thereby producing a theodicy (with what consequences we shall examine in chapter 3) that Santmire, with his traditional understanding of the divine nature, is not warranted in adopting. The upshot is that Santmire depicts God as having created a world that is good and en route to perfection; but the pilgrimage is marred by such evils as disease, suffering, and death. And we are given—in light of Santmire's traditionalist understanding of God—no reason why we should not expect the Creator to have done better.

It must be granted that Santmire's chief mentor does go much further. Barth develops an elaborate doctrine of evil that appears to come down— if a brief characterization of Barth's complex doctrine is permitted—to a unique version of the Augustinian notion that evil is a privation of the good. Thus, for Barth, sin, death, and the devil all belong to the realm of the Nihil or nothingness.[76]

> . . . this whole realm that we term evil—death, sin, the Devil and hell—is *not* God's creation, but rather what was excluded by God's creation, that to which God has said "No." And if there is a reality of evil, it can only be the reality of this excluded and repudiated thing, the reality behind God's back, which He passed over, when He made the world and made it good.[77]

Evil in Barth's perspective, the realm of *das Nichtige*, is "the impossible possibility." It is "non-real"; yet it is actual, having "the power of being which arises out of the weight of the divine 'No'."[78]

Although the Barthian treatment of evil is more thorough-going than that found in Santmire's Neo-Orthodox theology of nature, it is not clear that Barth can finally incorporate any more successfully than Santmire such features of the newly emergent view of nature as those that indicate "natural evils" to be ingredient to the creative process as such. Barth, as Santmire has elaborately shown in *Creation and Nature*, deals with the deeper implications of the new view of nature largely by ignoring them.

---

[76]*Church Dogmatics*, 3:3, par. 50 and elsewhere. Rendering *das Nichtige* by the Latin term *"the Nihil"* preserves Barth's sense of the reality and power of evil better than the term "nothingness" which is employed by the translators of Barth's multi-volume work.

[77]Karl Barth, *Dogmatics in Outline*, trans. G. T. Thomson (New York: Harper & Row; Harper Torchbooks, 1959), 57.

[78]Ibid.

And Santmire, to a greater extent than we should expect, follows Barth's example.

Santmire's discussion of the third moment of the creative rule of God, his "joyous valuing of nature," represents our author's attempt to affirm the goodness and "intrinsic value" of nature.[79] Santmire is searching here for a way of transcending the purely utilitarian definition of the value of nature that is so common among us. Nature does indeed have economic and aesthetic utility for man, and Santmire wants to affirm with Scripture that God values nature for this reason. Nature *is* the stage for the human drama, and Santmire wants to affirm with Scripture that God values nature for this reason too. But unlike theologians such as Barth—for whom the goodness of the created realm is purely its function as the setting for the covenant of grace[80]—Santmire wants to move on to an affirmation of an additional dimension of value of the natural order; and he believes Scripture warrants this further move. "The theology of the Bible suggests that the created realm *has* value in itself for God."[81] The "congruity" of the created realm is the moment that corresponds to "its determination by the joyous valuing of God."[82]

Here we come to one of the more significant aspects of Santmire's attempt to construct a new theology of nature. In fact, his attempt to provide the foundation for a new valuational perspective on nature is essentially the highpoint of his labors. The beginnings consist of the biblical theme of God's delight in that which he has created: "And God saw that it was good." But Santmire attempts to explicate the meaning of the divine delight by setting forth the rudiments of a value-theory fashioned of insights drawn largely from Jonathan Edwards.

It should be noted that at this point in particular Santmire's efforts make contact with the theological work of H. Richard Niebuhr. Santmire refers to the valuational perspective elaborated by Niebuhr as a means of translating the biblical motifs of the goodness of, and divine delight in, creation into contemporary philosophical-theological idiom.[83] Regrettably, Santmire does not explore in specifically Niebuhrian terms the rich possibilities afforded the theologian of nature by the thinking of Niebuhr.

---

[79] *Brother Earth*, 126-31 and 137-39.

[80] See, e.g., *Church Dogmatics*, 3:1, par. 41.

[81] *Brother Earth*, 128. Santmire appeals to such biblical passages as Ps. 104, Pr. 8:30, Gen. 1:21, Mt. 6:26, 30, and Lk. 12:6.

[82] *Brother Earth*, 137.

[83] See especially *Radical Monotheism and Western Culture* (New York: Harper & Row; Harper Torchbooks, 1970).

He does, however, express his intent to set forth the value of nature from the standpoint of the "center of value"—God, the ultimate giver of value. Further, he executes this intent, in a way congenial to Niebuhr, by employing certain insights and distinctions from Jonathan Edwards.

Edwards distinguishes between subordinate and ultimate ends or (a) purposes aimed at the actualization of further purposes and (b) purposes that are ends in themselves.[84] Among the latter he further distinguishes between "original and independent ultimate ends" and "consequential and dependent ultimate ends." Following Edwards, Santmire argues in effect that in divine perspective, as indicated by Scripture, nature has the character of both a subordinate end and an ultimate end. Nature is valued by God as the stage for human life and the drama of redemption; hence, it is the means to the realization of a further end. But this does not exhaust the value nature has for God, according to both Edwards and Santmire. In Edwardsean terms, the created order is valuable because it is an exercise *ad extra* of the divine goodness: being good, God delights in communicating himself. God's primal goal in creating—the "original and independent" type of ultimate end—consists of God's propensity to be what he is: self-communicating good. Goodness emanates good, and God's delight in the self-expressive act of creating gives value to the creation. "But," says Edwards, "after the world was created, and such and such intelligent creatures actually had existence, in such and such circumstances, then a wise, just regulation of them was agreeable to God, *in itself* considered."[85] That is to say that God delights in what he has made "in itself considered" as well as in the self-expressive act of creating. Thus, God's delight in his creation becomes a "consequential and dependent" ultimate end. God takes joy in what he has made as well as in the making; and his joy in creation, including nature, is a further ground of the affirmation of the goodness and value of nature.

It is the "congruity" of nature that provides the foundation of the divine rejoicing in creation, according to Santmire. Nature's congruity is conformity in both of its other moments (spontaneity and continuity) to the establishing and shaping moments of the divine rule. Without the notion of congruity God's rejoicing in creation might be considered "purely an inner-Divine act." With this notion, the divine rejoicing can be

---

[84]See *A Dissertation Concerning the Chief End for Which God Created the World* in *The Works of President Edwards*, vol. 3 (New York: S. Converse, 1829). Also, *The Nature of True Virtue* (Ann Arbor: University of Michigan Press, 1960).

[85]*A Dissertation Concerning the Chief End*, 10. Santmire's discussion does not make clear the distinction between the two types of ultimate ends, a distinction which I have attempted to stress here.

reckoned as resultant upon the actual character of the created order: God delights in creation because it really is good in the sense of being capable of fulfilling the divine ends in both the ultimate and subordinate senses. Such features as the variety, immensity, and complexity of nature provide the actual occasion for God's rejoicing in nature as an ultimate end. The aesthetic and economic utility of nature for man provides the actual occasion for God's rejoicing in nature as a subordinate end. "In these two ways, then in itself and as a servant for mankind, nature perfectly serves the Divine joy."[86]

Although Santmire's intention is to set forth a theoretical framework within which nature can be properly thought of as having genuinely intrinsic value, it is questionable whether he has succeeded. Strictly speaking, for something to be intrinsically valuable it must be valuable in itself for itself. Employing the idea of congruity, Santmire treats nature as valuable in itself for God (and, as we shall see, for humanity): God delights in nature and thus regards it as valuable. Since we are given no theoretical justification for affirming that nature is valuable in itself for itself, we must judge that Santmire's attribution of value to the created order is still imputed rather than intrinsic value. It is imputed value of a higher order, so to speak, since nature is now regarded as valuable to the ultimate value-giver as well as to humanity; and its value to God is judged to be "ultimate" as well as "subordinate." But this is not yet an affirmation of the intrinsic value of nature, or, if it is, it is so by virtue of a somewhat peculiar (even if common) employment of the notion of "intrinsic value." Nonetheless, the attempt to provide a new valuational perspective on nature is itself valuable.

The Relationship between Humankind and Nature. Having described the moments of the creative rule of God and the corresponding moments of the created realm apart from man, Santmire turns his attention to humankind and the relationship obtaining between the human and the natural orders.[87] Here it becomes important to find a way of speaking of both humanity's participation in nature, understood as the physical-vital dimension of creation, and humanity's transcendence of nature.

Human participation in nature is described as having both an intensive and an extensive aspect. Since the physical-vital element of personal existence is the body, the issue here is the one which has traditionally been framed in terms of the relationship between the soul and the body. It is the

---

[86]*Brother Earth*, 139.

[87]Ibid., 139-61. Also, "Reflections of the Alleged Ecological Bankruptcy of Western Theology," esp. 150ff. and "I-Thou, I-It, and I-Ens."

mind-body problem. Santmire's treatment of this issue is not elaborate. However, enough is said to indicate Santmire's intention of moving beyond any form of Cartesian dualism. Such a dualistic perspective survives, he suggests, in the theology of Karl Barth, for whom the relationship is essentially that of an I to an It. According to Barth, "man *is* the soul of his body."[88] The emphasis in Barth is therefore on the distinction between personal and bodily existence and on the transcendence of the corporeal element by the personal dimension. In consonance with the dominant thrust of modern biblical scholarship as well as with the consensus of humanistic psychology, Santmire stresses the psychosomatic integrity of man: "*I am the body of my soul* as well as the soul of my body."[89] I am neither body nor soul alone but "body-soul," with distinguishable but inseparable aspects of one personal existence. While such a view involves us in certain difficulties, it provides a way of affirming our participation in nature and paves the way for an appropriate acceptance, release, and celebration of the vitalities of the body. It allows us with Francis and, of late, Martin Buber, to speak of "Brother Body"[90]—a phrase that recognizes the legitimate place within personal existence of the vitalities of the body, a recognition difficult to come by within more dualistic theories of the nature of human existence.

This is the intensive aspect of our participation in nature. The extensive aspect consists of our personal (body-soul) involvement in the created realm as such. It is the fact that selfhood as we know it is always embodied selfhood—selfhood that is given only with a body and also with a "world," in this case the entire physical-vital dimension of creation. That is, nature is the "home" (cf. *oikos*) of our personal existence, without which there is no "I." As Santmire puts it, "just as one does not say 'I' without referring at least implicitly to one's body as a constituent of the self, so one does not say 'I' unless one refers at least implicitly to one's

---

[88]*Church Dogmatics*, 3:2:426. Although there is warrant for Santmire's reading of Barth, Santmire has clearly done Barth an injustice at this point. The full sentence from which this excerpt is taken reads: "The one man is the soul of his body and therefore both soul and body." In the same passage Barth uses the phrase "body of his soul" as well as "soul of his body" in reference to "the one man." And he says, "If man understands himself in his relation to God as established and ordained by God, in relation to soul and body as the two moments of his being he can in no case understand himself as a dual but only as a single subject, as soul identical with his body and as body identical with his soul" (ibid.). Clearly there is in Barth more of a penchant for a whole man psychology than Santmire recognizes.

[89]*Brother Earth*, 141.

[90]Martin Buber, "Brother Body," in *Pointing the Way: Collected Essays* (London: Routledge and Kegan Paul, 1957), 20-24.

union with the whole of nature."[91] Human existence is participatory existence: it is existence *in* nature, both "intensively" and "extensively."

But human existence also transcends nature. It is existence "above-and-with" nature, again both intensively and extensively. Santmire's treatment of the peculiar and even superior character of the human dimension is informed by those modern philosophers and theologians who have given most eloquent expression to our understanding of the uniqueness of human existence, among them Barth, Buber, and Reinhold Niebuhr. In fact, it can be said that his differences with such thinkers have to do not with what they affirm about "man" so much as with their treatment, or the absence of it, of "nature." Humankind alone is addressed by God and given the capacity to respond. Adam alone stands in an I-Thou relationship with his Creator. With man alone does God enter into personal communion, and man alone is capable of personal communion with his own kind. Moreover, only man has consciousness of his own selfhood. Only man has that freedom consciously to open himself to new possibilities, to transcend his own past and present, to order his life in the world. Only man can consciously worship his Creator, or refuse to do so.

These unique human capabilities that are collectively affirmed by the conviction that humankind alone is created in the image of God (Gen. 1:26a) bespeak humankind's transcendence of the mode of existence characteristic of other creaturely kind. They are marks of man's life "above" nature. But the very character of human transcendence involves, argues Santmire, life "with" nature. Ours is a "concomitant transcendence." Adam "is created not to turn away from but to engage himself consciously with nature."[92] By virtue of being created *imago Dei* he is, as it were, equipped to engage in a relationship with nature that is immediately analogous to the Creator's rule of the created realm.

Corresponding to God's powerful establishing of nature is man's career as caretaker. Here Santmire picks up the dominion motif (Gen. 1:26b) which is basic to the exploitative attitude toward nature. As overlord, man legitimately engages nature as an "it," treating the natural world as resource and instrument of human ends. We appropriately recognize that "human rights take precedence over nature's rights.";[93] accordingly, we utilize the stuff of nature to provide for human need. Santmire affirms the overlord role as being an essential aspect of the

---

[91]*Brother Earth*, 143.

[92]Ibid., 146.

[93]"Reflections on the Alleged Ecological Bankruptcy of Western Theology," 151.

biblical and traditional Western concern with social justice. The dominion role is divinely ordained for the provision of human need. But
Santmire stresses limits to human dominion that set his position apart
from that of the ethic of exploitation and the cult of compulsive manipulation that he has so roundly castigated. Essentially, the limits are of two
kinds. The one has to do with the (divinely ordained) egalitarian sense
that natural resources should be garnered for the good of all people, not
just a few.[94] The other has to do with appreciation of the (divinely
ordained) rights of nature and the recognition that the proper exercise of
dominion includes caretaking as well as exploiting. "We are still concerned with an I-It relation, but the accent here is no longer on the motif
of manipulation for the sake of the subject, but on manipulation for the
sake of the object."[95] Man's role as caretaker represents a stewardly
continuation of the divine shaping of nature—for the welfare of otherkind as well as humankind. This caretaking motif accomplishes a number
of things. It picks up the biblical perception of the integrity of the created
order and of human responsibility for it. Moreover, it allows for the
responsible garnering of natural good in the interest of human need
(social justice), but in a way that relativizes human manipulation of
nature. As a caretaking overlord, man attends to nature not in a compul-
sively exploitative fashion but in a manipulative mode that is sensitive to
the needs of the natural order as well as to the genuine requirements of
humankind.

Through the first two ethical modes that Santmire employs to describe humankind's concomitant transcendence of nature—overlord and
caretaker—he attempts to salvage the legitimate elements of the ethic of
exploitation and the cult of compulsive manipulation. In his description
of the third ethical mode—that of "wondering onlooker"—he attempts to
pick up the legitimate insights thath have found distorted embodiment in
what he has called the ethic of adoration and the cult of the simple rustic
life. This third mode of man's relatedness to nature corresponds to the
moment of the divine creative rule described as God's joyous valuing of
nature. In his discussion of this mode of human-nature relatedness, as in
his discussion of the divine delight in nature, Santmire moves to the
threshold of the sacramental approach to nature; but he does not fully
explicate a sacramental theology.

The problem with which Santmire is wrestling is that of finding a way
of recovering a preternatural sense of the world. He does not utilize this

---

[94]Ibid.

[95]*Brother Earth*, 149.

terminology, but he recognizes that he is attending to a mode of relatedness with nature that has become alien to many technologically oriented moderns. Hence he confesses:

> This motif [that of wondering onlooker] represents a radical break with the (modern) Protestant ethic. *We are turning abruptly toward the pre-modern period, toward the thought of the reformers, the intuitions of St. Francis, and the dreams of the biblical poets.* In this respect, nature is the garment of God, glowing with majesty and mystery, full of miracles everywhere. In this context, one perceives oneself interdependently, as a member of a cosmic whole, the wondrous household of God (*oikos Theou*).[96]

Santmire finds this preternatural sense of things powerfully embodied in the musings of the American naturalist John Muir. For him, the wonder elicited by our experience of nature clearly functions as a signal (Berger) or "hint" of the reality of transcendence. Muir moved behind—or beyond—the modern experience of the "desacralization of nature" to a recovery of a sense of the mystery of nature and the dimension of depth (Tillich) that the experience of genuine mystery elicits.

Santmire's task is to find a way of giving contemporary theological expression to this preternatural sense of the world. To do so he turns to the language of Martin Buber and modifies it.[97] Buber's distinction of the two modes of human relations, I-Thou and I-It, has been utilized in a variety of ways by a number of recent theologians. Although Buber himself allowed the possibility of entering into a relationship with elements of the natural world, say a tree, that is not exhaustively accounted for by the I-It mode of relatedness,[98] most of those who have employed his distinctions seem to have been content to limit I-Thou relations to the realm of human or human-divine encounters and to relegate all human engagements with nature to the I-It category.[99] Buber himself posited mutuality as a defining characteristic of the I-Thou encounter; hence, his generous attempt to extend the category to include his experience of the tree was unwarranted by his theory. Most of those taking up his distinctions appear to have been less restless than he with the limitations of his own categorical postulations.

Buber sensed that in his wondering (rather than manipulative) engagement of the tree and, even more so, of animals, he was at the "threshold of mutuality."[100] Santmire attempts to give forthright categor-

---

[96]"Reflections," 151. Emphasis added.

[97]Martin Buber, *I and Thou*, trans. Ronald G. Smith (2nd ed.; New York: Charles Scribner's Sons, 1958).

[98]Santmire, "I-Thou, I-It, and I-Ens." 267.

[99]Ibid., 267-268.

[100]See *I and Thou*, 124ff.

ical status to this experience by positing a third mode of relatedness, the "I-Ens" relationship. Conceptually, he is not certain exactly how to place the additional alternative:

> We might want to say that, ontologically, the I-Ens relation partakes of the pre-personal moment that precedes the I-Thou relation. But, on the other hand, it could be maintained that the I-Ens relation is given with the I-Thou relation *or* that it is mediate between the I-Thou and I-It relations.[101]

But, functionally, its character can be specified:

> There is . . . a certain immediacy to the I-Ens relation: the objectifying mode of human consciousness does not come between a man and a tree, as it does come between the two in the I-It relation. In this sense the I-Ens relations is not a juxtaposition of a *mere* subject pole and an objective pole bound together in an intimate community.[102]

Santmire proceeds to try to characterize the two poles of the I-Ens relationship, emphasizing that to separate them is to transform the relation into an I-It mode.[103] The "Ens" or objective pole of the relation is marked by its sheer givenness, a certain mysterious activity, and by beauty. The subjective pole experiences in this relation such moods as wonder, repulsion, or delight, and on occasion a sense of a dimension of depth or transcendence which leads to celebration (praise and thanksgiving). Here wonder functions in Santmire, as in Muir—as well of course as in Calvin, the psalmist, Loren Eiseley, and numerous others—as a "signal of transcendence."[104] And here, as indicated, Santmire comes to the threshold of a sacramental theory of nature; but he does not proceed to explore in any detail the new vistas thus opened up.[105]

---

[101]"I-Thou, I-It, and I-Ens," 267, n. 24.

[102]Ibid, 267-268.

[103]See Ibid., 268ff. and *Brother Earth* 154ff. Santmire postulates that an I-Ens relation might obtain between a person and "a constellation of natural entities," perhaps even between a person and "the universe as a whole," as well as between a person and an individual entity such as a tree ("I-Thou, I-It, and I-Ens," 270).

[104]Peter Berger and Rudolph Otto both have important bearing upon what Santmire is about at this point. Sam Keen's *Apology for Wonder* also is helpful in grasping the *"anatomy* of wonder."

[105]Santmire appears to sense that he has arrived, as it were, at a new beginning point. At the end of "I-Thou, I-It, and I-Ens" (272-73) he can quote Buber's statement "Because God is immanent in the world, the world becomes in a general religious sense—a sacrament." (Mamre: *Essays in Religion*, trans. Greta Hort [Melbourne: Melbourne University Press, 1946] 103.) And in his recent essay "Reflections on the Alleged Ecological Bankruptcy of Western Theology" 148), as well as in other places, he notes that theologians like Sittler and Galloway have opened up options compatible with, but largely unexplored, in his own theology.

TOWARDS AN ETHIC OF ECOLOGICAL
RENEWAL: RESPONSIBILITY AND ECSTASY

We have examined Santmire's analysis of our ethical and cultural dilemma before nature and its theoretical foundations. We have explored the contours of his proposals for theological reconstruction. Now, in concluding our examination of his theology of nature, we need to trace briefly the outlines of the ecological ethic to which he believes his vision conforms. The most prominent motifs of his ethic for ecological renewal are responsibility, love, and ecstasy. Many of the elements of his ethic have already been considered, and we need but highlight a few points in conclusion.

Santmire's discussion in *Brother Earth* culminates in a proposal that "an ethic of responsibility"—grounded in the theocentric vision embodied in the metaphor of the Kingdom of God—be adopted as the required corrective to the ethic of adoration and the ethic of exploitation with their attendant cults. "The present situation in our society and in our Church calls urgently for an *ethic of responsibility* build on a deeper understanding of our relationship to nature."[106]

The ethic of adoration is born of the tendency to regard nature as something to worship: it is cosmocentric in character. Within the cult of the simple rustic life "nature" is regarded as the highest good and becomes the focus of ultimate concern. The ethic of exploitation is expressive of the tendency to regard human good as ultimate: it is anthropocentric. And the ethos characterized as the cult of compulsive manipulation provides religious and philosophical legitimation of the exploitative relationship to nature. The cosmocentric and the anthropocentric orientations alike involve a rejection of the challenge of historical existence. The ethic of responsibility arises out of the recognition that God alone is worthy of our highest allegiance: it is theocentric. The radical faith that centers in responsible participation in the Kingdom of God relativizes the claims of both nature and humankind and directs our ultimate concern toward (in Niebuhr's language) the One beyond the many (nature and civilization) from whom the many derive their being. In doing so, this radically monotheistic form of faith *requires* that we attempt to come to terms with the challenge of historical existence—in both its natural and its societal dimensions.

> Theocentrism, in the tradition of an Isaiah or a Jesus, will be the ultimate framework for defining human existence. And this theocentrism will have a concrete shape, allegiance *to the universal history of God* : the Divine rule

---

[106]*Brother Earth*, p. 181.

with all his creatures, man and the whole of nature, from the very beginning through the present to the final consummation. When I identify myself existentially with that universal history, than I am responding to the challenge of historical existence.[107]

Here Santmire's theology makes contact with the rich legacy of H. Richard Niebuhr. We have noted the parallel between Santmire's and Niebuhr's vision of the Kingdom of God.[108] That basic parallelism includes the nisus toward a "radically monotheistic" or thoroughly theocentric orientation, although Santmire stops short of exploring the full resources that Niebuhr's theology provides. The parallel extends to Santmire's promotion of an ethic of responsibility. But Santmire again fails to appropriate the rich ethical insights that Niebuhr's treatment of responsible selfhood makes available.[109] In fact, our brief characterization of Santmire's Niebuhrian tendencies has already extended the specifically Niebuhrian language and insights beyond what Santmire's discussion explicitly warrants. We regard this parallelism with Niebuhr as at the same time one of the strongest and weakest features of Santmire's theology of nature and ecological ethic. He has appropriated some of the suggestive elements that can collectively be dominated "the ecological motif" in Niebuhr's theology, but most of them are left only partially explored (the exception is the Kingdom image itself) and others—such as the dialectical relationship between the secularization and the sanctification of all things required by radically monotheistic faith—are left altogether unattended.[110] This failure to appropriate and extend a wider range of the Niebuhrian insights represents a curiosity in Santmire's theology of nature—one which leaves it somewhat less adequate than it might otherwise have been.

In any case, Santmire's treatment of the ethic of responsibility is, as he says, "predicated on a vision of the Kingdom of God and his righteousness as the ultimate framework for judging and inspiring moral action."[111] It involves an affirmation that the ethics of the Kingdom

---

[107]Ibid., 182.

[108]See James Fowler's characterization of the latter's orientation under the descriptive title *To See the Kingdom: The Theological Vision of H. Richard Niebuhr* (Nashville: Abingdon Press, 1974).

[109]See especially the posthumous collection of essays entitled *The Responsible Self* (New York: Harper & Row, 1963).

[110]*Radical Monotheism and Western Culture*, 52-53. Robert H. King gives a brief characterization of "The 'Ecological Motif' in the Theology of H. Richard Niebuhr" in an essay by that title published in the *Journal of the American Academy of Religion* 62:2 (June 1974):339-43.

[111]*Brother Earth*, 182.

requires a subordination of the claims of both nature and civilization to the claims of God and his Kingdom. Since the Kingdom includes nature and humankind as "fellow citizens," those whose highest allegiance is directed towards God find that they must promote the welfare of all our "companions in being," natural as well as human. The ethic of responsibility required by faithful participation in the Kingdom of God entails that we work for both social justice among men and the sustenance of "brother earth." This latter theme of our responsibility towards nature Santmire delineates in terms of the overlord, caretaking, and wondering onlooker roles that we examined above.

In his more recent essay "Catastrophe and Ecstasy," Santmire has extended his ethical reflections somewhat, giving attention especially to the theme of love as it bears on ecological renewal. In the practically oriented musings contained in this essay, he has suggested that ethical reconstruction that is ecologically relevant will need to take seriously all the forms of love. The flavor of his speculations can be briefly indicated by a number of quotations.

As a corrective to the suppression of the bodily element—including the larger body, the environment—characteristic of much Christian theology and piety, Santmire finds Norman O. Brown's (Lutheran- as well as Freudian-inspired) call for a rebirth of *eros* helpful.

> With this emphasis on being in the flesh and sinking into the unconscious, Brown also paints a picture of a unified relationship with the whole material world. Nature is thereby eroticized. It is no longer that *thing* out there, which I transcend, and which I may manipulate as I see fit. Nature is, as it were, my greater body. One participates mystically in nature, rather than manipulating it and exploiting it. One has a love affair with every tree. Every meal is holy communion.[112]

To supplement the call for a renewal of love for nature, Santmire turns to an emphasis upon *philia* and social justice as represented by the liberation theology of James H. Cone. Continuing the attempt to balance ecological and societal concerns characteristic of his earlier work, he concludes:

> Renewal of the earth would be a travesty without liberation of the wretched of the earth. . . . *Eros* to be *eros*, and not just another name for death, needs *philia*.[113]

Finally, Santmire turns to Teilhard's emphasis on cosmic redemption to say that concern for natural vitalities and for human liberation must both be seen in the context of "the process of universal reconciliation."

---

[112]*Ecological Renewal*, 95.

[113]Ibid., 100.

> Still, there *is* an era beyond the revolution. And that is what Teilhard helps us
> to see. This is the universal era of reconciliation, the era of *agape*. This is the
> goal toward which history is moving, penultimately and ultimately.[114]

Here Santmire picks up the eschatological emphasis that we found in his
earlier work. In spite of his more positive employment of Teilhard in this
later essay, however, his eschatological affirmations remain largely
informed by biblical rather than "scientific" images.

> The universe is a cosmic and historical symphony of divine life and righteous-
> ness, shaped along the way by the grace of God, proceeding to a glorious
> climax of consummated *agape*. God is drawing all things and all peoples
> forward, everywhere at all times, toward the mysterious Day of his new
> heavens and new earth, toward the perfected City of God. In the words of
> Colossians, so cherished by Teilhard de Chardin, God is at work in all things,
> from the beginning to the very end, "to reconcile to himself all things" (Col.
> 1:20). On that final Day, according to St. Paul, God will be all in all (I Cor.
> 15:28). That is the transcendent goal toward which all things and all men are
> moving every day, the final banquet of divine grace.[115]

Like Tillich, Santmire affirms the ultimate unity (we might say coinherence) of the three forms of the one reality of love, implicitly rejecting
the tendency of Nygren and others to pull the forms of love apart by
turning distinctions into separations. Ultimately his discussion is a call
for ecological renewal through the development of "an ecstatic lifestyle"
inspired by a recovery of the capacity to love—in every sense of the word
"love."

> What is required is nothing less than a total transformation of the lifestyle to
> which we have grown accustomed. What is required is *ecstasy*, which literally
> means "standing outside of" oneself. We must learn how to stand outside of
> the patterns of life that we have inherited and that we take for granted. We
> must learn how to be beside ourselves: to be *beside ourselves* with love. Life
> on the good Spaceship Earth [and, in terms of Santmire's dominant meta-
> phor, within the Kingdom of God] will require a style of life that is a living
> embodiment of *eros*, *philia*, and *agape*. The competitive, manipulative,
> consumptive American pattern of "business as usual" must be quickly
> brought to an end. Without delay we must create a new universal pattern of
> life as love.[116]

CONCLUSION

In concluding Chapter 2 of our study let us pull together the results of
our analysis of the attempt to do the theology of nature on the basis of the

---

[114]Ibid., 101.

[115]Ibid., 115f.

[116]Ibid., 119.

constructive employment of socio-political imagery. We have focused on Paul Santmire's theology of nature and its correlative ecological ethic since his is the most comprehensive and thorough-going recent attempt to construct a theology of nature by consistent adherence to and elaboration of the socio-political metaphor of the Kingdom of God.

We have noted that in its basic imagery and at a number of specific points Santmire's theology of nature shows a kinship with the ecological motif in the theology of H. Richard Niebuhr, although several of Niebuhr's significant leads go unattended or are developed in only a cursory fashion in Santmire's theology. We have found it regrettable that Santmire did not attend to those leads more rigorously; such elements in Niebuhr's theology appear to be eminently compatible with Santmire's program and following them out more fully would have dramatically enhanced the quality of Santmire's result. In our evaluation of the contributions and limitations of the theology of nature that is forged within the framework of socio-political imagery we must have an eye both for the results that are actually before us in the work of Paul Santmire and for the results that might have been achieved if the Niebuhrian leads had been pursued more extensively. We should be sensitive, too, to the possibilities for the theology of nature of the employment of the socio-political image(s) in a fashion that involves less dependency upon Karl Barth's theological program than that which we have found to color Santmire's theological efforts.

A large part of Santmire's significance lies simply in the fact that he has taken "nature" seriously in his theological work. In so doing he, along with others, has begun to provide a partial corrective to much recent Protestant theology, especially in its Neo-Orthodox and existentialist modes. We have emphasized repeatedly the Neo-Reformation character of Santmire's own orientation, while pointing out prominent points of divergence from major Neo-Orthodox spokesmen. In his recent essay "Reflections on the Alleged Ecological Bankruptcy of Western Theology," Santmire has made absolutely clear his intention of *reappropriating and developing* further the ecological motif in the thinking of the great sixteenth century reformers. In this essay he maintains that, although the theologies of Luther and Calvin are primarily concerned with God and humankind, they include a definite concern with nature also. While the orientation of each reformer is "the-anthropological," in Barth's terminology, it is, in Santmire's qualification, "*inclusively* the-anthropological." Creation, including prominently the physical-vital aspect of the world, is viewed as a "mask of God" (Luther) and as the "theater of God's glory" (Calvin). For a number of interrelated reasons, the orientation of later Protestant theologians, including especially influential thinkers of our own time (Barth, Brunner, Bultmann, et al.), has become more narrowly focused upon God and humanity, with the natural order being at the same time neglected, misrepresented, and generally relegated to a position of theological inferiority. Recent Neo-Reformation thinking, in other words, has been "*exclusively* the-anthropological." In simplest terms, Santmire has taken it as his project to provide a corrective by developing a pattern of Neo-Reformation thought that is again, like the theology of Luther and Calvin, "inclusively the-anthropological." This he has tried to achieve by adopting many Neo-Orthodox perspectives on the nature of God and humanity, and the relationship between them, on the nature and role of Christ, and, basically, on the nature of the theological enterprise itself; but these Neo-Orthodox perspectives have been conjoined and adapted to a renewed theological interest in nature.

We judge Santmire's efforts as significant, first, simply because they represent a revitalized theological interest in the meaning and value of "nature." But secondly, we note that his efforts have provided us with an updated Reformation theology of nature, as it were; and this theological thought-experiment—fashioned at once over against and along Neo-Orthodox lines of thought—provides us with the occasion to evaluate the potential of a Neo-Reformation pattern of Christian thinking to meet our reconstructive needs as we ask what can and ought to be said theologically about nature in our time.

Beyond simply getting nature back into our conversation about God and humanity in a vital fashion, Santmire's orientation accomplishes several things. The grandest achievements are associated with the employment of the Kingdom metaphor. As we have noted, this is the most comprehensive and thoroughgoing attempt to do the theology of nature by consistent adherence to and elaboration of socio-political imagery. Utilizing the motif of the Kingdom of God has made it possible to bring a concern for social justice into a concern for nature and an interest in ecological renewal into an interest in promoting social justice. It has, to pick up Perry Miller's language, effectively brought together civilization and nature and ended the adversative relationship between them which Santmire characterizes so colorfully.

This achievement is resultant upon another. Employing the Kingdom metaphor as central makes Santmire's orientation radically theocentric. Here the character of Santmire's vision reaffirms the dominant thrust of the Judeo-Christian tradition; and the God-centered character of the vision relativizes the claims of both civilization and nature.

Surely these are important accomplishments. No theology of nature can pretend to adequacy when judged by Christian criteria unless it somehow affirms that the source of being is the only proper center of value. Likewise, no ecological ethic can pretend to adequacy when judged by Christian criteria unless it includes within itself a social ethic directed at the welfare of "the least of these, my brethren." The imagery of the Kingdom of God provides a powerful way of protecting these two central concerns of the Christian vision; and making this imagery dominant, as Santmire does, assures that a theological interest in nature will not result in a lessening of interest in the pursuance of social justice or a deflection of devotion from the One whose cause is the promotion of justice.

Thus, Santmire has managed to affirm a grander understanding of the nature and value of nature than that characteristic of much recent Protestant theology; but he has done so without denigrating the significance of humankind. Within an ultimately theocentric orientation he recognizes (by virtue of the character of the Kingdom imagery) the penultimate legitimacy of a certain "anthropocentrism." This contrasts sharply with the calls of some theologians of nature (such as Elder) for the abolition of all anthropocentric bias. The peculiar and even superior character of the human dimension is recognized and appreciated in concert with the fine sensibilities of Kant, Ritschl, Barth, and others on this point. At the same time, Santmire's employment of the Kingdom imagery provides for the penultimate legitimacy of a certain "cosmocentrism."

Moreover, as we should expect of an essentially Neo-Orthodox theology, Santmire's work is biblically informed in a sensitive fashion. And, while his discussion of the program of the theology of nature is not extensive, he proceeds in a way that appreciates the point that Christian reflection about nature must be done, not over against, but in the light of the faith response to what has been revealed to and among us.

These things, and others, Santmire has done rather well. We regard these results as positively contributory to the theological reconstruction regarding the meaning and significance of nature that is so urgently required today. But Santmire's efforts are vitiated by several serious deficiencies. We have noted a number of them along the way. At this point we shall review some of them and make a few further observations.

We have noted that Santmire nowhere attends in an extensive fashion to exactly what it is he is theologizing about when he does the theology of "nature." This is not, of course, a peculiarity of his approach; but it does leave the result rather the satisfactory.

Second, we have seen that Santmire implicitly calls for a type of theology of nature that he does not provide: a theology of nature vitally related to and informed by a contemporary philosophy of nature. At point after point Santmire's theological positions are marred by unresolved issues, cognitive tensions, and suggestions of dubious intelligibility. These difficulties are resultant in part from the absence of a good philosophy of nature, based upon the best modern understanding of "nature." The philosophy of nature that does occasionally surface in Santmire's theologizing is not fully warranted in being there, nor is it consistently adhered to and employed. We judge Santmire's difficulties here to be parallel to those for which he faults Karl Barth. Barth's refusal to elaborate a doctrine of nature, Santmire tells us, has left him dependent upon currents that slip into his doctrine of creation uninvited, as it were, and unrefined. In the same way, Santmire's refusal consistently to forge or adopt a philosophy of nature as the handmaiden of his theology of nature leaves him with both an inconsistency and a vacuum in his theology of nature. Such a difficulty is not ingredient to the employment of the Kingdom imagery, but it does suggest some of the problems associated with attempting to do the theology of nature within an essentially Neo-Orthodox framework. The Kingdom metaphor remains helpful, however, and could be developed without some of Santmire's Neo-Orthodox liabilities.

Third, we have found Santmire coming to the threshold of a processive philosophy and theology of nature (in his eschatological emphasis, et cetera) and to the threshold of a sacramental view of nature (in his understanding of the divine delight and the I-Ens relation). But in neither case does he "pass over" and provide what his position leads us to anticipate with longing. In so far, the difficulty lies in what he has omitted rather than in what he has affirmed.

Fourth, we should note difficulties associated with Santmire's choice of imagery. His dominant images are socio-political in character. Both familial and political metaphors have a prominent place in his theology of nature. The title of his pivotal work is borrowed from Francis's familial imagery: *Brother Earth*. But the dominant image is not familial; it is rather the political image of the Kingdom of God. The political image has primacy even in the work whose title borrows the familial metaphor.

This mixing of metaphors within the framework—consistently adhered to—of the socio-political approach is not without its rationale. Santmire himself does not appear to be consciously sensitive to the interplay of these two distinctive types of socio-political metaphors in his work. But they can be perceived as finally compatible, and Santmire's tendency to slip back and forth between them can be said to have a certain merit. The intrinsic aim, as historically perceived, of the Kingdom of God is the development of a brotherhood of love. Hence it can be argued that the logic of the political imagery (Jesus) leads directly to the familial (Francis). *Brother Earth*, a book about the co-citizenry of nature and humanity in the Kingdom of God, has the merit of bringing together the emphases of Jesus and Francis.[117]

There *is* a certain compatibility between the familial and the political metaphors which needs to be recognized and appreciated, but there is tension too. The principle of the familial metaphor is egalitarian in character; the principle of the monarchical image is hierarchical and elitist. Francis's reticence about employing the monarchical imagery seems to attest his sensitivity to this disparity. Santmire's indiscriminate mixing of the two kinds of socio-political metaphors is finally something of a liability; for while attesting a certain compatibility, the interweaving of the two types of imagery tends to be obfuscatory of the differences between them. If both familial and political images are to be used in the construction of a systematic theology of nature—and there are good biblical, sociological, and scientific reasons for employing both types of imagery—they must be carefully discriminated, their differences as well as their similarities recognized, their respective merits and limits made clear.[118]

Fifth, we should note that not only is the monarchical imagery in tension with modern democratic sensibilities, it is also in tension with the rising feminist consciousness—given the historical association of monarchy with a patriarchical tradition.

In conclusion, then, we can say, in the handy typology Elder has provided us, that what Santmire has done is develop one type of "inclusionist" position. He has done so by borrowing an image not from the shop but from man's social life. The dominant inclusionist image in Santmire is political: nature is (like) a fellow citizen. Closely related to it is

---

[117]It is noteworthy that the theology of Walter Rauschenbusch achieves the same result, although Rauschenbusch limited his concerns to the social dimension. See, e.g., *A Theology for the Social Gospel* (New York: Abingdon Press, 1945; first published, 1919). Rauschenbusch in effect attempts to democratize the monarchical conception of God by vigorously emphasizing the brotherhood of man within the framework of the Kingdom of God. The result is powerful and in large part legitimate, for there are significant similarities between a benevolent monarch and a kindly father. But there is friction too. I am not aware that Rauschenbusch ever forthrightly confronted the tension between his democratic/familial and his monarchical metaphors.

[118]The reasons for employing both types of imagery include the following: (a) both familial and political images are employed in Scripture, (b) both types of imagery continue to have social relevancy and power in the West in spite of the modification of monarchical political institutions in a democratic direction, and (c) the science of ecology suggests that the natural order is characterized both by "fraternal" interdependence and cooperation and by competition and hierarchical ordering (to wit, food chains and increasing orders of complexity of organization).

the familial image: nature is (like) a brother.

The political (and the familial) image implies several things of significance. Most strikingly, it suggests that humanity and nature alike belong to a greater commonwealth of some kind and that they participate in that commonwealth not as lord and vassal, but generally speaking, as "equals." The image suggests both dependence and independence, continuity and discontinuity, between humankind and nature. That is, the two "citizens" are intimately related to each other; they are *fellow* citizens; they belong to the same whole, the same commonwealth. But they are at the same time partially free with respect to each other and valuable independently of each other as well as in relation to the other. The value of one member of the commonwealth is not one-sidedly dependent upon the value of the other, but each citizen is of especial, if not altogether "intrinsic value" (as Santmire would have it). This is to say that whereas the exclusionist tends to be simply anthropocentric, the theistic inclusionist tends to be holistic—anthropocentric and cosmocentric at the same time—because in a profounder sense he is finally theocentric. He considers not just humanity to be a source and center of creaturely value but also the entire biotic community and ultimately all of nature. Nature is not, for the inclusionist, a mere means to an end; it is rather, like humanity, an end-in-itself.

Santmire's attempt to provide a "new" valuational perspective on nature is itself valuable; in fact, it is the single most significant aspect of his attempt to elaborate a theology of nature for our time. This is the case in spite of the truncated character of Santmire's excursion into value theory as such. The contribution of his entire enterprise, based as it is on the imagery of co-citizenry, is to provide a valuational perspective on nature that offers a genuine alternative to the dominant ways of regarding nature in the West.

Thus, Santmire's labors have resulted in certain theological and ethical conclusions that we regard as indispensable to a viable contemporary theology of nature and its correlative ecological ethic. But these achievements are associated, in his reconstructive efforts, with shortcomings and problematic perspectives that we can but regard as unacceptable. Consequently, as we conclude our examination of this attempt to found the theology of nature on socio-political imagery, we find ourselves only at the beginning of our quest for a viable contemporary theology of nature.

CHAPTER 3

A WHITEHEADIAN THEOLOGY OF NATURE: THE APPROACH OF JOHN B. COBB, JR.

Not surprisingly, theologians who adopt the conceptual apparatus elaborated by Alfred North Whitehead have been among those who responded most readily to the challenge of attempting to create a new theology of nature. The Whiteheadian conceptuality is deeply informed by modern developments in the natural sciences, and it includes an elaborate philosophical attempt at the formulation of "the new view of nature" which those special sciences have made imperative. Accordingly, theologians who have found the Whiteheadian conceptuality compelling have been quick to identify with the need for a new *theology* of nature— one based on recent scientific and scientifically informed philosophical developments—and several such Whiteheadian theologians have been eager to supply the required theological construction. None has done so with more thoroughness or imaginative power than John B. Cobb, Jr. Consequently, our detailed examination of the Whiteheadian approach to the theology of nature will focus on the work of Cobb.

Cobb's treatments of issues ingredient to the theology of nature and ecological ethics are to be found in numerous products of his prolific career. The pivotal work, as far as our interests in this essay are concerned, is the volume entitled *Is It Too Late? A Theology of Ecology.*[1] This little book is supplemented by others that bear importantly upon our theme; chief among them are *Living Options in Protestant Theology: A Survey of Methods; A Christian Natural Theology: Based on the Thought of Alfred North Whitehead; The Structure of Christian Exis-*

---

[1](Beverly Hills CA: Bruce, 1972).

tence; God and the World; Christ in a Pluralistic Age; and *Process Theology: An Introductory Exposition.*[2] Besides these volumes Cobb has authored several shorter essays dealing with aspects of the theology of nature and ecological ethics.[3]

In his inquiry *Is It Too Late?* John Cobb speaks both of "the need for a new vision" and "the new vision we need." We shall adopt this handy parallelism as the framework for our consideration of the major features of Cobb's ecological vision, although our analysis will diverge rather markedly at certain points from Cobb's own ordering of materials and issues. To this basic organizing structure we shall append, in the beginning, a consideration of some foundational foci of Cobb's work and, at the end, a discussion of ecological vision and venture; and we shall take a "methodological interlude" along the way.

---

[2]All published at Philadelphia by Westminster Press in 1962, 1965, 1967, 1969, 1975, and 1976 respectively. The latter book, *Process Theology*, was co-authored with David Ray Griffin; but since Cobb identifies himself with the entirety of the volume (p. 11), it is treated here as simply his work. Certain sections of the book represent the most forthright statement of his theology of nature found outside *Is It Too Late? A Theology of Ecology.*

This analysis of Cobb rests on the conviction that his work is marked by an overall consistency in his theological development. There have, of course, been changes through the years, and some of these are noted. But few, if any, of the shifts at the time of this writing represent really drastic departures from the main lines of thought laid down in his earliest works. For an account of Cobb's "subtle shifts" see David Ray Griffin and Thomas J. J. Altizer, eds., *John Cobb's Theology in Process* (Philadelphia: Westminster Press, 1977), especially 5-24 and 150-92.

[3]They include, in chronological order, the following:

"The Population Explosion and the Rights of the Subhuman World," *IDOC-International: North American Edition* (12 September 1970): 40-62; abridged in *Dimensions of the Environmental Crisis*, ed. John A. Day, F. F. Fost, and P. Rose (John Wiley & Sons, 1971), 19-32;

"Ecological Disaster and the Church," *The Christian Century* 87 (7 October 1970): 1185-1187; also as "Out of the Ashes of Disaster," *Resource* 12 (March 1971):20-23;

"Christian Theism and the Ecological Crisis," *Religious Education* 66 (January-February 1971):31-35;

"Natural Causality and Divine Action," *Idealistic Studies* 3 (September 1973):207-22;

"Ecology, Ethics and Theology," *Toward a Steady-State Economy*, ed. Herman E. Daly (W. H. Freeman and Company, 1973), 303-20;

"A New Christian Existence," *Neues Testament und Christliche Existenz*, ed. Hans Dieter Betz and Louise Schottroff (Tubingen: J. C. B. Mohr, 1973), 79-94;

"The Local Church and the Environmental Crisis," *The Christian Ministry* 4 (September 1973):3-7; also in *Foundations* 17 (April-June 1974):164-72;

"The Christian Concern for the Non-Human World," *Anticipation* 16 (March 1974):32-34;

"Men and Animals," *The Christian Science Monitor*, (6 May 1974); and

"The Christian, the Future, and Paolo Soleri," *The Christian Century* 91 (30 October 1974):1008-1011.

For a bibliography of Cobb's writings through 1977, see *John Cobb's Theology in Process*, 193-201.

FOUNDATIONS:
THE MAJOR FOCI OF COBB'S THEOLOGICAL CONCERNS

John Cobb's early important theological works were aimed at clarifying his methodological convictions and hence at stating the context and character of his theological program. These efforts found embodiment in the two essays which dealt with the nature and possibility of natural theology, *Living Options in Protestant Theology* and *A Christian Natural Theology*. These writings were followed by an ambitious attempt to analyze the history and character of the structures of human existence in a work entitled *The Structure of Christian Existence*. This was followed by an attempt to think through the relationship between God and the world. In these initial volumes, as well as in subsequent writings, Cobb set forth the shape of the central foci of his theological concerns: "visions of reality" and "structures of existence." We must attend to his understanding of these correlative notions in order to explicate his view of the nature of the theological enterprise and to get before us the larger context of his theology of nature.

Structures of Existence. Like other moderns, Cobb experiences the radically problematic character of his religious heritage. He is faced then with the necessity of trying to specify what "Christianity" is about, its distinctive "essence." One of his initial approaches to clarifying the content of his religious heritage has taken the form of a dialogue with the existentialist theologians: Bultmann, and thus Heidegger, in particular. Like the existentialist thinkers, Cobb focuses on Christian *faith* as a mode of existence rather than a mode of belief as such. That is, he approaches the question of the content of his religious heritage in terms of an analysis of the existential possibilities it makes available to human beings rather than in terms of the rationalist tendency to define it as assent to certain doctrines asserted to be of the essence of Christian faith. However, Cobb disagrees with the existentialist tendency to make what he regards as an overly simple equation between Christian existence and authentic human existence. His objections are several. First, the existentialist position obscures the developmental process leading to the emergence of the complex structure found among modern Western human beings—the kind of structure of existence illuminated by Heidegger's analyses.[4] By default, if not by conscious intent, existentialist authors have tended to suggest that this complex mode of being "emerged full-blown with the first appear-

---

[4]*The Structure of Christian Existence*, 17.

ance of beings worthy of the name 'human.' "[5] Second, the existentialist position obscures the relative values achieved in modes of existence as diverse as those found in Eastern mysticism and Western "other-directed" individualism by lumping together everything other than the Christian mode under the label of the "inauthentic." Third, Cobb regards the existentialists as giving too much specific content to the notion of "human nature," insofar as this term is defined in reference to what is distinctive of human beings over against other creatures and to what all human beings share in common. Cobb's analyses lead him to emphasize continuities as well as discontinuities between human and other beings and to limit the attribution of universal and distinctive qualities of "human nature" to the capacity for language and, alternatively, to historicality.[6] In effect, Cobb asserts that the universally distinctive quality of "human nature" is the capacity for diversity. Finally, the existentialist notion that the possibility of authentic, or Christian, existence is universally present to humankind obscures the historically conditioned character of Christian existence and renders the continuing appeal to Jesus and Scripture rather arbitrary.

Thus, while taking his lead from the existentialist thinkers in his attempt to delineate the distinctively Christian by focusing on structures of existence rather than, in the first instance, on ideas and beliefs, Cobb diverges from the existentialists by replacing the two categories of authentic and inauthentic existence with the recognition that human being assumes a plurality of structures. Moreover, he identifies diverse "modes" of existence within the various "structures."

By "existence" Cobb intends "what a subject is in and for himself in his givenness to himself."[7] By "structures of existence" Cobb refers to the total psychical-ontological patterns and contexts within which beings—human and (higher) animal—live and move and have their being: the

---

[5]David Ray Griffin, "Post-Modern Theology for a New Christian Existence," in *John Cobb's Theology in Process*, 7. My characterization of Cobb's positions in this section is informed to some extent by Griffin's analysis as well as by Cobb's own work in *The Structure of Christian Existence*, especially. Griffin, however, identifies the two central foci of Cobb's interests with Christian existence and a Christian natural theology (*John Cobb's Theology in Process*, 6). This is misleading, both because it narrows Cobb's concerns overly much and because it unduly emphasizes the methodological dimension of his thinking. It is fairer to say that his work focuses broadly upon structures of existence, on the one hand, and upon visions of reality, on the other. These general concerns do *culminate* in the primary attention directed by Cobb toward Christian existence and Christian vision(s) of reality. But natural theology is merely one enterprise by which Cobb seeks to clarify and fortify these Christian theological concerns, especially the Christian "vision."

[6]See especially *A Christian Natural Theology*, 6163.

[7]*The Structure of Christian Existence*, 16.

fundamental ways life is experienced and, for human beings, understood. Cobb includes unconscious as well as conscious elements in his description of the psychical-ontological patterns or structures of existence, and he allows for the interplay between the two kinds of elements. With this flexible analytical tool in hand (the category of "structures of existence"), Cobb is able to differentiate a wide variety of ways of being in the world, distinguishing as he does so elements of both continuity and discontinuity between the various "structures" and their attendant "modes." He is able, moreover, to encompass not only a greater diversity of structures and modes of being but a profounder appreciation of the evolutionary-historical character of those modes, including the emergence of novel ones, than his existentialist mentors from whom he takes his initial leads.

In *The Structure of Christian Existence* Cobb attempts to set forth a typology of structures of existence that ranges from animal through primitive and archaic human existence to civilized and axial forms of existence. The various structures are differentiated by a shift in the "seat of existence" or determining perspective of the self from the unconscious to the conscious—a shift that is characterized by a corresponding increase in rationality, freedom, and a sense of individuality and responsibility.[8] Cobb describes the emergence of each new structure as providing the occasion for the actualization of an unprecedented array of possibilities of experience and (self-)understanding. The emergence of the novel structures, and of new modes within the various structures, is seen as the result of the heightening or intensifying of particular potentialities within existing structures. Thus, new structures are depicted as developing in a way analogous to modern biological theories of speciation: by incremental changes marking continuity but resulting in qualitative changes that represent the crossing of "thresholds" and the emergence of novel structures essentially (but not developmentally) *dis*continuous with what has gone before.

We shall return below to a consideration of the distinction between subhuman and human forms of existence that results from this analysis. At present we need only get before us the major features of this typological treatment of the diverse modalities of human history. Uniquely human structures of existence are depicted by Cobb as putting in an appearance at the time that "reflective consciousness" arises out of a

---

[8]Strictly speaking, the term "seat of existence" applies only to the highly organized human structures of existence that characterize "axial man" in his various forms; thus, for some, the seat of existence is in the will, for others in reason, and so on. See *The Structure of Christian Existence*, 54ff. I have here used the term in a looser and more metaphorical sense than is Cobb's usual wont.

dramatic intensification of the purely "receptive consciousness" characteristic of animals. Thus, early or "primitive" humans represent the stage in evolutionary history in which the capacity for the symbolic ordering of experience emerged and made possible a more complex relationship to the environment[9] as well as the (psychical) capacity to aim at the well-being of the psyche as its own end rather than merely at the satisfaction of bodily needs of the organism. The reflective consciousness became further refined into the "incipient rationality" of early civilization. This movement in turn culminated in a stage of development that Cobb characterizes by a notion suggested by Karl Jaspers: axial existence.[10] Axial man is marked by a fully developed rational consciousness that has made possible much more complex understandings of the self and its environment than was possible heretofore.

The burden of Cobb's analysis in the book to which we are primarily attending is the delineation of the distinctive characteristics of several types of axial existence, culminating in an attempt to clarify the uniqueness and "finality" of the Christian pattern.[11] He characterizes pre-axial man as having taken the organizing principles of his existence from the unconscious elements of his psyche and thus as being best understood in terms of the projections of his unconscious, namely his myths.[12] Cobb describes axial man—who emerged in India, Persia, China, Greece, and Israel in the millennium before Christ—as developing unifying centers of experience in the reflective consciousness and thus as being best understood in terms of his diversely developed rationality. Various "seats of existence" are seen as involved in a struggle to gain dominance over the other elements of experience, and diverse cultures are depicted as developing differing structures of existence accordingly. Cobb attends to the traditions that emerged in India, Greece, and Israel, identifying the successive stages of development: Buddhist existence out of Hindu, Socratic from Homeric, and Christian existence out of prophetic.

In India the emergence and heightening of the rational consciousness was accompanied by an awakening of a painfully acute awareness of the

---

[9]Cf. Susanne Langer, *Philosophy in a New Key*, 3d ed. (Cambridge: Harvard University Press, 1957).

[10]Karl Jaspers, *The Origin and Goal of History*, trans. Michael Bullock (London: Routledge & Kegan Paul, 1953). Cobb's employment of the notion of axial existence is marked by several divergences fron Jasper's own analysis, including the treatment of the emergence of axial man as one of several "threshold crossings" rather than (as in Jaspers) an unparalleled occurrence. See *The Structure of Christian Existence*, 52-53.

[11]*The Structure of Christian Existence*, chs. 6-12.

[12]See especially ibid., 42.

sorrowful round of life. This led to a structure of axial existence in which
the changing phenomenal world and the transcendent and unchanging
self were elaborately distinguished. Buddhism carried the process
through by denying the reality of the "I" itself, thereby challenging the
significance of the rational consciousness.

In Greece, in contrast, a structure of existence was fashioned around a
positive valuation of the phenomenal world and of selfhood. In Homeric
existence objective reality was recognized and appreciated in its objective
givenness; it was distinguished from the subject by what Cobb describes
as the psychic act of aesthetic distancing. In Socratic existence the process
was carried further with the awareness and appreciation of the experiencing subject being sharpened to the point where reason was identified as
the very center or "seat" of human existence.

In Israel still another structure of existence emerged.

> The Hebrews adopted a third path. As their power of rational reflection
> grew, they accepted the tribal myth of a divine law-giver, much as the Indians
> accepted the myth of transmigration and the Greeks that of their ancestral
> gods. Their critical and reflective activity was directed toward rationalizing
> the understanding of their relationship to this deity. This unconscious deci-
> sion turned out to be just as determinative of their whole cultural and
> intellectual development as had the corresponding choices in India and
> Greece for those civilizations.[13]

Cobb describes the structure that emerged in Israel as that of "personal"
existence and points out that it was fashioned in terms of the perceived
relationship with Yahweh. Strictly speaking, "prophetic" and "Christian"
existence are, within Cobb's typological analysis, distinguishable modes
of the personalistic structure of existence. Personal existence is the structure within which the awareness of selfhood is intensified through ethical
experience requiring decisions. Thus, the seat of personal existence is in
the will. Prophetic existence is that mode of personal existence in which
the "person" is shaped by the assumption of responsibility for his actions.
In Israel this mode of responsible personhood emerged in response to the
prophetic announcement of the moral character and requirements of
deity. Christian existence, which Cobb depicts as healthy spiritual existence, is that mode of intensified personal existence in which the "person"
assumes responsibility for his motives as well as his actions.[14] Spiritual
existence involves the emergence of awareness that the self transcends all

---

[13]Ibid., 94.

[14]Self-preoccupation represents unhealthy spiritual existence; it involves obsession
with moral purity. Cobb appeals to the experience of acceptation by the other or, in
classical terms, justification by grace as the occasion of release from self-concern into the
state of genuine concern for others which is the mark of healthy spiritual existence.

dimensions of the psyche, even its feelings and motives, and is accordingly responsible for them. It represents self-conscious self-transcendence and involves one in an indefinite process of self-transcendence in which the will itself and every stage of development is objectified and made the subject of personal responsibility.[15] According to Cobb, "Jesus and the Easter experiences of the community were the occasion for crossing the new threshold" into spiritual existence, for with Jesus there occurred the renewal of the prophetic sense of the present immediacy of God involving "the radicalization of trust in God" with an accompanying "radicalization and interiorization of the ethical demand."[16] In this intensification of the sense of interiority and personal responsibility, the proper motive principle of the will, the seat of personal-spiritual existence, is accentuated: the nature and requirements of love emerge with new power, and the deepened understanding of love results in a new community.

Thus, Cobb's sweeping analysis culminates in the conclusion that the distinctive characteristic of Christianity, insofar as Christianity embodies authentic Christian existence, is found in the fact that it is only within this structural perspective that humankind clearly confronts the possibility of freely choosing a love that makes for the transcending of self-centeredness and the embracing of all the companions of the self. In this deepening of the consciousness of personal responsibility and of the continuous challenge of self-transcendence through love is found the grounds of the Christian claim to uniqueness and finality. For in an important, if slightly paradoxical sense, this self-transcending structure of existence cannot be itself transcended, although it can and must undergo enrichment through internal transformation.

It has not been possible in this review of Cobb's account of the structures of existence to deal with all the nuances of his analysis;[17] but this overview gets several considerations important to our theme before us, and we shall return to them at the appropriate points. We conclude with three observations. The first is that Cobb recognizes that the Greek

---

[15]Cf. *John Cobb's Theology in Process*, 68; see *The Structure of Christian Existence*, 121ff.

[16]*The Structure of Christian Existence*, 110, 111, and 115.

[17]Nor do we attempt a critique at this point. Although we shall engage certain motifs ingredient to Cobb's typological analysis of the structures of existence in our evaluation of his theology of nature, we shall not attempt to assess in comprehensive terms his phenomenological analysis of human history, especially human religiousness, as such. That task lies beyond the parameters appropriate to this study, but it is to be noted that important critical assessments of this part of Cobb's program are provided by Traugott Koch and Robert Neville in *John Cobb's Theology in Process*, 39-53 and 67-83 respectively.

structure of existence has been taken up into, or combined with, the Hebraic-Christian structure and that the Western tradition is the heir to this joint heritage. This leads him, second, to identify Christianity and Buddhism in their developed forms as the major religious alternatives confronting humankind today. His early tendency was to juxtapose rather sharply these two options, but in more recent writings he has recognized that his own (Whiteheadian) principles dictate that the proper way of dealing with the differences between Christianity and Buddhism is "to convert them into contrasts capable of joint realization and contributory of new intensities." Hence, he says,

> I look for a movement toward unity through the actual encounter of two highly diverse structures of existence, each being modified by its specific appreciation for the other. Instead of directly seeking a universal structure that synthesizes all, I hope for a transformation of the Christian structure through Buddhism and a transformation of the Buddhist structure through Christianity.[18]

Third, Cobb's predilection for the Christian alternative, a preference that remains in spite of his appreciative response to Buddhism, is shaped in part by his conviction that the Christian structure of existence affords the greater promise of survival in a world marked by technological advance with its related ecological threat to all forms of existence.

Vision of Reality. The second over-arching focus of Cobb's concern has to do with that which he calls a "vision of reality." With regard to this point too he defines his position over against the existentialist theologians. Their focus upon human self-understanding, including their perception of Christian faith as a mode of existence, is frequently associated with a disparagement of the significance of cognitive beliefs. Pointing out that human structures of existence have emerged in intimate conjunction with visions of reality, Cobb argues that the existential structures tend to lose their power when the visions with which they are correlated vanish. Existentialist thinkers generally grant the historical association between modes of existence and diverse "visions" and cognitive perceptions of reality; but they are concerned to isolate the peculiar types of self-understanding associated with various doctrines and belief systems, and they tend to regard the latter as secondary and even dispensable. Bultmann's program of demythologizing the New Testament represents perhaps the most powerful expression of this tendency. Cobb's fear and

---

[18]*John Cobb's Theology in Process*, 161. On this topic in general, cf. ch. 12 in *The Structure of Christian Existence* with the "Responses to Critiques" in *John Cobb's Theology in Process*, 150ff. and the treatment of the encounter of Buddhism and Christianity in *Process Theology*, 136ff. and *Christ in a Pluralistic Age*.

hence his contention—which, regrettably, is not very well documented by historical references—is that when the vision goes the demise of the associated existential possibilities is not far behind. His dominant (and perhaps his only relatively clear-cut) argument for this tendency arises out of his description of what *appears* to be happening in the modern West to the historic Hebrew-Christian structures as the Judeo-Christian vision of the world as creation undergoes erosion.

In the preceding paragraph the terms "vision of reality" and "cognitive belief" are used interchangeably; such usage denotes the close association of these notions in Cobb's mind, but they must now be distinguished. "Vision of reality" is a technical term for Cobb that refers initially to a preconscious and basically precognitive way of ordering and interpreting the data of experience.[19] He compares his intention in the employment of the term to that behind the British analysts' "blik" (regarded as too artificial) and some existentialists' usage of "self-understanding" (regarded as either too narrow or else misleading); it also has affinities with the German *Weltanschauung* (too intellectualistic) and, we might add, with Whitehead's "climate of opinion" (presumably, too vague). Better than these alternatives, Cobb thinks, the term "vision of reality" specifies that "perception of the locus and the character of the real *that is taken for granted in all our ordinary judgments.*"[20] It is on the basis of this initial preconscious interpretation of the data of experience that our intellectual structures, or cognitive beliefs, receive articulation. But our conscious, cognitive beliefs are not merely incidentally related to their presupposed vision of reality. Rather, they articulate and support the vision; and the vision itself, argues Cobb, cannot long endure without this conscious intellectual buttressing any more than the existential structures can long survive after the vision of reality with which they are associated cease to be functional.

The notion of vision of reality throws additional light on the diversified and historically conditioned character of the structures of existence.

---

[19]I use the term "initially" in this specification of the meaning of "vision of reality" since it appears to me that Cobb is not altogether consistent in his employment of the term. The strict definition of "vision of reality," indicated in these pages, tends to slide over into a more inclusive understanding that includes elements of conscious as well as preconscious belief; and Cobb actually utilizes the term in both the stricter and the looser senses, as in the phrase "the new vision we need." Moreover, Cobb takes the fact that we can and have become conscious of our underlying visions to indicate the necessity of renewing the Christian vision at the conscious level, if it is to be renewed at all (cf. *Process Theology*, ch. 2).

[20]"A New Christian Existence," 8. Emphasis added. Cf. *God and the World*, 117ff. and 136ff.

Each structure of existence has emerged under determinate conditions that included particular visions of reality. The Hindu structures rest on the vision of the world as perpetual round involving transmigration. The Hebraic-Christian structures of existence assume the vision of the world as creation.

> Taking, then, as my starting point the decisiveness of man's vision of reality for all experience and thought, I affirm that the distinctiveness of the Judeo-Christian vision of reality lies in its vision of the world as creation. This does not mean that the *doctrine* of creation is a unique possession of this tradition. Other traditions have myths of creation and conceptions of creator deities, but in no other case does the creation idea constitute a fundamental basis for interpreting the world, history, and man's self-hood. In other instances, it is *a* belief about the world alongside other beliefs, invoked for special occasions; something else determines the forms of thought and life and self-understanding.
>
> In the Judeo-Christian tradition, however, the essential truth about the world is that it is created by God. This fact determines what is indubitable and what is problematic. It is itself never problematic. Therefore, it is not constantly repeated as we repeat ideas that we fear may not be accepted. It is not argued for nor defended. The world is simply seen as God's creation, and this vision is the starting point for worship and prophecy alike.[21]

In Cobb's perspective the emergence of Christian existence, as well as the prophetic personal existence out of which spiritual existence arose, is inexplicable apart from the vision of the world as creation. This preconscious, precognitive judgment is determinative for all other Hebrew-Christian judgments and provides the context for those peculiar modes of self-understanding and ways of being-in-the-world that are distinctive of the Hebrew and Christian traditions.[22] The understanding of the world as the result of divine agency and the further perception of the Creator as personal, purposive, knowledgeable, and righteous made possible the emergence of a sense of the human self as personal, historical, and radically responsible; it encourages the identification of the "will" (the locus of motivation or purposing) as the "seat" of existence. When the implications for the self of this vision of God and the world are taken with utmost seriousness—as they are in Jesus—then the sense of absolute responsibility and the correlative sense of our radical freedom that are distinctive of full spiritual existence emerge with clarity and life-

---

[21]*God and the World*, 120.

[22]Cobb acknowledges that "the thesis that the vision of the world as creation is decisive for the Judeo-Christian tradition could be justified only by taking, one by one, all the problems and doctrines that have arisen within this tradition and showing that each presupposes and is given its characteristic form by this "vision" (*God and the World*, 121-22).

transforming power.[23] Self-conscious self-transcending existence becomes both a possibility and a moral imperative.

Cobb goes further. Besides linking the emergence of the Hebraic-Christian structures of existence with the vision of the world as creation, he maintains, as we have suggested, that these structures require the vision in order to endure. And the endurance of the Hebraic-Christian vision of reality rests upon its conscious articulation in appropriate doctrines.

This is the case, it appears, because human beings ineluctably fashion conscious as well as preconscious modes of belief. That is, thinkers (within the axial cultures especially) construct philosophical and religious doctrines. And these doctrines are either compatible with the *cognitive implications* of the dominant preconscious vision of reality of a given cultural epoch or they are incompatible with it. If the former is the case then psychic integrity and a sense of meaningfulness prevail; if the latter, then disorientation and widespread ennui result.

Now, of course, some deny that modes of human self-understanding bear any positive relationship to objectifying assertions about the way things are. Here the difference between Bultmann and Cobb emerges sharply, with Cobb's Whiteheadian predilections clearly governing the pattern of his thinking. Bultmann's position is that an understanding of existence is non-cognitive in the sense that distortion is resultant upon the attempt to cast such understanding into the language of objective assertions about God and world. Cobb's position is that a vision of reality has certain cognitive implications that are compatible with specific objective assertions about God and the world and incompatible with others. This position leads him to modify Bultmann's demythologizing program by denying that demythologizing properly means total de-objectifying. Rather than trying to translate the objective assertions about God and the world found in Scripture and tradition exhaustively into statements about human existence, the theologian should seek to translate the ancient assertions into analogous contemporary statements about God and the world, as well as about human existence—statements that are intellectually viable and supportive of Christian existence. Without such conscious articulation of the implications of the preconscious vision out of which Christian existence derived, its continuation as a positive human possibility becomes problematical.

---

[23]See *God and the World*, pp. 120-23 and *The Structure of Christian Existence*, chs. 10-12.

What we have here, in sum, is an attempt to bring together the deep insights into human existence that have characterized modern existentialism, including especially the biblical scholarship that has been informed by it, with the conviction that some form of ontological realism is requisite to the survival of the modes of human existence that existentialist scholarship has helped clarify. We began this section by noting that Cobb was taking up again the task of identifying the "essence" of Christianity. We found that the first result of his inquiry into this question is the identification of a distinctive structure of existence: self-conscious self-transcending existence. We have seen that this in turn leads him to a second result, the identification of a distinctive vision of reality: the world as creation. And we have found that he regards the two results as inextricably bound together. Thus, Cobb finally describes the essence of Christian faith in the correlative terms of "structure of existence" and "vision of reality." In so doing he is acknowledging that faith has both a subjective and an objective polar element. Cobb refuses to make either element the mere shadow of the other (contra Bultmann on the one hand and certain classical realists on the other) but posits what amounts to a dialectical relation between them, a relation in which each element finally presupposes and supports the other.[24]

Recently Cobb has ostensibly given up the quest for a distinctive essence of Christianity and has indicated that he has come to regard the *intention* behind his own earlier efforts as misplaced.[25] However, he continues to affirm the main lines and results of his previous inquiries into structures of existence and visions of reality, while preferring now simply to identify that which is distinctive of Christianity as a mode of relating to its own past, a mode which he has termed "creative transformation."[26] But Cobb's disavowal of his earlier intention of delineating an essence of Christianity may not represent as great a departure from his previous position as at first appears. For Cobb does not intend to allow that any type of transformation would be Christian simply because it stands in some kind of continuity with the historic Christian tradition (Nazism would not qualify, for example). Cobb retains a normative criterion that rules out a total relativism: the transformation must be "creative." And when we seek, in Cobbian terms, for some criteria by which creative transformations could be differentiated from noncreative ones we are

---

[24]Cf. Griffin, *John Cobb's Theology in Process*, 10.

[25]See *Christ in a Pluralistic Age* and *John Cobb's Theology in Process*, 157 and 169-70.

[26]This point is developed in my essay "Process Theology and the Protestant Principle," *Foundations* 21:4 (October-December 1978):356-64.

forced back upon our preconscious, precognitive vision of reality. Hence, his more recent formulation of the distinctive character of Christian faith is more accurately seen as a reaffirmation than a repudiation of his earlier intention and results, in spite of his avowed change of position.[27] Be that as it may, we must now proceed to examine how his understanding of structures of existence and visions of reality bears upon his attempt to construct a theology of nature.

CRITICAL ANALYSIS: "THE NEED FOR A NEW VISION"

As we have seen, "vision of reality" is a central technical term in Cobb's philosophical theology. The terms "modern" and "dominant" also assume a technical character in his writing. Modernity represents the climate of opinion that has been shaped by the dominant thought and achievements of the recent past. The chief shaping factor has been the rise and influence of the natural sciences. The success of the scientific mode of investigation has led to a widespread tendency to equate reality exclusively with that which is available to sensory experience, especially vision and touch; and this tendency has been in various ways embodied in and supported by the dominant Western academic philosophies of recent years. Since "indirectly, but pervasively, we are shaped by philosophy"[28]—in our "common sense" as well as in our theology—we shall review Cobb's perception of the rise and character of the dominant modern vision of reality, giving especial attention as we do so to the ecological bearing of these recent developments. Our review will of necessity be limited in scope; but it will be aimed at bringing out the main lines of Cobb's analysis and critique of modern philosophy, thereby setting the stage for grasping his understanding of the theological enterprise and the character of his own reconstructive efforts. The details of the story in themselves are commonplace; of interest is what Cobb does with them.

In Cobb's perspective the dominant philosophical schools of the modern West—however divergent in particulars—are linked together by a common propensity toward a vitiated understanding of the nature of experience, of subject and object, of the nature of relatedness, and of cause and effect.[29] Above all, they are characterized by a ubiquitous

---

[27]Cf. Griffin, *John Cobb's Theology in Process*, 23.

[28]*A Theology of Ecology*, 99.

[29]This analytical overview takes as its starting point chs. 11 and 12 of *A Theology of Ecology*; chs. 9 and 10 are also relevant. This resource is supplemented by Cobb's

tendency to deny significant reality to the subhuman order and, consequently, any genuine value to it as well.

The oft-told story begins with Descartes. The Cartesian philosophy involved a metaphysical separation of humankind from all else "in a way more drastic than had ever been done before in Western philosophy."[30] This bifurcation, as Whitehead termed it, involved the reduction of everything other than mind—the inanimate and the animate alike—to the status of mere bodies marked preeminently by extension in space. Descartes did grant the nonhuman world the status of objective being; it was marked by a substantiality not dependent upon human observation, but its "reality" was of an inferior order and its value limited.

Ontological objectivism met its initial nemesis in Berkeley, and the process was completed by Hume. As the epistemological question moved increasingly to center stage, the objective reality of the nonhuman became ever more difficult to affirm. The idea of "substance" began to appear altogether empty as "objects" came to be regarded as nothing more than what they seem to be, the objects, that is, of perception. Since the perceived qualities of objects are products of the perceiver and the conditions under which perceptions occur, the substantiality of objects was "reduced to a flow of qualities in endless flux."[31] The physical realities of the Cartesian system became sense data whose substantial existence was at best problematical. However, responding to the fact that sensory data appear to us as something given, Bishop Berkeley posited the divine mind as the source of the impressions that play upon our minds. For Cobb, let us note, this means that "trees and dogs do not exist as objects which can be appropriately loved."[32] Kant took the process a step further in attributing to the human mind the power of ordering the world of sensory data. "In his thought," Cobb concludes, "the movement toward a completely man-centered view of reality thus takes yet one step more."[33] More recent philosophies such as existentialism and phenomenology, as well as Hegelian and other forms of German idealism, follow Kant in affirming either forthrightly or implicitly that the human mind is essentially alone with itself.

---

historical excursions in *Living Options, God and the World, A Christian Natural Theology*, and various articles, especially "Nihilism, Existentialism, and Whitehead," *Religion in Life* 30 (Autumn 1961):521-33.

[30]*A Theology of Ecology*, 93.

[31]"Nihilism, Existentialism, and Whitehead," 521.

[32]*A Theology of Ecology*, 94.

[33]Ibid.

We may attend to Cobb's reading of Husserl as an example. In certain respects Husserl attempted to transcend the idealist tradition by granting substantiality to the object as well as to the subject of experience. Stressing that all experience is "intentional"—that is, experience of something—Husserl attempted to distinguish the object of experience from the experience as such. The object as intended is acknowledged to be more than the sensory data through which we experience it. Yet we are to put aside all theories about reality and give attention to the way in which the object presents itself to us as objective. To do this we attend to our own objectivizing process. "The objectivity of the object is its objectivity for us, and its objectivity as such along with all that is objectified must finally be understood as a function of the absolute subject."[34] In spite of his interest in objects as well as the experiencing subject, Husserl then is still not talking about "things-in-themselves" but about the objects of human mind. Hence, in Cobb's perspective the ecological results of phenomenology are existentially identical to those of Berkeleyan idealism. The existentialists transcend the phenomenologists in their understanding of human existence, but they do not assist in the process of attributing significant reality and value to the nonhuman order.

The results of the "empirical" tradition, at least in its initial forms, are even more devastating ecologically than those of the "idealist." The latter provided a powerful vision of the reality and value of the human dimension, the world of mind; thereby it established a ground for the concern of human beings for one another. But the empiricist tradition followed Hume in undermining the substantial reality of mind as well as objects. Essentially Hume turned Berkeley's own methods against him, reducing "mind" to a "flux of sensuous forms and concepts devoid of being and value."[35] Although it emphasized sense data, the Humean empirical tradition resulted in a positivism that renders considerations of reality and value meaningless. Although a product of the empirical tradition, language analysis softens certain results of the radical forms of empiricism; but by its nature ordinary language philosophy cannot provide the reconstruction that is needed.

Cobb notes that the results of the collapse of ontological objectivism were minimized for a time by the success of the scientific mode of investigation, based as it was on a kind of naive realism. But with the more recent developments in theoretical physics the remnants of the older

---

[34]"Nihilism, Existentialism, and Whitehead," 522.

[35]*A Theology of Ecology*, 95.

confidence in a given world have largely dissipated.[36] Cobb notes too that various forms of materialism, especially the Marxist versions, have attempted to hold out against the idealist and empiricist erosion of the notion of the objective reality of the "physical" world. But the dominant Marxist tendency remains that of regarding "matter" in terms of its economic utility alone, thus relegating its value solely to its instrumental function.

As this brief historical review suggests, what Cobb has done is emphasize the widespread negative agreement of several quite diverse schools of thought: they all draw back from granting significant reality and/or significant value to "things-in-themselves," especially to the subhuman world. The immediate result is to render the development of an ecological consciousness and attitude impossible: we cannot love what we do not regard as real or genuinely valuable.[37] Cobb's analysis goes on to argue that the dominant modern vision involves other results that are ecologically pernicious: several of them are implicit in the foregoing. The descriptions of the nature of experience, of subject and object, of relatedness, and of causality found in "the dominant" philosophical perspectives are inadequate.[38] Moreover, the modern vision is one that leads toward a complete relativism, toward total nihilism, and toward the "death of God."[39] The phenomenalistic-materialistic-positivistic vision does not leave a "place" for God or for the recognition of relations between God and the world.

Thus, the dominant modern vision is, in Cobb's view, in significant tension with the historic Christian vision of reality. Whereas the Christian vision of the world as creation involves certain presuppositions about the nature of reality and value, the exaggerated relativism characteristic of the modern vision makes these presuppositions difficult to support. Whereas the Christian vision affirms the meaningfulness of an existence

---

[36]For a systematic discussion of the consequences of the collapse of naive realism in scientific circles see Ian Barbour, *Issues in Science and Religion* (Englewood Cliffs NJ: Prentice-Hall, 1966), especially 284-86. Barbour himself defends a "critical realism"; and, like Cobb, he appeals to the Whiteheadian conceptuality for support.

[37]A practical result is that defenders of the environment are forced to rely exclusively upon utilitarian considerations to promote their interests. See *A Theology of Ecology*, 99-100.

[38]We shall attend to certain of these points in more detail as we examine Cobb's positive theological developments.

[39]See *God and the World;* "From Crisis Theology to the Post-Modern World," in *Radical Theology: Phase Two*, ed. C. W. Christian and Glenn R. Wittig (J. B. Lippincott Company, 1967), 191-205; "Nihilism, Existentialism, and Whitehead"; *Living Options*, 24.

grounded in the divine will, the modern vision presses toward an essentially nihilistic conclusion. And whereas the Christian vision is articulated in "God-talk," the modern vision renders all such language exceedingly problematical. In this situation a number of theological responses have been attempted.

One response is to attempt to proceed as if nothing has changed. Cobb regards this to be the route chosen by some Thomists and Personalists, as well as by Protestant conservatives.[40] The opposite alternative is, of course, to give up the Christian vision in deference to the dominant modern vision and become purely "secular."[41] One result of this choice would be the loss of spiritual existence, since in Cobb's view it cannot long survive the vision that supports it; another result would be finally to render Christian theology impossible and meaningless.[42] A third alternative is to opt for an uneasy compromise. Cobb regards this to be the route actually chosen by most important modern theologians of the last generation. "Barth, Bultmann, and Tillich achieved a delicate balance between the two visions of reality."[43]

Barth and Bultmann essentially accepted the dominant modern vision of reality and defined the legitimate province of theology both in the light of and over against it. In effect, these theologians recognized the modern vision to be controlling in our understanding of the world and thus to rule out the possibility of doing theology on the basis of our knowledge of the world. Hence, (for this and other reasons) Barth rejected natural theology and restricted the theological enterprise to reflection on God's activity as that has been disclosed in revelation. Theological assertions are not to be

---

[40]See *God and the World*, 127-28.

[41]It is now widely recognized that acceptance of the modern vision entails either the abandonment of God-talk or the radical reconception of the notion of God, and some theologians are attempting to reformulate Christian doctrine within the context provided by what Cobb calls the dominant modern vision of reality. Although they understand the modern vision in differing ways, Paul van Buren and Gerhard Ebeling, among others, have provided examples of theology that attempt to take seriously the theological implications of modernity. See *The Secular Meaning of the Gospel* (New York: Macmillan Company, 1963) and *God and Word*, trans. James W. Leitch (Philadelphia: Fortress Press, 1967), respectively. Cobb himself concludes that Christian theology is simply no longer possible once the dominant modern vision triumphs in our consciousness. Thus, insofar as works like the aforementioned still deserve the name Christian theology, Cobb thinks that it is by virtue of the resistance of the total triumph of the modern vision and the persistence of some elements of the Christian vision.

[42]See Cobb's essay "Is Christian Theology Still Possible?" in *God and the World*, especially 117ff.

[43]*God and the World*, 137. See the longer analyses of these, and other thinkers, in *Living Options*.

based on our natural knowledge, nor do they inform us about how the physical world came to be or about the process of our own appearance within it. The grounds of the authentication of God-talk, so to speak, lie altogether outside the province of the dominant modern vision or any other human construction. Similarly, Bultmann accepted "modern" man's inability to understand theological affirmations about divine cosmic activity; but he continued to make theological affirmations. In doing so, he effectively isolated our Christian consciousness from our world or cosmic consciousness, affirming that the "faith event" is altogether discontinuous with physical and psychological events. Hence, theology can proceed as an account of the occurrence of faith and existence in faith without becoming implicated in cognitive assertions about either the nature of the cosmos or of world history. Both Bultmann and Barth, then, have attempted to preserve faith, and theology, by adopting a perspectival duality which, on the one hand, accepts the dominant modern vision and, on the other, proceeds independently of it.

Tillich did not go so far. Standing "on the boundary" between the modern and the historic Christian vision, he attempted to "correlate" the two more systematically than either Bultmann or Barth. Tillich recognized that modern man has lost the depth dimension of his being—a dimension that Cobb considers essentially equivalent to the vision of the world as creation. Hence, in combined Tillichian and Cobbian terminology, the dominant modern vision of reality poses the question to which the Christian vision supplies the answer. Tillich did not attempt to renew belief in the meaning-giving vision of the Creator God within the context of the modern vision; but he attempted to identify the ultimate creative Ground of Being as the source of meaningfulness which modernity anxiously longs for and is incapable, in its own terms, of finding. Says Cobb:

> Translated in terms of what is here regarded as the crucial element of the depth dimension, i.e., a fundamental vision of reality, Tillich's view may be stated as follows: Modern man can be saved only as his false or inadequate vision is shattered and healed by the encounter with the Ground of his Being. Life recovers meaning as it becomes transparent to its Ground, or in my terms, when the vision of the world (including, of course, the self) as *creation* is restored.[44]

Cobb considers Tillich's result to be an unstable compromise, in effect because those who stand within the modern vision have learned to get along without the concept of "Being" and have even come to regard the notion as unintelligible. Hence, the "correlation" between the modern

---

[44] *God and the World*, 126.

and the Christian vision proves ineffective because those conditioned by the modern vision simply cannot recognize the salvific potential of an alien vision and, especially, of one couched in the pre-modern substantialistic language that Tillich employs to explicate the meaning of "God."

What is required, then, in Cobb's view, is neither neglect of the modern vision, nor a total or near total acceptance of it, nor an attempt to "answer" the questions implicit in it by reference to an alternative vision. What is required is something more radical: the confrontation, critique, and transcending of the dominant modern vision of reality by the creation of a "post-modern" vision within which the Christian vision might be recovered in renewed form. Thus, to the three alternatives identified above, Cobb adds a fourth; and it leads us to a consideration of his proposals for a "Christian natural theology."

METHODOLOGICAL INTERLUDE:
A CHRISTIAN NATURAL THEOLOGY
AND A CHRISTIAN THEOLOGY OF NATURE

In the concluding chapter of *God and the World* Cobb asks, " Is Christian theology still possible?" He concludes:

> My answer to the question that is the title of this chapter is, then, No and Yes. No, Christian theology is not possible if the dominant modern vision of reality is accepted as context and norm. . . . Yes, Christian theology can become possible again when this dominant vision is challenged and replaced.[45]

The collapse of the vision of the world as creation renders theologizing— including Christian theologizing about "nature"—ineffectual and, in a very real sense, even impossible. Yet, there is no remedy for our current theological dilemma in attempting to return to a pre-modern mode of theological reflection. The only effective response to the religiously and theologically debilitating power of the dominant vision lies, Cobb argues, in the creation of a new, post-modern vision. The fashioning of such a vision is the peculiar task of the enterprise of natural theology in our time. Only on the foundations laid down in natural theology can a new theology of nature be fashioned.

Cobb's attempt to repristinate the notion of natural theology begins with the acceptance of the modern critique of the enterprise as traditionally defined. The collective influence of the contributions of Hume, Kant, Barth, and others has left no doubt about our inability to "move from a

---

[45]Ibid., 138.

universally given starting point to conclusions that are both theologically important and rationally probable or certain."[46] Confidence in the powers of an essentially a-historical and universal reason has given way to the recognition of the intrinsic historicity of all human ratiocination. Grounds for the affirmation of a purely neutral starting point have been eroded as the awareness of the conditioned and limited character of all our cognitive orientations has permeated our consciousness. Hence, natural theology in its various historical modes (Thomistic, Protestant Scholastic, Liberal Protestant, et cetera—all bound together by a confidence in the objective or unconditioned powers of human reason) has simply collapsed.

Yet Cobb argues that natural theology is still possible and, moreover, that it is widely practiced even by its critics. A major point of *Living Options* was to show the presence and character of a "natural theology" in the work of numerous major Protestant theologians of the previous generation.[47] But the assumptions and developed implications that Cobb recognizes as belonging to the sphere of natural theology and that he finds so pervasively present in recent theological constructions consist simply of "*some* vision of the nature of things . . . that is to some degree distinctively Christian."[48] This would mean that "a *Christian* natural theology" is unconsciously presupposed in almost all Christian theologizing.

Cobb defines theology broadly as "any coherent statement about matters of ultimate concern that recognizes that the perspective by which it is governed is received from a community of faith."[49] Christian theology, accordingly, is theology done with the recognition that it is informed or conditioned above all by the theologian's participation in the Christian

---

[46]*Living Options*, 313.

[47]The only exceptions that Cobb recognizes are Bultmann and Barth, and possibly Reinhold Niebuhr; Cobb concludes that they *almost* avoid the employment of a natural theology. To the degree that they succeed they do so (and here Cobb is thinking especially of Bultmann and Barth) by affirming "a strictly supernatural occurrence as the basis for Christian existence," saying "nothing about the cause of Christian existence that either presupposes or implies anything about nature or history as they are visible from any other vantage point," and formulating Christian faith in such a way "that it has no implications that are in principle relevant to any perspective other than that of faith" *Living Options* 320). Santmire's analysis of Karl Barth's doctrine of nature suggests that Barth may not have been nearly as successful as Cobb allows, although he does perhaps come closer than any other theologian to avoiding the employment of philosophy as a natural theology in Cobb's sense.

[48]Ibid., 313; cf. *A Christian Natural Theology*, 11.

[49]*A Christian Natural Theology*, 252.

faith community; hence, it is theology that is elaborated on the assumption of the veracity of the Christian "vision of reality," the perception namely of the world as creation, as that vision has been shaped and mediated by the influence of Jesus Christ. Christian *natural* theology is then any *philosophical* "vision of the nature of things" that is "to some degree" distinctively informed by the vision of reality assumed and borne by the historic Christian community of faith.

On the basis of the analyses contained in *Living Options* Cobb postulates that all (or almost all) theologians assume, consciously or unconsciously, "*some* [philosophical] vision of the nature of things" that functions as their natural theology. Theological integrity requires that the philosophy thus employed be both forthrightly recognized and selected by virtue of its compatibility with the Christian vision as well as its "intrinsic excellence" when judged in terms of the criteria of consistency and coherence.[50] Much mischief has been done by unwitting and hence uncritical acceptance of philosophical perspectives that are in marked tension with the Christian vision.[51] But the employment of some philosophical perspective is, Cobb argues, virtually unavoidable. Accordingly,

> . . . natural theology is the overlapping of two circles, the theological and the philosophical. Natural theology is a branch of theology because the theologian in appropriating it must recognize that his selection expresses his particular perspective formed in a community from which he speaks. On the other hand, it is also philosophy because it embodies thinking that has been done and judged in terms of philosophical norms.[52]

Cobb assigns basically three distinguishable but interrelated tasks to the postive theological employment of philosophy in its function as natural theology. The first and second roles involve world view explication. Philosophy is utilized, as has been the case classically, to articulate Christian cognitive beliefs and to explicate the underlying Christian vision. It is also employed to clarify the character of alternative visions and patterns of belief. The third role of philosophy in Christian theology is that of "critical, self-transcending argumentation"—by which is meant the employment of philosophy to critique, purify, and enrich the vision and beliefs previously explicated.

David Tracy has recently urged Cobb to distinguish these three roles of philosophy in his natural theology more sharply than has been the case

---

[50]See especially ibid, 264ff.

[51]See especially ibid, 262-63.

[52]Ibid., 266-67.

heretofore.[53] Tracy has further argued that only if the function of philosophy is limited to the first two (world view explication) is the appellation "Christian" appropriate. When the theologian engages in the third philosophical task, as Cobb continuously does, he is doing simply "natural theology," not *Christian* natural theology, since the criteria of adequacy employed are purely philosophical. Cobb's conviction that the thinker can never completely escape cultural conditioning or the relativism of his own position, even when engaged in "critical, self-transcending argumentation," leads him to insist on the retention of the qualifying adjective to distinguish the resultant natural theology produced within a Christian context (or under the influence of the Christian vision of reality) from that elaborated in, say, a Buddhist context. In any case, natural theology is understood by Cobb as a philosophical activity which employs philosophical criteria and appeals only to evidence that is generally accessible (rather than the special claims of a particular community for its unique sources); but Christian natural theology will be peculiarly informed by the underlying and presupposed Christian vision of reality, as Buddhist natural theology will be peculiarly informed by the underlying and presupposed Buddhist vision of reality—while both types of natural theology remain purely philosophical enterprises.

As we have suggested, Cobb regards the special role of natural theology in our time to be that of articulating and reinforcing the Christian vision of reality *over against* the debilitating dominant modern vision. In Cobb's view, the only successful resolution of the challenge posed the Christian vision by the modern is through the elaboration of a "postmodern philosophy." The peculiar challenge of natural theology in our time is the production of a comprehensive post-modern philosophy which will incorporate the legitimate insights and motifs of "modernity" while avoiding the pitfalls and, in this way, make possible a recovery and renewal (Cobb now speaks of "reform") of the Christian vision of reality and the correlative Christian structure of existence. Happily, Cobb has found the groundwork for the required reconstruction already laid in magnificent fashion in the philosophy of Alfred North Whitehead. Hence, Cobb's own considerable contributions to the development of the requisite post-modern philosophy have the character of a "Whiteheadian Christian natural theology."[54] In the next section we shall examine the shape of the Whiteheadian-Cobbian reconstruction as it bears on the

---

[53]See Tracy's essay "John Cobb's Theological Method: Interpretation and Reflections" in *John Cobb's Theology in Process*, 25-38.

[54]*A Christian Natural Theology*, 12; cf. 268-270.

issues central to the theology of nature and will see why the philosophy of Whitehead is regarded as "post-modern" in the required sense.

Now, however, we must ask how a Christian theology of nature is related, in Cobb's work, to a Christian natural theology. And we must acknowledge at the outset that the lines of distinction are not clearly drawn. Cobb does evidently intend a distinction: he speaks of the "theology of nature" and a "theology of ecology" over against "natural theology," but he nowhere spells out clearly and precisely his understanding of the former in the way that he does his view of the latter. So once again we find (as we did in Santmire's case) a new theologian of nature failing to specify forthrightly and exactly what it is he is about when he does the theology of nature; and the omission is the more puzzling in Cobb's case because of the careful and extensive consideration he has given to theological methodology, especially in regard to natural theology.

What Cobb has done is distinguish in a general way between "Christian natural theology" and "the other tasks of theology" or "Christian theology proper."[55] He defines his view of the relations between the two kinds of theology over against three tendencies: to wit, (a) the tendency to subordinate theology proper to natural theology, (b) the tendency to subordinate natural theology to theology proper, and (c) the tendency (which he calls the Augustinian position) to "stress the homogeneity and continuity of Christian natural theology and theology proper in such a way that no line of distinction would be made."[56] About the latter—which involves the perception of Christian philosophy and Christian theology as a unified act of reflection under the influence of divine grace—Cobb can say that he sees "no serious objection to this course as long as it is a matter of emphasis rather than of principle." Then, he adds:

> However, there remains within the starting point given in faith a distinction between the fundamental vision of the world and the specifically Christian affirmations consciously referred to God's revelation in Jesus Christ as their warrant. Some conclusions can be drawn from the starting point in the general vision. Others require avowed commitment and quite specific experience as their warrant. *The two should prove coherent and mutually supportive, but their distinction is not unimportant.*[57]

What we miss in Cobb's work, in spite of this concluding statement, is any sustained attempt comparable to his detailed examination of the nature of natural theology to set forth the nature of Christian theology proper. Those Christian affirmations that "require avowed commitment

---

[55]See *A Christian Natural Theology*, 277ff. and *Living Options*, 318ff.

[56]*Living Options*, 319.

[57]Ibid, 319. Emphasis added.

and quite specific experience as their warrant" are never clearly and systematically differentiated from those "conclusions . . . drawn from the starting point in the general vision." This failure to attend at length to the methodological foundations of "theology proper" vitiates the results of even those essays that (one would suppose) would most clearly fall under the rubric. Such is the case with Cobb's *Christ in a Pluralistic Age*. In this work we may assume we have "theology proper," but the precise relationship between Christological formulation and natural theology remains vague. For Christian natural theology presupposes the shaping impact of the life of Jesus of Nazareth as does the explication of the possibility of "creative transformation." Moreover, Cobb's development of the various sub-themes falling under the heading of theology proper are, like his natural theology, characteristically dependent upon the Whiteheadian conceptuality. The categories derived from Whitehead tend to govern his formulations in rather decisive ways even when the technicalities of the Whiteheadian vocabulary are avoided: God is "the One Who Calls," that is, God acting "superjectively"; Christ is the Christian proper name of "creative transformation," a formulation not unrelated to Whitehead's understanding of "creativity."[58]

As indicated above, Cobb nowhere spells out precisely and in detail his understanding of a Christian theology of nature. Presumably, it belongs under the heading of "Christian theology proper." But in this as in other cases—perhaps more in this case than in others—no sharp line can be drawn between Cobb's understanding of Christian natural theology and Christian theology proper. Cobb's theology of nature is heavily informed by his Whiteheadian natural theology, although one could argue that it tends to transcend the enterprise of natural theology precisely to the degree that his theology of nature is wedded to the Christological motif of "creative transformation"; for, as we shall see, integral to Cobb's theology of nature is a call for a new (and more ecologically acceptable) mode of Christian existence correlative to the renewal of the vision of the world as creation. But his analyses of the nature of Christian existence and of the Christ "event" itself do not manifest a clear-cut distinction between the moments of reflection he refers to as Christian natural theology and Christian theology proper. Hence, what we have in Cobb is, in effect, a Whiteheadian Christian natural theology and a Whiteheadian Christian theology of nature conjoined in a way that is, as Cobb wishes, "coherent and mutually supportive"; but their distinction,

---

[58]Tillich's understanding of Christ as the New Being and the Bearer of the New Being has also clearly influenced Cobb's Christological formulation. See *Christ in a Pluralistic Age*. 21-22. and my "Process Theology and the Protestant Principle."

which is "not unimportant," is also not clearly indicated. And this we must regard as a regrettable methodological failure.

Numerous other questions of significance are raised by Cobb's understanding of the nature of the theological enterprise, but we shall defer our consideration of the relevant issues until we have examined the main lines of his theology of nature as such. Before proceeding to that task, however, Cobb's understanding of the nature of nature needs to be indicated.

Somewhat surprisingly, Cobb's obscurity about the methodological foundations of the theology of nature is paralleled by a failure systematically to investigate the concept of nature. "Nature" is certainly a crucial concept in his theology, but he nowhere critically attends in length or detail to the content and function of this pivotal notion. Such discussions as are to be found note the ambiguity in the usage of the term "nature,"[59] especially as it is employed by Whitehead.[60] For the latter—and for Cobb himself—"nature" is occasionally used inclusively to refer to all that occurs.[61] On other occasions "nature" is used to designate that which is studied by the natural scientist, and in this sense it stands in contrast to culture and history.[62] Like Whitehead, Cobb reckons the attempt of the scientist to abstract from "the meaning, purpose, and subjectivity of things" as inevitably to distort even the physical objects under investigation. Accordingly, he concludes:

> The effort to treat nature as a mere object of the scientist's investigation must finally break down, even in the scientist's own province. When it does, the deeper underlying unity of the reality of physical objects and of historical events can be grasped without minimizing the decisive differences that also obtain.[63]

The nisus in both Cobb and his mentor is toward a comprehensive vision of nature in which human selfhood is taken as the key to the nature of nature. "The knower, the percipient event, provides the clue to nature

---

[59]*A Theology of Ecology*, 84.

[60]Cf. *A Christian Natural Theology*, 60-61. At one point Cobb makes the following startling revelation: "I have called attention to Whitehead's lack of terminological consistency on this point [the meaning of "nature"]. . . . However, *there is no substantive problem*" (ibid., 136, 4; emphasis added)!

[61]Alfred North Whitehead, *Adventures of Ideas* (New York: Macmillan Company, 1933), 99, 237; *Modes of Thought* (New York: Macmillan Company, 1938), 214; *A Theology of Ecology*, 84, 89.

[62]Cf. Whitehead, *Science and the Modern World* (Macmillan Company, 1926), 171 and *Modes of Thought*, 100, 174. In *Adventures of Ideas* (265), Whitehead identifies nature as "a complex of enduring objects."

[63]*A Christian Natural Theology*, 61.

in general."[64] We shall trace in the pages that follow some of the implications of this position. At present we conclude by noting that Cobb regards the result of Whitehead's and his own decision to take human selfhood as the key to the understanding of the whole perceived as "nature" to be a position quite different from most forms of both idealism and naturalism. This "new vision" is, in Cobb's characterization, an "idealistic naturalism" or a "naturalistic idealism."[65]

RECONSTRUCTION: "THE NEW VISION WE NEED"

John Cobb considers the vision of reality underlying an age to be the basic clue to thought and sensibility in that age. He regards the vision of the world as creation to be the determinative formative factor in the Judeo-Christian tradition. He notes that this vision of reality is in tension with the dominant modern vision and is, accordingly, increasingly inaccessible to modern consciousness. He makes much of the fact that we have recently acquired the capacity to "objectify" our basic visions; that is, we have become self-conscious about both our own presuppositions and alternatives to them in a way no previous age has done. He considers the recovery and renewal of the Christian vision to be imperative—for ecological as well as other reasons. Cobb interprets this to mean that we must work to create a new intellectual climate in which the power and veracity of the vision of the world as creation can once again be appreciated. And he adopts as the presupposition behind this call to the renewal of natural theology the following conviction: "Once the vision has entered consciousness as an object, confidence can be restored only at the level of conscious persuasion."[66]

Cobb turns to the philosophy of Whitehead for the rudiments of the requisite "post-modern" vision. Whitehead's philosophy is considered promising for several reasons. In broadest terms, Cobb's appreciation of his mentor stems from his conviction that Whitehead has drunk as deeply from the waters of modernity as anyone but without being poisoned by the reductionistic and nihilistic tendencies ingredient to them. More precisely, Whitehead's philosophy begins with and incorporates the modern scientific worldview but presses on to develop a form of "radical empiricism" which refuses to follow recent empiricist orthodoxy into an

---

[64]Ibid., 136.

[65]Ibid.

[66]*Living Options*, 317.

affirmation of the primacy of sense data. Taking the assumptions and implications of the scientific enterprise as seriously as anyone (Cobb thinks *more* seriously), Whitehead has deigned to show that the conclusions of the dominant modern schools of philosophy are in serious tension with their own adopted foundations. Whitehead's epistemological critique of dominant philosophies—a critique that centers in the rejection of the primacy of sense data—enables him to move beyond the notion that there is no warrant in experience for the affirmation of genuine and valuable reality to a neo-classical ontology that is at once post-sensationalistic and post-nihilistic. In short, Whitehead has demonstrated (so it appears to some) the continuing possibility of ontological realism in philosophy and theology; and it is a demonstration that stems not from the rejection of the legitimate accomplishments of science and "modernity" but from their more faithful interpretation.[67]

For our purposes it is the ecological availability of Whitehead's philosophy that is of overriding interest. Through repeated attention to certain themes, Cobb suggests that a theology of nature or a "theology of ecology" must accomplish several things and that Whitehead's thought as "an ecological philosophy"[68] par excellence assists in every respect. Most importantly, a theology of nature must show the reality and interrelations of things and thereby provide the grounds for the positive valuation of them. It must provide for the meaningful incorporation of the scientific unveiling of the historical character of nature. The theology of nature must also be able to speak of the uniqueness and genuine superiority of the human dimension within nature. And it must present an intelligible description of the relationship between God and the world, including nature. Moreover, a viable theology of nature must include the development of a theodicy consonant with the picture of nature, humanity, and God that emerges within it; and it must result in the clarification of the grounds for ecological responsibility and the hope of survival. In the pages that follow we shall attend to the way in which Cobb treats of these themes with the help of Whitehead and, in some measure, Charles Hartshorne.

A "New" Vision of Reality.
      Foundations of an Ecological Attitude. Cobb's theology of nature is

---

[67]Cobb repeatedly affirms the virtues of the Whiteheadian achievement. The most sustained exposition of the promise of Whitehead is found in *A Christian Natural Theology*, but numerous other writings reflect the themes briefly laid out in this paragraph: among them, *God and the World*, 73-76, 135ff., "Nihilism, Existentialism, and Whitehead," and *Process Theology*.

[68]*A Theology of Ecology*, 109ff.

grounded in an attempt to demonstrate both the reality and the interrelatedness of things. Establishing the reality and interdependency of things is regarded as foundational to affirming their value and cultivating an attitude of respect or even reverence toward them. It is noteworthy that the idea of an "ecological attitude" has taken on these twin connotations.[69] In the strict sense the term "ecology" refers to the scientific study of the interrelationships among things, especially the relations between organisms and their environments. Thus, an ecological attitude is first of all one in which the complex mutual relations and dependencies among "real" things are recognized. But beyond that, an ecological attitude is marked by respect, possibly reverence, and even a sense of kinship with (in Niebuhr's phrase) our companions in being.

The chief philosophical problem is that of identifying on what basis the reality of "things-in-themselves" can be affirmed. Most modern philosophers have found talk about things-in-themselves very problematical. Whitehead's attempt to reinstate belief in the reality of the entities constituting our world and to repristinate confidence in our capacity to talk about things-in-themselves takes its clue from human (subjective) experience. In this sense the Whiteheadian metaphysic has a Cartesian postulate at its base: I think—feel, experience—therefore I am. But Whitehead leaves Descartes behind by universalizing this subjectivist starting point, inviting us, as it were, to see what results in our attempt to understand reality if we assume that all things are characterized by interiority, that is, by experience or "feeling." In this way Whitehead has sought to get beyond modern skepticism about our capacity to know phenomena rather than merely experience it. The skepticism, in his view, results from our looking at entities always from the outside: as mere things that somehow occasion our sensory experience. Whitehead strives, therefore, to transcend the Cartesian "bifurcation" by postulating the interiority of all entities; that is, by treating them as subjects of experience. In doing so, he was assisted by William James's identification of "droplets of experience" as the ultimately "real things."

John Cobb adopts this Whiteheadian starting point, asking what it means for things to have reality in themselves for themselves and answering that "to have reality for itself an entity must feel."[70] Following Whitehead, Cobb rejects the tendency (manifested, for example, in Descartes and existentialism) sharply to distinguish human experience from everything else and regards it instead as a high-level exemplification of reality in general. All entities "feel" or experience; what is more, they are

---

[69]See *Process Theology*, 76.

[70]*A Theology of Ecology*, 111.

constituted as entities by their "feelings." And it is on the basis of the recognition of their character as subjects that the reality of "things-in-themselves" can be affirmed. In this way Cobb attempts to overcome the ecologically devastating consequence of the dominant modern schools of philosophy: the tendency namely to deny significant reality to non-human entities, or at least to make that reality highly problematical.

Cobb's challenge to the second ecologically pernicious result of modern philosophy builds on the perception of entities as constituted by their experience. Whitehead answered the question of what entities feel by reference to other feelings: all actual entities, from the most obscure "puff of existence" to God, are constituted by their feeling of feelings. The concrescing subject "prehends" or "takes account of" (the technical meaning of "feeling") the experiences in its immediate past (the objective data of experiencing subjects) as well as of the pure possibilities for its own becoming (the relevant "eternal objects"). On the basis thus of its "physical prehensions" and its "conceptual prehensions," the concrescing subject selects what it will become (the "subjective aim") and actualizes itself (achieving "satisfaction"), thereby becoming an objective datum for other actual entities. Thus, the "actual entities," the finally real things of which the world is constituted, are in the Whiteheadian schema actualizations of experience. And the whole of the Whiteheadian philosophy consists of an analysis of such entities and of their relations with one another.

The important point here is that the individuals who collectively make up the world are constituted precisely by their relations. That is to say that in Whiteheadian perspective relations are "internal" rather than "external" to the entities involved. This means that interdependence is affirmed and emphasized rather than independence.

Cobb considers it a major failing of traditional substance-oriented philosophies and theologies that they defined entities primarily in terms of independence, as discreet individuals. He sees the same kind of error perpetuated by various modern philosophies, otherwise quite different from their precursors. Whitehead, on the other hand, views the world as an arena of events that occur only in the process of taking account of other events. Relations are internal to or constitutive of the entities characterized by them. Thus, the Whiteheadian perspective is ecologically available and helpful precisely at a point at which other perspectives are ecologically disastrous. Whitehead, Cobb thinks, makes it possible to affirm the interrelatedness and interdependencies of all things in exactly the fashion indicated by modern ecology and necessitated by environmental disruption. In this philosophy, "The whole universe is one vast ecological system."[71]

Whitehead's depiction of a world of real events, organically related, provides the basis on which Cobb sets out to fashion a theory of value in which the *intrinsic* worth of all entities can be affirmed. Neither the dominant modern systems nor the traditional Western philosophies and theologies have been very successful in attributing genuinely intrinsic value to non-human creatures. Santmire speaks of their intrinsic value, as we have seen; but he has no philosophical grounds for employing the notion of intrinsic value in the strict or proper sense. Finally he affirms that non-human creatures are valuable because they are valued by God and also by man, the "wondering onlooker." And this is all that he, along with most classical theologians, is warranted in claiming. He, like others classical and modern, has no real basis for speaking of the genuinely intrinsic value of the subhuman order.

The reason is that, for an entity to have intrinsic value in the fully proper sense, it must have value in itself and for itself. And this can be affirmed with integrity only if there is present a vision of the nature of things that makes the affirmation intelligible. Cobb finds this warranting vision in the Whiteheadian metaphysic. That which has value in itself for itself is that which has the capacity for experience or feeling or, most properly, enjoyment.[72] Indeed, the Whiteheadian analysis leads to the conclusion that all entities whatsoever, all units of process, are characterized by enjoyment; accordingly, all actual entities and groups of actual entities possess intrinsic value. They are valuable in themselves for themselves precisely because they "enjoy" their own existence.

Certain distinctions are important at this point. First, it is to be remembered that in attributing "enjoyment" to all occasions of experience Whitehead and Cobb are not thereby necessarily also attributing consciousness to them. Consciousness in fact is thought by our authors to arise only at a relatively advanced stage of what Cobb, following Teilhard's lead, calls the complexification process. In Whitehead's oft-quoted phrase: "Consciousness presupposes experience, and not experience consciousness."[73] This means that, while all actualities experience, not all rise to the level of consciousness. Where consciousness does appear it tends to illuminate certain elements unconsciously experienced in the process of concrescence, thereby selectively accentuating the significance of a few of the innumerable factors in experience. In doing so consciousness multi-

---

[71]Ibid., 113.

[72]Cf. Whitehead: "the experience enjoyed by an actual entity" is "what the actual entity is in itself, for itself" (*Process and Reality* [New York: Macmillan Company, 1929], 81).

[73]Ibid., 83.

plies the enjoyment of experience; but it is not itself the basis of, or synonymous with, either experience or enjoyment.[74]

This distinction already suggests a second of immense import—the distinction, namely, between momentary actual entities and enduring individuals. We do not confront individual actual occasions in our ordinary experience; if detectable at all, it is by means of intense introspection and the employment of scientific instruments.[75] What we do confront in ordinary experience are entities which are groupings of actual occasions.

In the technical vocabulary of Whiteheadian philosophy, any group of occasions marked by any real measure of interconnectedness is called a "nexus." If the members of a nexus exemplify a trait characteristic of the grouping of occasions as a whole, the nexus is called a "society." Societies of many different kinds and degrees of complexity of organization abound. Moreover, they exemplify perdurance; and it is because of their self-identity through time (as opposed to the instantaneous origination and vanishing of actual occasions as such) that we can become aware of them. In the technical jargon, a society of actual entities that is marked by temporal contiguity and successiveness is known as an "enduring object." The components of such a society are said to have "serial" or "personal" order, since each component is constituted by its prehensions of the preceding occasions in the society and, through its own reenactment of the defining characteristic of the society, mediates the pattern to its successors. Thus, enduring objects are the basis of such stability as we find in the world.

As we have little if any direct experience of individual actual occasions, so we have but limited direct experience of enduring objects as such. However, the latter are accessible in a way that the former are not. The molecule is an example. This enduring route of occasions—marked by the overwhelming preponderance of the physical pole of its existence—can be detected under certain specifiable conditions. But the ordinary objects of our experience are macrocosmic entities made up of innumerable molecules complexly interrelated.

---

[74]Whitehead defines experience as the "self-enjoyment of being one among many, and of being one arising out of the composition of many" (*Process and Reality*, 220). It is in this sense that each and every unit of process is said to "enjoy" its own existence. It is to be noted that Whitehead does not recognize the notion of *actual* entities lacking enjoyment. The notion of an entity without enjoyment suggests to Whitehead a "vacuous actuality, void of subjective experience" (ibid., 253). In rejecting this notion Whitehead is affirming the Cartesian dualism between experiencing and nonexperiencing actualities to be erroneous. (Cf. Cobb, *Process Theology*, 17.)

[75]Cobb evidently thinks it possible to identify certain actual occasions by these means. See *A Christian Natural Theology*, 40.

The simplest of these are "corpuscular societies" or "aggregates," such as tables and stones. Such relatively simple societies do not have dominant members and are constituted (in large part) by strands of enduring objects. This being the case, they themselves perdure.

These remarks prepare us for a third distinction, again implicit in the foregoing; and with it we return to a direct consideration of Cobb's value theory. While Whitehead and Cobb reject *ontological* dualism by affirming that all existing things are either actual entities or groups of actual entities, they do allow, even affirm, an organizational duality.[76] "Those things," says Cobb, "which *seem* to be mere objects are still affirmed by process thought to *be* mere objects."[77] Rocks, stars, and corpses are examples. "These entities have no coordinated originality of response," as Cobb nicely puts it.[78] They are composed of myriads of experiencing subjects loosely related, but are not themselves subjects. Hence, they have no intrinsic value in themselves; rather, "their intrinsic value is simply that of the sum of their lowly members."[79]

With living cells and plants we come to a more difficult stage of analysis. Again following Whitehead, Cobb defines "life" by reference to the psychical component in a subject's existence. This means that in a general sense every entity is "living," for even the most obscure actual entity has a psychic pole. But the psychical element is negligible at the levels of actual occasions, enduring objects, and corpuscular societies. All such individuals are constituted in overwhelming proponderance by their physical prehensions of the occurrences in their past environments. With the "living" cell, however, the psychical component has become dramatically more pronounced. The cell perdures because it is composed of subordinate societies of enduring objects such as molecules. But the cell manifests a capacity for novelty that its component enduring objects as such do not. Hence, it marks the crossing of a threshold, the emergence of "life" in the ordinary and, in this case, proper usage of the word.

(We need not explore in any detail the technical Whiteheadian account of how this is possible, but we may note that this account proceeds by the postulation of the occurrence of psychically dominated actual occasions in the interstices between the space occupied by the

---

[76]See *Process Theology*, 78; also *A Christian Natural Theology*, 40ff.

[77]*Process Theology*, 78.

[78]Ibid., 78. Whitehead even puts plants in the category of mere aggregates. Cobb, awaiting the results of research into the psychic life of plants, appears to have suspended judgment on this point for the time being.

[79]Ibid., 78.

physically dominated occasions that constitute the enduring components or molecules within the cell. Since the occasions that give the cell its greater capacity for novelty are primarily psychical in character, they cannot be detected by the methods available to scientific investigators.)[80]

Plants and animals represent, of course, the organization of cells into "complex societies." Although interested in claims about the psychic capabilities of plants (capabilities which, if actual, would imply the presence of a "presiding" occasion), Cobb continues to follow Whitehead in describing them as "democracies," without a single "dominant" member or occasion. They are more complex than rocks but not as complex as animals in which a "dominant," "presiding," or "final percipient" occasion does exist. But both plants and animals, being complexly ordered societies of experiencing occasions, are capable of much greater enjoyments than actual occasions and strands of actual occasions as such. The animal in particular (with various gradations running from, say, amoeba to ape) is capable of a rich "coordinated originality of response"; that is, it has a highly advanced capacity for novelty and for the rich measure of enjoyment that attends highly developed psychical "life."

With these kinds of considerations Cobb seeks to present rational underpinnings for our sense of kinship with, respect for, and responsibility toward the subhuman order.

> Whitehead's philosophy pictures for us a world filled with real events, each having its own intrinsic value. Especially those that are alive significantly share with man in feeling and activity. It is therein that the needed attitude of love, concern, or reverence for living things is adequately and rationally grounded.
>
> This philosophy also describes these real and valuable events as interrelated and interconnected in just the way that is implied by the ecological attitude. We ignore this at our peril. As Whitehead says in *Science and the Modern World*, "The two evils are: one, the ignoration of the true relation of each organism and the environment: and the other, the habit of ignoring the intrinsic worth of the environment which must be allowed its weight in any consideration of final ends."[81]

In Cobb's presentation the notion of the mutual relatedness and dependency of the various levels of enduring individuals (the one aspect of an ecological attitude) supports the attribution of enjoyment and hence intrinsic value to every level of actuality (the other aspect). As long as the subhuman order is supposed to be devoid of either significant reality or the capacity for enjoyment it cannot be considered to have intrinsic value.

---

[80]*A Christian Natural Theology*, 43.

[81]*A Theology of Ecology*, 112-13.

Its value is in that case imputed only and hence purely instrumental in character. Even aesthetic value is value imputed by the observer or appreciating subject. Moreover, as long as the subhuman order is thought to be devoid of significant reality including, decisively, an element of interiority, it cannot but be considered as something fundamentally alien to human existence which is marked above all by subjectivity. Still further, as long as the subhuman order is viewed as a concatenation of objects in purely external relations with one another it cannot be regarded as a community whose members and relations are intrinsically worth preserving and enhancing; it is in such a case incumbent upon us to preserve the environment for utilitarian reasons alone.

As long as such attitudes toward the subhuman order prevail, a sense of kinship with, respect for, and even love of it can only be regarded as quaint romanticizing. Only when the subhuman order is perceived to be marked with capacities that are continuous—albeit marked by great gradations of difference—with our own mode of being can such a sense of kinship, reverence, and love be rationally grounded. However, when the various members of the subhuman *community* are perceived as sharing in a capacity and propensity for enjoyment common to us and them, then it becomes both sensible and incumbent upon us to reverence and love these, our experiencing companions in being, *to the degree* warranted by their capacity for enjoyment. Then, "reverence for the neighbor becomes reverence for all creatures."[82] Such is Cobb's position.

He goes a step further, rooting an ethic of responsibility in the recognition of the intrinsic value of all creatures.

> The belief that all levels of actuality can enjoy some degree of experience provides the basis for a feeling of responsibility directly to them. It is precisely the knowledge that other human beings enjoy experience, and hence have value in and for themselves, that grounds our sense of obligation toward them. This is true even for Kant (who is generally viewed as having a strictly deontological ethic, i.e., one not based upon an anticipation of the values that an ethically right action would create). Thus, one of Kant's formulations of the categorical imperative was that we should treat other human beings as ends in themselves, not merely as means to our own ends. Accordingly, if all actualities, not simply human ones, are constituted by the enjoyment of experience, and hence are to some degree ends in themselves, then we should, *to the appropriate degree*, treat them as ends and not merely as means to our ends.[83]

Cobb has not fully worked out the principles of the ethic that would stem from his delineation of an "ecological attitude"; he has, rather, tried

---

[82]*Process Theology*, 77.

[83]Ibid. Emphasis added.

to provide the theoretical basis for such an ethic, the detailed elaboration of which will be a lengthy and arduous task. But Cobb has suggested certain principles, and we can glean some of them from the pages of his writings. One principle is that actions that affect members of the subhuman order must take account of the diverse capacity for enjoyment characteristic of the members of that order. Cobb rejects the notion of a "democracy of value" advocated by Lynn White and implicitly supported by Albert Schweitzer (since Schweitzer refused to set forth a theoretical justification for preserving one life at the expense of another, although in practice he continually did so). The diversity of the capacity for enjoyment means that the intrinsic value of creatures is diverse, requiring us to work out a discriminating theory that recognizes a hierarchy of values.

> Destroying the life of some types of actualities is more serious than destroy-
> ing that of others. Everything else being equal, those with greater intrinsic
> value are to be preferred, when a choice must be made.[84]

A second principle involves the continuing recognition of the validity of instrumental considerations regarding the subhuman order—as long as such utilitarian attitudes are balanced henceforth by the appreciation of the intrinsic values ingredient to the new ecological attitude. Plants and animals *are* legitimately valued as food, for example; and the intrinsic value of the "higher" herbivores and carnivores (ourselves included)— and especially of the total biotic community which is supported by the predatorial characteristic of "nature"—means that it is still okay to eat! A third principle, indicated above, is that it is appropriate to recognize that some things are mere things. Since a brick is not a subject (although, in Whiteheadian perspective it is composed of subjects), a brick has no intrinsic value to be considered other than that of its component subjects, which is essentially negligible. All of this suggests the fourth principle: the principle, namely, that an ecological ethic of responsibility must involve a complicated calculus of considerations of both instrumental and intrinsic value. Action entails choices, and those choices often involve the loss of certain intrinsically valuable actualities in the interest of other intrinsic goods and the instrumental goals of creatures of superior intrinsic value. The calculus will be complex, and its detailed elaboration awaits still further scientific information concerning the mutual interdependencies of the order of nature.

In summary, then, we can say that with the help of Whitehead, Cobb has elaborated the foundations of an "ecological attitude" that affirms at once the reality, interrelatedness, and intrinsic value of all things.

---

[84]Ibid., 79.

Moreover, he has done so in a way that allows for the recognition of the "common sense" perception of gradations of value and encourages a responsible elaboration of an ecological ethic of responsibility.

God as Creative-Responsive Love. Nothing that was said in the previous section necessitates the notion that Cobb is doing the *theology* of nature, much less a *Christian* theology of nature. We turn now to the relationship between an ecological attitude and the Cobbian doctrine of God. On philosophical grounds alone Cobb has argued that the various components of nature are of intrinsic value. This argument, based on Whitehead, supplies an ingredient absent from Santmire and largely absent from most philosophical and theological treatments of "nature." Now, on combined philosophical and theological grounds Cobb argues that the components of the natural order are valuable also because they are appreciated by God. This argument is in line with Santmire's Neo-Reformation position and with virtually the whole historic tradition of Christian theologizing; but Cobb utilizes Whiteheadian insights to explicate this traditional theme in a rather novel fashion.

Cobb's doctrine of God has as its point of departure the conviction that traditional ways of imaging the divine reality have failed by virtue of their having become inaccessible to modern consciousness. In a famous passage, Whitehead distinguished three historically interrelated images of deity that have dominated the history of Western theistic philosophy: God as imperial ruler (associated with the Roman Caesars), as a personification of moral energy (the Hebrew prophets), and as an ultimate metaphysical principle (Aristotle).[85] Under the impact of recent challenges to Western theism, Cobb expands the list of inadequate images to five: God as cosmic moralist, as the unchanging and passionless absolute, as controlling power, as sanctioner of the status quo, and as male.[86] Cobb's analysis reflects especially the sensibility that found expression in the nineteenth century in Nietzsche and more recently (in especially poignant fashion) in Thomas Altizer: the protest against the heteronomous and dehumanizing effects of various images of the divine reality.[87]

Whitehead identified "in the Galilean origin of Christianity yet another suggestion."

---

[85] *Process and Reality*, 519-21.

[86] *Process Theology*, 8-10; cf. *God and the World*, ch. 1.

[87] Many modern writers have, of course, sensed the life-distorting effects of traditional theistic imagery and have responded to the problem in various ways. It is through Altizer's vision, however, that the protest has affected Cobb's efforts at reformulation most vitally, and several aspects of his understanding of God and of Christian existence are clarified it seen in the light of his continuing dialogue with Altizer.

It does not emphasize the ruling Caesar, or the ruthless moralist, or the unmoved mover. It dwells upon the tender elements in the world, which slowly and in quietness operate by love. . . .[88]

Cobb's doctrine of God represents an attempt to follow through this Whiteheadian lead, exploring and developing as fully as possible—with the help of Hartshorne and Whitehead himself—the image of the divine thus suggested. The result has important bearing on Cobb's theology of nature.

Cobb's starting point is experiential. We experience a "call forward," that is, we are aware of ideal and normative possibilities available for our actualization. This awareness may take the form of recognizing the claim of truth upon us, or the claim of the neighbor, or of some creative possibility open to us. In any case, the normative possibilities we become aware lure us out of bondage to the past and established patterns and, insofar as they are pursued, lead to growth and the enrichment of our experience. Moreover, says Cobb, "this call forward is the aspect of human experience in relation to which we as Christians have reason to approach the question of God."[89]

Cobb's analysis of the power of the ideal is indebted to Dewey and Wieman.[90] But more than either of these thinkers, Cobb feels compelled to attribute objectivity to "that which calls." At issue is the ontological status of that which has agency. Dewey's understanding of ideals as projections leaves unexplained the power which they are capable of exercising. Similarly, Wieman's rich description of the creative growth process leaves unclarified the nature of the power operative within the process. Moreover, both Dewey and Wieman attend to what the latter calls "the source of *human* good," so that neither throws much light on the nisus toward fuller being which appears to Cobb to be operative in the subhuman order. Although Wieman does not focus as exclusively upon consciously entertained ideals as does Dewey, he fails nonetheless to provide a conceptuality capable of clarifying the "creative interchange" present in subhuman nature. There too, Cobb argues, the power of the "ideal" is experienced as the call forward, albeit in a largely pre-conscious fashion (with the partial exception of the higher mammals).

The clarification of the call forward as it functions in man's consciousness, in his total growth, and in the totality of nature was the peculiar achievement of Alfred North Whitehead. Whitehead saw that all growth requires the

---

[88]*Process and Reality*, 520.

[89]*God and the World*, 49-50.

[90]See ibid., 50ff.

achievement of a novel concreteness. The introduction of novelty requires the confrontation of each situation by the realm of pure possibilities, the reality of which precedes man's experience. The achievement of concreteness requires that these possibilities are so ordered as to be relevant to the actual situation of each becoming entity. This ordering, too, is given for man and not projected by him.[91]

Cobb's reasoning is based on what Whitehead called "the ontological principle." One formulation of this principle is that only that which is actual can have agency. Ideals as such, normative possibilities, are abstract. And from Plato on, maintains Cobb, the attempt to attribute superior reality and the capacity for agency to possibilities as such has remained obscure and problematical. If possibilities unactualized in the past are to have effective relevancy for present and future occasions of experience, those possibilities must be presented as relevant by the agency of something actual. Moreover, effective agency is the prerogative of unitary actualities, for group action must finally be attributed to members of the group. "Therefore,"

the agency by virtue of which possibilities gain effective relevance, like all agents whatsoever, is an individual or unitary actuality. Since we have attributed cosmic functioning to the call forward, that which calls is best understood as universal in scope and everlasting in duration.[92]

The traditional name of this universal and everlasting agent is "God." The refusal to recognize the objective reality of that which embodies the ideals that lure us forward is possible, as Dewey attests; but it represents an unstable position, vitiated by the failure to account for the effective agency of that which in itself is merely abstract.[93]

It is along these lines that Cobb defends the need for the recovery of ontological realism in theology. The mode of reality to be attributed to God, his relation to space and time, and the reconceptualization of the nature of the divine influence on the world Cobb regards as having been illuminated by Whitehead and Hartshorne. Although each of these topics is immense and important in itself, we shall focus on the third—which involves a fuller exploration of Cobb's understanding of divine agency— and treat of the first two topics along with others, as they bear on our main theme.[94] Our dominant concern will be to delineate Cobb's view of

----

[91]Ibid., 54.

[92]Ibid., 58.

[93]Cf. ibid., 62.

[94]The substantive statement of Cobb's doctrine of God which is least dependent upon heavy employment of the technical Whiteheadian vocabulary is found in the recent systematic work, *Process Theology*. The volumes *God and the World* and *A Theology of*

how God functions as the One Who Calls human and subhuman entities alike to the actualization of novel and greater possibilities.

God functions as the One Who Calls by the way in which he constitutes himself. The distinctively Christian coloring of Cobb's doctrine of God results from his adopting, as the essential clue to the divine nature, a motif drawn from "the Galilean origin of Christianity": the motif of love. The notion of "agape" has been historically the preeminent category in terms of which Christian understandings of God have been forged. But the meaning of the affirmation "God is love" is not altogether clear; moreover, many historic Christian claims about the nature of the divine have been in prima facie tension with this central Christian conviction.

Whitehead and, especially, Hartshorne have emphasized the tension present in the classical tendency to link the Hebraic conception of a "God who acts" with the Greek notion of divine impassibility. The dual claims that God is compassionate and yet passionless have not been easy to reconcile, although subtle efforts have been expended in the attempt to hold the two together.[95] At the least, the element of "sympathetic responsiveness" has often been obscured or even denied to the divine love. The result has been to make the love of God entirely creative in character; God's love for us is his active goodwill towards us. The divine does good things for us but does not actually suffer with us or receive from us.[96] Thus runs the tendency of the classical positions.

Both Whitehead and Hartshorne have attempted to resolve the tension between the active and responsive elements properly present in the notion of the divine character, including divine love, by developing a form of what the latter calls "dipolar theism"; and John Cobb follows

---

Ecology also set forth salient features of Cobb's position. Each of these works presuppose the technical discussion of the nature of God found in *A Christian Natural Theology*. Taking the account in *Process Theology* as a pivotal formulation, I attempt in this analysis to set forth the substance of Cobb's position while keeping the employment of the technical jargon to a minimum.

[95]See, e.g., Anselm, *Proslogium*, 6 and 8 and Thomas Aquinas, *Summa Theologica* 1, Q 20.

[96]The most thoroughgoing interpretation of agape as entirely outgoing or "active goodwill," devoid of sympathetic responsiveness, is found in the work of Anders Nygren, especially *Agape and Eros* (Philadelphia: Westminster Press, 1953). Paul Tillich, among others, has effectively challenged Nygren's divorce of the various "loves," arguing that agape, eros, and philia represent diverse qualities or aspects of the one reality of love. Thus, Tillich moved in the direction of recovering the element of sympathetic responsiveness for the divine love. This represents one of several points of parallelism between Tillich's position and that of the process thinkers. Cf. Tyron Inbody, "Paul Tillich and Process Theology," *Theological Studies* 36:3 (September 1975):472-92 and my essay "Process Theology and the Protestant Principle."

their lead. Charles Hartshorne's description of the polar aspects of the divine nature distinguishes between the abstract essence of God and the concrete actuality.[97] The former—which alone was emphasized by the dominant classical tradition—is absolute, independent, immutable, and eternal in character; the latter is relative, dependent, changeable, and temporal. This distinction has enabled Hartshorne and his followers, including Cobb, to maintain that the divine attributes such as power, knowledge, and love are *both* absolute (a point the dominant Western theistic tradition clearly affirms) and relative (a point the tradition obscures). In Hartshornean and Cobbian perspectives the "absolute" quality of the divine attributes lies in their unique adequacy; and this is invariant. For example, God's omniscience is affirmed in the sense that the *character* of the divine knowing is said to be completely and constantly adequate to its objects. But the *content* of divine knowledge varies (and here "varies" essentially means "increases") with the changes in what there is to be known.[98] Similarly, the character of the divine love is constant—pure and unbounded (that is, all-inclusive) compassion. But the "concrete" content and expression of the divine love, in both its receptive and active aspects, varies with variations in what is available to be loved and in what circumstances.

   Whitehead's formulation of the divine polarity is not identical with Hartshorne's. But his doctrine of the Consequent Nature, the aspect of

---

[97]See especially Charles Hartshorne, *The Divine Relativity: A Social Conception of God* (New Haven: Yale University Press, 1948).

[98]What Whitehead pioneered, Hartshorne explored, and Cobb inherited is an altered perception of "the logic of perfection." (See Hartshorne's work by that title [Lasalle IL: Open Court Publishing Company, 1962]). The traditional understanding of perfection has involved the assumption that perfection is a static notion. In effect, what the process philosophers have done is challenge that assumption—by "dynamizing" the notion of perfection—and then proceed to explore the logic of the understanding of the divine reality that follows from this altered perception. This has resulted in the affirmation that God is "perfect" but "growing." He is "the self-surpassing surpasser" (Hartshorne) who is completely or "perfectly" adequate to all occasions of experience, but his concrete actuality increases as more occasions of experience are actualized in the natural-historical processes of the world. Thus, God can be perceived to be both perfectly adequate in character (that is, absolute) and perfectly responsive (that is, relative; in Hartshornean terminology, "sur-relative" or "supremely relative"). Speaking of divine perfection, then, no longer entails defending complete immutability or "unresponsiveness."
   The eighteenth century American theologian Jonathan Edwards developed a position which anticipated the thought of Hartshorne and his followers in important particulars. Edwards developed both a dynamic doctrine of divine perfection and the notion that (internal) relations are constitutive of being. For the Edwardsean doctrines of creation and God see Herbert W. Richardson, *"The Glory of God in the Theology of Jonathan Edwards"* (Ph. D. dissertation, Harvard University, 1962).

God that is constituted by the divine perception and appreciation of what occurs in the world, is basically parallel to what Hartshorne has identified as God's concrete actuality. The consequential "aspect" of God is God as fully actual in Whiteheadian perspective,[99] and God's actuality includes his response to and reception of worldly actualizations. Accordingly, the term "consequent" is employed by Whitehead to maintain much the same thing that Hartshorne affirms with the term "relative."

Whether in the language of Whitehead or Hartshorne, Cobb's intent is to bring the notion of sympathetic responsiveness into our understanding of the divine character in general and divine love in particular. Both the content of the divine knowledge and "God's own emotional state" (!) are dependent upon his perception of and response to what is going on in the world. The divine love, or agape, is not properly perceived as a contradictory state of "passionless compassion" but rather as compassion in the fully proper sense—that is, as inclusive of the element of sympathetic feeling, divine feeling of and with the feelings of worldly beings. God then is to be understood as "*responsive* love." The ecological bearing of this Cobbian emphasis will be rendered explicit below, but first it is vital to bring out that in Whiteheadian-Hartshornean-Cobbian perspective God is also to be understood as "*creative* love."

Cobb's Whiteheadian doctrine of God seeks to hold together sympathetic responsiveness and creative activity as polar aspects of the divine nature. These elements roughly correspond to Whitehead's distinction between the Consequent Nature, on the one hand, and the Primordial and "Superjective" Natures of God, on the other. And it is in Cobb's development of the theme of the divine creative love that the agential character of the One Who Calls is most fully developed.

In spite of the prevalence of the notion of divine impassibility, classical theology affirmed in various fashions the creative activity of God. All worldly events were understood to be caused by God either directly or through the mediation of natural or secondary causative factors. With the emergence of the scientifically informed modern vision of reality in which all events are thought to be sufficiently accounted for in mundane terms alone,[100] the notion of divine causal efficacy has become increasingly problematical. Several prominent theologians of the previous generation attempted to retain the notion of divine activity in nature and history by appealing to one or another form of what can be called the double

---

[99] *Process and Reality*, 524, 530.

[100] This general conviction seems to prevail even among those who appreciate the Humean critique of the notion of causality.

perspectival theory. Barth retained the scheme of primary and secondary causality, emphasizing the gracious and hidden character of the divine workings.[101] Bultmann granted that every event is adequately accounted for via natural causality alone, but he added that the perspective of faith allows us to confess that "nevertheless" an event is an act of God. We have seen, too, that Santmire's essentially Barthian approach to the theology of nature adopts this double perspectival position.

As suggested in the previous chapter, the essential problem of all such approaches, whether classical or recent, is one of intelligibility.[102] Cobb's sensitivity to this issue in regard to traditional approaches (including those of Barth and Bultmann) informs his efforts to provide a doctrine of God that includes an intelligible affirmation of the divine creative and shaping activity. "Process theology provides a way of recovering the conviction that God acts creatively in the world and of understanding this creative activity as the expression of divine *love* for the world."[103]

Cobb's attempt to recover in intelligible form the conviction that God does exercise causal efficacy takes the form of emphasizing the (Whiteheadian) category of persuasion, as the discussion of God as the One Who Calls has already suggested. The adopting of agape as the normative clue to the divine nature requires the rejecting of the notion of coercive controlling power. Indeed, Cobb regards much of the classical understanding of God to be vitiated by the tendency to make divine love secondary to power rather than interpreting divine power in the light of God's love—as Cobb, influenced by Bonhoeffer as well as Whitehead, thinks a sensitive response to the Christ event requires. Love, as we experience it in our relations with our companions, seeks to work through persuasion; and when it must resort to coercion for the sake of the general welfare, it does so with a sense of unease and partial failure. Analogously, divine love characteristically operates through persuasion even, we may suppose, when the persuasive efforts assume coercive proportions—as in the face of the threat of impending ecological disaster.

Cobb's reconceptualization of the notion of divine creativity can be briefly set forth in the technical vocabulary borrowed from Whitehead. God, suggested Whitehead, primordially envisions all possibilities for worldly actualization. In accordance with the "ontological principle," everything must be somewhere; and the locus of the pure potentials of the

---

[101]See *Church Dogmatics*, 3:3:31, 99-100, 118, 146-47.

[102]There are also other problems: prominent among them, the issues of "theodicy" and creaturely freedom.

[103]*Process Theology*, 51.

universe, the "eternal objects," is the Primordial nature of God. This polar element of the divine being is described as non-temporal and unchanging: the infinite number of potentialities available for actualization "exists" eternally in the conceptual nature of God. Moreover, potentialities become effectively available for actualization only through the mediation of some actuality; this, too, is required by the ontological principle. Thus Whitehead (and Cobb following Whitehead) suggests that God perpetually·correlates what might be with what is, weaving together, as it were, the content of his physical pole (the Consequent Nature, constituted by his prehension of what has occurred and is occurring in the world) with the content of his conceptual pole (the Primordial Nature, consisting of his prehension of all potentialities). From this perpetual correlative activity God selects the possibilities for all concrescing subjects that would result in the maximum intensification of experience for each and all and "presents" to each worldly actuality in its process of becoming the "lure" of actualizing the best possibility open to it. This lure functions as the "initial aim" of the actual occasion, but it becomes the "subjective aim" of the concrescing subject only if selected by the occasion. The subject may select another aim provided by its concrete situation, such as the perpetuation of a past pattern when novel opportunities are available to it. In any case, God can only attempt to "persuade" each among the welter of subjects conjointly constituting the world at each moment to select the possibility for actualization that would be best for it and, at the same time, for all. This persuasive activity of God, resultant upon the perpetual correlation of the actual and the possible, represents the Superjective Nature of God or, better perhaps, the one God (who is at once and always both "consequential" and "primordial" in character) acting "superjectively."[104]

In sum, then, Cobb's Whiteheadian understanding of God—which is open to statement in general theological terms but is buttressed by the technical philosophical analysis—is one that affirms that God is best understood as creative-responsive love and that the mode of God's operation is persuasion. Now we must add the element that connects Cobb's understanding of God with the general theory of value discussed in the previous section: the object of the divine love is to promote enjoyment.

---

[104]Various elements of his system, including his doctrine of God, were left rather loosely connected by Whitehead himself. He did not always carefully emphasize the essential unity of the polar elements within the divine nature, not did he fully integrate the four ultimate elements of his system (God, actual occasions, eternal objects, and creativity). One of Cobb's tasks in *A Christian Natural Theology* was to reduce the remaining incoherence in Whitehead's own work (see especially ch. 5).

The One Who Calls and exercises his call through persuasion aims at the promotion of both creaturely and divine satisfaction: he perpetually calls all creatures to the realization of the one intrinsic good, the enjoyment of intense experience.[105]

> Process theology sees God's fundamental aim to be the promotion of the creatures' own enjoyment. *God's creative influence upon them is loving, because it aims at promoting that which the creatures experience as intrinsically good.* . . . God's creative love extends to all the creatures, since all actualities, as experiential, have some degree of enjoyment. *The promotion of enjoyment is God's primary concern throughout the whole process of creative evolution.*[106]

Nature as Historical. The doctrine that the divine aim is the promotion of enjoyment provides the occasion for Cobb to incorporate the modern dynamic view of nature as evolutionary process into his theology in a vital fashion. Those traditional theologians who perceive God as *actus purus* encounter some difficulty in accounting for the fact that there is a world at all. Divine action *ad extra* adds no values not already (eternally) actualized within the divine being itself. Such theologies encounter additional difficulties in accounting for the fact that the world in which we find ourselves is marked by evolutionary process. If the notion of God as pure actuality is replaced or somehow supplemented by the notion of God as all-controlling power, it is not clear why the most, or only(?), valuable player in the drama of creation should not have been posited at once (as indeed was long held to have been the case).

Cobb's response to both sets of difficulties is based on his perception of God as the promoter of intense experience or enjoyment. On the first issue—why a world?—he agrees with the traditional perspective in the assertion that God is the locus of all possible values; but he differs by his insistence that values subsist in God initially *only* as possible, not actualized, values. "They are in God only conceptually, or in the mode of appetition, not physically, or in the mode of enjoyment."[107] Accordingly, a world of finite actualities is required if any values are to be realized, or enjoyed. And since God's aim is to promote enjoyment, a world is necessary to the realization of his aim. Regarding the second issue—why an evolutionary process?—Cobb does basically two things. He argues that there are gradations of value since some actualities are capable of a larger measure of enjoyment than others. Moreover, he rejects the notion of God as controlling power in favor of the view that God is One Who

---

[105]Cf. *Process Theology*, 59.

[106]Ibid., 56. Emphasis added.

[107]Ibid., 63.

Calls, exercising his creative and shaping function by persuasion alone. This mode of divine operation entails that God can produce only such order as is possible.[108] And this view of divine action implies what is suggested by observation: ". , . that the more complex forms of order presuppose the simpler forms, and hence can only come after them."[109]

Basic to the Whiteheadian-Cobbian understanding of the world as evolutionary process is the notion that a positive correlation pertains in the relationship between the complexity of organization and the measure of enjoyment—and hence value—characteristic of experiencing entities. The degree of enjoyment possible for any entity is a function of the two variables, harmony and intensity.

> Obviously, for experience to be enjoyable, it must be basically harmonious; the elements must not clash so strongly that discord outweighs harmony. Also, for great enjoyment there must be adequate intensity of experience. Without intensity there might be harmony, but the value enjoyed will be trivial. Intensity depends upon complexity, since intensity requires that a variety of elements be brought together into a unity of experience. To bring a variety of elements into a moment of experience means to *feel* these elements, to prehend them *positively*. Now, the more complex an actuality is, the more elements from its environment it can feel, and thereby take into itself. The simpler occasions of experience must exclude from feeling more of the potential values in the environment. This is why intensity depends upon complexity, and hence why the higher grades of enjoyment finally depend upon complexity. Furthermore, a complex actuality is possible only on the basis of an ordered environment. This is why order is promoted for the sake of increased enjoyment.[110]

Since his description of the variables involved in the degree of enjoyment was informed by categories drawn from aesthetics, Whitehead could employ the language of aesthetics to speak of the divine purpose. God aims at maximizing enjoyment or, what comes to the same things for Whitehead and Cobb, beauty. "To maximize beauty is to maximize enjoyment."[111] The criteria in each case are the same: harmony and intensity, with intensity of experience resulting from variety held in contrast. It is above all on the basis of what is involved in the employment of these criteria of intrinsic value that Cobb develops his case for viewing the evolutionary process as the result of divine creative and providential workings.

------

[108]Cf. Whitehead, *Adventures of Ideas*, 139.

[109]*Process Theology*, 64.

[110]Ibid., 64-65.

[111]Ibid., 65.

Like other process theologians and Whitehead himself, Cobb rejects the notion of creation "out of nothing" insofar as the classical forms of this doctrine involve an affirmation that God is the sole source and determiner of all that is. The Whiteheadian emphasis upon the essential correlative character of God and world entails the recognition of their coeval status. With Plato and "more Old Testament passages than those supporting the doctrine of creation out of nothing," Cobb affirms a doctrine of creation out of primordial chaotic stuff.[112] Thus, in process perspective, "creation" means ordering and, specifically, an ordering directed toward the production of occasions of greater complexity and value.

What answers to the notion of absolute chaos within the Whiteheadian perception is the state in which nothing but very simple actual occasions occur at random. There is in such a state no identifiable route of occasions; rather, each entity inherits equally from all previously actualized contiguous entities. Since all actual occasions enjoy some intrinsic value, even in chaos there is a measure of worth; but the value realized is "extremely trivial."

The development of "enduring individuals" (protons, electrons, molecules) marks the first moment in the evolutionary transcendence of triviality. Being a series of occasions that inherits more significantly from its precursors in the series than from other environmentally proximate actualities, the enduring individual represents the initial stage in the achievement of greater value; for the simple repetition of form "adds intensity to the actualization of the value in question."[113] Hence, this initial increment in value is the result of the actualization of the greater order realized when the enduring individual emerged out of the primitive chaos.

But the new measure of order not only contributes to the immediate intensification of experience, that is, to the emergence of greater enjoyment; it also provides the conditions that render possible the emergence of even greater degrees of order and enjoyment. Thus order and novelty are interrelated: achievements of new dimensions of orderliness become in turn the base for the realization of yet other novel forms of order, and so on. Possibilities cannot be actualized at random; "rather, some become *real* possibilities only after others have been actualized."[114] Thus, enjoy-

---

[112]Ibid.

[113]Ibid., 66. See Whitehead, *Science and the Modern World*, 137, 152-53, 278, *Modes of Thought*, 87, and *Process and Reality*, 373-74.

[114]*Process Theology*, 66.

ment or intrinsically valuable experience is positively correlated with order, novelty, and intensity of experience. The emergence of the molecule waits upon the appearance of the more primitive enduring individuals (electrons, etc.); the emergence of the living cell presupposes the appearance of complex molecules; the emergence of the animal can only follow the evolution of vegetation; and the development of humankind follows the flowering of otherkind.

Such considerations enable Cobb to appropriate the modern evolutionary picture of the structuring of the world. What is more, he is able to do so not grudgingly, or as if the evolutionary insights were an addendum, but in a way that depicts the scientific picture of the process of "complexification" and the processive view of God as interrelated:

> On the basis of this correlation between novelty and increasingly complex order, on the one hand, and increased capacity for enjoyment, on the other, the evolutionary development of our world propounded by modern science can be interpreted in harmony with the character and purpose of God. This creatively and responsively loving God is incarnately active in the present, bringing about immediate good on the basis of activity in the past, and with the purpose to bring about greater good in the future—a greater good that will involve a fuller incarnation of the divine reality itself.[115]

A Process Theodicy. One problem that is acute for the theologian of nature is the problem of theodicy. While Walt Disney's aseptic presentations have tidied up the natural world for tender American sensitivities, modern no less than ancient people have been unable to forget that nature is "red in tooth and claw."[116] Even Charles Darwin could postulate that the menagerie of the natural world—marked as it is by what Herbert Spencer called "the survival of the fittest"—is a bloody concatenation befitting the work of a demonic more than a divine artificer. Indeed, the spectacle of nature leads some not toward "nature's God" but away from the notion of a theistic ground of "creation" entirely.[117] In recognition of

---

[115]Ibid., 68.

[116]Is this awareness one of the psychological sources of the compulsive war on subhuman creatures? Does a death-dealing evolutionary process inspire the killing of subhuman beings in the names of "sport" and "progress" as part of an attempt to stop death by inflicting it?

[117]Cf. Darwin's comments to Asa Gray in a letter of 22 May 1860 in *The Autobiography of Charles Darwin*, ed. Francis Darwin (New York: Dover Publications, 1958; first published, 1892), 249: "I cannot persuade myself that a beneficent and omnipotent God would have designedly created the Ichneumonidae with the express intention of their feeding within the living bodies of caterpillars, or that a cat should play with mice." See also ibid., 63-64. and Charles E. Raven, *Natural Religion and Christian Theology*, 2 vols. (Cambridge: Cambridge University Press, 1953) 2:115-16.

this, the theologian of nature must address the issue of "why so much evil in the world?"[118]

Cobb has set forth a process theodicy in some detail, and he has made its relevancy to the theology of nature apparent. The pivotal issue for every attempt at theodicy is the question of how to distinguish between divine responsibility for the way things are and divine culpability. The emphasis in classical theology upon the sovereignty of God—understood by some as an affirmation of all-controlling power—made the distinction difficult. Insofar as God was understood to be the source of the prevailing order of things in such a way that states of affairs could not really have been otherwise, God could be exonerated only by logical strategems—which not infrequently took the form of denying that which appears evil is *really* evil. Acknowledging that evil is in fact evil, Cobb attempts to draw a distinction between divine responsibility and blameworthiness by elaborating three notions.

The first has to do with the way in which divine power is conceived. "It is my conviction that the proper conception of divine power holds the key to the Christian solution to the problem of evil."[119] Cobb's following of Whitehead and Hartshorne in describing the divine power as persuasive rather than coercive allows him to deny that God is all-controlling. He attempts on the basis of the perception of divine power as persuasive to affirm that God is responsible for the character of the world, including its evil, but not blameworthy. Since God's influence is persuasive only, the finite members of the world can fall short of God's good intentions for them. And in Whitehead's words, "So far as the conformity is incomplete, there is evil in the world."[120] Says Cobb,

> This deviation is not necessary; hence evil is not necessary. But the possibility for the deviation is necessary; hence the possibility of evil is necessary.[121]

The latter possibilities follow, of course, from the fact that divine power functions persuasively only; for the character of persuasive power necessarily entails the possibility of its rejection.

The redefinition of divine power is the primary element in Cobb's process theodicy. It provides for a partial explanation of the *fact* of evil

---

[118]See the section by this title in *Process Theology*, pp. 69-75. Cobb also addresses the problem of theodicy in ch. 4 of *God and the World*. Cf. David Ray Griffin's contribution, written from a Cobbian perspective, *God, Power, and Evil: A Process Theodicy* (Philadelphia: Westminster Press, 1976), especially part 3.

[119]*God and the World*, 87.

[120]Whitehead, *Religion in the Making* (Macmillan Company, 1926), 60.

[121]*Process Theology*, 69.

and permits an affirmation of divine goodness in spite of the evil present
in the world. To the redefinition of divine power Cobb adds a distinction
between kinds of evil. This distinction allows him to give a partial
explanation of the extent of evil.

Cobb follows Whitehead in identifying enjoyment as the one intrinsic
good. Enjoyment arises out of harmonious and intense experience. "Harmony" and "intensity" alike are ingredient to "rich" experiences. Accordingly, the two forms of evil represent the two ways in which richness of
experience can be diminished: through inordinate discord and unnecessary triviality.[122] Both forms of evil are in fact evil because they block the
fullest actualization of the one intrinsic good, namely, enjoyment.

Cobb regards the distinction between the forms of evil as important if
certain pitfalls are to be avoided. Oftentimes nonmoral evil is simply
identified with the discordant elements in our world or, more precisely,
with those resulting in physical and mental suffering. Discord, understood as the occasion of such suffering, "is simply evil in itself, whenever it
occurs."[123] Accordingly, it is thought that if God is good his aim should be
to prevent or eliminate discord. This, of course, could be accomplished in
fullest measure only if God were prepared to acquiesce in a very trivial
form of created existence, or none at all!

This negativistic definition of moral goodness obscures the fact that
unnecessary triviality is itself evil. To be sure, triviality is not always evil:
trivial experiences are better than none and in some cases—as in the
electron or even the insect—relatively harmonious but trivial experience
is all that is possible of actualization. But moral goodness, positively
defined, entails the promotion of "worthwhile experience to the quantita-
tively and qualitatively greatest possible extent."[124] From this, the aim of
a morally good agent, including preeminently God, cannot properly be
conceived as simply the avoidance of discord; it must also be perceived as
the intention of promoting as much good or (harmonious and intense)
enjoyment as possible and thus as involving a nisus toward the overcoming of unnecessary triviality. Hence, for the good God to create a good
world the risk of discord had to be borne in the interest of promoting
intensity. This means that considerable evil, understood as the discordant
element of physical and mental suffering, will likely accompany the
achievement of high orders of good, understood as significantly harmonious and intense experience. The alternative is not a good world devoid

---

[122]Ibid., 70; cf. *God and the World*, 93ff.

[123]*Process Theology*, 70; cf. Whitehead, *Adventures of Ideas*, 329-30, 342.

[124]*Process Theology*, 70f.

of evil but no world or a world marked by a greater measure of harmonious experience purchased at the price of the evil of the divine acquiescence in unnecessary triviality. Given the capacity to stimulate the worldly actualization of rich experience at the cost of the evil of discord, God's failure to do so would be far more reprehensible than the course God has actually taken. The fact that he would not be present to raise the question of theodicy should convince anyone who values his own existence that this is in fact the case! Thus the extent of evil is accounted for, in Cobbian terms, by the extent of good itself—and by understanding the correlative character of the chief "ingredients" of the good. "God by creating good provides the context within which there is evil."[125]

These remarks already suggest the third major aspect of Cobb's process theodicy. It consists of the recognition that there is a positive and necessary correlation among a number of factors: namely, (1) the capacity for intrinsic good, (2) the capacity for intrinsic evil, (3) the capacity for instrumental good, (4) the capacity for instrumental evil, and (5) the capacity for self-determination.[126]

We have already attended to the correlative character of the capacity for intrinsic good and for intrinsic evil. As greater complexity of experience involves the transcending of triviality it opens up the possibility of great discord: the more an individual can feel the more the risk that "the sympathetic appropriation" of the feelings of others will become the occasion of suffering. At the human level, this can lead to the choice of a

---

[125] *God and the World*, 96.

[126] *Process Theology*, 71; cf. *God and the World*, 93. The correlation among these factors is both positive and necessary. Cobb links his affirmation of the (eternally) necessary character of the principles governing the relations among worldly actualities, and the divine relations with them, to the Whiteheadian affirmation of the eternality of the world. Thus, he allows that for traditional theism, in which the existence of worldly actualities was strictly contingent, the principles governing their interrelations was also strictly contingent; but in a worldview that affirms the necessarily coeval character of God and the world "it also makes sense to think of eternally necessary principles descriptive of their possible relationship" (*Process Theology*, 72).

It is not clear that in this allowance Cobb has accurately characterized the dominant strands in Western theistic philosophy. To be sure the Occamist tradition affirmed the radical contingency of all worldly existence *and* relations; but, outside of that and a few other schools, the logical necessity of certain ideas and relations were thought to be compelling even for God. (Not even God could create a round square or abolish yesterday). A Thomist, convinced of the veracity of the traditional doctrine of *creatio ex nihilo*, might consent as readily as Cobb himself to the linkage of the five factors listed above. The difficulty for the Thomist is less likely to lie in the recognition of the "positive" and "necessary" character of the correlation of these factors than in consenting to the Whiteheadian definition of "intrinsic" good and evil. It is the Whiteheadian doctrine of intrinsic value that introduces a somewhat novel element, not the notion of the correlative character of the five capacities listed above.

trivial form of existence in order to avoid the pain that accompanies intensity of experience.

We have noted the correlation between intrinsic and instrumental good in our review of the historic character of nature. As the capacity for more complex forms of experience, and hence greater intrinsic good, increases, so increase the possibilities for the emergence of novel forms of existence and experience. Newly achieved good becomes the occasion for the realization of further good. At the same time, the capacity for instrumental evil also increases. The bodily developments that lead to the greater enjoyment of, say, food and sex, can lead to greater suffering if, for example, the bodily needs are frustrated.

> On the basis of the positive correlations among these first four dimensions of experience, we see that the development of beings with the capacity to enjoy significant values, and to contribute significant values to those beyond themselves, necessarily meant the development of beings with the capacity to undergo significant suffering, and to contribute significantly to the suffering of others beyond themselves. The good cannot be had without the possibility of the bad. To escape triviality necessarily means to risk discord.[127]

The capacity for self-determination is correlative with the other four factors.

> This increased capacity for self-determination is part of the increased capacity for intrinsic and instrumental good and evil, since increased freedom means the capacity to synthesize the data from one's environment in a disharmonious way. Hence, even if the environment in which we find ourselves is not objectively negative, we can make ourselves miserable. Also, we can form ourselves in such a way as to make ourselves objectively destructive elements in the environment of others. We can even do this deliberately— which is the essence of moral evil. Hence, increasing the freedom of the creatures was a risky business on God's part. But it was a necessary risk, if there was to be the chance for greatness.[128]

The Cobbian theodicy then comes down to the allowance that God is partly responsible for much of what is called evil, the evil of discord; but he is not indictable for the evil present in the world, since he "risks" the occurrence of evil in order to promote the good. God works to "persuade" worldly actualities to realize the fullest measure of good possible. In Cobb's view, not this course but the other—acquiescing in unnecessary triviality—would render God culpable; for "the positive values enjoyed by the higher forms of actuality are worth the risk of the negative values, the sufferings."[129]

---

[127] *Process Theology*, 73.

[128] Ibid., 73-74.

[129] Ibid., 75.

A "New" Christian Existence. As we have noted, Cobb continually emphasizes the interdependent character of vision of reality and structure of existence. Accordingly, correlative with his call for the development of a new, post-modern vision of reality is his attempt to delineate the shape of a new, post-modern, mode of Christian existence.

The Creative Transformation of Christian Existence. By "a new Christian existence" Cobb intends more than simply the exorcism of distorted elements from traditional forms of Christian faith and life. To be sure, the "new Christianity" which centers in the new mode of existence must be rendered as devoid as possible of the distortions—legalism, authoritarianism, sexism, exclusivism, and superstition—that have marred the old; else it will not meet our needs. Indeed, much of Cobb's polemic is directed against heteronomous and exclusivistic elements in Christian understanding, and his program can be seen as fundamentally an attempt to discover the contours of a theonomous style of Christian vision and existence. His doctrine of God as the One Who Calls represents an attempt to replace the conception of deity as alien other (all-controlling power, cosmic moralist, etc.) with a perception of God as the companion who understands and shares in the lives and fortunes of his creatures. Furthermore, Cobb's perception of the nature and function of morality represents a repudiation of anything that hints of heteronomy and an effort to formulate, within the Whiteheadian framework, the rudiments of a theonomous ethic.

But Cobb's attempt to delineate the shape of a new Christian existence involves more than the determination to purge Christian existence of traditional, and now widely recognized, distortions. The challenge of modernity has done more than expose the illnesses of traditional expressions of Christian existence; it has called in question the viability of "the Christian ideal, normative Christian existence."[130] And it has done so in several ways.

First, the association of Christian or spiritual existence with the particular vision of reality that has become problematical has tended to result in a parallel weakening of Christian existence itself. The Christian sense of responsibility, of freedom, and interiority developed in the context of the conviction that life is lived *coram Deo*; but when God vanishes much of the traditional impetus for the pursuance of righteousness appears to follow suit. Moreover, the waning of a sense of grace renders difficult the breaking of the bondage of self-concern in the

---

[130]"A New Christian Existence,". 79.

interest of concern for the neighbor. Cobb's conviction that spiritual existence can be sustained only if there is "a vision of reality which in critical respects parallels the traditional Christian one"[131] has led him, as we have seen, to elaborate a new theistic vision, one which he feels transcends the problems presented by the dominant modern mentality.

But spiritual existence is in trouble today for other reasons, too, suggests Cobb.

> Where once it was experienced as liberating and healing, today it is felt as restraining and restrictive. Creative energy has passed over into the exploration of dimensions of existence which spiritual existence has traditionally neglected or condemned. Viewed from the perspective of these dimensions, Christian existence, even at its best, appears repressive.[132]

The dimensions to which "creative energy has passed over" Cobb identifies as three: the bodily and emotional life, the new concern for nature, and interest in new forms of community. The three are not unrelated, but we shall attend only briefly to the first and third dimensions and focus our attention on the way in which Cobb thinks the new concern for nature could affect the shape of "a new Christian existence."

In a recent essay on Cobb's ethics, his position has been characterized by the term "somatic ethics"; and joy and adventure have been identified as the two major internal elements in this theory of the embodied moral life.[133] This characterization correctly suggests the difference between Cobb's ethic-in-the-making and much conventional Christian morality. Christians have always attended to their emotions, but the concern has been directed principally toward the disciplining of the interior life rather than its enjoyment. Moreover, the somewhat inchoate awareness of the positive biblical valuation of the body, including sexuality, has preserved Christians from sheer enmity towards this dimension of their life; but this aspect of life, too, has been the subject of much fearful discipline rather than an occasion for spontaneity and enjoyment. Without denying the actualization of values rendered possible by conventional morality or denigrating the necessity of discipline in both emotional and bodily life, Cobb, like other contemporary Christians, wonders whether the time has come for an enlargement of Christian existence. He asks whether Christianity—now that modern culture, under the influence of depth psychology, is raising the question of the role of emotion and sexuality in

---

[131]Ibid., 85.

[132]Ibid.

[133]Charles Reynolds, "Somatic Ethics: Joy and Adventure in the Embodied Moral Life," in *John Cobb's Theology in Process*, 116-32.

human life in a new way—"can accomplish an inner transformation that will enable it to do justice to the body, its needs, and its potential contribution to joy."

> Is spirit now sufficiently strong, sufficiently established, sufficiently secure that it can welcome as friend and ally its ancient enemy? And can spirit grant that former enemy full freedom without finally abandoning to it the reins of government?[134]

The complete reversal of the classical Christian insights called for by Norman O. Brown, for instance—a reversal consisting of the identification of our organic basis with our true being—is clearly unacceptable; but, Cobb suggests, we are currently just on the threshold of the exploration of "the possibility of a new spiritual existence within which the unrepressed body can find its fulfillment."[135]

Similarly, Cobb maintains that contemporary cultural currents call us to explore the possibility that a new spiritual existence could include, and even help give rise to, a new form of communal being. In Whiteheadian perspective the self is constituted by its relations. But with the rise of axial existence and the transference of the organizing center of the psyche, or "seat of existence," from the unconscious to the conscious aspect of experience the self became not only more individualized but more alienated. Since, as Cobb emphasizes, much of our experience of others and of the divine reality is at the unconscious level, this change in the locus of the psychic center led to a sense of estrangement. At the same time, since psychic life became identified with a temporal thread of conscious experience, individuality was accentuated. Now,

> Christian selfhood has been developed in the context of a strongly individualized psyche and has encouraged that individualization. But its essential genius and value are not necessarily bound up with it. This genius resides in a structure that characterizes the individual moments of experience. The center from which those experiences are organized transcends and objectifies all their aspects. The self is not reason, or will, or emotion, or bodily feeling, but a perspective from which all these are evaluated and related and which determines its own relation to all of them. Such a center could never have arisen apart from a highly individualized and separated psyche. But once it has arisen and achieved strength, perhaps it no longer requires such a separated individuality. Perhaps it is no longer necessary to shut out or distance the others in the environment in order that the organization of experience be radically free and responsible. Perhaps the fuller and more positive inclusion of the feelings, purposes, and attitudes of others can

---

[134]"A New Christian Existence," 89; cf. Nikos Kazantzakis's moving presentation of the same question in *Report to Greco*, trans. P. A. Bien (New York: Bantam Books, 1966), 290.

[135]"A New Christian Existence," 89.

contribute to a richer experience, and perhaps this is compatible with free, transcendent selfhood or spirit.[136]

While appreciating the positive effects that have accrued from the heightening of the sense of individuality, Cobb empathizes with those contemporaries who wish to return to a more primitive, communal, type of existence. But he urges instead that we seek to move forward to what he has called a "post-personal" mode of existence,[137] using "personal" in the above sense of an exclusivistic individuality. Cobb accepts the need to recover a greater measure of wholeness and community—something akin to the sense of unity characteristic of primitive existence. But he favors a dialectical or synthetic movement rather than a simple return in which the gains of axial existence are denied. If primitive tribalism (in which the seat of existence is unconscious) is taken as the thesis and individuality (in which the seat of existence is conscious) as the antithesis, what Cobb calls post-personal existence would be the synthesis—a synthesis that both preserves and transcends the best achievements of the earlier and more partial modes of existence. Cobb might speak of what he envisions as a "new tribalism," but if so it would be a form of corporate existence in which the universal community constitutes the "tribe."

> The new community which I propose would be not a return to tribal community but a movement beyond what we have known as Christian community. Each would reach out to the other not only with the indispensable concern for the neighbor as an other but also in openness to being personally affected and informed by the neighbor's feelings alongside his own past feelings, giving them an equal share in the formation of his new experience. Yet he would not allow his selfhood or his ultimate purpose to become only a reflection of others. His openness to the neighbor would enable him in each moment to become more free from his own past, but that would only heighten his final responsibility in each moment for what he becomes out of the vast richness of feeling and thought that inform his being.[138]

As these examples suggest, Cobb's understanding of "a new Christian existence" essentially consists of a widening, or "reaching out," of Christian love. Cobb wishes to extend Christian affection in such a way as to embrace the body, its feelings, and the selfhood of others both more fully and more intensively than has been the case heretofore. And this "reaching out" of love is directed also at the subhuman world of nature.

Cobb claims that the historic structure of Christian existence itself must be changed if we are "to gain an experience of actual participation

---

[136]Ibid., 92-93.

[137]Cobb, "What Is the Future," in *Hope and the Future of Man*, ed. Ewert H. Cousins (Philadelphia: Fortress Press, 1972), 11.

[138]"A New Christian Existence," 93.

and interpenetration with our environment."[139] This change in the existential structure must rest on, as well as contribute to, the kind of changes in the underlying vision of reality of which we have spoken; but the new vision in itself "remains insufficient." What is needed is the kind of opening up of Christian existence that can come only with a fairly dramatic modification of the kind of sensibility about the self and its relations with the "not-self" of the natural environment that has been dominant in much of Christian history. Again, Christian existence "has tended toward self-enclosedness," thinks Cobb.

> It has moved out from itself in concern for others, but it has sustained and strengthened its selfhood by establishing its own self-identity through time. To do so it has contrasted this continuous line of selfhood with the essentially alien environment. Even the body has suffered from this alienation, but more critically still, the self in its struggle for transcendence of the wider nature has refused participation in it. Until we feel that the killing of the oceans, the extinction of species of wildlife, the impoverishment of the soils, and the poisoning of the air diminish *us now*, in our very being, we will not be moved to the dimensions of concern and action that can save our children from catastrophe.[140]

Cobb's understanding of a new or enlarged Christian existence implicitly calls for a dramatic modification of the dominant historical forms of distinguishing the natural and the human. Throughout the ages, Christian faith has centered in the perception that the transcendent Creator is alone ultimately sacred. All else is derived from the Creator, and the final value of all else—natural and human alike—is derivative.

> From this agreed point, there can be two lines of development. It is possible, on the one side, to stress that all God's creatures are valuable to God and, hence, in themselves. In this case it is natural and proper to emphasize man's cocreaturehood with all and to extend love to all. But on the other side, Christianity teaches that man alone is made in the image of God and that God has established him as lord over all other creatures. It sometimes so accentuates man's supreme and unique importance that all other things become mere means to his ends. This tendency has dominated Western Christendom.[141]

The emphasis upon the uniqueness and superiority of the human dimension of creation has, of course, tended to promote a widening of the gulf between humankind and otherkind. It has, to use language which Cobb himself adopts, tended to promote an exclusionist attitude toward the relation of the human and the natural orders. In recent times this has involved a sharp contrast between history and nature—a contrast said to

---

[139]Ibid., 90.

[140]Ibid., 90-91.

[141]*A Theology of Ecology*, 117.

be rooted in differences in modes of inquiry as well as in the objects of inquiry.

Cobb considers the adoption of the other line of development foundational to a new Christian existence. The recognition of cocreaturehood and the extension of love to all creatures is a subdominant motif in Christian history, as the examples of Francis of Assisi and Albert Schweitzer suggest. Now it has become imperative that the subdominant motif become the dominant.

Cobb is self-consciously aligning himself with the "inclusionist" position and even makes explicit his conviction that inclusionism "will further that next step in the development of Christian existence" for which he is calling.[142] Moreover, the inclusionist position is closer to the facts as these have been disclosed by modern evolutionary science.

> Man evolved with and from the subhuman world, and although he has crossed many thresholds in his development, none of them constitutes the sort of divide that would justify the exclusionist view. Man's difference from a chimpanzee is analogous to a chimpanzee's difference from a sardine or a sardine's difference from an amoeba. These differences are vast, but they do not justify views of total discontinuity when the evidence of evolutionary continuity is so great.[143]

Still further, Cobb notes that "there is as much ground for inclusionism as for exclusionism in the Bible."[144] The Genesis account of creation depicts humankind and otherkind alike as having been constituted out of earthly stuff. The scriptural accent falls at least as heavily upon the motif of cocreaturehood as upon that of the distinguishing *imago Dei*, thinks Cobb; although it is to the latter that Christian thinkers have chiefly attended. The interest of the biblical authors focuses upon the distinction between Creator and creation; the threefold distinction of God, man, and nature represents a refinement by later thinkers. Cobb is, however, careful to emphasize that in biblical perspective Adam is the apex of creation; but Cobb does deny that this high valuation of man necessarily leads either biblical or later interpreters of the human situation to an exclusivistic attitude toward the relation of human and other kind.

Within the framework of the new Christian vision-existence that Cobb advocates, the distinctiveness of humankind is that of "a unique being within nature."[145] Adam is "the apex and summation" of nature—

142Ibid., 85.

143Ibid., 84.

144Ibid., 87.

145Ibid., 89.

nature's finest flowering, as it were. Hence, the enhanced love of nature "involves no disparagement of man."[146] "By distinguishing within nature the human and the subhuman," says Cobb, "we can continue to recognize man's superior value without disparaging or denying the intrinsic value of other living things."[147] Thus, Cobb's neo-naturalistic view of man and of the relation of the human and subhuman orders is proffered as "a continuation and development of our biblical heritage rather than its repudiation."[148]

This neo-naturalistic inclusionist doctrine of humanity and nature entails, of course, a repudiation of the contrast of history and nature that has characterized much modern theologizing. The repudiation follows basically from a rejection of the widespread understanding of history as an arena of unique and irreversible events over against nature as a complex of relatively stable and recurrent patterns. Now that time has gotten into our conception of nature with the emergence of the evolutionary perspective, the contrast is, Cobb argues, no longer tenable. Nature, too, is characterized by the unique and unrepeatable; moreover, history contains more pattern than is often allowed.[149]

Cobb appeals to the image of the biotic pyramid suggested by Aldo Leopold to sum up the new consciousness which he considers basic to the new mode of Christian existence.[150] The foundations of the pyramid are constituted by the inorganic reals, including especially the soil. The rich variety of the organic realm constitutes the various layers of the pyramid of life which culminates in the most complex of all creatures, humankind. The evolutionary process promotes the maximization of the pyramid

---

[146]Ibid., 51.

[147]Ibid., 52.

[148]Ibid., 52.

[149]Cf. ibid., 80-81 and *A Christian Natural Theology*, pp. 60ff. Cobb thinks that methodological conclusions have drastically influenced our tendency to contrast too sharply history and nature: "Our exaggerated distinction between methods of inquiry in science and history has misled us into supposing that their objects—'natural' and 'human' events—are fundamentally distinct and separable" (*A Theology of Ecology*, 81). Another process thinker, Ian Barbour, has argued at length that the differences in methods appropriate to the human (including historical) and the natural sciences must be seen in terms of a continuun rather than in terms of sharp, discontinuous, divergences (*Issues in Science and Religion*, chs. 7 and 8).

The theology of Carl Michalson represents one of the most vigorous attempts to clarify and affirm the uniqueness of both "nature" and "history." See *The Hinge of History* (New York: Charles Scribner's Sons, 1959) and *The Rationality of Faith* (New York: Charles Scribner's Sons, 1963).

[150]Aldo Leopold, *A Sand County Almanac* (New York: Ballantine Books, 1970), 254.

through the production of both variety and complexity in the constituent members of the whole.

> The new Christianity must substitute a vision of a healthy biotic pyramid with man at its apex for the absoluteness of man. This negation of the sacredness of human life is not without biblical grounds. Indeed, in its purest form prophetic faith has affirmed that only God is sacred or absolute. That doctrine *can* have profoundly negative consequences by reducing man and all creation to mere instruments of God. Humanism has often been justified in criticizing certain types of theism for their depreciation of human value. But if God is understood as concerned for and involved in the whole evolutionary process culminating in man, then these negative consequences can be avoided. In that case, renewal of the biblical vision of God as alone sacred would undergird and direct appropriate [sensibility and] action in God's world.[151]

Of Vision and Venture. Christian existence is that peculiar possibility of self-conscious, self-transcending human existence which came into being through the divine workings in the history of the people of Israel and, supremely, in Jesus of Nazareth. In one sense such existence cannot itself be transcended; as a mode of existence characterized by self-transcendence it is in an important sense "final." But in another sense Christian existence by its very nature leads those who share in it ever again into new dimensions of consciousness and being. Cobb's call for a new Christian existence is, as we have seen, basically a call for the extension of Christian love to *all* our companions in being—and to the working out of the consequences for action of such an extension. As such, it requires a new vision of reality—in the sense of both being rooted in and leading to such a new vision. The vision and the mode of existence, while distinguishable, are really inseparable.

The possibility of such a vision and existence, Cobb maintains, became decisively actual in Jesus Christ. "My view of Jesus Christ, then, is primarily an understanding of his role in the formation and renewal of Christian existence as a possibility within history."[152] Cobb's chief Christological image, that of "creative transformation," suggests that the new Christian existence which Cobb hopes is emerging in response to—among other things—the ecological crisis is in an important sense the work of Christ. Christ as the Logos is the Transformer of human existence. Thus, insofar as the call for an extension of love to the subhuman order represents a potential transformation of human existence, Cobb's theology of nature—with its dual concerns of a new vision of reality and a

---

[151]*A Theology of Ecology*, 55-56.

[152]Cobb, "Christian Natural Theology and Christian Existence," in *Frontline Theology*, ed. Dean G. Peerman (John Knox Press, 1967) 43.

new structure of existence—has a Christological character throughout. This conclusion comes, however, by way of inference from our overview of Cobb's work as a whole; for it must be admitted that he has not made very explicit the interrelationship between his Christology and his theology of nature. In the latter his characteristic tendency is to speak of God, not Christ. And he speaks of God as the One Who Calls us to both a new vision and new ventures aimed at ecological renewal.[153]

It is because of the promise of a new style of existence and of the new vision of reality, including especially the kind of understanding of God that he has set forth, that Cobb thinks that hope is possible in the face of the unprecedented threat to life on this planet; and not only hope, but constructive action. Cobb recognizes that both complacency and despair are inimical to hope, and he contends that both can be rooted in inadequate understandings of God.[154] The one response assumes that God (and/or other authorities) will take care of everything; the other that no one, not even God, can effect a repair. In both cases the springs of effective action are destroyed. Like visionaries of old, Cobb roots his call for a new style of existence, including redemptive action, in the hope born of confidence that there is One working in and with us to effect purposes that we cannot effect alone. This is "the realistic hope apart from which there is no hope." "It is because of God," Cobb thinks, "that it may not be too late."[155]

God functions not only as the ground of hope in the face of the threat of ecological disaster but also as the ground of the spirit of sacrifice and as the ground of moral openness and responsibility.[156] The motif of bearing the cross is given environmental relevancy by Cobb in the notion of what he calls a new "ecological asceticism."[157] And we have seen something of

---

[153]Cobb's intention and the reasons for the absence of much explicit Christological language in his theology of nature are not altogether obscure. Cobb identifies the Logos with the Primordial Nature of God and suggests that God or the Logos leads his creatures into "creative transformation" through persuasion—by providing the most promising "initial aim" in relation to which each worldly actuality decides how to constitute itself. "The source of the novelty [in the world] is the Logos, whose incarnation is Christ. Where Christ is effectively present, there is creative transformation" (*Process Theology*, 100). Thus, given this linkage of ideas, Cobb can speak alternatively of God (the One Who Calls), the Logos, and Christ as the source of creative transformation.

[154]*A Theology of Ecology*, 141ff. and "Christian Theism and the Ecological Crisis," 34.

[155]*A Theology of Ecology*, 143 and 144.

[156]"Christian Theism and the Ecological Crisis," 34-35.

[157]*A Theology of Ecology*, ch. 7.

how he thinks responsiveness to the One Who Calls can lead to the emergence of new patterns of responsible thought and action.[158]

Such responsiveness is not adequately symbolized, Cobb suggests, by either the imagery of commitment to the whole viewed as sacred or by the notion of stewardship. Viewing all that is, or at least all of life, as sacred obscures the tragic side of the creaturely order; we do not properly give unqualified assent to a process that is marked by destructive elements. The imagery of stewardship provides a better way of expressing the concern which we are called upon to extend to all things, for the stewardly vocation is "governed not only by respect for the goodness things embody but also by a vision of the good that is yet to be realized."[159] Yet stewardship, too, has its limits as an image: it obscures the fact that humankind is a part of that for which we are called to be concerned and responsible, making humankind an outsider and perpetuating the nature-history distinction that provides the context within which stewardly imagery is at home. Moreover, such an image suggests that man has the requisite knowledge and capability to manipulate the subhuman order when it is in fact just such manipulation that has led to the current difficulties.

Cobb opts for a third image, that of "a participant in a process of healing and growth."

> The better image is of a participant in a process of healing and growth. Such a participant has responsibilities, but he is not the master. There is something going on that he does not manage, something that he must learn to adjust to and work with. Since he is himself part of nature, he can recognize that process working in himself, both in his body and in his personality, as well as in his environment. He can develop sensitivity to that process and by restraint and openness assist its working both within and without.

> The process which we cannot manipulate, but whose working we can facilitate, must be discriminated from the totality of events in the universe. It is not expressed in hurricanes, or earthquakes, or the force of gravity, although these, too, are parts of nature. It is the process that makes for life and the enrichment of life, variety of forms, intensity of experience, consciousness, and love.[160]

This imagery of participation allows Cobb to distinguish between our appropriate relative concerns and our ultimate concern. Toward the

---

[158]We dealt above with the foundations of Cobb's ecological ethic. Admittedly, that ethic is not fully worked out, but elements of it can be discerned throughout his pages. Our chief interest, however, in this present study has been focused on the theoretical foundations such an ethic might have; and it is to these that we have largely attended.

[159]*A Theology of Ecology*, 124.

[160]Ibid.

various entities and sub-processes within the whole, love and concern are indeed appropriate; but the loving concern is relativized. Yet toward the One who is working in all entities and processes to promote the good, an ultimate or absolute commitment is appropriate. Thus Cobb utilizes the imagery of participation to avoid obscuring the tragic element within the world and the setting of humanity sharply over against the rest of creation and, at the same time, to promote the inclusive kind of commitment to ecological renewal that seems called for by the new vision and the new mode of Christian existence.

CONCLUSION

No contemporary theologian has gone further than John Cobb in elaborating a new theology of nature. Not only has he responded to the challenge of engaging in the reconstruction of Christian theology that seems to be required, but he has done so in a way that is sensitively informed by relevant scientific, philosophical, cultural, historical, and biblical currents; and he has elaborated his theology of nature in the context of a theological program that is marked by both breadth and depth of vision. For his efforts we must be grateful.

The achievements of Cobb's theological creativity—and of his "theology of ecology" in particular—are many and notable. Some of these he shares with Santmire and others who are engaging in the rethinking of the Christian attitude toward the category of "nature," but in important respects Cobb's program transcends the limitations of these other theologies of nature. We need to direct our attention to these singular achievements of Cobb's work before examining the limitations and problematical aspects of his perception of the new—ecological—vision we need.

More clearly than any other contemporary theologian of nature, Cobb has maintained that a viable theology of nature must root its affirmation of the value of the subhuman order in a comprehensive vision that includes a convincing affirmation of the reality of nature—and God. That is, Cobb recognizes what Santmire and several other theologians of nature evidently do not: that the theology of nature, including an ecological ethic, needs to be rooted in a metaphysical vision that grants significant reality to the extra-human order. The affirmation that "nature" is valuable to God is intelligible only if God is depicted as One who is capable of a positive valuational response, which, in Cobb's language, means that God must be marked by "sympathetic responsiveness." More than that, Cobb has striven to give substance to the claim that subhuman nature has "intrinsic" value. Since genuinely intrinsic value is the value an entity has in itself for itself, the attribution of such value is intelligible only if it rests in a metaphysical vision of the nature of things that supports the attribution. As we have seen, Santmire has, strictly speaking, no warrant for the usage of the language of intrinsic value. The Whiteheadian doctrine of the world as a complex of experiencing subjects, however, legitimates Cobb's attribution of intrinsic value to subhuman entities. Moreover, it provides a basis for distinguishing various degrees of intrinsic value, thereby supporting our "common sense" judgment that an ape is a "higher" animal than an amoeba and—apart from instrumental considerations—"worth" more.

The Whiteheadian-Cobbian vision of the world also involves an assertion of the interrelations and interdependencies of the world in a way that appears to be consonant with what is indicated by modern science. Whitehead's *is* an "ecological philosophy"; this can be granted even by those with serious reservations about the specifics of the Whiteheadian vision. The recognition that the world, including the "world of nature," is a nexus of relations bears importantly upon value theory. Cobb has perceived this and has employed the Whiteheadian perception of the interrelations of things to bring together the notions of instrumental and intrinsic value. While all actualities possess intrinsic value, nothing is without instrumental significance. Accordingly, the "worth" of an entity must be judged in terms of both its intrinsic capacity for significant experience and its capability to contribute to the experiences of others. Thus, in at least these two ways the value theory is rooted directly in the metaphysical vision: the doctrine of intrinsic value arises out of the understanding of occasions of experience, and the notion of instrumental value follows from the perception of the interdependencies of experiencing occasions. Furthermore, Cobb's ecological ethic rests directly on the foundations laid down in both metaphysical vision and the associated theory of value. Again, it is possible to appreciate Cobb's achievement in elaborating the grounds of his value theory and his ethic whether the particulars of his Whiteheadian perspective are accepted or not. Most other theologians of nature have not been so thoroughgoing.

We have found that the new theologians of nature are concerned not only with elaborating an ecologically relevant theory of value but also with affirming that God is at work in the world of nature. We have found further that the work of such theologians is oftentimes marred by a problem of intelligibility at both points. Not only, for example, does Santmire fail to legitimate his talk about intrinsic value and his affirmation that God loves the world; but he fails particularly to render intelligible his claims that God is a "God who acts" in the realm of nature as well as in human affairs. Santmire provides neither a theory of the nature of nature nor an interpretation of the nature of the divine that would warrant his claims. What he does in this respect amounts to little more than an affirmation that biblical writers and classical theologians, especially Luther and Calvin, were right in their claims about God's action in the created order of history and nature. He does not give us significant help in seeing how we can responsibly make the same affirmation in our time—although he purports to be proffering a *contemporary* theology of nature.

John Cobb's work transcends these limitations. Cobb's Whiteheadian theory of the nature of nature enables him not only to affirm the intrinsic value of the subhuman order and meaningfully to link instrumental with intrinsic value; it allows him, at the same time, to show how the world of nature might be open to divine influence. Moreover, Cobb utilizes Whiteheadian and Hartshornean insights into the nature of the divine to set forth a meaningful theory of how God is related to, and acts in and on, the world. We shall consider the panentheistic model of the God-world relation in more detail in Part Two, but it can be said at this point that it does provide a framework for an affirmation of the reciprocal influence of God and the world. And the adoption of the (neo-Aristotelian) category of persuasion as the mode of the divine operations in the world— linked as it is with the peculiar Whiteheadian doctrine of the nature of all actualities as percipient occasions of experience—provides, *within the framework of the conceptuality* that is proffered, an intelligible account of how God acts in nature.[161]

Cobb has achieved other things as well. Ingredient to much of what is said above is the judgment that he incorporates the deliverances of modern science, especially the biological sciences, in a significant fashion. Surely no contemporary theology of nature can achieve adequacy if it fails in this respect; for it is the very success of the natural sciences that, more than anything else, has precipitated the new theological concern with nature. Cobb's appropriation of scientific insights, both directly and through the mediation of Whitehead, has led him to bring together the human and the subhuman orders in an emphasis upon the lines of continuity existing between them that is missing in much recent theology. Over against metaphysicians, like Whitehead himself, who have attended to cosmological problems to the detriment of human issues and over

---

[161]It is possible, of course, to challenge the veracity and the meaningfulness, if not the intelligibility as such, of the Whiteheadian-Cobbian claim that all entities experience. If this claim is denied, that is, if the Whiteheadian conceptuality is denied, then the account of how God acts in nature breaks down.

against existentialists and neo-orthodox thinkers who have attended to human concerns to the neglect of the natural order, Cobb attempts to bring together in a comprehensive vision both dimensions of the creaturely order, the natural and the human.

However, it is precisely at this point of success, as it were, that some of Cobb's greatest difficulties lie. More generally, it can be argued that it is the very conceptuality that makes possible Cobb's most significant achievements that is the source of the profoundest problems. Let us look first at the key concept underlying this Whiteheadian theology of nature.

We have noted that John Cobb never critically examines in any detail what is involved in either Whitehead's or his own employment of the concept of nature. Rather, Cobb acknowledges the extreme ambiguity of the concept of nature; and he endorses Whitehead's intention of taking "the percipient event" as "the clue to nature in general." But instead of basing his theology of nature and his neo-naturalistic theology as a whole on a sustained critical examination of this crucial concept, he moves, almost hurriedly, to theological reconstruction on several fronts. This move is facilitated in his theology of nature as such by the adoption of the language of the "subhuman" and "human environment" in preference to talk about "nature." Moreover, he subtitles his main work on this subject "a theology of ecology" rather than a theology of nature, although he utilizes both terms at various points to refer to this dimension of his work. In other words, Cobb appears to try to skirt the critical task by a shift in terminology. Yet his entire theological enterprise is so pervasively dependent upon the notion of nature that the failure to wrestle forthrightly and extensively with the content, character, and function of this crucial concept is at best obfuscatory and at worst subversive of the results of his theological program. The plain fact is that a theology of nature *or* "a theology of ecology," cannot be successfully elaborated without a critical examination of the concept of nature. And certainly Cobb's kind of orientation cannot lead to a satisfactory result apart from the doing of this kind of "preliminary" task; for in the same work in which he most consistently adheres to the alternate language (of subhuman, environment, and ecology), Cobb refers to "nature as historic," "man as part of nature," and he blasts the traditional ways of distinguishing "history and nature." He even describes humankind as "the apex and summation of nature" and endorses the enterprise of "distinguishing *within nature* the human and the subhuman."[162] Surely the issues underlying such language

---

[162] *A Theology of Ecology*, 51 and 52. Emphasis added.

cannot be resolved by a mere shift in terminology—even if the alternate language were more consistently adhered to than it is by Cobb.

We shall attend to the multiple meanings of the concept of nature in Part Two of this study, but we have noted in the introduction that ordinary usage of the concept involves a basic ambiguity. On the one hand, the term "nature" refers to the totality of reality, that complex of processes and powers that constitute the universe in which we live and move and have our being; as such, "nature" is essentially equivalent to "world" and, in some usages, to "creation." On the other hand, the term "nature" has a more limited meaning, referring to that which is distinguished from culture or human artifice. This ambiguity (and others) respecting the meaning of "nature" is present throughout Cobb's work. He utilizes the term as a virtual synonym for creation or world, as when he speaks of "distinguishing within nature the human and the subhuman." This appears to be his usual wont. At times, however, especially when he wants to emphasize the uniqueness of the human dimension, Cobb tends toward the identification of nature with the subhuman environment. It is not clear that a theology of nature, or ecology, can be successfully executed unless this basic ambiguity is attended to (even if it cannot be fully resolved); for our understanding of the meaning of "nature" affects our selection of root metaphors, our definition of the human both in its uniqueness and in the modes of its relatedness, and many other matters as well.

Cobb's specification of the character of human existence and divine reality is affected throughout by these basic unresolved problems in his work. With respect to the former, it is clear that Cobb's intent is to emphasize the lines of continuity linking humankind with otherkind both temporally and environmentally. And we may appreciate the importance of such efforts as a kind of corrective to the tendency of doing theology in isolation from the revolution in human world consciousness effected by modern (especially natural) science. It is difficult to see how theology can any longer responsibly ignore, say, either the scientific account of origins or the ideological roots of the environmental perturbations that plague our planet.[163] What is not clear is whether Cobb has adequately protected the insights and sensitivities concerning the uniqueness of the human dimension which have come to powerful expression in precisely those theologies and philosophies that have emphasized the peculiar properties

---

[163]This is not to say that all theologians have ignored such matters; it does represent a concurrence in the judgment that much recent theology—especially in its existential and neo-orthodox expressions—has failed to give due attention to these insights and concerns.

of human selfhood and have in so doing frequently sharply contrasted "history" and "nature."

To get at this question we need to examine, if briefly, the kind of clarification of the meaning of human selfhood that has emerged in our history; and for this task the insights of the philosophical idealists may prove helpful.[164] These thinkers have helped us see that human selfhood is characterized above all by self-reflexivity. That is, the self, unlike any other reality of which we have experience, is capable of becoming object to itself. More precisely, the human self can, as subject, become aware of itself as subject at the same time that it is aware of other realities as objects. This is the peculiar property of selfhood, and it is one that distinguishes selfhood from all other forms of being. "Nature" and "natural," then, are terms that refer to those other forms of being, either collectively or individually: those forms of being which are devoid of the capacity for self-reflexity. Accordingly, the human self and its products, history and culture, can legitimately be subsumed under the category of "nature," the realm of objects, only if the latter is imbued with at least as much self-reflexive complexity as the former. Such an understanding of nature is, it at first appears, possible. Hegel himself projected an understanding of nature as ultimately characterized by subjectivity such that it could incorporate other modes of self-reflexivity into itself. Cobb's understanding of nature seems to be moving in a similar direction, a la Whitehead. However, such a movement—whether in Hegel, Whitehead, or Cobb—involves a rejection of the paradigm in terms of which the concept of nature has been shaped under the influence of the special sciences; and it may well tend in the direction of a coalescing of categories that is more confusing than clarifying.

What Cobb has done, whether wittingly or unwittingly, is suggest that the diverse components of the subhuman order of nature—from subatomic "electromagnetic event" to highly developed anthropoid—are possessed of some measure of the self-reflexivity that has finally flowered in evolutionary history with the emergence of humankind. That this is the case follows from his adoption of "the percipient event [as] the clue to nature in general" and thus from his attribution of "feeling" and interiority to subhuman entities. It follows also from his insistence upon the notion that each such actuality possesses value—and hence reality, it

---

[164]See especially G. W. F. Hegel, *The Phenomenology of Mind*, trans. J. B. Baillie rev. ed. (London: George Allen & Unwin Ltd., 1931). My employment of Hegel and my distinction between selfhood and nature, as set forth here, is indebted to Gordon D. Kaufman, especially his discussion in "A Problem for Theology: The Concept of Nature," 360-61.

would seem—not only "in itself" but also "for itself." When pressed, Cobb has on occasion retreated from the conclusion that he is in fact attributing a measure of self-reflexivity to subhuman creatures;[165] yet his language and the logic of his position seem to require the recognition that this is in fact precisely what is happening in his philosophical theology. If so, the distinction between the human and the subhuman dimensions, or between personal and natural actualities—and conversely, the "uniqueness" of each of these dimensions—is significantly obscured in Cobb's theology by the character of his attempt to delineate and emphasize the lines of continuity between them.

The difficulty which Cobb's position thus seems to entail leads us to question the plausibility of regarding the human sense of subjectivity and interiority as the essential clue to the character of all dimensions or levels of reality. If we take the highly developed "structures of human existence" as seriously as one line of Cobb's own thinking seems to require us to do, we find significant impetus for recognizing a qualitatively unique form of self-reflexiveness that is indispensably constitutive of human subjectivity, a peculiar mode of selfhood which cannot have any clear approximations or analogies in subhuman forms of being and psychic constitution. The structure of human consciousness alone, then, would have the requisite reflexivity for the self to turn back on itself in such a way as to make it possible for it to be "for itself" in any significant measure. To the degree that the Cobbian modification of the discontinuities between humankind and otherkind rests upon the hypothesis that the reflexive character of human consciousness provides the clue for understanding and recognizing our kinship with otherkind, including subatomic events, Cobb's position is in need of a great deal more metaphysical buttressing; and the tension between his own understanding of the uniqueness of human or self-reflexive existence and his attribution of something approximating that to subhuman actualities remains to be ironed out. Moreover, these considerations raise significant problems concerning his attribution of intrinsic value to the subhuman order, since this attribution, like the affirmation of the kinship between human and otherkind, rests upon the doctrine that subhuman entitites have reality in themselves and for themselves.

One further point in regard to Cobb's discussion of the nature-history relationship ought to be mentioned at this point. It is not clear that

---

[165]In a discussion of Cobb's *A Theology of Ecology* and Kaufman's "A Problem for Theology: The Concept of Nature" at the annual meeting of the American Academy of Religion at Chicago in the fall of 1973.

Cobb's treatments of nature and human selfhood and the forms of their relatedness are such as adequately to allow for or support the development of the kinds of moral sensitivities and actions to which he calls us before "it is too late." Cobb appears to have immersed humankind so completely and, as it were, undialectically within "nature" as to render problematical his call for the development of the mode of responsible selfhood that would result in the kind of sensitive reflection, self-denial, and action that is required for ecological repair. Such ethical thought and moral action seem to presuppose a fairly clear differentiation of the responsible moral agent from the arena and objects of his reflection and action. This is to say that the possibility of responsible ecological action rests upon the presupposition that those effecting the action stand in some sense outside of, beyond, or over against the object of their action—which in this case is "nature." The fact that humankind alone among earthly kind can recognize the damage he has done to his supporting environment implies that he stands apart in a significant fashion from all the otherkind constituting his environment or natural world. Hence, man is participant, as Cobb suggests; but he is a participant with a difference. And it has been the peculiar burden of the traditional image of stewardship to call attention to precisely this difference between human and otherkind and to accent the responsibility of the former—cocreature though he is—for the latter. It is questionable whether Cobb has made sufficient allowances for humanity's differentiation from nature to account for the peculiarities of his moral and responsible selfhood. Additionally, it is doubtful that Cobb has been able adequately to account for the human capacity to create and shape new "structures of existence," including cultural patterns marked by new degrees of ecological sensitivity. A theology of nature that regards humanity as so easily and completely included within nature cannot readily make sense of humanity's capacity to mold nature or to exercise his creative powers to create a new realm of being, which we know as culture, above nature.[166]

For John Cobb, selves are understood to be highly complex forms of natural process; it is questionable whether there is any genuinely qualitative difference between the processes of nature and human selves. God, too, is perceived not as a creator self whose being is of a qualitatively different order than that which constitutes the natural world but as the process of creativity that is—or, more precisely, that includes and is included within—the world. In Part Two we shall devote considerable attention to the issue of the models of God and the God-world relation-

---

[166]Cf. Kaufman, ibid., 363-64.

ship that are available to the theologian of nature; in doing so, we shall attend to some of the strengths and weaknesses of the panentheistic model that are found in the work of John Cobb. At present, however, we need to raise, in a preliminary fashion, the question of whether the understanding of God proffered by Cobb is marked by a serious tension between diverse elements. In his *Theology of Ecology* Cobb goes so far as forthrightly to identify God as "creative process."[167] Yet his development of the main lines of his processive understanding of God is marked by an attempt to interpret God in terms of the notion of love, with special attention being given to a certain dialectic between the creative and responsive moments in the divine loving. Given this wedding of impersonal (processive) with personalistic imagery (loving agent), the question of compatibility between the two partners thus conjoined comes inevitably to mind. Is the notion of creative process really essentially equivalent to a Christian conception of God? Or has Cobb appropriated elements of a personalistic conception of God—love, sympathy, et cetera—to his basically impersonal image? And if the latter is the case, what transformations of both kinds of images has occurred? Can the image of God as creative process really bear the kind of personalistic meaning that Cobb's appropriation to it of the more anthropomorphic attributes of deity seems to require? Or do we not have here once again an example of the pernicious results of Cobb's failure to examine carefully and critically the content, character, and function of his pivotal category—nature?

In sum, we can say that Cobb's attempt to produce a comprehensive characterization of nature, humanity, and God in their mutual interrelatedness has turned on an effort to identify and emphasize the lines of continuity pertaining among the three. And this emphasis has been purchased at the price of obscuring the distinctiveness of each of these realities—by tending toward the "reduction" of both human and divine selfhood to a process within nature.[168] Hence, we must finally conclude that in important respects Cobb's theology of nature confuses as much as it clarifies and that a viable theology of nature must be based on a

---

[167] *A Theology of Ecology*, 125.

[168] Striving as they do to understand "nature" on the model of human selfhood, Whitehead and Cobb, like other modern naturalistically inclined philosophers, have produced a more sophisticated or neo-naturalistic vision that avoids the crudely reductionistic character of the older forms of naturalism—some of which are still widely current. Nonetheless, the effects of what we might call naive naturalism and neo-naturalism are similar: they both tend to "reduce" all reality to the status of a natural process, although the neo-naturalistic tendency is to accomplish the reduction more gently, with more finesse—and more obscurely—than its older sister.

conceptuality that clearly affirms the discontinuities and the distinctions within being as well as the continuities and the similarities.

CHAPTER 4

A NEO-CATHOLIC THEOLOGY OF NATURE: THE APPROACH OF PIERRE TEILHARD DE CHARDIN

If for no other reason, the priest-paleontologist Marie-Joseph-Pierre Teilhard de Chardin (1881-1955) demands attention in a study of the theology of nature because of the tremendous influence which he has exercised upon others concerned with rethinking Christian attitudes toward nature. While the "Neo-Catholic" thinkers share many things with the Neo-Reformation and Neo-Naturalistic theologians (and, indeed, both of the latter are themselves influenced in some measure by Teilhard), the Neo-Catholic thinkers give a position of dominance to motifs that play only a subordinate role, at most, in the constructions of those building upon the foundations laid by the Reformers and White-head. These additional motifs need to be identified and examined. A number of Neo-Catholic or, more broadly, Neo-Thomistic thinkers have addressed themselves to the problem of defining a new theological under-standing of nature; but none has done so with more imaginative power than the Jesuit paleontologist to whom we now turn our attention.

While the entirety of the available Teilhardian corpus underlies our treatment, the chief features—and most details—of the vision of Teilhard can be found in *The Phenomenon of Man* and *The Divine Milieu* supplemented by a few collections of essays, *The Future of Man, Christianity and Evolution, The Heart of Matter, Science and Christ, Writings in Time of War,* and *Toward the Future.*[1] It is on these works that our analysis will largely turn.

---

[1]Several of Teilhard's works have been issued in a variety of editions with differing paginations. The editions cited in the present study are the following (listed in alphabeti-order):

Teilhard's project, like that of Cobb, can be described as a quest for a new vision. He wanted, above all, "to *see* and to *make others see*."[2] To see the "huge past" and the "fantastic future," the subhuman and the human, the individual and the social, the natural and the divine conjoined in a unitary meaningful vision—that was, and is, the essence of Teilhard's project. "But to do this we must focus our eyes correctly."[3]

TEILHARD AS THEOLOGIAN OF NATURE

What are we to make of Teilhard? Was he scientist or mystic? The answer is—both, and more. Ian Barbour has identified "five ways of

---

Building the Earth, trans. Noel Lindsay (New York: Avon Books; Discus Edition, 1969);

Christianity and Evolution, trans. René Hague (New York: Harcourt Brace Jovanovich, 1971);

The Divine Milieu, trans. Bernard Wall (New York: Harper & Row, 1960);

The Future of Man, trans. Norman Denny (New York: Harper & Row, 1964);

The Heart of Matter, trans. René Hague (New York: Harcourt Brace Jovanovich, 1978);

Human Energy, trans. J. M. Cohen (New York: Harcourt Brace Jovanovich, 1969);

Hymn of the Universe, trans. Gerald Vann (New York: Harper & Row; Perennial Library Edition, 1972);

Letters from a Traveler, trans. René Hague et al. (New York: Harper & Row; Torchbooks Edition, 1961);

The Making of a Mind, trans. René Hague (New York: Harper & Row, 1965);

Man's Place in Nature (London: William Collins Sons, 1966);

The Phenomenon of Man, trans. Bernard Wall (New York: Harper & Row; Torchbooks Edition, 1961);

Science and Christ, trans. René Hague (New York: Harper & Row, 1968);

Toward the Future, trans. René Hague (New York: Harcourt Brace Jovanovich), 1975;

The Vision of The Past, trans. J. M. Cohen (New York: Harper and Row, 1966);

Writings in Time of War, trans. René Hague (New York: Harper & Row, 1968).

Since several of these works are collections of essays and since Teilhard released different editions of the same essay—and even different essays bearing identical or similar titles—all notational references to his briefer works will include the essay title, the date of writing, and the title of the English volume in which the essay is to be found.

Variation in the spelling and capitalization of a number of terms (hominisation/ hominization; centre/center, etc.) reflects the fact that Teilhard's English translators and interpreters live on both shores of the Atlantic; some mystification about what to do with his idiosyncratic terminology is also reflected in the variation. My wont has been to follow standardized American patterns as much as possible in my treatment of Teilhard, but several decisions about linguistic form have had to be made in the absence of a consensus regarding the translation of Teilhardian terminology. In quoted materials I have, of course, retained the British and other variations; the one exception is that the employment of quotation marks has been "Americanized" throughout.

[2]*The Phenomenon of Man*, 31.

[3]Ibid., 33.

reading Teilhard," all of which have much to support them.[4] We shall briefly review these options and suggest, with only slight modifications of Barbour's conclusions, that Teilhard was finally a process theologian with a special concern with and interest in the theology of nature and that he elaborated his theology (of nature) via the partial development of a process metaphysics.

Teilhard was an evolutionary natural scientist, and his least ambiguous works belong to this category. But Teilhard, motivated in part perhaps by the desire to appease his theological censors, seems to have overemphasized the scientific character of his various writings. While, as Barbour argues, there may be in them little or nothing that is "unscientific," in the sense of contradicting established data and theories, there is in them a great deal that is "nonscientific." Teilhard's "hyperphysics" is at the least "science-in-ecstasy"; it is not merely science as understood in the consensus of informed opinion. Except for the technical essays released in scientific journals, the vast majority of Teilhard's works include poetic, mystical, theological, and metaphysical elements: among them, the notions of the "within" of things, the "noosphere," and "Omega."

In polar opposition to his own overemphasis on the scientific character of his work, some have regarded Teilhard as "*primarily* a Christian mystic and only secondarily a scientist."[5] Such critics point to the fecundity of poetic imagery (most of it organic and physical: for example, human beings are "molecules") and to the process of mystical resacralizing of the world that goes on in the writings of Teilhard (to wit: development of the notion of the divine milieu centering in "Omega"). Undeniably, Teilhard was a great poet, mystic—and mythmaker. And we shall suggest in the conclusion to this chapter that Teilhard's greatest significance finally lies in his (unconscious) function of "remythologization." But this perspective on Teilhard—Teilhard as mythmaker—must be developed in a way that respects his concern for conceptual synthesis. The tendency of some critics to treat the poetic, mystic, and even mythic elements in the Teilhardian vision in such a way as to denigrate the cognitive content and truth-value of his perceptions is pernicious; it represents a misunderstanding at one and the same time of this imaginative writer and of the function(s) of nonliteral language.

---

[4]Ian G. Barbour, "Five Ways of Reading Teilhard," *Soundings* 51:2 (Summer 1968):115-45; reprinted in *The Teilhard Review* 3:1 (Summer 1968). References here are to the printing in *Soundings.*

[5]George Gaylord Simpson, *This View of Life* (Harcourt, Brace and World, 1964), 225.

Teilhard is widely regarded as a natural theologian and a Christian apologist.[6] He does often address himself to the (scientifically) "cultured among the despisers." He does appear frequently to be drawing theistic inferences from scientific data; above all, he gives the impression that he is employing evolutionary science as the basis for a reformulated version of the argument from design. But Father Teilhard also regularly addresses himself to believers and seems to have been as much interested in helping the believer bewildered by the impact of science on faith "to see" as he was to assist the scientific unbeliever. Moreover, Teilhard's primordial desire seems to have been to effect a reconciliation between the religious and scientific aspects of his own life; this means that he ineluctably approached the deliverances of science with a variety of questions and predilections formed by his heritage and experience of faith. Accordingly, it is difficult to see how his major conclusions could have emerged *simply* as inferences from scientific data. Barbour's conclusion is compelling:

> . . . whatever his *intentions* he has not in practice limited himself to the phenomena and has raised what would classically have been called meta-physical questions. Moreover, . . . his ideas represent a genuine synthesis of scientific and religious insights rather than an inference from science alone.[7]

More adequate than any of the perspectives on Teilhard suggested so far—scientist, mystical poet, natural theologian—is that in which he is seen as a Christian theologian, and a Christian theologian who is preemi-nently a theologian of nature.[8] Whether or not *The Phenomenon of Man* lends itself to an unambiguous reading, in much of his work Teilhard is clearly engaged in an attempt to rethink the nature and meaning of nature—from a theological perspective. Moreover, he is involved in an attempt to rethink the nature and meaning of classical Christian doctrines as these present themselves within a universe-in-the-making. In fact, since the new situation within which the task of theology must be done in our age involves, as much as anything else (perhaps more than anything else), the new view of nature presented to us by the special sciences, the two tasks are really inseparable: theological reflection on the world, including nature, as currently understood and reflection on the classical doctrines

---

[6]See, e.g., Henri de Lubac, *Teilhard de Chardin: The Man and His Meaning*, trans. René Hague (New York: Hawthorn Books, 1965) and Stephen Toulmin, "On Teilhard de Chardin," *Commentary* 39:3 (March 1965):54.

[7]"Five Ways of Reading Teilhard," 128.

[8]Cf. Bernard Wall in his Introduction to Teilhard's volume *Man's Place in Nature*, p. 5. Christopher F. Mooney's discussion implies that Teilhard is a theologian of nature as well as something of a natural theologian; see *Teilhard de Chardin and the Mystery of Christ* (New York: Harper & Row, 1964).

of creation, providence, redemption, eschatology, and the like in the light of the new view of nature. The two are quite clearly seen coming together in Teilhard's "cosmic Christology," and we shall examine how this is the case in some detail in the pages that follow.

In this view the primary sources of Teilhard's religious ideas lie outside science. The primary sources would be historical revelation as reported and interpreted in both Scripture and tradition and Teilhard's own religious experience as molded by his Christian heritage. Far from simply beginning with nature and rising in some neutral fashion to a knowledge of God, Teilhard's understanding of nature is itself perfused throughout by his Christian consciousness. He himself admits the primacy of the latter on several occasions, as when he confesses that in respect to his doctrine of the cosmic point of convergence which he calls "Omega," "doubtless I should never have ventured to envisage the latter or formulate the hypothesis rationally if, *in my consciousness as a believer*, I had not found not only its speculative model but also its living reality."[9] Barbour, who adopts this view, sums up some of its advantages while he sets the stage for his own contribution to the reading of Teilhard:

> Let us assume that the primary sources of Teilhard's theological ideas were religious experience and historical revelation. Like those who see Teilhard as a mystic, we can recognize the importance of his own devotional life; but religious experience is always interpreted in terms of a particular historical tradition. Like the "natural theology" school, we can allow for the influence of science on Teilhard's thought. But science was not the primary source of his understanding of God; his evolutionary outlook influenced his theological views more indirectly through his metaphysics. Like those who see his writing as Christian theology, we can acknowledge his dependence on historical revelation. But theology is not itself revealed; it always involves the human interpretation of events in which God is understood to have acted. Both Protestant and Catholic writers have maintained that revelation occurs not in a fixed set of theological propositions but in historical events—events which elicit man's ever-new response and which are understood only in the changing categories of his thought. In Teilhard's case these categories reflect a metaphysics of process.[10]

Barbour argues that regarding Teilhard as a process philosopher represents a fifth way of reading Teilhard and one that has been, somewhat strangely, neglected. Although Teilhard was not chiefly a philosopher and although he disparaged metaphysics, "it is in his informal metaphysics that one must seek the unity of his thought."[11] Teilhard, Barbour contends with considerable supporting evidence, proffered an

---

[9]*The Phenomenon of Man*, 294. Emphasis added.

[10]"Five Ways of Reading Teilhard," 132.

[11]Ibid., 115.

inchoate but crucially significant process metaphysics that functions as the point of meeting between his biblical concepts and his evolutionary insights.

Teilhard's opposition to the term "metaphysics" appears to have been rooted in a particular understanding of the enterprise as abstract a priori deduction from first principles. But what he attempted under the alternative rubric of "hyperphysics" appears to be synonymous with another— and classical—understanding of metaphysics as the enterprise in which the attempt is made to interpret and integrate the widest possible range of diverse types of data towards the end of producing a coherent view of that which is. This is an understanding of metaphysics that has found powerful recent expression in the philosophy of Alfred North Whitehead. Classically, metaphysics involved the search for the most general categories for interpreting experience and for analyzing the structures of reality; and the enterprise was nourished by experiences, ideas, and data drawn from a variety of sources. Thomas Aquinas, for example, constructed a view of reality that was formed, preeminently and with some inherent tensions, from the dual sources of biblical religion and Aristotelian philosophy. His basic categories were those of being and substance. Teilhard, however, who was attempting (as he repeatedly affirmed) a synthesis of ideas deriving from his religious and his scientific background, gave primacy to the categories of becoming and process. Treating the world as a complex evolving ecosystem, he exalted time, transformation, and interaction. The adoption of this evolutionary perspective simultaneously reflected Teilhard's perception of God as agent and influenced him to emphasize the dynamic aspects of the biblical vision of God acting continuously to fashion his creation. "Teilhard's view of reality as temporal process was thus the 'middle term' through which scientific ideas indirectly affected theological ones and vice versa."[12] While not a professionally trained philosopher, "his partially developed metaphysics shows the same kind of double origin and two-way influence that is evident in Aquinas; specifically, we can trace the interaction of evolutionary science and biblical theology in his thought."[13]

That Teilhard is basically a process philosopher Barbour attempts to demonstrate by a detailed comparison between Whitehead and Teilhard. He points out the similarity of their views in several particulars:[14] the

---

[12]Ibid., 133.

[13]Ibid.

[14]Sketchily in ibid.; in considerable detail in "Teilhard's Process Metaphysics," in Ewert H. Cousins, ed., *Process Theology: Basic Writings* (New York: Newman Press,

understanding of reality as temporal process, the notion of a "within" of things, their treatment of freedom and determinism, the notion of continuing creation, the understanding of God and time, the problem of evil, and their perspectives on the future of the world. Barbour concludes:

> Teilhard's most significant intellectual contribution is a *process theology* which combines the fourth and fifth classifications, Christian theology and process philosophy. His more strongly theological writings represent explorations of the doctrines of man, creation, and redemption in an evolutionary universe. *The Phenomenon of Man* represents a "theology of nature" rather than a natural theology; it is an attempt to view nature, as understood by modern science, from a perspective which is both evolutionary and biblical. This conclusion enables us to see Teilhard's total thought as a synthesis of scientific and religious ideas, and it provides a rationale for the interaction which is so evident among the components of his thought.[15]

Thus, in spite of his emphasis upon Teilhard's accomplishments as a process philosopher, Barbour really seems to think of Teilhard—and, in any case, this is the more accurate view—as a Catholic process theologian who arrived at an underlying process metaphysic on his own. Unlike the majority of process theologians, who have borrowed their philosophical vision from Whitehead, Teilhard was in effect his own Whitehead as well as a creative Christian theologian.[16] He was, as Barbour argues, a process philosopher whose variegated works find their unity in his partially formed metaphysic; but his process philosophy was forged along with and functions in service of his Neo-Catholic process theology.

In this study, then, we shall treat Teilhard as finally a Christian theologian and preeminently a theologian of nature who was vitally interested in a comprehensive intellectual synthesis. He was scientist. He was poet. He was mystic. He was to some extent a natural theologian of a (Neo-)Thomistic type. He was a philosopher of sufficient aptitude to identify and develop several important metaphysical implications of recent science which have proven elusive to many professional philosophers. He was a Christian theologian—of nature—who employed his various resources and capabilities to mark out the possible foundations and contours of a new Christian synthesis.

1971), 323-50. This essay by Barbour was orginally printed in *The Journal of Religion* 49 (1969):136-59. References here are to the printing in the volume edited by Cousins. We shall compare Teilhard with Cobb—and thus, implicitly, with Whitehead—in some detail in Chapter 5.

[15]"Five Ways of Reading Teilhard," 138.

[16]There is no evidence that Teilhard had read Whitehead, or vice versa. The two thinkers did, however, drink from a common fountain philosophically: both were influenced by Henri Bergson.

THE TEILHARDIAN VISION: FOUNDATIONS

Teilhard de Chardin was above all a visionary, a seer, whose intent it was to help others to see. Starting as a scientist concerned with the history of life, Teilhard extended his vision of the past into an elaborate interpretation of the present and a grand vision of the future. We shall examine the shape of these moments of the Teilhardian vision in order to lay the foundations for our examination of his promise as a theologian of nature. In this section we are attending to what he regarded as a strictly "phenomenological" analysis of the process of evolution, even if (as he himself allows) it is improbable that he would have arrived at some of the positions set forth without the conditioning of his acumen by his participation in "the Christian phenomenon." We begin with a brief examination of his analysis of the cosmic process from its inception up to the coming of life and the birth of thought. Then we examine his treatment of the present state and future projections of evolutionary development.

The Vision of the Past: From Cosmogenesis to Anthropogenesis. In 1949 Teilhard produced an essay bearing a title which the editors of his works were later to employ as the rubric under which they would issue a collection of his shorter reflections on the nature of evolutionary development. In "The Vision of the Past" Teilhard reflects his tendency to trace all the radiating lines of his interpretation of present trends and future projections to his scientifically informed reading of human and, especially, natural history. "I am," he wrote a friend, "a pilgrim of the future on my way back from a journey made entirely in the past."[17]

Teilhard's explorations of the past led to the conclusion—which is at the same time the starting point of his thought—that ours is a universe-in-the-making. The world with which we have to do is "no longer the cosmos, but cosmogenesis."[18] Genesis on a prodigious scale hitherto unsuspected is the reality which modern science has disclosed to us and which must henceforth be incorporated in all our thinking.

Teilhard begins his pivotal work on the phenomenon of man by rehearsing, almost poetically, the deliverances of recent science regarding the origination of the cosmos: the formation of molecules, the dispersal of the galaxies, and the emergence and development of our own planet. His panoramic sweep moves from the "pre-life" determinations of matter through the emergence of life to the flowering of thought and society. But our concern here must be less with the particulars of his depiction of the

---

[17]*Letters from a Traveler*, 101.

[18]"The Vision of the Past" (1949), *The Vision of the Past*, 238.

development of the cosmos in its various phases than with the way in which he seeks to synthesize the deliverances of the various sciences (astronomy, geology, physics, chemistry, paleontology, biology, anthropology, sociology) into one comprehensive and coherent picture.

Teilhard searches for dynamic principles in the vast concatenation of phenomena to which he is attending. The most significant principle that emerges from Teilhard's "hyperscientific" examination of the evolutionary process is that of the "law of complexification."[19] By "complexification" Teilhard refers to a movement within the world process—a movement susceptible to empirical discernment and confirmation—towards increasing complexity of structure accompanied by the development of greater internal unity and concentration. Throughout nature there are to be seen developed unities, internally unified wholes; and these entities manifest increasing complexity of organization. This trend towards increasingly centered complexity is manifested in atoms, molecules, planets, organisms, and societies. The world is a dynamic process marked by the emergence of novel entities which are both more complex and more "centered" or unified.

Teilhard traces the tendency towards the production of increasingly centered and complex entities to the nature of energy itself. Science had taught him to understand energy to be the most primitive stuff of the universe and to recognize the capacity of energy to take material form (as in molecules) with a capacity for action.[20] Moreover, by the collective bonds of energy each bit of matter is related to, is affected by, and affects all other material particles. Thus, the character of energy accounts, in the first instance, for the basic coherence of the universe, its capacity to "hang together." (Teilhard will go on to say that finally the unity and coherence of the universe comes "from above," as we shall note momentarily.) And the character of energy accounts for, again in the first instance, the movement of various members of the universe—and the universe itself—towards greater centered complexity. But to follow Teilhard's line of thinking further we must introduce another notion.

Teilhard accepts the deliverances of science, even when he tries to supersede them. And at the physical level science has affirmed the operation of two principles in regard to primordial stuff: one is the principle of the conservation of energy (the first law of thermodynamics) and the other is the principle of increasing entropy (the second law of thermodynamics). The first principle indicates that the amount of energy available

---

[19]See, e.g., *The Phenomenon of Man*, 48.

[20]Ibid., 42-43.

in the universe is constant. It follows that the energy available to the process of evolutionary development is limited. But the second principle formulates the observation that in a particular system the *available* energy decreases as work is done. It follows from this that the energy available to the process of evolutionary development is not only limited but is decreasing. Entropy is the measure of the loss of available energy. And since energy is continuously entropized (in the form of heat), the available energy of the universe is being dissipated, a condition that threatens the specter of a final cosmic state of static equilibrium.

Now some, of course, simply do not believe the second law of thermodynamics. Proponents of the "steady state" theory of the cosmos, for example, hold that the universe is nonentropic in character. Teilhard, however, attempts no such direct challenge of the dominant scientific consensus. His is an almost childlike acceptance of the deliverances of science:

> A rocket rising in the wake of time's arrow, that only bursts to be extinguished; an eddy rising on the bosom of a descending current—such then must be our picture of the world.
>
> So says science: and I believe in science. . . .[21]

But Teilhard immediately questions whether this picture—accurate insofar as it goes—is the full picture: "Up to now has science ever troubled to look at the world other than from *without*?"[22]

Teilhard attempts both to accept and correct the picture of the cosmos proffered by science, not by a denial of the deliverances of science, but by a questioning examination of the nature of energy. Taking man, and thus the flowering of interiority or consciousness, as the key to the whole world process, Teilhard theorizes that there is another kind—or "face"—of energy. And this inner aspect of energy—this "within"—which we know introspectively points, Teilhard suggests, to an interior aspect of the whole universe.

> It is impossible to deny that, deep within ourselves, an "interior" appears at the heart of beings, as it were seen through a rent. This is enough to ensure that, in one degree or another, this "interior" should obtrude itself as existing everywhere in nature from all time. Since the stuff of the universe has an inner aspect at one point of itself, there is necessarily a *double aspect to its structure*, that is to say in every region of space and time—in the same way, for instance, as it is granular: *coextensive with their Without, there is a Within to things.*[23]

---

[21]Ibid., 52.

[22]Ibid.

[23]Ibid., 56.

This stance brings Teilhard to the conclusion—or rather assumption—that "all energy is psychical [*psychique*] in nature"[24] and that physical energy is but one dimension of the total phenomenon. Teilhard postulates two complementary dimensions or aspects of energy: a "tangential" component (corresponding to the "without") and a "radial" component (corresponding to the "within"). The former, he maintains, "links the element with all others of the same order (that is to say of the same complexity and centricity) as itself in the universe."[25] In this way, tangential energy gives shape to the outward form of the evolutionary process. Its results can be observed scientifically, for they constitute the material complexity of organization of the various units of process. Radial energy, on the other hand, draws the element "towards ever greater complexity and centricity—in other words forwards."[26] It is the radial component that is responsible for the movement to novel and "higher" entities/levels (when judged in terms of complexity of organization) within the evolutionary process. And it is likewise responsible for the increase in the degree and quality of interiority and the heightened unity that accompany the greater degree of organization. Thus, energy in its radial aspect accounts for the development of more centered molecules early in our planetary history and, later on, for the emergence of highly complex and intelligent organisms; while the tangential component of energy explains the proliferation and interaction of molecules, cells, and organisms at their respective levels of organization.

What Teilhard has done by this bold theory is twofold. He has incorporated man squarely into the world that science depicts to us. A coherent view of the cosmos inclusive of humankind is not possible as long as science attends only to the "without" of things. By inviting science to enlarge its scope and attend to the "within" as well as the "without" Teilhard converts the human phenomenon from the status of an anomaly or epiphenomenon to that of a pivotal position holding the key to all the rest.[27] Moreover, Teilhard's theory of the two aspects of energy provides him with an explanation of how a (directed) evolutionary movement

---

[24]Ibid., 64. The translator has misconstrued the term *psychique* as "physical" in the 1959 edition of *The Phenomenon of Man*. The error has been corrected in subsequent editions, and it is corrected here.

[25]Ibid., 65.

[26]Ibid.

[27]By the same token—and this is simply another way of putting the point—Teilhard has ostensibly overcome the persistent dichotomy between mind and matter; and he has done it in the same way that Whitehead and Cobb do, by postulating that all energy has a dipolar (within and without, psychical and physical) character.

towards higher complexity and centricity could have occurred. As one of Teilhard's interpreters sums it up:

> Using only the one energy of science, tangential energy, we are at a loss to explain evolution's direction and man's place in nature. Tangential energy alone can account only for chance physiochemical interchanges, leaving unexplained the growing unification and centeredness of evolving matter and finding no definable place in the cosmos for man.
>
> By postulating a radial or centering energy in matter, one can explain the increasing complexification of matter. This radial energy accounts for the imponderable action whereby matter arranges itself, under pressure of the environment's scattered tangential energies, into more complex arrangements and, therefore, into more centered unities. The presence in matter of a self-organizing energy explains both the direction of evolution and the very centeredness or unity of atoms, molecules, cells, animals and men.[28]

The law of complexification and interiorization that the Jesuit paleontologist finds operating in the evolutionary process is thus given an ontological basis in energy itself. And it is specifically the radial component of energy that accounts for the evolutionary advances which the law describes. Teilhard speaks of certain "critical points" or "thresholds" that are crossed in the process and at which novel phenomena appear.

> In every domain, when anything exceeds a certain measurement, it suddenly changes its aspect, condition or nature. The curve doubles back, the surface contracts to a point, the solid disintegrates, the liquid boils, the germ cell divides, intuition suddenly bursts on the piled up facts. . . . Critical points have been reached, rungs on the ladder, involving a change of state—jumps of all sorts *in the course* of development.[29]

Teilhard accounts for the evolutionary "jumps" or threshold-crossings by setting forth a theory (Is it science or poetic imagery?) of "involution" or "coiling up." "Regarded along its axis of complexity, the universe is, both on the whole and at each of its points, in a continual tension of organic doubling back upon itself, and thus of interiorization."[30] Teilhard illustrates his point by setting forth the image of a vortex in which the central core consists of a continually growing "consciousness"; this "core" becomes deeper as the degree of interior organization increases or, that is, as the vortex undergoes a greater tightness of coiling.

Examples of such critical points are several. In each case quantitative changes have accumulated to the point that a qualitative change occurs. The appearance of life and the emergence of humankind are dramatic

---

[28]W. Henry Kenney, *A Path through Teilhard's Phenomenon* (Dayton OH: Pflaum Press, 1970), 83-84.

[29]*The Phenomenon of Man*, 78.

[30]Ibid., 301.

instances. In the former case, protein-type molecules undergo complexification until a point of supersaturation is reached and life bursts forth.[31] Life then assumes a multitude of forms which "grope" their way toward greater complexity and richer interiority. This "groping" Teilhard describes as "directed chance."

> Once more, this time on the plane of animate particles, we find the fundamental technique of *groping*, the specific and invincible weapon of all expanding multitudes. This groping strangely combines the blind fantasy of large numbers with the precise orientation of a specific target. It would be a mistake to see it as mere chance. Groping is *directed chance*. It means pervading everything so as to try everything, and trying everything so as to find everything. Surely in the last resort it is precisely to develop this procedure (always increasing in size and cost in proportion as it spreads) that nature has had recourse to profusion.[32]

Teilhard accounts for the prodigious wastefulness of nature—its profusion of forms and multiplication of individuals—in terms of the tendency, born of the radial component of energy, to seek a way forward. The seemingly random activity on which the theory of natural selection focuses attention is less than fully random; for it is somehow shaped by an inner nisus, governed in overall pattern if not in particulars, then by an internal organizing principle. Simpler entities are taken up into the process of constituting more complex wholes. Accordingly, there is in the evolutionary process a lack of regard for all that does not lie ahead or possess a tendency towards a centered wholeness. "Groping profusion; constructive ingenuity; indifference towards whatever is not future and totality;—these are the three headings under which life rises up by virtue of its elementary mechanisms."[33] The simpler individual, the product of the lower level of evolution, is incorporated into the new whole of the higher level and thus carried into the future movement of the process. And the whole process is governed or "motivated" by a principle of organization which, while it is opaque to science, is not incompatible with the laws pertaining at the physical level (with which ordinary science deals), but rather operates within them.

Teilhard frankly admits the orthogenetic character of his account of evolutionary process. Because of the scientifically suspect status of orthogenesis this has been one of the factors which has brought down upon Teilhard's vision the opprobrium of certain members of the scientific community. George Gaylord Simpson who takes Teilhard to task at this

---

[31]Cf. ibid., 72ff.

[32]Ibid., 110.

[33]Ibid., 111.

point, defines orthogenesis as "a tendency for evolution to continue steadily in the same direction over indefinitely prolonged periods of time regardless of influences directly involved in the interaction of organism and environment."[34] Clearly, orthogenesis understood in this fashion is scientifically spurious. But this is not what Teilhard means by the term. For the Jesuit, who might better have avoided the term because of its troublesome connotations, orthogenesis refers to the directional drift of evolution on the whole towards increasing complexification and interiorization. This is not what most biologists understand by orthogenesis. Theodosius Dobzhansky, himself a Neo-Darwinian biologist, acknowledges that Teilhard's employment of the term is unusual in that it carries for Teilhard "philosophical and mystical" meanings rather than strictly biological ones. Dobzhansky goes so far as to allow that Teilhard's "mystical 'orthogenesis' need not be incompatible with modern biological theory."[35] Thus, even after it is admitted that orthogenesis is a useless concept within the strictly biological sphere—since a functional definition cannot be set forth in terms of which the notion could be tested by empirical data—the question remains as to whether in a "hyperbiology" orthogenesis functions as a structural concept which is valid and significant in dealing with the expanded range of data.

With or without the term "orthogenesis," Teilhard treats life as a story of ascending complexity of organization accompanied by a tendency towards increasing involution and deepening interiorization. A variety of evolutionary stems "grope" upwards in pursuance of increasing centricity; but it is in a single stem, that of the zoological group Vertebrata, that the process of "coiling up," interiorization, becomes astonishingly pronounced. In the endothermic animals in general and in the primates in particular the process of complexification becomes centered in the central nervous system, including especially the brain. With the emergence of the primates in the Eocene period, the evolutionary movement takes the form of increasing cerebralization and, accordingly, of increasing consciousness. The influence of the radial component of energy becomes ever more pronounced. Consciousness flowers into self-consciousness; and a new evolutionary trend—new in its scope and significance—sets in: conver-

---

[34]Quoted in George B. Murray, "Teilhard and Orthogenetic Evolution," *Harvard Theological Review* 60 (1967):285. For a fuller treatment by Simpson of the notion of orthogenesis see the revised edition of his volume *The Meaning of Evolution* (New Haven: Yale University Press, 1967), 131-59. Simpson's evaluation of Teilhard's vision is found in *This View of Life*, 224-33.

[35]Theodosius G. Dobzhansky, *Heredity and the Nature of Man* (New York: New American Library; Sequet Books, 1966), 151-52.

gence. The early stages of the evolution of life are marked by divergence, the radiation of life into multiple forms. In this phase the role of the tangential component of energy is prominent; but increasing cerebralization carries life across a major new threshold, and the capacity for advanced forms of reflection is born. Along with the capacity for reflection the unparalleled ability for self-reflexivity emerges: a creature is born who can say "I." "The cell has become 'someone.' "[36] And this quintessence of the radial component of energy sets the stage for a new evolutionary drama, one that is marked by the phenomenon of convergence as the "noosphere" envelopes our planet.

> When compared to all the living verticils, the human phylum is not like any other. But because the specific orthogenesis of the primates (urging them towards increasing cerebralisation) coincides with the axial orthogenesis of organised matter (urging all living things towards a higher consciousness) man, appearing at the heart of the primates, flourishes on the leading shoot of zoological evolution.[37]

What Teilhard affirms, then, in this first stage of his analysis is that the cosmos is a coherent but dynamic unity, that a single pattern runs through cosmic evolutionary development, and that the dominant nisus of this pattern is towards humankind. This is the "Ariadne's thread" of evolution.[38] In this part of his phenomenological analysis, Teilhard is attempting to specify the meaning with which evolution invests "man." Far from being an epiphenomenon or an anomoly within biological evolution, humankind is really the key to the biological—and cosmic—process; for the evolutionary process is "no more than a movement of consciousness veiled by morphology."[39] In the second stage of his analysis, Teilhard focuses on the meaning humankind invests in evolution.

The Vision of the Future: From Anthropogenesis to the Omega Point. The world is still in process of development, according to Teilhard. But

---

[36] *The Phenomenon of Man*, 173. Teilhard's term for this event is "hominization." In a colorful passage (180) he defines it in the following fashion:

"Reflection conserves even while re-shaping all the lines of the phylum on which it settles. . . . Man only progresses by slowly elaborating from age to age the essence and the totality of a universe deposited within him.

"To this grand process of sublimation it is fitting to apply with all its force the word hominisation. Hominisation can be accepted in the first place as the individual and instantaneous leap from instinct to thought, but it is also, in a wider sense, the progressive phyletic spiritualisation in human civilisation of all the forces contained in the animal world."

[37] Ibid., 180.

[38] Ibid., 142ff.

[39] Ibid., 167.

the "scene of the action" has shifted from the biological to the psycho-social sphere. "Man," in fact, "*is nothing else than evolution become conscious of itself.*"[40] Humankind represents "the arrow pointing the way to the final unification of the world in terms of life."[41] *"The social phenomenon is the culmination and not the attenuation of the biological phenomenon."*[42]

Teilhard regards the emergence of the noosphere—the capacity for thought and socialization—as marking a critical turning point for life in its organic totality, as well as for the individual and the species. Once hominization occurs and the noosphere begins to take shape, the evolutionary process centers its creative energies in its newest emergent.

> This sudden deluge of cerebralisation, this biological invasion of a new animal type which gradually eliminates or subjects all forms of life that are not human, this irresistible tide of fields and factories, this immense and growing edifice of matter and ideas—all these signs that we look at, day in and day out—seem to proclaim that there has been a change on the earth and a change of planetary magnitude. . . .
>
> The greatest revelation open to science today is to perceive that everything precious, active, and progressive originally contained in that cosmic fragment from which our world emerged, is now concentrated in and crowned by the noosphere.[43]

Teilhard regards the appearance of man and "the phosphorescence of thought"[44] that marks noospheric evolution as at once continuous and discontinuous with what has gone before. The new arises out of and continues what has gone before, but the new thing cannot be exhaustively accounted for by its precursors. It represents the crossing of a threshold and, in the case of the shift from biologic to noospheric evolution, "an infinite leap forward."[45]

The emergence of "the psychozoic era,"[46] the era of noetic evolution, is marked by the phenomenon of social and psychic convergence. Once the critical point of hominization was passed humankind began rapidly to radiate around the planet. The species multiplied and differentiated itself under the influence of the tangential component of energy, and it began to develop control over the planet and the biosphere. Then another critical

---

[40]Ibid., 220. The phrase is derived from Julian Huxley, as is my term "psycho-social."

[41]Ibid., 233.

[42]Ibid., 222.

[43]Ibid., 183.

[44]Ibid.

[45]See ibid., 169ff.

[46]Ibid., 183.

point, as it were, was reached; and divergence tended to give place to the opposing trend. The phenomenon of convergence—the flowing together or "coiling up" of people and ideas—reflects a necessity imposed by the character of the planet on which man has emerged: limited space and geodesic curvature. Coupled with the propensity of the species to "be fruitful and multiply," the size and shape of the planet guaranteed that the radiating lines of human evolution would meet. As the "human mass" increased and radiated into confined areas, social pressures increased. Goods and ideas were exchanged. Physical, intellectual, and spiritual interactions and interdependencies multiplied, as men and women forged complex networks of trade, communications, learning, and technological prowess.

Teilhard interprets the phenomenon of social and psychic convergence as a continuation of that tendency towards "coiling up" or increasing complexification and interiorization present throughout evolutionary history. In fact, the concept of convergence is contained, as it were, within the law of complexity-consciousness; but the employment of the concept of convergence renders explicit the inner dynamic of evolution towards unification, as this dynamic manifests itself at the human level. Operating under the influence of the radial component of energy, the process of interiorization, which moved through long ages of increasing cerebralization to the emergence of humankind, continues its centralizing function within the human phenomenon itself. The increase in numbers, the occupation of all available spaces, the increasing socialization and collectivization of humanity, the development of a planetary envelope of ideas—the noosphere—all represent the further unfolding of the nisus universally operative in nature, the nisus towards greater complexity and interiority. "We begin to realize that, under the veil of human socialization, there may be the same basic and universal force operating which, since the dawn of the world, has constantly striven towards an evergrowing organization of Matter."[47]

The noosphere is, thus, marked by the evolution of the social and the personal along with the intellectual and the technological. Teilhard's interpretation of recent and present trends focuses on the evolutionary significance of the various experiments in the organization of human life that have marked our recent and continuing history.[48] Democracy, communism, and fascism (by which Teilhard means all forms of authoritarian

[47]"The Psychological Conditions of Human Unification" (1948), *Building the Earth*, 104.

[48]See, e.g., ibid., 51ff.

nationalism) offer themselves as competing ways of organizing human aspirations and energy. The personal element, produced by hominization, developed itself until in the West during the past century or so the value of the autonomous individual attained a high water mark. This high valuation of the individual has been fostered and institutionalized in democracy; but the growth of this noble respect for personal integrity has been accompanied by no corresponding development of universally powerful integrating visions and structures that could effect a really vital cohesion of the autonomous individuals. The result has been, says Teilhard, a "disastrous equalitarianism which constitutes a threat to any serious construction of a new earth."[49]

> By confounding individualism and personalism, crowd and totality, by fragmenting and leveling the human mass, democracy has run the risk of jeopardizing our innate hopes for the future of mankind. For that reason it has seen Communism break away from it to the left, and all the forms of Fascism rise against it on the right.[50]

As with democracy, Teilhard appreciated aspects of communism while fearing others. Its appreciation of matter and the earth ("The true name of Communism should be 'terreniam'"[51]), its wish to fulfill the earth, its confidence in the future, its determination to overcome human alienation—all of these are to be applauded. But, "here too, the human ideal was defective or very quickly became deformed."[52] Communism depersonalizes human beings: by suppressing the individual, it "has turned man into a termite."[53] It denigrates or denies personal freedom, and undercuts the aspiration toward more-being by stressing mere well-being. Above all, "in its unbalanced admiration of the physical powers of the universe, it has systematically excluded from its hopes the possibility of a spiritual metamorphosis of the universe."[54] By denying the reality of a transcendent focus of human affection and aspiration, communism cuts itself off from both sufficient motivation for and an adequate vision of the ultimate consummation appropriate to humankind. In similar fashion, fascism promotes a vision too narrow and constricting to bind up the energies operating in the modern world.

---

[49]Ibid., 52.

[50]Ibid.

[51]Ibid., 53.

[52]Ibid.

[53]Ibid.

[54]Ibid.

We rehearse these rather commonplace observations to suggest that Teilhard is looking for a new way forward. He perceives forces working within the noosphere to produce the convergence of the human group(s) into a new phase of intensified social interiorization. In short, earth has experienced in recent history a sharp rise in its "psychic-temperature."

> It takes the form of the all-encompassing ascent of the masses; the constant tightening of economic bonds; the spread of financial and intellectual associations; the totalisation of political regimes; the closer physical contact of individuals as well as of nations; the increasing impossibility of being or acting or thinking *alone*—in short, the rise, in every form, of the *Other* around us. We are all constantly aware of these tentacles of a social condition that is rapidly evolving to the point of becoming monstrous.[55]

Does the recent and present turmoil represent a crisis of death or a crisis of birth? Turning his attention from present currents to possible future trends, Teilhard opts energetically for the latter. The present turmoil and the conflict of ideologies is not just a natural catastrophe to be stoically accepted; it has rather a deeper import, argues Teilhard, an import that can be seen in the light of the law of complexity-interiority. The present turmoil is a "crisis of birth." And Teilhard, acting as a midwife of the future, hopes to help bring forth a new option for the human family-in-the-making:

> How can we unite all the positive values of civilization in a totality which will also respect individual values? How can we attain that higher passionate unity in which we shall find rooted and consummated in a new synthesis the Democratic sense of the rights of the person, the Communist vision of the potentialities contained in matter, and the Fascist ideal of an organized elite?[56]

The route by which Teilhard attempts to go forward involves extrapolating past and present trends into the future in such a way as to identify the conditions that make the (desirable) future thinkable. Following the trajectory of increasing complexification into the future leads him to project a point upon which the entire evolutionary process is converging and in which its nisus towards greater interiority and centricity will find completion. Since the universal process of complexification-interiorization has led to the emergence of the personal as its highest form of expression, Teilhard argues that *the true extension of the noosphere— and thus of the evolutionary process as such—must be towards the (ultra-)personal.* A movement towards the impersonal would be regressive; so, unless the movement ceases altogether, it must advance in the

---

[55] *The Future of Man*, 113.

[56] *Building the Earth*, 55.

direction of a heightening of the personal. The tendency of radial energy to "inspire" the evolutionary emergence of greater unity out of greater complexity can only result, thinks Teilhard, in the convergence of the universe upon some ultimate center marked by maximum interiority or consciousness. And such supreme consciousness cannot be the prerogative of the impersonal but only that of the "hyperpersonal" mode of reality. This center, this ultimate pole of convergence, Teilhard denominates "Omega," since it will be found at the terminus of the entire evolutionary process.

The reality of such a personal center provides the primary condition that makes "the future of man" both thinkable and possible. Only a vision of something supremely attractive and lovable ahead can enable human beings to overcome their deep-rooted tendencies towards the repulsion and exclusion of one another that express themselves in various forms of social philosophies and organization. Such a vision, if true, means that the era of increased socialization into which we have entered need not mean the end of the personal but rather its genuine beginning; for, Teilhard argues, it is the function of genuine union to differentiate and complete the united elements. Teilhard supports this contention by appeal to organic as well as social phenomena:

> In any domain—whether it be the cells of a body, the members of a society or the elements of a spiritual synthesis—*union differentiates*. In every organised whole, the parts perfect themselves and fulfil themselves.[57]

Thus, the individual becomes genuinely personal only as he/she becomes "universalized."

Teilhard's point is discerned most readily perhaps in the good marriage, an image that he himself employs. In such a union the individual personalities are not dimished but rather enhanced by the union. The marital partners become more—in their individuality as well as in their togetherness—by virtue of their togetherness. This image lends itself to his emphasis upon love as the form of energy which issues in a creative socialization that is also a "personalization." It is the property of love, the highest form of the radial component of energy, precisely to bind persons together in ways that make for mutual enrichment. This is the case in the sexual relationship, in the family, in friendship, and to some measure in the nation. Above all, this is the case with our love for the Whole.

It appears that Teilhard distinguishes various qualities of love (Tillich) but not various types or forms (Nygren). His biological starting-point, with its emphasis upon continuity, would suggest this.

---

[57] *The Phenomenon of Man*, 262.

> Considered in its full biological reality, *love*—that is to say *the affinity of*
> *being with being*—is not peculiar to man. It is a general property of all life
> and as such it embraces, in its *varieties and degrees*, all the forms successively
> adopted by organised matter.[58]

This universal and internal "propensity to unite" takes a unique "hominized" form as man appears,[59] and it manifests a tendency to enlarge itself by uniting ever larger and more complex entities. In its most refined form, natural love flowers into full Christian charity. But whatever its "varieties and degrees," love appears to be a unitary reality which works for unification. Like Tillich, Teilhard evidently regards eros, philia ("natural" and human love?), and even agape ("Christian charity"?) as manifestations of a single reality and as marked by common properties.

Teilhard's ultimate concern is with love directed towards the All or the Whole. "A universal love is not only psychologically possible," he suggests; "it is the only complete and final way in which we are able to love."[60] Like every sensitive thinker within the Judeo-Christian tradition, Teilhard understands that love by its nature requires universalization; absolute love directed to the finite is idolatry. But Teilhard the scientist influences Teilhard the Jesuit mystic and theologian to add that it is "biologically necessary" that we develop "our power of loving . . . until it embraces the total of men and of the earth."[61] It is just such a universal love or "consent to being in general" (Edwards) that will lead to the ultimate personalization of man—and the universe in man—through the process of totalization.

All of this says a great deal about Teilhard's understanding of the Omega Point. Following the Thomistic-Aristotelian tradition, Teilhard postulates a Prime Mover ahead. But what he intends by Omega remains, in the end, rather elusive, although several things are clear.

Most important, Teilhard utilizes the term Omega in two distinct senses, which are nonetheless blended together. The Omega Point represents that state of ultimate centricity and collective "hyper reflection" which will mark the terminus of the evolutionary process. Omega thus understood is an extrapolation of the trends observed in the process itself, and it will be constituted by the fullest flowering of the potentials of the world. But this understanding of Omega passes into another: Omega as the Center of centers—autonomous, presently actual, irreversible, and

---

[58]Ibid., 264. Emphasis added.

[59]Ibid.

[60]Ibid., 266.

[61]Ibid., 265.

transcendent[62]—whose attractive action assures the realization of the proper terminus of the evolutionary process. Omega understood in this way is independent, as far as its reality is concerned, of the process whose success it renders possible. Thus, the term "Omega" is employed by Teilhard to denominate both the outcome of evolution and the transcendent goal that draws the process forward: "While being the last term of its [evolution's] series, it is also *outside all series*."[63] Point Omega, understood comprehensively, represents the coming together of these two types of termini.

> Unless it is to be powerless to form the keystone of the noosphere, "Omega" can only be conceived as the meeting-point between a universe that has reached the limit of centration, and another, even deeper, centre—this being the self-subsistent centre and absolutely final principle of irreversibility and personalisation: the one and only true Omega.[64]

At this point the idea of God is forthrightly interpolated into the evolutionary process.

> And it is at this point, if I am not mistaken, in the science of evolution (so that evolution may show itself capable of functioning in a hominised milieu), that the problem of God comes in—the Prime Mover, Gatherer and Consolidator, ahead of us, of evolution.[65]

Like Thomas, Teilhard ostensibly arrives at the notion of God by reason alone—in Teilhard's case, by reason reflecting on the complexifying evolutionary process.[66] But his elaboration of the doctrine of God is done in the light of revelation. This is shown by the fact that no sooner has he identified God with the Omega Point of evolution than he further identifies God-Omega with Christ. And it quickly becomes apparent that Teilhard's understanding of Christ functions as the key to his understanding of the entire process of evolution—past, present, and future. Thus, His, is ultimately a Christocentric vision of the world.

THE THEOLOGY OF NATURE AS CHRISTOLOGICAL PROBLEM

Human reason has led the Jesuit paleontologist to postulate a transcendent personal Center and Goal for the evolutionary process. His

---

[62]Ibid., 267-72.

[63]Ibid., 270.

[64]*Man's Place in Nature*, 121.

[65]Ibid.

[66]Here is found one line of evidence which suggests that Teilhard is basically a natural theologian. But, as noted above, Teilhard himself admits that apart from the informing

Christian faith has led him to identify this Center with Jesus Christ. In light of this, Teilhard illustrates the fact that the affirmation and interpretation of the classical doctrine of the incarnation becomes complicated as soon as the universe is thought in terms of "cosmogenesis" rather than mere "cosmos"; for from that moment on there exists the problem of reconciling two different and partially autonomous axes of evolutionary development: cosmogenesis or "natural" evolution and Christogenesis or "supernatural" evolution. This tension places Teilhard under an obligation to develop a Christology in which there exists a correspondence between the natural-human point of planetary maturation and the supernatural-*Christic* point of the parousia. Accordingly, his theological project becomes that of rethinking the person and work of Christ in terms of the category of *genèse*.[67] Near the end of his life he confesses:

> Recently, the whole "nucleus" of my interior perspective has again come to appear to my mind as entirely dependent on, and "deducible" from, nothing but the transposition into cosmogenic dimensions of the traditional view expressed in cosmic terms: Creation, Spirit, Evil, God (and, more specifically, original sin, the Cross, the Resurrection, the Parousia, Charity . . .) —all these notions, once they are transposed to a "genesis" dimension, become amazingly clear and coherent.[68]

But the emphasis on "genesis," in Teilhard's thinking, directs attention less to beginnings than to process and, especially, endings. "Nothing in our progressive world is truly intelligible until it has reached its end."[69] As the adult form of life illuminates the development of the embryo rather than vice versa (note the biological pattern of Teilhard's thinking), so the whole evolutionary process is illuminated by its term. The parousia assumes great importance in Teilhard's thinking because it marks the final maturation of God's plan for the salvation of the world; thus it corresponds to Teilhard's initial perception of Omega as humankind's "natural" planetary maturation. But Omega means more than the state of ultimate planetary cohesion and reflection; Omega is also and even more fundamentally the everlasting and supreme personal reality who initiates,

---

character of his Christian faith, he might never have arrived at the (scientific) hypothesis of Omega.

[67]It is to be noted that the French term *genèse* is broader in meaning than the corresponding English word, as ordinarily used. Whereas the latter refers most frequently to the initial stage of a series or to "beginnings," the French term commonly refers also to the series itself if that series involves successively produced stages that are oriented towards some goal.

[68]Correspondence of 1 January 1951, in Claude Cuénot, *Teilhard de Chardin*, trans. Vincent Colimore (London: Burns & Oates, 1965). 273.

[69]"Pantheism and Christianity" (1923), *Christianity and Evolution*, 66.

motivates, and shapes the evolutionary process itself. Therefore, if the
Christ of revelation and Catholic teaching is to be identified with the
Omega of evolution—and Teilhard thinks that this identification is absolutely necessary—then that eternal Omega which is able to effect and
integrate both the parousia and humanity's planetary maturation must
already be present in history in the person of Jesus of Nazareth. In fact,
for Teilhard, the two—Omega-terminus and Omega-God, as we might
call them—can be integrated only if the latter has become part of the
evolutionary process for which he is responsible; and precisely this he has
done by taking flesh in Jesus. By virtue of the incarnation Omega-God's
work of salvation is rooted in space-time, and the incarnate Omega
continues to work within the material world until the final fulfillment of
all things is effected. This means that all the great Christological
"moments" (birth, life, cross, resurrection, parousia) must have found
expression within a process governed by genesis and complexification-
interiorization. It means, moreover, that in a world in genesis we need to
find a way of speaking of two faces of *genèse*: the one "Christic" and the
other cosmic. And we need to be able to speak of them as finally one,
distinguishable but inseparable moments or aspects of a unitary world
process. "It is," notes Christopher Mooney, "precisely to speak in such a
way, while yet remaining faithful to the testimony of revelation, which is
the aim of Teilhard de Chardin's Christology."[70]

Teilhard's attempt to construct a Christology in which he can establish a connection between the natural process and the supernatural
guidance and consummation of the process moves in three distinguishable, if inseparable, directions. The first involves an attempt to establish
the nature of the relationship existing between the "Body of Christ,"
humankind, and the material world. Teilhard's thinking in this regard is
based on the cosmic motifs in Paul, John, and the early church fathers,
especially the Pauline tradition as represented by Colossians and Ephesians. What Teilhard attempts in this first line of thought is to interpret
the nature and meaning of both humankind and otherkind in the light of
the motifs of incarnation and eucharistic transformation. The second
direction involves an attempt to rethink the meaning of death and evil,

---

[70]Mooney, *Teilhard de Chardin and the Mystery of Christ*, 63. The analysis of
Teilhard's Christology that follows is deeply indebted to Mooney's study. The intent of
Mooney's analysis and the present one differ, however. It is Mooney's wish to show, above
all, that the significance of Teilhard lies in his responding to "modern man's most pressing
psychological need" by providing "an assurance that some successful outcome exists for
that progress on earth for which he knows himself to be responsible" (67). The interest of
the present study lies in delineating the shape of Teilhard's "cosmic Christology" in order
to evaluate its potential contribution to a reconstructed theology of nature/creation.

both physical and moral evil, in the light of the notion of Christogenesis. To do this Teilhard elaborates a distinction between Christ the Redeemer and Christ the "Evolver." And, as part of his theology of redemption, he defends a version of the notion of "cosmic fall." The third direction of Teilhard's Christological thinking involves the completing of the previous two: Teilhard tries to carry further his understanding of the relationship between cosmic history and salvation history by attending to the "cosmic" function of the Church as it becomes the agent through which Christ the Evolver effects "pleromization," thereby bringing creation to completion.

"Christogenesis": Incarnation and Eucharistic Transformation. In his first theological essay, written in 1916, Teilhard brought together a number of ideas about Christ and the cosmos which were to receive restatement and fuller development in the years that followed. In that early essay, "La Vie cosmique," as in many that followed it, Teilhard purports to be transposing into an evolutionary framework the great cosmic claims regarding the person and work of Christ made by Paul and other early Christian writers. That essay shows Teilhard beginning his search for "organic" and "physical" modes of understanding the work of Christ and his relationship to the cosmos, ways of understanding that would supplement the "juridical" (moral and logical) modes which theology in the West has favored. Says Teilhard:

> Minds that are afraid of a bold concept or are governed by individualistic prejudicies, and always try to interpret the relationships between beings in moral or logical terms, are apt to conceive the Body of Christ by analogy with human associations; it then becomes much more akin to a social aggregation than to a natural organism. Such minds dangerously weaken the thought of Scripture and make it unintelligible or platitudinous to thinking men who are eager to trace out physical connexions and relations that are specifically cosmic. They unjustifiably diminish Christ and the profoundly real mystery of his Flesh. The Body of Christ is not, as some unenterprising thinkers would have us believe, the extrinsic or juridical association of men who are embraced by one and the same benevolence and are destined to the same reward. It must be understood with boldness, as St John and St Paul and the Fathers saw it and loved it. It constitutes a world that is natural and new, an organism that is animate and in motion, one in which we are all united, physically and *biologically*. The exclusive task of the world is the physical incorporation of the faithful in the Christ who is of God. . . . By means of sacramental communion he consummates the union of the faithful in Himself through an individual and integral contact of soul with soul, flesh with flesh: . . . in the first place through the Incarnation, and then through the Eucharist, he organizes us for himself and implants himself in us.[71]

---

[71]"Cosmic Life," (1916), *Writings in Time of War*, 49-51.

Still further:

> By grace, Jesus Christ is united to all sanctified souls, and since the bonds
> that link souls to him in one single hallowed mass end in Him and meet in
> Him, and hold together by Him, it is He who reigns and He who lives; the
> whole body is His in its entirety. Souls, however, are not a group of isolated
> monads. As the "cosmic view" specifically shows us, they make up one single
> whole with the universe, consolidated by life and matter. Christ, therefore,
> cannot confine his body to some periphery drawn within things; though he
> came primarily, and in fact exclusively, for souls, he could bring them
> together and give them life only by assuming and animating, with them, all
> the rest of the world; through his Incarnation he entered not only into
> mankind but also into the universe that bears mankind—and this he did, not
> simply in the capacity of an element associated with it, but with the dignity
> and function of directive principle, of centre upon which every form of love
> and every affinity converge. Mysterious and vast though the mystical Body
> already be, it does not, accordingly, exhaust the immense and bountiful
> integrity of the Word made Flesh. Christ has a *cosmic Body* that extends
> throughout the whole universe: such is the final proposition to be borne in
> mind. "*Qui potest capere, capiat.*"[72]

These early lines contain a number of ideas that are central to Teilhard's mature theological program. They give expression to Teilhard's
peculiar cosmic Christocentrism, his thoroughgoing emphasis upon the
Incarnation, and his perception of the eucharistic extensions of the
Incarnation. They express, moreover, the fierce ontological "realism"
with which he understood the "Body of Christ"—the notion by which he
held together several of his leading motifs, including his understanding of
Christ, the cosmos, the Church, and the Eucharist.

In his employment of the concept of the Body of Christ, Teilhard
appears to make three central affirmations.[73] We shall attend to Teilhard's treatment of his notion in its three aspects, in order to get before us
the rudiments of both his theory of the Incarnation and his understanding
of the Church; then we shall examine in a preliminary fashion (the theme
to be taken up again towards the end of the chapter) his theology of the
altar insofar as it bears on his Christological understanding of creation.

The Incarnation as Historical Event. "Precisely because of those
characteristics that would at first appear to confine him too strictly to the
particular, *an historically* incarnate God is on the contrary the only God
who can satisfy not only the inflexible laws of a Universe in which nothing
is produced or appears except *by way of birth*, but also the irrepressible

---

[72]Ibid., 57-58.

[73]Mooney delineates these themes. For a fuller discussion of them see *Teilhard de
Chardin and the Mystery of Christ*, ch. 3. Mooney also discusses in some detail the
exegetical basis for the Teilhardian development of the Pauline metaphor of the body.

aspirations of our own mind."[74] This affirmation represents a motif that is primary for Teilhard: Christ for him always means first of all the historical personage of Jesus of Nazareth. Whatever else terms such as "Christ" and "Body of Christ" may refer to, they include a primary reference to "the Body-Person" of Jesus of Nazareth who lived and died at a particular time and place in human-cosmic history. Admittedly, this Jesuit theologian does not much discuss the Jesus of the Gospels; and the omission represents a deficiency in his total program.[75] But the reasons for his neglect are not hard to find. Teilhard was far more concerned with culminations than with beginnings; and, for him, the historical Jesus had the aspect of a beginning more than anything else—albeit the beginning of the Incarnation. "Nothing in our progressive world is truly intelligible until it has reached its end. . . . If, then, we are to obtain a true idea of the Incarnation we must not go back to its beginnings (the Annunciation, the Nativity, even the Passion); our standpoint, so far as possible, must be its final term."[76] Nonetheless, culminations represent the fruition of historically rooted and real processes:

> The immense enchantment of the divine milieu owes all its value in the long run to the human-divine contact which was revealed at the Epiphany of Jesus. If you suppress the historical reality of Christ, the divine omnipresence which intoxicates us becomes, like all the other dreams of metaphysics, uncertain, vague, conventional—lacking the decisive experimental verification by which to impose itself on our minds, and without the moral directives to assimilate our lives into it. . . . *The mystical Christ, the universal Christ of St. Paul, has neither meaning nor value in our eyes except as an expansion of the Christ who was born of Mary and who died on the Cross.* The former essentially draws His fundamental quality of undeniability and concreteness from the latter. *However far we may be drawn into the divine spaces opened up to us by Christian mysticism, we never depart from the Jesus of the Gospels.*[77]

Only by maintaining a firm linkage between the cosmic and the historical Christ could Teilhard affirm the reality of the divine omnipresence within the historical process. Accordingly, whenever he identifies the Christ of revelation and mystical aspiration with the Omega of evolution he is asserting, intrinsically, that the two meet in the Body-Person of Jesus of Nazareth.

---

[74]"The Heart of Matter" (1919), *The Heart of Matter*, 54.

[75]One suspects that, in various ways, Teilhard's program would have been both corrected and confirmed if he had devoted more careful attention to the results of modern biblical scholarship.

[76]"Pantheism and Christianity" (1923), *Christianity and Evolution*, 66.

[77]*The Divine Milieu*, 94-95. Emphases added.

The Incarnation as Personal Center of Creation. This identification involves Teilhard in another affirmation: the Body of Christ constitutes the personal center for humankind and indeed for the entire created order. This means that everything that God has brought (and is bringing) to be is being shaped into a unitary entity the center of which is the Word Incarnate. And this suggests, in turn, that created reality is being fulfilled and even elevated *in its entirety*—as it is being assimilated to its divine center.

That the Body of Christ constitutes the unique personal center for all creation Teilhard affirms on the basis of the confluence of two lines of evidence. Reason acting on scientific data leads him to set forth the hypothesis of a converging universe and to postulate that such a world requires at its summit a transcendent personal center that shapes the whole by activating and directing the radial component of energy. Scripture and Church teaching lead him to envision Christ as the Lord of all and hence as having a cosmic status and performing a cosmic function. Since "the world can no more have two summits than a circumference can have two centres,"[78] the two lines of evidence must point to a single reality as the apex of the entire created order. Hence, Teilhard concludes that in a converging universe Christ Jesus must fulfill the function of Omega; he who was born of Mary must be one with the transcendent personal center that exercises a shaping influence upon the entire evolutionary process.

While the whole creaturely order is being shaped into a unitary entity the center of which is the Word Incarnate, "Christ, it is true, is not the centre whom all things here below could *naturally* aspire to be one with." Rather, "To be destined for Christ is a gratuitous favour of the Creator we have no right to count upon."[79] Teilhard sought to safeguard the divine sovereignty and freedom by emphasizing the gratuity of the present order. Yet by virtue of God's action in Christ the "natural" has been so thoroughly permeated and taken up in the "supernatural" that it is now virtually impossible to conceive of the created order without thinking of nature as somehow caught up in the orbit of grace. "Nevertheless, it remains true that the Incarnation so completely *recast* the universe in the supernatural that, *in concrete fact*, we can no longer ask, or imagine, towards what Centre the elements of this world, had they not been raised up by grace, would have gravitated."[80] It should also be noted that it is not, according to Teilhard, the bare fact of the centricity of the world that

---

[78]Ibid., 137.

[79]"Creative Union" (1917), *Writings in Time of War*, 174.

[80]Ibid.

gives it its gratuitous character in the fullest sense; nor does its gratuity derive from the mere presence of an Omega Point beckoning the world towards completion. "What gives the world its 'gratuitous' character is precisely that the position of universal centre has not been given to any supreme intermediary between God and the universe, but has been occupied by the Divinity himself—who has thus introduced us 'in et cum Mundo' into the triune heart of his immanence."[81]

Thus, according to Teilhard, the world (a) has one center only and (b) it is being elevated in its entirety. "There is only *one single centre* in the universe; it is at once natural and supernatural; it impels the whole of creation along one and the same line, first towards the fullest development of consciousness, and later towards the highest degree of holiness; in other words towards Christ Jesus, personal and cosmic."[82] Teilhard considered the possibility of dividing the world into two parts, "natural" and "supernatural," each having its appropriate character and destiny or center. But he rejects such an option for two basic reasons. Such a bifurcation of the world into two realms denies implicitly the identity of God the Creator and God the Redeemer, making the one responsible for the natural order and the other responsible for the supernatural or higher order and destiny. Moreover, argues Teilhard, such a bifurcation corrupts the reality of grace, (unduly) restricting the sphere of the operations of grace and thus implicitly devaluing the whole realm of the "natural." Instead of dividing the world into two "parts," Teilhard affirms that *grace perfects nature.* Here his Thomistic predilections are clear. Grace leads not to the abolition of the natural but to its completion. "For grace does not force man to enter another universe; it introduces him into an extension of our own universe."[83] But Teilhard modifies this Thomistic motif in the direction of the more cosmically oriented Eastern thinkers such as John of Damascus. Like John, Teilhard argues that what is being elevated, what is being completed and perfected, by the ("supernatural") operations of grace is not humankind alone but the entire created order. Since the world has one center only and that "supernatural," there can be no merely natural end for evolutionary progress. Everything that moves towards greater complexity and interiority—this movement constituting Teilhard's definition of "progress"—is destined for fulfillment in the plentitude of Christ-Omega. If anything has a merely "natural" destiny it

---

[81]"My Universe" (1924), *Science and Christ,* 56.

[82]"Forma Christi" (1918), *Writings in Time of War,* 256.

[83]Correspondence of 29 December 1919, in *Archives,* 154; cited by Mooney, *Teilhard de Chardin,* 76.

is the tangential component of energy and the product of its operations. But even tangential energy contributes to the ascent towards higher degrees of consciousness and personality. Accordingly, "the distinction . . . between 'natural' and 'supernatural' remains, but it cannot mean that something has been created which is unconnected with the supernatural destiny of mankind and which would be without reference to the final Plentitude of Christ."[84]

The Incarnation as Physical Center of Creation. While maintaining the distinction, crucial to Catholic theology, between the natural and the supernatural, Teilhard rejects the notion of a merely natural goal for evolutionary development. "Christ is the term *of even the natural* evolution of . . . beings."[85] The natural is continuously being completed by virtue of its contribution to the supernatural. Conversely, the supernatural is continuously being nourished by the natural: "Heaven cannot dispense with Earth."[86] And Christ, as the telos of all creation "has the function of cementing the definitive concentration of the universe."[87]

In an attempt to explain how Christ can fulfill this function, Teilhard introduces an unusual notion: Christ is somehow an "organic" or "physical" center of the evolutionary process. "By the Universal Christ, I mean Christ the organic centre of the entire universe. *Organic centre*: that is to say the centre on which every even natural development is ultimately physically dependent."[88] While Teilhard has difficulty giving precision to his notion of Christ as physical-organic (he utilizes both terms, apparently synonymously) centre, he clearly intends to affirm certain things while rejecting others. He wishes, at a minimum, to affirm that Christ's relationship to the universe, including its material aspects, is more than merely "juridical." The kingship of Jesus Christ means more than appointment and ownership. Christ's kingship is also "physical," by which Teilhard appears to mean that it is personal and ontological (thus "real" to Teilhard's scientific bent of mind in a way "merely" logical and

---

[84]Mooney, *Teilhard de Chardin*, 76. Cf. Eulalio R. Baltazar, *Teilhard and the Supernatural* (Baltimore: Helicon Press, 1966).

[85]"Cosmic Life" (1916), *Writings in Time of War* 59. In a footnote on the same page Teilhard records his perception of the relationship of his position to that of Thomas Aquinas: "Once the universe (nature) is an evolution, we may say with regard to evolution what St. Thomas, speaking of the supernatural, said with regard to nature: *Non est aliquid naturae, sed naturae finis*—it is not something that belongs to nature, but nature's (final) end."

[86]"My Universe" (1918), *The Heart of Matter*, 203.

[87]"The Soul of the World" (1918), *Writings in Time of War*, 186.

[88]"Note on the Universal Christ" (1920), *Science and Christ*, 14.

legal, or "juridical," states of affairs are not). Moreover, we are assured that "there is nothing strange about this idea of a universal physical element in Christ."[89] To explicate and buttress this assurance, Teilhard sets forth a field theory of Christ's constitution and influence:

> *Each and every one of us*, if we care to observe it, is enveloped—is *haloed*—by an extension of his being as vast as the universe. We are conscious of only the core of ourselves. Nevertheless, the interplay of the monads would be unintelligible if an *aura* did not extend from one to another: something, that is, which is peculiar to each one of them and at the same time common to all.

> How, then, may we conceive Christ to be constituted as the cosmic centre of creation?

> Simply as a magnification, a transformation, realized in the humanity of Christ, of the *aura* that surrounds every human monad.[90]

Teilhard's understanding of Christ's "physical" relationship to the created order comes finally to this: that it is something that pertains within the realm of the personal and the human. Christ exercised his kingship over creation—physically—by virtue of his human-personal existence. Evidently, Teilhard is searching for language, appropriate to his biological-mystical pattern of thinking, for expressing the divine omnipresence and its influence. Hence, he maintains that by virtue of the incarnation, Christ "became coextensive with the physical immensities of duration and space, without losing the preciseness of his humanity."[91]

The Incarnation as Continuing Historical-Organic Event. Along with his evolutionary theory of the incarnation, Teilhard develops his theology of the sacraments, of the Eucharist in particular.[92] In the hands of this Jesuit priest, traditional doctrine undergoes two major transformations. In Catholic teaching, the Church has been regarded as the continuation of the Incarnation, an extension constituted of all those souls who are

---

[89]"Forma Christi" (1918), *Writings in Time of War*, 253.

[90]Ibid.

[91]"Esquisse d'un univers personnel," (1936), in *Oeuvres*, 6:113; cited by Mooney, *Teilhard de Chardin*, 80-81.

[92]Teilhard's sacramental theory centers in his theology of the sacrament of the altar: "In reality the eucharist belongs to an order of its own among the sacraments. It is the first of the sacraments, or rather it is the one sacrament to which all the others are related...." ("Introduction to the Christian Life" [1944], in *Christianity and Evolution*, 165). This being the case in Teilhard's view, our treatment of his sacramental theory will properly focus on his theology of the Eucharist.

Teilhard appears to have developed separately his speculation regarding Christ as "physical center" and his theory of the Eucharist. He brings the two together conclusively in *The Divine Milieu* (1927). For many details of the history of the development of Father Teilhard's thinking, see Mooney, *Teilhard de Chardin*.

incorporated into Christ by faith and the sacraments. Further, Catholic teaching states that the Eucharist has effected the transformation of believers even as the eucharistic elements themselves have undergone "transubstantiation." In the hands of Father Teilhard, the eucharistic transformation extends to all of the created order (at least potentially) and the Incarnation is thereby extended to include not only all souls but the entire material-vital "milieu" of souls as well. Christ comes sacramentally to the faithful soul "in order to join him, physically, a little more closely to himself and to all the rest of the faithful in the growing unity of the world."

> When, through the priest, Christ says, "*Hoc est corpus meum,*" "This is my body," the words reach out infinitely far beyond the morsel of bread over which they are pronounced: they bring the entire mystical body into being. The priestly act extends beyond the transubstantiated Host to *the cosmos itself*, which, century after century, *is gradually being transformed by the Incarnation*, itself never complete. From age to age, there is but one single mass in the world: *the true Host, the total Host, is the universe* which is continually being more intimately penetrated and vivified by Christ. From the most distant origin of things until their unforeseeable consummation, through the countless convulsions of boundless space, *the whole of nature is slowly and irresistibly undergoing the supreme consecration.* Fundamentally—since all time and for ever—*but one single thing is being made in creation: the body of Christ.*[93]

It is in Teilhard's treatment of the Eucharist that the diverse strands of his Christology come together: here the unity of the eternal Logos, the agent of creation, Christ Jesus who died in Palestine, and Christ-Omega, the telos of all creation is affirmed. Moreover, in his doctrine of the Eucharist the individual and the collective are brought together. In fact, "the whole of Teilhard's theology and cosmology is collected and focused at this point."[94]

From the beginning to the end Christ operates in and through matter-nature-history in order to actualize the potentials of creation. He works universally to transform and thus "save" the entire created order. This is the underlying principle of both the Incarnation and the Eucharist. In each case the Word becomes flesh and "flesh" (matter) becomes the sacramental vehicle of the Word. Christ enters the immense "host" which is the universe itself; and the universe, perfused by and centered in him, is transformed ("transubstantiated") into his body. The entire universe is assimilated and elevated, thus "divinized."

---

[93]"Pantheism and Christianity" (1923), *Christianity and Evolution*, 73-74; emphases added.

[94]Michael H. Murray, *The Thought of Teilhard de Chardin* (New York: Seabury Press, 1966), 81.

The salient elements of this cosmic eucharistic theory need to be distinguished and emphasized at this point. The one is that matter functions as the vehicle of the self-expression (and completion?) of God; it is through matter that God communicates himself to his creatures, and it is through matter that God communicates himself, so to speak, to himself. In the words of William Temple, who forged a vision of a "sacramental universe" that closely parallels that of Teilhard:

> So God, who is spirit, is His eternal self in and through the historical process of creating a world and winning it to union with Himself. His creation is sacramental of Himself to His creatures; but in effectively fulfilling that function it becomes sacramental of Him to Himself—the means whereby He is eternally that which eternally He is.[95]

The other notable element of Teilhard's eucharistic theory has to do with the valuation it places on matter/nature. The God who incarnates himself in matter and expresses himself through it thereby accentuates its significance. In Teilhard's terms, "the sacramental action of Christ . . . *sanctifies matter*";[96] through him, "the whole of nature is slowly and irresistibly undergoing the supreme consecration."[97] The world, in both its human and prehuman dimensions, is rendered sacred by the (continuing) incarnation. By this incarnational mode of omnipresence creation is transformed into a "divine milieu." Thus,

> we find ourselves (by simply having followed the "extensions" of the Eucharist) plunged once again precisely into our divine milieu. . . . Christ reveals Himself in each reality around us, and shines like an ultimate determinant, like a centre, one might almost say like a universal element. As our humanity assimilates the material world, and as the Host assimilates our humanity, the eucharistic transformation goes beyond and completes the transubstantiation of the bread on the altar. Step by step it irresistibly invades the universe. . . . In a secondary and generalised sense, but in a true sense, the sacramental Species are formed by the totality of the world, and the duration of the creation is the time needed for its consecration.[98]

Christ: Redeemer and "Evolver." Because of the inseparable character of the person and work of Christ we are, in treating of the mode of the Incarnation, already involved in explicating the nature of Teilhard's understanding of redemption. In order to proceed further, however, we must specify the character of that towards which the salvific work of Christ is directed. We must, that is to say, inquire as to how Teilhard deals

---

[95]William Temple, *Nature, Man and God* (London: Macmillan, 1964), 495.

[96]*The Divine Milieu*, 104.

[97]"Pantheism and Christianity" (1923), *Christianity and Evolution*, 74.

[98]*The Divine Milieu*, 104.

with the presence of evil in the world of which Christ is the center. We must treat the presence of suffering, death, and sin in a world that is undergoing consecration by virtue of its progressive assimilation to the Body of Christ. Then we must examine more particularly how these evils are dealt with by him towards whom all things move.

Original Sin Reconsidered. Teilhard de Chardin's understanding of evil and his theodicy are similar to John Cobb's. There are, however, some important differences—differences that have to do, in part, with Teilhard's greater emphasis upon the Incarnation and the sacraments.

Like Cobb, Teilhard transposes the concept of evil from a universe of static structures into a world of evolutionary becoming. If the creation of the world is seen as essentially complete with the appearance of humanity, then the manifestations of imperfection within our world, and their results, give rise to something of a scandal: reconciliation of the manifest evil in our world with a Creator possessed of perfect love and unlimited power is difficult to effect. If, however, the world is understood as still in the process of being created, then perfection cannot rightly be expected prior to the final completion of creation; and the urgency of the problem of evil is somewhat reduced.

For Teilhard, as for Cobb, evil is necessarily ingredient to finite, temporal existence. But whereas Cobb attempts to substantiate this conclusion by redefining divine power, by distinguishing the variables of intense experience and the corresponding two forms of evil (harmony and intensity; discord and triviality), and by pointing out the correlative character of certain experiential structures (the capacity for instrumental good and the capacity for instrumental evil, for instance), Teilhard attempts primarily to locate the roots of evil in multiplicity. Understanding creation as the process of creative union, Teilhard identifies as evil anything that resists and disrupts such unification.

> In the old cosmos, which was assumed to have emerged complete from the hands of the Creator, it was only natural to find it difficult to reconcile a partially evil world with the existence of a God who is both good and omnipotent. But with . . . a universe in a state of *cosmogenesis* . . . God can proceed to creation *in only one way*: he must arrange, and, under his magnetic influence and using the tentative operation of enormous numbers, gradually unify an immense multitude of elements. Initially, these are infinite in number, extremely simple, and hardly conscious—then they gradually become fewer, more complex, and ultimately endowed with reflection. What, then, is the inevitable counterpart to every success gained in the course of such a process, if not that it has to be paid for by a certain amount of wastage? So we find physical discords or decompositions in the pre-living; suffering in the living; sin in the domain of freedom. There can be no *order in process of formation* which does not at every stage imply *some disorder*. In this ontological (or, more correctly, ontogenic) condition inherent in the participated,

there is nothing which impairs the dignity or limits the omnipotence of the Creator, nothing which in any way smacks of Manichaeanism. In itself, the pure, unorganized Multiple is not evil: but because it is multiple, which means that it is essentially subject in its arrangements to the operation of chance, it is absolutely barred from progressing towards unity without sporadically engendering evil: and that *as a matter of statistical necessity. "Necessarium est ut adveniant scandala."*[99]

Teilhard identifies the locus of evil as the structure of created being itself. He argues that in a world in evolution evil is a structural ingredient. But in taking this position he attempts to avoid two pernicious alternatives which the classical doctrine of creation was designed to deny. Teilhard refuses, on the one hand, to attribute evil to matter or to multiplicity as such; and he refuses, on the other hand, to attribute it to God. Matter in itself is good—and good precisely insofar as it is responsive to God's creative organizing power. "In itself, the pure, unorganized Multiple is not evil," but rather is good insofar as it provides the grounds of the possibility of God's creative shaping of great (centered) wholes. But evil arises out of multiplicity "as a matter of statistical necessity." This is to say that some disorder and failure, some pain born of conflict, resistance, and decomposition are inevitable in a world marked by the interplay of large numbers—even though the existents themselves and the forms of their existence are essentially good.

But let us be more precise. What Teilhard is doing is offering a dynamic and even "eschatological" definition of both good and evil. The good is not really something intrinsic, an inherent property or an abstract essence; rather, the good within Teilhard's evolutionary perspective is defined by directionality. The good is "that which rises": it represents a tendency, or movement, towards greater synthesis, a fuller measure of spirit, and God. In a word, the good is that which promotes (the movement towards) "personalization." Evil, on the contrary, is that which inhibits the upwards-moving process; it represents a blockage, a reversal, a falling backwards towards the realm of multiplicity (and non-being) out of which God is creating the world. Hence, evil too is defined by directionality. This means that good and evil alike are not properly imputed to the elements of the world taken in isolation, for the progress of the whole process is the touchstone for the identification of each. Thus, the character of goodness is seen fully only as the evolutionary process converges towards its ultimate term, Omega, and as that ultimate term is manifested even now as incarnate in Christ Jesus. The character of evil is identified only negatively in contrast to the good. As sickness is to health, as

---

[99]"My Fundamental Vision" (1948), *Toward the Future*, 196-98.

blindness is to sight, so evil is to good: evil has no genuine being of its own but is merely a residue of the good, a relapse towards non-being. Accordingly, evil as such was not created, even though it arises ("statistically") out of the structure of being. And God, strictly speaking, is not the author of evil, although he is the author of the conditions within which evil appears.

"Perfect goodness, then," as one of Teilhard's interpreters sums it up,

> is a transcendental or an eschatological reality. In historical existence, every temporal good is a stage on the way toward perfect goodness. So in history, everything partakes both positively of good and negatively of evil in proportions which vary with the element's position on the evolutionary axis, with the direction of its movement, and with the contribution or hindrance which it makes to the system as a whole.[100]

Teilhard identifies several faces of evil, all of them forms of "disorder" and hence retrogression. "So we find physical discords or decompositions in the pre-living; suffering in the living; sin in the domain of freedom. There can be no *order in process of formation* that does not at every stage imply *some disorder*."[101] We need not trace the details of Teilhard's treatment of the various aspects of non-moral evil (although we shall have to return to some of them below); but we need to note his linkage of his theory of moral evil, or sin, to his understanding of the pre-moral forms of evil. And the first point to recognize is Teilhard's treatment of the two forms of evil as distinguishable aspects of the one evolutionary process. "There is *only one Evil*," he says, "disunity."[102] Moral and non-moral evil alike represent structural disorder and resistance to unification, although moral evil occurs on a different plane, as it were, from physical evil since moral evil originates in the free will of human beings. The second point follows from the first. Like the non-moral evils of suffering and death, sin is ("statistically") necessary within humanity-in-the-making: "There is no order under formation which does not at every stage imply disorder." As soon as the process of complexification-interiorization reaches the point at which reflective-reflexive consciousness and genuine freedom appear, sin enters the world; for Adam, like the prehuman orders of creation, is incomplete and hence imperfect. Accordingly, the probability of (moral) "disorder," both individual and social, occurring within the human "zone" is so great as to amount to a virtual inevitability. Still, sin arises from the freedom of humankind and is thus grounded in neither the

---

[100]Murray, *The Thought of Teilhard de Chardin*, 94.

[101]"My Fundamental Vision" (1948), *Toward the Future*, 197.

[102]"My Universe" (1924), *Science and Christ*, 80, n15.

Creator nor some (Manichaean) principle of evil that stands over against God. Viewed phenomenologically, moral evil is thus an inevitable by-product of human choice. From either perspective sin constitutes a "fall" and reflects the "fallen" character of the entire cosmos.

Teilhard's linkage of moral and non-moral forms of evil through the categories of disorder (disunion) and statistical necessity involves him in the universalizing of the notion of "original sin." (His theological motive for this movement of thought will be noted momentarily.) In an early essay which, by virtue of its circulation among the authorities in Rome, resulted in his being pulled from his teaching position at the French Institut Catholique and "banished" to China, Father Teilhard maintained that

> original sin expresses, translates, personifies, in an instantaneous and localized act, the perennial and universal law of imperfection which operates in mankind *in virtue* of its being "*in fieri*". One might even go so far as to say that since the creative act (by definition) causes being to rise up to God from the confines of nothingness (that is, from the depth of the multiple, which means from some other matter), all creation brings with it, as its accompanying risk and shadow, some fault; in other words, it has its counterpart in some redemption.[103]

In an essay written just two years earlier Teilhard had elaborated on these themes somewhat more fully:

> Original sin, taken in its widest sense, is not a malady specific to the earth, nor is it bound up with human generation. It simply symbolizes the inevitable chance of evil (*Necesse est ut eveniant scandala*) which accompanies the existence of all participated being. Wherever being *in fieri* is produced, suffering and wrong immediately appear as its shadow; not only as a result of the tendency towards inaction and selfishness found in creatures, but also . . . as an inevitable concomitant of their effort to progress. Original sin is the essential reaction of the finite to the creative act. Inevitably it insinuates itself into existence through the medium of all creation. It is the *reverse side* of all creation. By the very fact that he creates, God commits himself to a fight against evil and in consequence to, in one way or another, effecting a redemption. The specifically human Fall is no more than the (broadly speaking, collective and eternal) actualizing of this "*fomes peccati*" which was infused, long before us, into the whole of the universe, from the lowest zones of matter to the angelic spheres. Strictly speaking, there is no first Adam. The name disguises a universal and unbreakable law of reversion or perversion—the price that has to be paid for progress.[104]

Evil, then, is in Teilhardian perspective a universal phenomenon within an evolving world. It manifests itself in a variety of ways in the

---

[103]"Note on Some Possible Historical Representations of Original Sin" (1922), *Christianity and Evolution*, 51-52.

[104]"Fall, Redemption, and Geocentrism" (1920), ibid., 40-41.

various dimensions in the world that God is creating, but through all its forms there runs a structural similarity. Far from neglecting the reality of evil, as some of his critics charge, Teilhard magnifies and extends it to cosmic proportions. If he blurs the distinction between moral (personal) and non-moral forms of evil, it is a consequence which follows not from a neglect of the specter of evil but from the reverse tendency to be always haunted by the "shadowy" element that stalks all forms of finite existence and of trying to find a way to envision this mysterious "reverse side of all creation."

The result is a somewhat curious hybrid of processive and classical Catholic elements. Contrary to what at first blush appears perhaps as a new form of Manichaeism, the Teilhardian perspective on the problem of evil represents a dynamic type of Augustinian theory. Teilhard picks up on the Augustinian understanding of evil as privation of being and gives it a new form of expression; in his hands, the privative theory is transposed into evolutionary terms. All orders of creation carry within themselves the possibility of a great reversal, a collapse, towards lesser forms of being. Evil, therefore, consists precisely of "non-being," a gap, a privation of the real; it is the absence of wholeness—or order, union, centreity— where centered wholeness ought to be.

In certain respects, God is made responsible for the presence of evil in the world (since he chose to actualize the world in spite of the risks), but he is not thereby rendered culpable (since he did what was necessary to actualize good). To be sure, Teilhard does not make this conclusion as explicit as does Cobb; but it is an inescapable implication of the movement of his thought. This means, moreover, that there is implicit within the Teilhardian schema an inchoate recognition of the kinds of distinctions Cobb draws between the two forms of evil, discord and unnecessary triviality. It means, still further, that Teilhard recognizes a "positive and necessary correlation" among such factors as the capacity for rich experience, the capacity for self-determination, and the capacity for being both the patient and the agent of great evil. But at one point there is a dramatic divergence between the Cobbian and Teilhardian patterns of thinking about the problem of evil. Teilhard does not perceive the need to limit the operation of the divine power as severely as does Cobb. "In this ontological (or, more correctly, ontogenic) condition inherent in the participated, there is nothing which impairs the dignity or limits the omnipotence of the Creator. . . ."[105] Teilhard admits that God did not and could not create our kind of world without the occurrence of evil; this

---

[105]"My Fundamental Vision" (1948), *Toward the Future*, 197.

impossibility belongs to the same logical-ontological category as the divine inability to create a round square and abolish yesterday, and thus represents no more, or less, than an extension (warranted by the transposition of Christian thinking into an evolutionary mode) of Thomistic reflection on the character of divine power. Moreover, Teilhard moves in the Cobbian direction of a redefinition of divine power in terms of the category of persuasion—a movement that constitutes the primary plank in the Cobbian theodicy. But since Teilhard affirms, unlike Cobb, that evil is essentially privation of being, Teilhard is under no compulsion by virtue of his theory of evil as such to place severe strictures upon the extent and the efficacy of the operations of the divine power. Accordingly, since he retains a fuller portion of confidence in the divine omnipotence, Teilhard remains somewhat surer of a favorable outcome to the cosmic evolutionary process than does Cobb. For Teilhard as well as for Cobb, hope is grounded in God; but Teilhard's vision of an "almighty" God who is working powerfully to save limits his ability to acknowledge—in spite of his perception of the universality of evil—that the whole evolutionary process might abort. And herein lies the ground of what many perceive (Cobb among them) as Teilhard's hyper optimism.

Redemption of a World in Evolution. It is because of the scope and the seriousness of evil in the world that the world requires redemption. Precisely because the problem of evil is cosmic in character the redemption must be cosmic if the world process is to have a favorable outcome. Hence, Teilhard not only universalizes the "fall," he universalizes the remedy. This action requires that Christ be genuinely "universal," or "cosmic." "The *whole* universe, the faithful believe, was perverted by Adam's disobedience; and it is *because* of that universal perversion that the Redemption, in turn, was extended to the entire universe, and that Christ became the centre of the neo-creation. . . ."[106] But Teilhard's argument cuts the other direction also, and it appears that this is the characteristic movement of his thought: from the universality of Christ (the primary postulate, based on Scripture and tradition) through the universality of Christ's curative work to the universality of the fault. "*If Christ is to be truly universal*, the Redemption, and hence the Fall, must extend to the whole universe."[107]

In any case, whether the movement is from the universality of Christ to the universality of evil or from the cosmic fall to the cosmic Christ, the

---

[106]"Fall, Redemption, and Geocentrism" (1920), *Christianity and Evolution*, 37.

[107]"Note on the Universal Christ" (1920), *Science and Christ*, 16.

cross takes on new and comprehensive significance within the Teilhardian schema.

> When the Cross is projected upon such a universe [a universe in evolution], in
> which struggle against evil is the *sine qua non* of existence, it takes on new
> importance and beauty—such, moreover, as are just the most capable of
> appealing to us. Christ, it is true, is still he who bears the sins of the world;
> moral evil is in some mysterious way paid for by suffering. But even more
> essentially, Christ is he who structurally in himself, and for all of us, over-
> comes the resistance to unification offered by the multiple, resistance to the
> rise of spirit inherent in matter. Christ is he who bears the burden, construc-
> tionally inevitable, of every sort of creation. He is the symbol and the
> sign-in-action of progress. The complete and definitive meaning of redemp-
> tion is *no longer only* to expiate: it is to surmount and conquer.[108]

Classical theology has distinguished two aspects of the redemptive work
of Christ: a negative aspect consisting of the expiation and removal of sin
and a positive aspect consisting of the exaltation and sanctification of
humankind. Teilhard preserves and affirms both aspects, but in his quest
for a new theology—directed towards "bringing Christology and evolution into line with one another"[109]—he gives priority to the second. The
work of Christ is, above all, to promote evolutionary progress. Christ
"saves" a world in evolution by bringing it to completion. In order to do
so, he has to overcome the various forms which evil takes in an evolutionary cosmos: the evil of growth, the evil of disharmony and failure, the evil
of death or decomposition, and ultimately moral evil or sin.

The imagery of ascent is prominent in Teilhard's writings.[110] Life,
human and prehuman alike, even the entire cosmos, is involved in a quest
(a "groping") for fuller dimensions of being. Spirit lies latent in matter,
and matter finds its authentic fulfillment only when spirit is "released"
and enhanced. Complexification-interiorization represents a universal
axis of growth. But growth entails suffering, and the pain of growth gives
rise to an inclination to falter in the "ascent." At the human level, the
temptation becomes strong to go on "strike" against the painful demands
imposed by the evolutionary nisus towards heightened personalization—
unless that process can be perceived to have a satisfactory, and attractive,
term. The work of Christ consists, first of all, then, in establishing and
revealing a summit towards which the cosmic ascent moves. To save a
world in evolution Christ must establish or "reveal"—once the evolutionary process has become conscious of itself, as it has in man—that the
ascent is worth the price.

---

[108]"Christology and Evolution" (1933), *Christianity and Evolution*, 85.

[109]Ibid., 77.

[110]See, e.g., *The Divine Milieu*, 77ff.

Second, since a world-in-the-making is structurally and inevitably a world marked by multiplicity and hence disorder, the work of Christ consists of the organization and union of the multiple. Understanding redemption as the continuation and completion of creation, Teilhard must show that at all levels of reality Christ constitutes the many into appropriate wholes. This, Teilhard argues, Christ does in a variety of ways: preeminently through the power of attraction (or persuasion) which he exercises in his function of Omega. As Omega, Christ draws all dimensions of existence towards himself by eliciting the emergence of novel and appropriate entities at every level of existence. In regard to the prehuman moments of (cosmo- and bio-) genesis, this is explicated in terms of the category of radial energy; at the human level radial energy is depicted as flowering into human and, ultimately, Christian love. Christ's unitive influence operates, moreover, through human and churchly action (see below): by becoming "moment" in the Incarnation, Christ effects the further unification and "eucharistic transformation" of the world "from within." In such ways Christ works to unify, to personalize, to spiritualize, and thus to save all that can be saved.

The ultimate disharmony is death. Death is one form of the discord that God had to accept in order to create anything at all, to create in any case a world in which such creatures as we are could come to existence. Only a world marked by a death-dealing process at the level of life could be fashioned out of primordial multiplicity. Thus, the third form of evil from which Christ must deliver a world in evolution is death: the death not only of the individual components of the world process but "total death," the dissolution of the process itself.

> Death is the sum and consummation of all our diminishments: it is *evil* itself—pure physical evil, in so far as it results organically from the material plurality in which we are immersed—but a moral evil too, in so far as this disordered plurality, the source of all strife and all corruption, is engendered in society or in ourselves by the wrong use of our liberty . . . .[111]

> Now the great victory of the Creator and Redeemer, in the Christian vision, is to have transformed what is in itself a universal power of diminishment and extinction into an essentially life-giving factor.[112]

Thus Christ saves, third, by conquering death, "not only by suppressing its evil effects, but by reversing its sting."[113] He does so by breaking the "death barrier" and transforming this ultimate diminishment into an

---

[111]Ibid., 54.

[112]Ibid., 61.

[113]Ibid., 54.

occasion of growth, a second threshold of reflection, the critical moment in the "ascent" towards full personalization.

Regarding evolution as a "personalizing" process, Teilhard must show that death can be an occasion of the fulfillment rather than the extinction of personality. This Teilhard tries to do by interpreting death in terms of his distinction between the two types of energy. Radial energy is that which operates to draw the elements of the world forward and upward towards greater measures of centered wholeness, while tangential energy is that mode of energy which operates to link elements on the same level of organization. It is the radial component of energy, therefore, that enables evolutionary progress to occur. At the human level, radial energy has found psychosocial expression (in communications technology, the flowering of love, et cetera); and it compels humankind collectively and individually towards the realization of richer modes of personal exist-ence. But in the material world the radial component of energy "operates only in virtue of the 'tangential energies' of arrangement and thus under certain conditions of spatial juxtaposition";[114] it is not independent. The significance of human death lies in the fact that it marks the point in the evolutionary process at which the functioning of the radial component of energy ceases to be dependent upon the tangential.

> Once formed, a reflective centre can no longer change except by involution upon itself. To outward appearance, admittedly, man becomes corrupted just like any animal. But here and there we find an inverse function of the phenomenon. By death, in the animal, the radial is reabsorbed into the tangential, while in man it escapes and is liberated from it. So we come to escape from entropy by turning back to Omega: the hominisation of death itself.

> Thus from the grains of thought forming the veritable and indestructible atoms of its stuff, the universe—a well-defined universe in the outcome—goes on building itself above our heads in the inverse direction of matter which vanishes. The universe is a collector and conservator, not of mechani-cal energy, as we supposed, but of persons. All round us, one by one, like a continual exhalation, "souls" break away, carrying upwards their incom-municable load of consciousness. One by one, yet not in isolation. Since, for each of them, by the very nature of Omega, there can only be one possible point of definitive emersion—that point at which, under the synthesising action of personalising union, the noosphere (furling its elements upon themselves as it too furls upon itself) will reach collectively its point of convergence—at the "end of the world."[115]

For Teilhard, then, death functions as a threshold in the evolutionary process itself. It is the critical point of transition between one stage of

---

[114] *The Phenomenon of Man*, 239.

[115] Ibid., 271-272.

existence and another, a second threshold of reflection in the process of "hominization." The significance of death lies in its function as a point of metamorphosis between different stages in the ascent of personality. Like other thresholds in the evolutionary process, this one, too, is marked by both continuity and discontinuity with what has gone before. The new life that emerges rises out of the old, but it is genuinely new. Death represents the occasion for the emergence of a new relationship between matter and spirit; it is a relationship defined less by the separation of the one from the other than by the final transmutation of matter into spirit. And this is true for both the individual and the totality of the material-vital universe.

Growth in spirit, Teilhard claimed, occurs precisely in and through a transformation of matter.

> This is the *general "drift" of matter* towards spirit. This movement must have its term: one day the whole divinisable substance of matter will have passed into the souls of men; all the chosen dynamisms will have been recuperated: and then our world will be ready for the Parousia.[116]

Here we arrive at that feature of the Teilhardian vision which leads his critics—Santmire and Elder among them—to suggest that Teilhard is finally an "exclusionist" who denigrates the value of the material-vital aspect of creation. It is not clear, however, that his critics have properly understood Teilhard or done him justice at this point. Teilhard's vision of the ultimate destiny of the material aspect of creation must be seen in the light of *both* the second law of thermodynamics and the classical Catholic doctrine of divinization. Teilhard certainly takes seriously the thermodynamic principle of entropy, and he affirms that what will ultimately be "saved" is indeed "spirit." This, of course, is the grounds for Santmire's and Elder's reading of his intention. But a comparison of Teilhard with his contemporary, Nikos Kazantzakis, may help clarify another, and more faithful, reading of him. The Cretan novelist, like the French paleontologist, has deep roots in classical Catholic piety; and the latter, in both its Eastern and Western forms, centers to a significant degree in the hope of divinization. As Athanasius put it: "He [Christ] was made man that we might be made divine" or, more literally, "He was humanized that we might be deified."[117] To be sure, the East has tended to think in more cosmic terms, whereas the focus of concern in the West has revolved more specifically upon the human; but in the churches of both East and West the divinization theme has had a prominent place. This theme is reflected in the writings of both the novelist and the paleontologist. But the

---

[116]*The Divine Milieu*, 86.

[117]Athanasius, *On the Incarnation* 54:3.

resemblance does not stop there. Both thinkers are fiercely "modern"—if
modernity is marked by affirmation of this world and a positive valuation
of "matter." Moreover, the writings of both men are highly poetic or
symbolic in character. (As we have noted, the problem of judging what
kind of writing certain of Teilhard's works represent, *The Phenomenon
of Man* in particular, is notorious; but Teilhard clearly understood his
talk about Omega to be symbolic in character, whatever his claims about
the nature of particular works taken as a whole.) My contention is that
Teilhard's understanding of the destiny of "matter" should be interpreted
in a way parallel to Kazantzakis's understanding of the role of "flesh":
matter can and should be taken up into and transformed by "spirit." In
words that Teilhard could have written, Kazantzakis affirms Christ to be
one who "continually transubstantiated flesh into spirit, and
ascended."[118] Within the complex thought worlds of Kazantzakis and
Teilhard—at once mystical-symbolic and secular-scientific, archaic and
modern—the proper destiny of matter is not entropy but divinization: the
"complexifying" evolutionary process proceeds by the transubstantiation
of matter into spirit and the whole "ascends" towards the "summit"
(Kazantzakis) of "Omega" (Teilhard). Moreover, there are in Teilhard no
a priori limits upon what can be thus spiritualized and divinized, and
nothing is *ab initio* destined to "fall away." It may be, in fact, that the
second law of thermodynamics should be understood to function in a way
parallel to the religious doctrine of hell in Teilhard's vision: as a warning
and a negative limit rather than as an affirmation of a sure and certain
destiny.[119] It is, rather, the proper destiny of all things to be taken up into
the world of spirit, to contribute to, and to participate in the consummation of all things symbolized in Teilhard by Point Omega—a symbol
which, if this reading is correct, already includes the "world."

If Teilhard is properly understood in the way that is here suggested,
then Elder's condemnation of him as an "exclusionist" and Santmire's
caviling about the ecological availability of his vision are both based on
distortions of the Jesuit's thinking. Teilhard would properly be regarded
as a theologian of nature who—in the combined language of evolutionary
science and mystical sacramentalism—affirms with Paul that God is "the
source, guide, and goal of all that is."[120] The problems then, to, which we

---

[118]Nikos Kazantzakis, *The Last Temptation of Christ*, trans. P. A. Bien (New York:
Simon and Schuster; Touchstone Edition, 1960), 3.

[119]On Teilhard's understanding of hell see "Introduction to the Christian Life" (1944),
in *Christianity and Evolution*, 164-65.

[120]Romans 11:36; NEB.

shall have to address ourselves in evaluating Teilhard will be other than those suggested by Elder and Santmire.

In summary, the positive meaning of redemption in Teilhard's theology comes to this: it is the support provided by Christ's suffering, his death, and his resurrection to the upward or ascensional movement of the evolutionary process and especially of humankind in its noospheric evolution.

> In its highest and most general sense, the doctrine of the Cross is that to which all men adhere who believe that the vast movement and agitation of human life opens on to a road which leads somewhere, and that that road *climbs upward*. Life has a term: therefore it imposes a particular direction, oriented, in fact, towards the highest possible spiritualisation by means of the greatest possible effort.
>
> . . . [Christianity] unveils to our eyes and hearts the moving and unfathomable reality of the historical Christ in whom the exemplary life of an individual man conceals this mysterious drama: the Master of the world, leading, like an element of the world, not only an elemental life, but (in addition to this and because of it) leading the total life of the universe, which He has shouldered and assimilated by experiencing it Himself. And finally, by the crucifixion and death of this adored Being, Christianity signifies to our thirst for happiness that the term of creation is not to be sought in the temporal zones of our visible world, but that the effort required of our fidelity must be consummated beyond a total metamorphosis of ourselves and of everything surrounding us. . . .
>
> To sum up, Jesus on the Cross is both the symbol and the reality of the immense labour of the centuries which has, little by little, raised up the created spirit and brought it back to the depths of the divine context. He represents (and in a true sense, He is) creation, as, sustained by God, it re-ascends the slopes of being. . . . We can now understand that from the very first . . . the Cross was placed on the crest of the road which leads to the highest peaks of creation.[121]

Having examined the leading lines of Teilhard's treatment of the "positive" aspects of Christ's salvific work, we turn now to a consideration of his discussion of the "negative" aspect of the work of redemption. It is clear that, for Teilhard, the expiatory aspect of the theory of redemption has a secondary place.

> For obvious historical reasons, Christian thought and piety have hitherto given *primary* consideration in the dogma of redemption to the idea of expiatory reparation. Christ was regarded *primarily* as the Lamb bearing the sins of the world, and the world *primarily* as a fallen mass. *In addition*, however, there was from the very beginning another element in the picture—a positive element, of reconstruction or recreation. New heavens, a new earth: these were, even for an Augustine, the fruit and the price of the sacrifice of the Cross.

---

[121] *The Divine Milieu*, 77-79.

Is it not conceivable—I may put it more strongly, is it not now happening—
that . . . these two elements, the positive and the negative, of the Christic
influence, may be reversing their respective values, or even their natural
order, in the outlook and the piety of the faithful, under the guidance of the
spirit of God? . . .

Put this question to the rising masses of young Christians, put it to ourselves:
we are all looking and waiting, more or less consciously, for a religious
efflorescence, a religious impetus—must it not come from a renewed Christology in which, however fully reparation is retained, it ceases to occupy the
foreground (*in ordine naturae*) in the saving operation of the Word? *Prima-
rio*, to consummate creation in divine union; and, in order to do so, *secunda-
rio*, to annihilate the evil forces of retrogression and dispersion. No longer
first to expiate, and then *in addition* to restore; but *first* to create (or
super-create) and, in order to do so (inevitably, but incidentally), fight
against evil and pay for evil. Is not that the new order in which our faith is
now incontrovertibly arranging the age-old factors?[122]

Teilhard unhesitantly affirms the reversal, and hence, the priority of the
notion of redemption as the consummation of creation. But he affirms the
other notion too: redemption involves the expiation of sins.

Teilhard's approach to this, the "negative" aspect of redemption,
centers in his treatment of human freedom and love. According to the
results of Teilhard's phenomenological analysis of evolution, the process
has become conscious of itself in and through humankind. Having
become conscious in man, the evolutionary process is now free to further
itself or to frustrate the project of the ages. That is, since the axis of future
development runs through the noosphere and hence depends on the
agency of conscious and free beings, evolution in the future will advance,
or fail to advance, towards further complexity and interiority according
to the decisions and actions of the human "molecules" that constitute the
noosphere. The tangential component of energy will result in further
technical progress, perhaps inevitably; but the progress of radial energy is
in no sense inevitable at the human level. For love is the highest form of
radial energy; and the growth of love is, accordingly, the condition of the
future. Love is "that psycho-moral energy" which "physically builds up
the universe."[123] It is, hence, the key to the entire moral order. Love binds
the members of the community together in (ever-greater) wholes, and it is
ultimately centered on Omega. Precisely because of the priority of Omega
in the affections of persons the repulsions and hatreds that divide the
noosphere and block further evolutionary progress can be, and are being,
overcome.

---

[122]"Christ the Evolver" (1942), *Christianity and Evolution*, 145-46.

[123]"Esquisse d'un univers personnel" (1936), *Oeuvres*, vi, 90; cited by Mooney, *Teilhard de Chardin*, 125.

Moral evil, or sin, consists of the refusal to love (rightly) and to act in accordance with the dictates of love. That is, the essence of moral evil is the free rejection of Omega as the center of individual, social, and even cosmic life. And the refusal of Omega is the refusal of evolutionary progress, the rejection of the future; for it involves the repudiation of that alone which can unify humankind, overcome the obstacles to progress, and bring the entire process to its appropriate end.

As these considerations suggest, Teilhard depicts evolution as a process that is endangered from within. Since the successful completion of the process is contingent upon human freedom and love and since human love can be so easily deflected from its appropriate objects, the final outcome of cosmogenesis remains problematical right to the end. Sin may subvert the great project of the ages—unless it can be encountered and overcome. And this Teilhard affirms, with the testimony of the ages, Christ has done in his cross.

Teilhard is not as clear as some wish he had been about his treatment of Christ's work of reparation. One of his most perceptive and favorable interpreters argues that Teilhard utterly fails to connect reparation for sin with the success of evolution, even though such a connection is really demanded by his own system. Pointing to Teilhard's tendency to effect certain transpositions—such as the interpretation of Christ as "he who bears the sins of the world" into "he who bears and supports the weight of the world in evolution" and the notion of "sin" into that of (resistance to) "progress"—Christopher Mooney argues that Teilhard never speaks of the essential meaning of Christ's bearing of the sins of the world as a bearing of the burden of humankind's refusal to love. Rather, maintains Mooney, Teilhard depersonalizes sin in dealing with Christ's work of redemption by consistently disassociating the notion of reparation from the concept of love.

> The net result is not simply to consign reparation to a place of secondary importance, which Teilhard frequently states as his purpose and which is in itself a legitimate theological position. Rather what results is that, in spite of his protests to the contrary, the negative aspect of redemption disappears altogether and the positive aspect alone remains. Because it is never connected with man's refusal to love, reparation for sin tends to become absorbed and identified with the union of all creation in Christ by reason of the Incarnation. Redemption comes to mean *solely* that Christ, through his suffering, death and Resurrection, overcomes in himself (and therefore in humanity as a whole) that resistance to spiritual ascent which is inherent in matter. What Teilhard apparently never sees when dealing with redemption is that one essential condition for spiritual ascent, the one certain guarantee of evolution's success, can only be Christ's conquest of that mysterious capacity in man for disunion and hatred on the personal level. Now this is an

anomaly of the first order, an utterly illogical omission for a mind which in its own analysis of evolution saw spiritual tension as the key to the universe.[124]

Mooney may be correct in this assessment. There is certainly a great deal of evidence to support his reading of Teilhard at this point. However, there is reason to think that Teilhard was not as negligent as Mooney suggests. What Teilhard says, and fails to say, about the Catholic doctrine of redemption must be assessed in terms of his understanding of the evolution of doctrine. On this point he is orthodox: "In the history of the Church it is evident and accepted as such that dogmatic and moral views are continually being perfected by the development and inclusion of certain elements which, from appearing subordinate, gradually become essential and even preponderant."[125] That is to say, Teilhard affirms that "theology is evolving not by addition or subtraction of its content but by relative increase or decrease of the emphasis laid on different aspects of it—the process culminating, in fact, in the emergence each time of a concept or an attitude that is more highly synthesized."[126]

Now Teilhard knows the notion of Christ as agent of the completion of creation to be a part of Catholic teaching from Paul and Irenaeus onward, albeit a subordinate part; and in his notion of "Christ the Evolver" he is self-consciously raising a subordinate motif to an "essential and even preponderant" position. But in doing so, he is—if his statements about how he views the growth of dogma are given due weight— presupposing and affirming the Church's traditional teaching regarding the notion of "Christ the Redeemer" from sin. In his quest for a "more highly synthesized" soteriological statement, he does not elaborate what has been one-sidedly elaborated in the past; he, rather, takes it for granted. Thus, he can affirm without elaboration that "a spiritual transformation is going on, slowly but surely, at the end of which the suffering Christ, *without ceasing to be 'he who bears the sins of the world,' indeed precisely as such*, will become more and more in the eyes of believers 'he who bears and supports the weight of the world in evolution.' "[127]

In making such a statement, it can reasonably be assumed, Father Teilhard is affirming that Christ "bears and supports the weight of a world in evolution" precisely by—among other things—effecting the expiatory sacrifice in terms of which sins are forgiven and a free and

---

[124]Mooney, *Teilhard de Chardin*, 134-35.

[125]"Christ the Evolver" (1942), *Christianity and Evolution*, 144.

[126]Ibid., 145.

[127]"Introduction to the Christian Life" (1944), in ibid., 163; emphasis added.

loving mode of existence becomes a possibility for the believer. It would indeed be, as Mooney suggests, an anomaly of the first order if, within the context of the Jesuit piety that informed his theology, Teilhard had rejected (as Mooney implies) rather than simply assumed and affirmed this traditional motif. If this reading of Teilhard's soteriological theory is correct, it does not excuse his neglect to connect more explicitly Christ's conquest of sin and the human refusal to love with the conditions rendering possible the evolutionary ascent; but it does, at least partially, explain the omission.

In summary, then, we can say that Teilhard's several-faceted treatment of the notion of the redemption of a world in evolution culminates in his emphasis upon "Christ the Evolver"; but his elaboration of "the creative aspect of redemption"[128] presupposes and incorporates more traditional Catholic understandings of the work of Christ.

> The idea of pardon and sacrifice enriched, and so transformed into the idea of consummation and conquest.
>
> In other words, Christ-the-Redeemer being fulfilled, without this in any way detracting from his suffering aspect, in the dynamic plentitude of a Christ-the-Evolver.
>
> Such is the prospect which is without any doubt rising over our horizon.[129]

"Christogenesis": Creation and "Pleromization." By virtue of his resurrection, Christ has taken the position of "physical center" of a world in evolution. In a prayer to "the Ever-Greater Christ," Teilhard confesses his expanding faith in an expanding incarnation:

> In the guise of a tiny babe in its mother's arms, obeying the great law of birth, you came, Lord Jesus, to swell in my infant soul; and then, as you re-enacted in me—and in so doing extended the range of—your growth through the Church, that same humanity which once was born and dwelt in Palestine began now to spread out gradually everywhere like an iridescence of unnumbered hues through which, without destroying anything your presence penetrated—and endued with supervitality—every other presence about me.
>
> And all this took place because, in a universe which was disclosing itself to me as structurally convergent, *you, by right of your resurrection*, had *assumed the dominating position of all-inclusive Centre in which everything is gathered together.*[130]

This perspective enables Father Teilhard to discern a close connection between redemption and creation and to give his doctrine of creation an

---

[128]"Christ the Evolver" (1942), in ibid., 144.

[129]Ibid., 147.

[130]"The Heart of Matter" (1919), *The Heart of Matter*, 55-56; emphasis added.

eschatological focus. Creation, understood as creative union, is a continuous process; and, by virtue of the incarnation-resurrection, God exercises his creative power in and through his Word from the beginning until the eschaton.

We look now in more detail at Teilhard's treatment of how God performs his continuing work of creation-redemption from the event of Christ's resurrection until the final event, the parousia. The divine creative power finds expression concretely in two ways, says Father Teilhard: in Christian action (that is, in and through the Church), and directly within the evolutionary process itself. We shall attend to each of these elements in the pages that follow.

Building the Earth: The Sanctification of Endeavor. The aim of Christian action for Teilhard is to build up the Body of Christ, "which seeks to be realized in [and through] each one of us."[131] Now, as we have seen, the Body of Christ is understood by this Catholic thinker to be a "physical" reality inserted via the incarnation into an evolving humanity and thereby into the entire evolving cosmos. Somehow, moreover, the Body of Christ is inclusive of the evolutionary realities in which Christ has appeared and is taking (final) shape. Thus, the incompleteness of humankind and of the cosmos-in-the-making means that the Body of Christ is itself incomplete. Christ both is and is in process of becoming: "In you, [Jesus,] side by side with *Him who is*, I can passionately love *Him who is becoming*."[132] The incompleteness of the Body of Christ is, manifestly, within this framework of thought, a physical incompleteness; and it is to the filling up of the Body of Christ that the Christian is called to direct his labors. The Christian does this precisely by the human work of bringing to humanity, and the cosmos, a bit of completion. The Christian's efforts on behalf of his own (human) kind, therefore, are "not simply to forward a human task but, in some way, to bring Christ to completion."[133] Similarly, the Christian's efforts on behalf of otherkind—the "cosmos" or "nature"— has the same end:

> Since immanent progress is the natural Soul of the cosmos, and since the cosmos is centred on Christ, it must be accepted as proved that, in one way or another, collaboration with the development of the cosmos holds an essential and prime position among the duties of the Christian. *It is in one single movement that nature grows in beauty and the Body of Christ reaches its full development.*[134]

---

[131]"Cosmic Life" (1916), *Writings in Time of War*, 51.

[132]Ibid., 52.

[133]Ibid., 62.

[134]Ibid; emphasis added.

Here we come to the heart of Teilhard's value theory respecting the subhuman order and the foundations of what amounts in this thinker also to an "ethic of responsibility."

> In its dogmas and sacraments, the whole economy of the Church teaches us respect for matter and insists on its value. Christ wished to assume, and had to assume, a real flesh. He sanctifies human flesh by a specific contact. He makes ready, physically, its Resurrection. In the Christian concept, then, *matter retains its cosmic role as the basis, lower in order but primordial and essential, of union*; and, by assimilation to the Body of Christ, some part of matter is destined to pass into the foundations and walls of the heavenly Jerusalem.[135]

Teilhard sees creation as a process of (creative) union. It is a process that is continuing. Creation, then, is linked to redemption, for redemption involves not only (or, for Teilhard, not even primarily) reparation but also and especially fulfillment or completion. Christ's role is as the primary agent of creation-redemption. And his followers are called to assist in his work of creation-redemption.

> We may, perhaps, imagine that the Creation was finished long ago. But that would be quite wrong. It continues still more magnificently.... And we serve to complete it, even by the humblest work of our hands. That is, ultimately, the meaning and value of our acts. . . . With each of one of our works, we labour—atomically, but no less really—to build the Pleroma; that is to say, we bring to Christ a little fulfilment.
>
> . . . in action I cleave to the creative power of God; I co-incide with it; I become not only its instrument but its living prolongation.[136]

Teilhard seems to regard the constructive efforts of all men and women as contributory to the continuing creative-redemptive workings of God. Thus, all human endeavor is "sanctified," at least in principle. But not all contribute knowingly or with the proper intentions, nor do all realize the meaning of their daily labors. And since God's continuous creative action is directed towards the realization of the Pleroma, those who consent—in faith and love—to God's design are capable of participating and contributing most fully and. Therefore, Christians, motivated by their love for God and his purposes, find their labours inspired by their love: "We now unite ourselves to Him in a common love of the end for which we are working."[137] The resistances to "creative union" are broken down by love, enabling souls to embrace one another and join their

---

[135]Ibid., 64.

[136]*The Divine Milieu*, 31.

[137]Ibid., 32.

efforts with the efforts of others, thus contributing most richly to the Pleroma-in-the-making.[138]

Out of the rapprochement of the notions of Christian charity (as the motive of participation in the building of the Pleroma) and "natural" love energy (at work in the unification of the noosphere) comes a unique understanding of Christianity and the Church. "Christianity, I would dare to say, is neither more nor less than a 'phylum' of love in nature."[139] As we have seen, Teilhard regards the entire orientation of evolution as being towards the formation of the human phylum. Through the human "shoot," life crosses the (first) threshold of reflection and centers its creative energies in the noosphere whose growth is marked and motivated by the energy of love. Continuing his "phenomenological" analysis, Teilhard perceives the Christian Church as a phylum—a phylum of love that develops within the human phylum and moves in the same direction, towards greater consciousness and centricity. Moving from the phenomenological to the theological plane of reflection, Teilhard argues that the Church is the real source and bearer of the energy of love and that it is therefore the true carrier of human life, and thus of the whole evolutionary process, in its ascensional movement towards Christ-Omega and the second threshold of reflection. Put another way, the Church aims at a synthesis of centers in and around a single Center—a synthesis is to be based on love, the only kind of (genuine) synthesis appropriate to noospheric evolution. Accordingly, it is through Christianity that the principal axis of evolution now passes; for in its visible structure, the Christian phenomenon constitutes the unique current of energy in the noosphere within which faith and hope reach their fulfillment in love.[140]

The elaboration of this understanding of the Church as a phylum of love enables Teilhard to tie together a number of his salient theological motifs. He fuses this notion of the Church as an organic phylum to his concept of Christ as the organic center of evolution. This fusion is made possible by, and further contributes to, his concept of evolution as Christogenesis. In the process, Teilhard's conception of Christian activity (and its relation to human action in general) is further clarified and his eucharistic theory deepened.

In the broadest sense, Christogenesis refers to the entire movement of cosmogenesis. But, in a more restricted sense, Christogenesis specifies the growth of the "phylum of love" within the total process in general and the

---

[138]See, e.g., ibid., 125-26.

[139]"Human Energy" (1937), *Human Energy*, 158.

[140]Cf. Mooney, *Teilhard de Chardin*, 157-58.

human phylum in particular. The Church as the phylum of love provides the entire evolutionary movement with a nucleus or "axis" around which the various human and, through the human, natural "molecules" are destined to gather; and it motivates and shapes their concentric convergence upon Christ-Omega. Teilhard brings together the notions of Christ as organic center and the Church as organic phylum by attempting to show that Christ functions as the physical center of both humankind and nature precisely by virtue of his role as center of the Church. According to Teilhard,

> ... at the very heart ... of the social phenomenon, a sort of *ultra-socialization* is in progress. It is the process by which "the Church" is gradually formed, its influence animating and assembling in their most sublime form all the spiritual energies of the noosphere: the Church, the reflexively Christified portion of the world—the Church, the principal focus-point at which inter-human affinities come together through super-charity—the Church, the central axis of universal convergence, and the exact meeting-point that springs up between the universe and Omega Point.[141]

Thus, the axial place of the Church in the world derives first of all from the fact that in and through it the influence of the cosmic Christ is transmitted; secondly, the crucial role of the Church is seen in the fact that through it the merely "natural" and human are appropriated to the "supernatural." Both of these functions occur through the Eucharist and Christian action. Through the Eucharist, Teilhard claims, passes directly "the *axis* of the Incarnation, that is to say, of creation."[142] And the Eucharist is ultimately "simply the expression and the manifestation of God's unifying energy applied individually to each spiritual atom of the universe."[143] This being the case, when believers are united with Christ in the Eucharist they are "inevitably and *ipso facto*" incorporated "a little more fully on each occasion in *a Christogenesis which itself . . . is none other than the soul of universal cosmogenesis.*"[144]

Teilhard's understanding of the cosmic Christ who is the Omega of evolutionary development and his "sacramental intensifying"[145] of the relationship between matter, man, and Christ are markedly mystical in character; but they carry great import for human action. If the entire world is the Body-of-Christ-in-the-making, each and every contribution

---

[141]"My Fundamental Vision" (1948), *Toward the Future*, 191-92.

[142]"Introduction to the Christian Life" (1944), *Christianity and Evolution*, 166.

[143]Ibid.

[144]Ibid; emphasis added.

[145]The phrase is Hefner's, *The Promise of Teilhard*, (Philadelphia: J. B. Lippincott Company, 1970), 105.

to the world process is charged with significance. Teilhard's spirituality is aimed at a life of action. "Because we love, and in order that we may love even more, we find ourselves happily and especially compelled to participate in all the endeavors, all the anxieties, all the aspirations and also all the affections of the earth—*insofar as these embody a principle of ascension and synthesis.*"[146] Christians are, in a few words, called to participate fully in the labor of "building the earth."

Teilhard rounds out his analysis of the Church and Christian activity by developing the theme of what might be called the coinherence of the "Upward" and "Forward" thrusts of human endeavor. His elaboration of this theme demonstrates in some measure the legitimacy of his identification of Christogenesis and cosmogenesis. Like the Platonic philosophy with which it has been so deeply imbued, traditional Christianity has sought human completion by calling on humankind to "transcend" towards that which is above and beyond this world of time and change and matter. Contemporary humanistic faiths such as Marxism, on the other hand, have promoted a gospel of human fulfillment by urging humankind to "transcend" towards that which lies ahead in the human future; for such forms of faith salvation is sought within the temporal, mutable, and material world.

> The Higher Life, the Union, the long dreamed-of consummation that has hitherto been sought *Above*, in the direction of some kind of transcendency: should we not rather look for it *Ahead*, in the prolongation of the inherent forces of evolution?
>
> Above or ahead—or both? . . .[147]

Teilhard tries to provide a solution to the dilemma by attempting to effect, or at least initiate, a reconciliation between the two forms of faith. Each, he suggests, is partial by itself and is in need of the other. The faith that is oriented one-sidedly towards the Above is defective because it neglects unduly the development of the world as well as the cosmic implications of the Incarnation. The faith that is oriented exclusively towards the human future is defective because it neglects the one condition which can make the future desirable and even possible, namely the transcendent Center in the love and service of which all the barriers to human progress and unification can be overcome. Teilhard brings the two forms of faith together in what may appropriately be called a Christian form of humanism. According to this third form of faith, the divine and the human require each other, the Upward and the Forward meet,

---

[146]"The New Spirit" (1942), *The Future of Man*, 95.

[147]"The Heart of the Problem" (1949), in ibid., 263.

faith in the Above and faith in the Ahead are mutually supporting. To "transcend" towards God is already to move towards the fulfilled human future (the Kingdom of God, in Christian imagery). To direct our lives towards authentic human fulfillment is already to move towards God-Omega (the Vision of God, in classical imagery). Far from being in opposition to each other, the two forms of faith (faith in God and faith in humanity or the world) "represent the two essential components of a complete humano-Christian mysticism."

> There can be no truly live Christian faith if it does not reach and raise up, in its ascending movement, the totality of mankind's spiritual dynamism (the totality of the "anima naturaliter christiana"). Nor is faith in man psychologically possible if the evolutionary future of the world does not meet, in the transcendent, some focal point of irreversible personalisation. In short, it is impossible to rise Above without moving Ahead, or to progress Ahead without steering towards the Above.[148]

Alpha and Omega: Creation as Creative Union. The final phase of Teilhard's attempt to think out the relationship between Christ and the world in terms of the category of *genèse* results in his theory of "pleromization." The growth of the "organic phylum" of love, the eucharistic assimilation and transformation of the material elements of the world, the continuation of creation in human endeavor—all have their completion in the realization of the Pleroma.

Teilhard's work centers in the elaboration of a vision in which the Christian motifs of creation, incarnation, and redemption are brought together in terms of a single evolutionary movement directed towards the emergence of the final plentitude of Christ. The basis of his integration of the three motifs is his understanding of creation as the "creative union" of diverse elements. That is, he links creation, incarnation, and redemption through a particular metaphysical theory. It is a metaphysical theory that is Christologically centered and biblically grounded.[149] Teilhard appeals especially to certain texts found in the "cosmic" writings of Paul, texts such as Colossians 1:15-17, Ephesians 2:10, and 1 Corinthians 8:6.

---

[148]"The Religious Value of Research" (1947), *Science and Christ*, 203.

[149]Teilhard spells out his theory of creative union in some detail in the 1924 essay entitled "My Universe," in *Science and Christ*. But in that essay (44), he again denies that he is doing metaphysics: "Creative union is not exactly a metaphysical doctrine. It is rather a sort of empirical and pragmatic explanation of the universe, conceived in my mind from the need to reconcile in a solidly coherent system scientific views on evolution (accepted as, in their essence, definitively established) with the innate urge that has impelled me to look for the Divine not in a cleavage with the physical world but through matter, and, in some sort of way, in union with matter." Clearly Teilhard's mistrust of one *type* of metaphysics leads him to obscure the essentially metaphysical character of his own enterprise.

Teilhard's philosophical theory of creative union is rooted in his theological view of the relationship of Christ to the entirety of creation. Teilhard regarded "every cosmic particle, be it the smallest electron," as "strictly co-extensive with the totality of space and time." If this in fact represents the way things are, then "the *body* of each living entity does not act as a containing limit to the latter within the universe . . . : the body is only the expression of the living entity's interiority and 'centricity.' "[150] Teilhard considers that in the case of Christ, "this coextension of coexistence has become coextension of sovereignty"; and he attributes the privileged position of Christ's body in the universe to "the transforming influence of the Resurrection."[151] Thus, the theory of the creative union of all things is for Teilhard a "philosophical extension of faith in the Incarnation."[152]

> . . . the philosophy of creative union is simply the development—generalization, extension to the universe—of what the Church teaches us about the growth of Christ. It is the philosophy of the universe expressed in terms of the notion of the mystical body.[153]

What Teilhard is doing is attempting an explanation of the movement of evolution by appealing to the data of both science and Scripture—and by bringing the two sets of data together in a philosophical theory. Creation—that is to say, the creative union of all the elements of the world—is occurring; and it is occurring in Christ. "In him, 'the plenitude of the universe,' *omnia creantur* because *omnia uniuntur*—all things are created because all things are made one. . . ."[154] From the "organic and physical" point of view, "nothing in the world any longer subsists permanently . . . apart from the unifying influence of Christ. Throughout the whole range of things Christ is the principle of universal consistence: '*In eo omnia constant.*' "[155] Thus, the universe represents "above all a work of creation continued in Christ."[156]

Teilhard distinguishes four "moments" in his metaphysics of union. These moments of creative union deserve attention because what Teilhard says in regard to them bears importantly on the issue of whether he

---

[150]"My Fundamental Vision" (1948), *Toward the Future*, 169, n4.

[151]Ibid., 199.

[152]"My Universe" (1924), *Science and Christ*, 53.

[153]"Creative Union" (1917), *Writings in Time of War*, 174.

[154]Ibid.

[155]"Pantheism and Christianity" (1923), *Christianity and Evolution*, 70-71.

[156]"Essai d'integration de l'homme dans l'univers" (1930), 4th lecture, 13; cited by Mooney, *Teilhard de Chardin*, 171.

understands God to be affected in any significant fashion by the cosmic evolutionary process. Teilhard begins by delineating the meaning of being in terms of the drive towards union—the movement that is inseparably associated with being in any and all of its forms. He understands God as somehow involved in the movement towards unity. To explicate the nature of the divine involvement Teilhard distinguishes between what he calls "trinitization" and "pleromization."

The first two moments of creative union have to do with the dynamics of the inner divine life, or "trinitization." In his treatment of the first moment Teilhard simply affirms (with Thomas and classical Catholic theology in general) the reality of a divine and self-sufficient First Cause as the Alpha and Omega of finite existence. In discussing the second moment, Teilhard affirms traditional trinitarian dogma: the life of the eternal One who is both beginning and end of all else consists in the act of opposing and uniting himself triunely to himself.

The last two moments of creative union have to do with the dynamics of pleromization and are of particular import for our purposes, for in discussing them Teilhard attempts to indicate how God can be said to "complete" himself in and through the act of the creation which reaches its consummation in the Pleroma of Christ. While "God exists only by *uniting himself . . . ,* he fulfills himself only *by uniting.*" What Teilhard says is this:

> In the very act by which his reality asserts itself, God (we have just seen) makes himself triune. But, what is more, by the very fact that he unifies himself upon himself in order that he may exist, the First Being *ipso facto* stimulates the outbreak of another type of opposition, not in the core of his being but at the very opposite pole from himself (*phase three*). The self-subsistent unity, at the pole of being: and as a necessary consequence, surrounding it on the circumference, the multiple—the *pure* multiple (with full emphasis on *pure*), or creatable *nil*, which is nothing—and which nevertheless, by passive potentiality of arrangement (that is to say, of union), is a possibility of being, a prayer for being: a prayer (and here we are in such deep waters that our minds are completely unable to distinguish supreme necessity from supreme freedom) which it is just as though God had been unable to resist.

> In classical philosophy (or theology) the Creation, or Participation (which constitutes *phase four*) always tends to be presented as an almost arbitrary act on the part of the first cause, operating (by causality that is analogically "efficient") through a completely indeterminate mechanism: an 'act of God,' indeed, in the catastrophic sense of the term. In a metaphysics of union, however, while the self-sufficiency and self-determination of the absolute being are retained intact (since, let me again emphasize, the pure multiple at the opposite pole is merely potentiality and pure passivity), on the other hand the creative act takes on a very clearly defined significance and structure. Being, in some way, the fruit of a reflection of God, no longer in God but outside him, the pleromization (as St Paul would have called it)—that is to

say, the realization of participated being through arrangement and totalization—emerges as a sort of echo or symmetrical response to Trinitization. It somehow fills a gap; it fits in. And at the same time it becomes expressible in the same terms as those which served us for our definition of being. To create is to unite.[157]

There is little evidence to suggest that Teilhard (unlike Cobb and other process thinkers) questioned the classical doctrine of *creatio ex nihilo*. Rather, he appears to take for granted the classical view that God calls primordial stuff into being "out of nothing." Teilhard's divergence from tradition lies in his emphasis upon the lengthy process by which God completes creation by shaping the primordial multiplicity into the diverse, and successive, array of entities which he wills to bring into existence.

The questions that have urgency in regard to the third and fourth moments of Teilhard's metaphysics of union have to do with whether God is under some constraint to express himself *ad extra* and whether he is in any sense enriched by that which he creates. Teilhard's answers to both questions appear to involve both a yes and a no. In regard to the latter issue, Teilhard begins by maintaining that creation is an image or reflection of the divine trinitarian life. And it is precisely this relation of the created to the Creator which imbues the created order with an internal necessity to pass from a state of multiplicity to one of unity; moreover, it imbues the created, more particularly, with an internal nisus towards an ultimate unity with the Creator. But the unification of the many and the union of the unified with the eternal One does not mean, according to Teilhard, that "anything essential" is added to God, much less that "the One is composed of the Multiple."[158] Rather, after asking "What is the supreme and complex reality for which the divine operation moulds us?," Teilhard answers:

> It is revealed to us by St. Paul and St. John. It is the quantitative repletion and the qualitative consummation of all things: it is the mysterious Pleroma, in which the substantial *One* and the created *many* fuse without confusion in a *whole* which, without adding anything essential to God, will nevertheless be a sort of triumph and generalisation of being.[159]

The Pleroma consists, then, of "God plus the many." Nothing "essential" is added to the divine Being, yet "pleromization" represents "a real completion in the symmetry of the universal Being."

---

[157]"My Fundamental Vision" (1948), *Toward the Future*, 194-96.

[158]"My Universe" (1924), *Science and Christ*, 45.

[159]*The Divine Milieu*, 100.

> The idea we are trying to form today of multiplicity, its structure and function, is closely linked up with the Christian vision of the final consummation of the universe. . . . because of the Incarnation, God can no longer do without the many among whom he has immersed himself—at least from now on in the present order. . . . that reality which is to be found *in Christo Jesu*, namely "God plus the many," seems both in Christian practice and Pauline spirituality to represent a perfection which, however wholly extrinsic to God it may be, involves a real completion in the symmetry of the universal Being.[160]

This statement raises the other issue: whether God is under some necessity to create. After a few remarks about this we can return to a consideration of whether anything is added to God by pleromization.

In regard to the problem of the necessity of creation, Teilhard's intent seems twofold. He wants, first of all, to protect the initial freedom of the Creator; thus, he contends that God is under no extrinsic compulsion to create. God freely chooses to call a world into being and bring it to completion. But Teilhard wants, second, to ward off any suggestion that creation is a merely "arbitrary act." What he seems to be doing is giving expression to a theory of "internal necessity": God created because of what he is. It is the nature of goodness to communicate itself, of love to express itself. Accordingly, Supreme Love expressed itself—freely and sovereignly—in the formation of an object of the divine love; and once he has brought into being that which is other than himself, God—freely and sovereignly—weds himself to it (and it to him) in such a way as to "guarantee" its fulfillment: "because of the Incarnation, God can no longer do without the many among whom he has immersed himself." The acts of creation and incarnation are free acts arising out of the divine life of love, but God being "eternally that which eternally he is" (Temple),[161] must effect "a real completion in the symmetry of the universal Being." Any necessity that is involved in creation is an "internal" necessity, one that arises out of the very character of God; accordingly, it is a "necessity" entirely compatible with, and one that even represents the supreme expression of, the divine sovereignty and freedom. Thus, while "everything takes place as if God had not been able to resist this appeal" for creaturely being, it is an "appeal" that has its origin in the mysterious inner-trinitarian life of God and not in the "extrinsic" reality of created being as such.

Pleromization, it seems, then arises out of and completes trinitization. "Pleromization is thus the fruits of God's reflection, not upon himself but

---

[160]"La Route de l'Quest" (1932), 20; cited by Mooney, *Teilhard de Chardin*, 174.

[161]Temple takes a similar view to that of Teilhard. See *Nature, Man and God*, 479ff.

ouside himself; it appears somehow as a sort of replica or symmetry of Trinitization. Somehow its actuation fills a void. . . ." Paradoxically (for Teilhard is groping for ideas that never find full expression), "God is entirely self-sufficient; and yet the universe contributes *something that is vitally necessary to him . . . .*"[162] It appears that what Teilhard suggests but never adequately clarifies is a form of dipolar theism in which "trinitization" represents the primordial aspect of the divine reality and "pleromization" the consequential aspect. In both aspects God is fully God: nothing outside him conditions the fullness of his being. Yet in his eternal perfection he actualizes a state of being in which is included the rich fruits of his actions *ad extra*, but the "pleromized" pole of the divine reality is rooted in nothing other than his eternally triune mode of being itself.[163]

Teilhard concludes his treatment of the four moments of creative union with an observation that affirms the mutuality of the motifs of creation, incarnation, and redemption—a coinherence of these three motifs that comes to light as we attend to the "consequential" aspect of the divine being:

> And so we can see how a series of notions, long regarded as independent, gradually comes to form a linked organic pattern. No God (up to a certain point . . .) without creative union. No creation without incarnational immersion. No incarnation without redemptive repayment. In a metaphysics of union, the three fundamental "mysteries" of Christianity are seen to be simply the three aspects of one and the same mystery of mysteries, that of pleromization (or unifying reduction of the multiple).[164]

Creation, incarnation, and redemption are three aspects of God's unitary work and relationship with a world he is in process of shaping and fulfilling. Teilhard thus depicts the world as a unitary process—Christogenesis—"considered either in its motive principle (creation), or in its unifying mechanism (incarnation), or in its ascensional work (redemption).[165]" Seen from the vantage of "pleromization"—by which Teilhard means "the mysterious 'repletive' (if not 'completive') relationship which links the first being with participated being"[166]—the unity of the whole comes into view. "Christogenesis," "creative union,"

---

[162]"Christianity and Evolution: Suggestions for a New Theology" (1945), *Christianity and Evolution*, 177.

[163]It is worth comparing Teilhard to Jonathan Edwards whose theory of creation involved just such a "dipolar" affirmation of divine being and action.

[164]"My Fundamental Vision" (1948), *Toward the Future*, 198. Cf. *Christianity and Evolution*, 182-83.

[165]"Introduction to the Christian Life" (1944), *Christianity and Evolution*, 155.

[166]"Reflections on Original Sin" (1947), in ibid., 198.

"pleromization"—all these are terms that Teilhard utilizes to speak of the exercise of Christ's function as organic Center of a universe-in-the-making, a continuous influence which is at the same time creative, unitive, and redemptive and which culminates in Christ's plenitude manifested at the parousia.

Creation and Incarnation: The Fulfillment. The parousia marks the completion of Christogenesis. Teilhard's doctrine of the final appearance of Christ reflects the same double-sidedness that is found in his doctrine of Omega. As Omega both exists already and is in-the-making, so the event of the parousia will involve the actualization of the potentialities of the universe and a further divine "in-breaking" or manifestation of One who exists before all worlds (the Alpha). But Teilhard is clear: the final manifestation of the divine splendor is not caused by the ripening of the potentials of creaturely being. Rather, planetary (and/or cosmic) maturation is the necessary preparatory condition for the occurrence of the parousia. The completion of evolution will represent a critical point—the maximization of the possibilities of complexity and consciousness—which will coincide with the parousia of Christ. The emergence of the "ultra-human" is the necessary condition for that transposition by which humankind—and nature (in and through humanity)—will be finally and completely incorporated into the Body-Person of Christ. But this ultimate "assimilation" is a work not of man but of God in Christ.

Teilhard's vision of the end involves a blending of diverse New Testament perspectives. The one (seen, for example, in 2 Peter 3:7-12) asserts the cataclysmic nature of the eschaton: the world is annihilated and a new order established. The other (seen, for example, in Romans 8:19-23) suggests that the "end of the ages" will be marked by a deliverance of the present age and a renewal or "rebirth" in a higher state of being. Within the evolutionary perspective of Teilhard the two traditions are brought together and, in effect, their complementarity affirmed. The eschaton will be a time of crisis (paroxysm and ecstasy) which awaits and involves the unification of humankind and the (spiritual) consummation of the universe. Says Teilhard:

> It is then, we may be sure, that the Parousia will be realised in a creation that has been taken to the climax of its capacity for union. The single act of assimilation and synthesis that has been going on since the beginning of time will then at last be made plain, and the universal Christ will blaze out like a flash of lightning in the storm clouds of a world whose slow consecration is complete. The trumpets of the angels are but a poor symbol. It will be impelled by the most powerful organic attraction that can be conceived (the very force by which the universe holds together) that the monads will join in a headlong rush to the place irrevocably appointed for them by the total adulthood of things and the inexorable irreversibility of the whole history of

the world—some, spiritualised matter, in the limitless fulfilment of an eternal communion—others, materialised spirit, in the conscious torment of an endless decomposition.

At that moment, St Paul tells us (1 Cor. 15. 23ff.), when Christ has emptied all created forces (rejecting in them everything that is a factor of dissociation and superanimating all that is a force of unity), he will consummate universal unification by giving himself, in his complete and adult Body, with a finally satisfied capacity for union, to the embrace of the Godhead.

Thus will be constituted the organic complex of God and world—the Pleroma—the mysterious reality of which we cannot say that it is more beautiful than God by himself (since God could dispense with the world), but which we cannot, either, consider completely gratuitous, completely subsidiary, without making Creation unintelligible, the Passion of Christ meaningless, and our effort completely valueless.

Et tunc erit finis.

Like a vast tide, Being will have engulfed the shifting sands of beings. Within a now tranquil ocean, each drop of which, nevertheless, will be conscious of remaining itself, the astonishing adventure of the world will have ended. The dream of every mystic, the eternal pantheist ideal, will have found their full and legitimate satisfaction. "Erit in omnibus Deus."[167]

CONCLUSION

The man whose thinking we have examined in this chapter has been called, along with Bonhoeffer, one of "the two most significant theological minds of our times."[168] This estimate does not reflect the judgment that Teilhard was the greatest of recent theological thinkers, but it reflects instead the judgment that Teilhard has sensed earlier and more clearly than most the issues that need to be addressed theologically in our day and that he has made some imaginative suggestions in response to his perceptions of current needs. Along with Bonhoeffer, Teilhard sensed early on the demand ingredient to recent and contemporary culture that faith be brought into a creative and affirmative relationship with "secular" life, that theology find a way of embracing the world. The vision with which he responded is admittedly incomplete; what he has bequeathed later generations theologically has more the character of a stimulating agenda than a well-rounded system. But by his insightful reading of the issues ingredient to our science-shaped culture and by the remarkably

---

[167]"My Universe" (1924), *Science and Christ*, 84-85. Emphasis added.

[168]J. V. Langmead Casserly, "Teilhard de Chardin as Theologian," in *Teilhard de Chardin: Re-Mythologization* (Waco TX: Word Books, 1970), 55. This volume also contains another significant essay to which reference will be made below: "Teilhard de Chardin as Philosopher," by Robert V. Wilshire.

original if partial character of his theological response, it may be that "Teilhard has laid [some of] the foundations of theological renewal in the twenty-first century, the century perhaps to which he truly belongs."[169]

Teilhard has seen that the discovery of spatial and (especially) temporal immensity, accompanied by the emergence of the new perspective on man as both the spearhead and agent of evolutionary development, has led us to the point at which a fundamental revision of Christian confession and sensibility—a new theology and a new saintly ideal—is needed. He was among the first to suggest that this far-reaching transformation is to be effected by focusing attention not on beginnings and past realizations as the key to understanding reality but on the future. To that end he engaged in a life-long project of advanced imagining, if we may put it so, in which he attempted to delineate the shape that might be taken by a new theology and a new spirituality informed by the postulation of the ontological and axiological priority of the future consummation and informed as well by the scientific and cultural currents which have made possible the re-emergence of eschatological expectations and modes of thinking. This pioneer of a new theology and a new spirituality, this remarkable intellectual and spiritual adventurer, has opened up for us and for generations to come horizons that will be neglected only at the peril of a vast diminishment of our human potential. To vary the image, Teilhard has engaged in a vast and sophisticated "thought experiment" in which he boldly, even audaciously, aimed at a grand new synthesis. He may have failed. But if so, his was the failure that accompanies the greatest successes in the history of the life of the mind: the Teilhardian synthesis is vitiated by, among other things, the inevitably partial character of so bold a construction. Aware of this and, seemingly aware too that the urgency of the issues and the challenge of new directions, some of which he had pointed up, would claim the energies of new adventurers and experimenters, Teilhard confessed near the end of *The Phenomenon of Man*, "I may have gone astray at many points." Then he added, "It is up to others to try to do better."[170]

As we have seen, Teilhard's explorations of the past led to the highlighting of a number of motifs ingredient to the evolutionary process. The first motif is that ours is a universe-in-the-making. The world with which we have to do is "no longer the cosmos, but cosmogenesis."[171] Genesis on a prodigious scale hitherto unsuspected is the reality which modern

---

[169]Ibid., 41.

[170]*The Phenomenon of Man*, 289-290.

[171]"The Vision of the Past" (1949), *The VIsion of the Past*, 238.

science has disclosed to us and which must henceforth be incorporated in all our thinking.

Teilhard suggests that for the proper appreciation of the dimensions of the world—and of our place in it—a whole series of new "senses" are necessary.[172] We need geometrical senses attuned to the spatial, temporal, and numerical immensities of the universe; we need a sense of proportion, a capacity to perceive the differences which separate "both in rhythm and dimension" the microscopic and the macroscopic features of the world; and we need evolutionary senses by which we can appreciate the radical novelty, the dynamic(s), and the organic oneness of an involuting cosmos. It may be that a Pascal, among others, possessed the first four senses; but the development of the three evolutionary senses awaited the emergence and maturation of modern science, especially biology. In "the vision of the past" that unfolds via the operation of these senses, Teilhard finds the history of a genesis, a "cosmogenesis." A cosmos is in-the-making: a cosmic process marked by the successive (but overlapping) stages of geo-genesis, bio-genesis, anthropo-genesis, and ultimately Christogenesis.

This suggests other major motifs in Teilhard's vision of the past. The world, he says, is "a *whole* which unfolds."[173] Teilhard's vision is unitary or holistic in character. The cosmos is not only dynamic; it is a dynamic unity. Thus, it is marked by continuity and interconnectedness. Moreover, there is a directionality inherent within the world process: the "unfolding whole" tends toward the production of increasingly complex entities marked by greater degrees of "consciousness." And this process of "complexification" is, thus, productive of novelty; so there is discontinuity within an overall process characterized by continuity.

---

[172] *The Phenomenon of Man*, 33-34. These "new senses" are part of the empirical paraphernalia, as it were, of hyperphysics. My discussion of these senses is indebted to Kenney, *A Path through Teilhard's Phenomenon*, 73ff.

[173] *The Phenomenon of Man*, 35. Teilhard thinks that we are possessed of a "cosmic sense" by which we intuit the holistic or unitary character of the cosmos. "Does not," he asks (in "How I Believe" [1934], *Christianity and Evolution*, 102), "the presence of the Whole in the world assert itself for us with the direct evidence of some source of light? I do indeed believe that that is so. And it is precisely the value of this primordial intuition which seems to me to hold up the whole edifice of my belief. Ultimately, and in order to account for facts which I have met at the deepest level of my consciousness, I am led to the conclusion that man, in virtue of his very condition of 'being in the world,' possesses a special *sense* which shows him, in a more or less ill-defined way, the Whole of which he forms a part. There is nothing astonishing, after all, in the existence of this 'cosmic sense.' Because he is endowed with sex, man undoubtedly has intuitions of love. Because he is an element, surely he must in some obscure way feel the attraction of the universe." (Compare "My Fundamental Vision" [1948], *Toward the Future*, 202.)

As a result of his emphasis on the centrality of the human phenomenon in the evolutionary process, Teilhard postulates a "within" of
things. His principle of universal interiority[174] goes beyond that which is
allowed by the orthodox empirical sciences, but Teilhard thinks that it is
required if we are to give due place to the human element within the
whole. Only if we allow that matter at all levels has an inner side, a psychic
as well as a physical aspect, can we account for the flowering of interiority
in the advanced levels of life. Teilhard speaks of the "psychic" aspect of
matter as "consciousness," a somewhat ill-chosen term; for Teilhard does
not regard prehuman entities as possessed of the capacity for thought.
Rather, the term "consciousness" is employed by Teilhard in the way
"feeling" is used by the Whiteheadian thinkers—to denote every kind of
psychism, from the most primitive types of interiority to the most
advanced flowering of reflective thought.[175]

By postulating the reality of the "within" of all phenomena, Teilhard
achieves some important results. He at once transcends the bifurcation
between mind and matter which Whitehead also wrestled with, and he
eliminates the sharp dualism in exactly the way that the Whiteheadian
process thinkers have done. Teilhard also overcomes the conflict between
the Darwinian and Lamarckian approaches to the understanding of
living matter; he reconciles these seemingly irreconcilable approaches by
connecting the development of the "within" (at least in the advanced
stages of evolution) with the Lamarckian inner principle of development
and by attributing the transformation of the "without" to the Darwinian
mode of explanation.

These results are not inconsequential, and they (especially the first)
clearly reflect Teilhard's deep psychological drive towards coherence and
a unitary vision of things. But it is important to note that these results are
rooted in a methodological decision. Teilhard chooses to adopt man as
the key to the whole and to ask what the whole looks like when the
decision is made to regard the human phenomenon—marked by a rich
interiority above all else—as the key to all the rest. Thus, what Teilhard
has done, along with William Temple and Alfred North Whitehead, is
engage in a kind of thought experiment in which the entire evolutionary
process is interpreted from the human standpoint, with the inner life of
man being taken as the key to the whole. The initial postulate of such a
program can be justified, if at all, only by the whole experiment in
thought (and that, of course, is what Teilhard, like Temple and White-

---

[174]Cf. *The Phenomenon of Man*, 143-44.

[175]Ibid., 57, n1.

head, intends); but the factors leading to the "bifurcation" against which Teilhard and others war cannot be overcome by a methodological ploy in and of itself. A panpsychic conclusion may follow from a particular methodological stance, and it may be buttressed by the results that proceed from the working out of that initial decision; but if it is to stand it must find support in other quarters as well.

As a summary of the first phase of his thinking, we can say that Teilhard has chosen evolution as the all-embracing framework for his thought. This "paradigm" (Kuhn) carries with it a number of the most important presuppositions *and* conclusions of the basic Teilhardian vision: namely, that the world is dynamic or processive in character, that it is unitary process, continuous and interrelated in its temporal-spatial dimensions, and that it is "going somewhere" (although whether its directionality is the result of mere drift, blind "groping," or of something else is not given in the paradigm itself). To this body of presuppositions-/conclusions that Teilhard shares with others who operate within the evolutionary paradigm, Teilhard adds the assumption—derived from his methodology—that the psychic element is universal and even primary in the stuff of the universe. And by this methodology (hyperphysics, which adopts man as the key to the rest), with its accompanying presupposition, Teilhard opens up his basic paradigm to some interesting and novel developments.

As we have seen, Teilhard's primary efforts in regard to theological reconstruction were directed at rethinking Christology in the light of our new understanding of the cosmos and, conversely (but almost inevitably), rethinking the nature and meaning of the cosmos in the light of Christ. Father Teilhard, quite simply wished to broaden and enlarge Christian thinking about Christ. He attempted to do so (a) through recovery of and reemphasis upon certain classical motifs which have played generally a minority role in the theological development of the West and (b) through the elaboration and completion of certain ideas which have been made accessible by the emergence of the evolutionary form of consciousness. But to "complete" Christology in this fashion, Teilhard had also to elaborate a theology of nature, something he was apparently eager to do. Indeed, for Teilhard the two are inseparable, as we have seen: Christ and the cosmos require each the other in order for each to be what he/it authentically is. Thus, the theology of nature is ineluctably, for Teilhard, a Christological problem. And Christological (re-)construction entails, again ineluctably, the elaboration of a theology of nature. In more traditional terms, Christology and Christian cosmology must be thought out together.

By bringing cosmology into the arena of theological concern, Teilhard, along with other theologians of nature, has performed a valuable service. By making Christology the key to cosmology he has gone beyond the perspectives of others whom we have examined. Whatever their intent, neither Santmire nor Cobb enlarge their Christological theories to the cosmic proportions achieved by Teilhard. This is to say, too, that Teilhard carries further than our other authors the emphasis upon the ultimate unity of the processes of creation and the processes of redemption. This enlargement and "completion" of Christological theory, along with the linkage of creation and redemption that is part and parcel of it, is achieved by Teilhard primarily through the renewal and extension of two classical motifs: eschatology and eucharistic theology.

Combining his heritage of faith with his scientific vision of things through the mediation of his metaphysics of process, Teilhard assigns to Christ the place in the universe that coincides with the place at the head and term of things that he denotes as Point Omega in his portrayal of the world process. This identification means that Christ is linked with the cosmos in a structural and organic fashion, rather than in a merely moral and juridical manner. All things are created in him, through him, and for him. This organic-structural identification of Christ and Omega means that it is through Christ that the world acquires its power of cohesion and its ultimate unity. Towards Christ-Omega all the strands of nature and history converge, and in him they cohere. Christ-Omega is the goal and, as such, the drawing power or motive force inspiring the entire process of convergence-coalescence. By his power of attraction (compare Aristotle-Thomas and Whitehead-Cobb) and through eucharistic transformation, Christ exercises the energy by which all things are drawn towards himself. All this means that, in the eschatological-sacramental perspective of Teilhard, Christ becomes the very meaning of nature and history. Christ-Omega provides the evolutionary process with direction; it is oriented toward him as its final term. Thus, not only are the structures and laws operating in nature and history governed finally by him towards whom all things move, but the *meaning* of the movement derives from him, as he is the goal and center of all things. In classical Christian expression: ". . . all are yours; and you are Christ's; and Christ is God's" (1 Corinthians 3:22-23). In Teilhardian terminology: Cosmogenesis gives rise to and is included in, biogenesis; biogenesis becomes, and is included in, anthropogenesis; anthropogenesis becomes, and is included in, Christogenesis; Christogenesis is mysteriously identical with Theogenesis. For both Paul and Teilhard the entire prehuman created order is centered in humankind; humankind is centered in Christ; and Christ is centered in God.[176]

Now, in all this Teilhard surely succeeds in elevating the value of matter and, more comprehensively, the natural world in general. The meaning of nature, like that of history, is to be found at the summit of creation—a summit which is being attained by evolutionary and eucharistic transformations within the processes of nature and history. At Omega the cosmic or "natural" and the Christic or "supernatural" become finally one. Until that point is reached nature remains, as it were, the base of something, or Someone; and its full meaning and value remain somewhat obscure. In the meanwhile, nature proceeds towards fulfillment and the Body of Christ grows by "nourishing itself" on—and completing—the natural world. Matter/nature is progressively "Christified," and in that is its glory.

What we finally find going on in Teilhard is an elaborate process of *resacralization* of the natural order *through remythologization.* His grand conceptual synthesis passes over into, and the results function as, a new creation myth. Francis also engaged in a process of resacralization of the natural order, and in that lies his significance. But, unlike Francis, Teilhard roots his renewed sense of the sacred and sacramental nature of all things in a grand conceptual synthesis informed by the best available science as well as by the biblical vision of the world as creation. The Franciscan "synthesis" was much less formal and rigorously executed than the Teilhardian. If, however, we view Teilhard only in this intellectualistic mold, we cannot do justice to the poetic and mystic elements which constitute such a prominent feature of his writings. Teilhard's majestic intellectual synthesis finally functions in a way that ordinary canons of scholarship do not allow. Poetry, science, theology, philosophy— Teilhard finally gives us more than any of these taken alone or even conjointly: he gives us myth. And unless we see his various capabilities and accomplishments as contributing to the (unconscious) process of remythologizing, Teilhard will remain enigmatic. His conceptual synthesis—which, as we have argued, is best viewed on one level as a thought experiment in the area of the theology of nature—functions finally as a new myth.

Teilhard has attempted in grand fashion the important work of relating the particular signification of the world which is ingredient to the Judeo-Christian tradition with the empirical data about the world as that data has been disclosed by science. In so doing he has not attempted

---

[176]Cf. N. M. Wildiers, *An Introduction to Teilhard de Chardin*, trans. Hubert Hoskins (New York: Harper & Row, 1968), 138-39.

anything new in principle. The process of synthesizing the deliverances of religion and science is ancient and widespread. Some of the grandest results are contained in the first two chapters of Genesis. Today this result is viewed as a "creation myth." The science reflected in this ancient story is now universally recognized by informed opinion to be inadequate; the ancient account is "demythologized." The religious sensibilities and the theological insights of the Hebraic accounts of origins—Yahwist and Priestly—have been affirmed, refashioned, and adapted to the further insights of both Hebrew religion and Christian experience. This process of remythologization is a continuing process. The burden of Genesis 3 has been repeatedly translated—that is, remythologized—in the light of modern depth psychology and other cultural-intellectual trends. Teilhard himself has contributed, as we have seen, to the remythologizing of the subject of Genesis 3. But no new creation myth grand enough to weld together the permanent insights of the Hebrew accounts of origins (Genesis 1 and 2) with the recent vast increase in knowledge of the physical universe has appeared—prior to Teilhard. The controversy between science and religion of the eighteenth and nineteenth centuries prevailed into this century, with tensions between the two human enterprises unresolved. Into this continuing controversy stepped Teilhard early in this century, attempting to bridge the gap by the elaboration of a new conceptual synthesis—a synthesis that functions, essentially, as a new creation myth.[177] The prospects for the further development and employment of the Teilhardian creation myth will be examined in Part Two of this study. But we turn now, in concluding Part One, to a brief consideration of the limitations of this Neo-Catholic approach to the theology of nature.

---

[177]Cf. Wilshire, *Teilhard de Chardin: Re-Mythologization*, 79. My treatment of Teilhard as a "re-mythologizer" is indebted to Wilshire and Casserly: also, James P. Reilly, Jr., "A Student of the 'Phenomena,' " in *The World of Teilhard*, ed. R. T. Francoeur (Baltimore: Helicon Press, 1961), 49-63. Reilly compares Teilhard's *Phenomenon of Man* with Plato's *Timaeus*. In both works socio-cultural, scientific, and religio-theological assumptions and insights all play a part. Says Reilly (61): "Plato distinguishes being from becoming, the ideal from the phenomenal. To this latter category belongs the visible universe. Since the phenomenal order is not the proper subject of metaphysical investigation, and since any strictly scientific report can be only a partial account, any attempt at a unified version of the phenomenal order admits only a likely story, a myth. Now Teilhard's ultraphysics, despite his assurances, is not, strictly speaking, science. Nor is his ultraphysics a metaphysics. If ultraphysics is neither science nor metaphysics, perhaps his ultraphysics embodies a myth, a likely account, which serves to give the unified description of reality and knowledge demanded by Teilhard's phenomenological approach."

It is painfully easy to critique Teilhard. The magnitude of his project and his methodological obscurantism taken together make him highly vulnerable to the censures of both specialists (scientific, philosophical, theological) and methodological purists. A multitude of critics willing to take advantage of his vulnerability has not been wanting. The result is a spate of criticisms that point out the obscurities, ambiguities, contradictions, and violations of orthodoxy (scientific, philosophical, theological, methodological) ingredient to Teilhard's thinking. Little would be gained by engaging in still another detailed cataloging of these problems, so we shall simply call attention to some of the most commonly noticed of them and focus on the more serious among them. An appreciative interpretation of Teilhard as an intellectual trailblazer in the area of the theology of nature, and a remythologizer, is compatible with a frank recognition of his limitations.

Teilhard's project is admittedly incomplete, and its execution lacks rigor at numerous points. His work is seminal, suggestive, but not rigorously carried through at all points. Many of his most obvious deficiencies are rooted in the unfinished character of his project. His insightful but inchoate metaphysics, for example, moves to the threshold of a vital new vision of God; but, unlike Whitehead, Teilhard fails to clarify the implications of his process cosmology for the doctrine of God. His understanding of the divine reality remains a curious hybrid of traditional Thomistic and recent processive insights, with the two ontological strains remaining only partially integrated. Moreover, Teilhard refrains from demonstrating as fully as is to be wished how faith in the Above and faith in the Ahead—the mystical and humanistic forms of faith—are henceforth to be integrated. And, as is universally pointed out by his critics (perhaps with more opprobrium than would be the case were not his position in tension with both Catholic and Calvinist orthodoxy), Teilhard's teachings regarding the origins and character of evil, including especially moral evil, raises several issues requiring a sustained reflection that Teilhard himself did not provide.

Related to the issues that are rooted in the inchoate character of his project are those that arise out of his methodological innovations and obscurantism. Teilhard, like all great mythmakers, was governed above all by intuition. Impatient with hyperspecialization, he grasped—intuitively—the total picture and the grander patterns. Constitutionally an holistic thinker, he sought an approach that would allow him to dispense with examining phenomena alternately from a scientific, philosophical, and theological perspective; his wont was to merge the different modes of knowledge and to move immediately from the scientific to the philosophical and the theological points of view. Like other process thinkers (Cobb, Barbour; unlike Santmire), Teilhard employs his (imperfectly formed) metaphysics to achieve this integration. His "system" is essentially premised on the concept of evolution, and he employs the notion of evolution to integrate diverse dimensions of meaning. By means of the evolutionary metaphysic, he holds together his scientific and humanistic perceptions of nature and history with his Christian (theological, mystical) insights into the signification of the whole.

As an intuitive thinker and finally a mythmaker—we should remember that he considered himself a "seer," a visionary—Teilhard was probably not fully aware of the character of his own methodology. The alternative to this conclusion is the hard judgment that with respect to his methodology this truth-seeker was less than truthful. His imperfect awareness of salient features of his own methodology, if granted, raises problems in itself; but, if Teilhard is to be understood as we are suggesting, they are not unique nor unforgivable. They are rather the kinds of problems ingredient to the vocation of all tellers of stories of cosmic dimensions—that is, mythologizers. And they are forgivable in at least a few among us, because without some neglect of methodological finesse on the part of intuitive thinkers like Teilhard, the grand new visions, the reformulated myths, would probably not be forthcoming.

Still, even if the imprecision of his understanding of his own methodology is overlooked, the problems that arise out of his way of proceeding remain. For Teilhard is a mythmaker in a new mode: his telling of the cosmic story is rooted in the new and highly sophisticated science of recent times, and his "story" has the character, first of all, of a grand cognitive synthesis. Accordingly, even if we view him as ultimately a mythologizer, we must put to him the hard questions appropriate to the penultimate dimensions of his work. We must ask if Teilhard has not moved somewhat too easily back and forth between the "data of revelation" and the deliverances of modern science. Can the cosmic affirmations of Paul and others regarding the person and work of Jesus Christ be transposed into an evolutionary framework in quite the facile fashion that Teilhard has suggested? And a related question: Can the "Jesus of history" and the "Christ of (mystical) faith" be integrated quite as readily as Teilhard has proposed? Or is the ease of his integration of the man Jesus with the cosmic Christ shaped by, as well as reflected in, his almost total neglect of modern New Testament scholarship in particular and modern historiography (other than that ingredient to scientific anthropology) in general?

Moreover, we must inquire about the legitimacy of Teilhard's tendency to group together so many diverse realities under the same universal categories of interpretation. Teilhard employs the theory of complexification to tie together his study of inorganic, organic, and personal (and even "super-personal") dimensions of reality. This procedure provides the foundation for affirming the lines of continuity by which the various dimensions are tied together; it enables him to move back and forth between biology and sociology, natural science and history, the past and the future. But does it not also, and thereby, function as the basis for an obscuring of the uniqueness of the various dimensions of the real? Can amoebas and men, the cosmos and Christ, be subsumed under the same general categories of interpretation in the fashion of Teilhard (and Cobb) without the losses exceeding the gains? This query brings us to the consideration of the most problematic, as well as the most promising, aspects of Teilhard's program.

Teilhard has sought to affirm both the continuity and the discontinuity of the various dimensions of reality: "Discontinuity in continuity: that is how . . . the birth of thought, like that of life, presents itself and defines itself."[178] Teilhard strives mightily to tie together in an holistic vision the human and the prehuman. To do so, he adopts "the biological point of view." This leads him finally to talk about the pre-personal/natural and the personal/historical in ways that threaten to obscure the uniqueness of the latter. "In reality," he says, "there is no breach of continuity between the two," history and pre-history.[179] The history of humankind "really does prolong—though in its own way and degree—the organic movements of life. It is *still* natural history through the phenomena of social ramification that it relates."[180] This emphasis on the principle of continuity, developed via biological/natural modes of thought, represents one thrust of Teilhard's program.

But there is in Teilhard another movement of thought, and it is one that is equally prominent. In this other mode, Teilhard accents discontinuity and gives priority to the category of the personal. While maintaining that interiority characterizes all levels of being, Teilhard affirms that self-reflexivity has appeared only at the human level. Although "hominization" represents "the progressive phyletic spiritualisation in human civilisation of all the forces contained in the animal world,"[181] with the appearance of man "another world is born,"[182] a major "threshold" is crossed. A creature appears who can say "I." "The cell has become

---

[178] *The Phenomenon of Man*, 169.

[179] Ibid., 205.

[180] Ibid., 107.

[181] Ibid., 180.

[182] Ibid., 165.

'someone.' "[183] In man, reflection, and the power of self-reflexivity, emerge. And, says Teilhard, "reflection is, as the word indicates, the power acquired by a consciousness to turn in upon itself, to take possession of itself *as of an object* endowed with its own particular consistence and value: no longer merely to know, but to know oneself; no longer merely to know, but to know that one knows."[184]

In the light of such affirmations, we may conclude that Teilhard escapes the more regrettable consequences of the Cobbian position. Whereas Cobb's way of accounting for interiority and evolutionary development (in terms of the self-shaping actual entities) runs the risk of an implicit attribution of self-reflexivity to the prehuman dimensions of reality, Teilhard's account of interiority and the "mechanism" of development (the two energies) allows him to avoid this risk to a greater degree. Teilhard is able to maintain that self-reflexivity is "the evolutionary lot proper to man and to man *only*."[185] This provides the foundation for a fuller appreciation of the character and superiority of human personal being than is to be found in the Whiteheadians. Teilhard, like Cobb, has humanity immersed in nature; but for Teilhard the immersion is more "dialectical," as it were, and thus less reductionistic in its consequences. But tension remains.

This tension between the evolutionary-natural and the personal-historical perspectives on humankind is reflected in Teilhard's treatment of Christ-God-Omega. Here again Teilhard's thinking is marked by two tendencies, without the relationship between them being very fully clarified. In one line of Teilhard's thought, Christ, God, Omega are all described in cosmic and impersonal terms. God-Omega is the Whole. Christ is the Evolver and "physical" center of creation. In the other line of Teilhard's thinking, God-Omega is described as hyperpersonal; the entire thrust of evolution is towards personalization; and Christ is the prime agent of the cosmic process of person-formation. Moreover, the energy and the mode of evolutionary advance—disclosed fully only after the crossing of the threshold of hominization—are themselves personal: love, expressing itself in union.

Thus, we have in Teilhard an evolutionary, or process, theologian of nature who perceives and appreciates the uniqueness of the personal mode of being, both human and divine—as well as the significance of the subhuman order. But we must finally judge that his project concludes

---

[183]Ibid., 173.

[184]Ibid., 165.

[185]Ibid.

with the impersonal processive categories being left in significant tension with the personal-historical categories. To anticipate our discussion in Part Two, we may suggest that Teilhard presents us with a theology of nature rooted in both a processive-organic (impersonal) model and an agential (personal) model, without the lines connecting and distinguishing the two ways of thinking being very clearly drawn.

PART TWO

SURVEYING
THE HORIZONS:
TOWARDS AN
ALTERNATIVE APPROACH
TO THE THEOLOGY
OF NATURE

CHAPTER 5

THE THREE APPROACHES: A RETROSPECTIVE SYNOPSIS

We have traveled far and recorded much. The landscape has proven rugged and challenging. Our three pathfinders have opened up exciting vistas before us. Now the landscape has been explored and our work of cartography is largely done. It remains to review and recollect what we have seen and recorded, to compare and contrast further the results of our retracing of the steps of our Neo-Protestant, Neo-Naturalistic, and Neo-Catholic trailblazers. Then we must utilize the results of our work of cartography to suggest where yet another, and more promising, path may lie.

As we have traveled, and recorded, we have had an eye for a number of interrelated features of the theological trails which we have followed. We have examined methodology, metaphysics and theology proper, value theory, and ecological ethics. We have attended with care to issues belonging to each of these categories, and the results are several.

CONCLUSIONS FOUNDATIONAL AND METHODOLOGICAL

With respect to methodology, we have discovered that those purporting to do the theology of nature have no clearly defined understanding of the work they are about. While the theology of nature explicitly belongs to the area of "theology proper" for two of the theologians we have examined (Santmire and Cobb) and implicitly for the third, there is no clear line of demarcation (for Cobb and Teilhard, especially) between a Christian natural theology and a Christian theology of nature. Hence, we are confronted with considerable confusion concerning precisely what the theologian of nature is about in his theological program. As part and parcel of that confusion we find the question of the role from science and philosophy in the elaboration of a Christian theology of nature. This methodological obscurity is most pronounced in Teilhard, but it is not absent from Cobb and Santmire. The latter tells us in Neo-Orthodox fashion that the theology of nature can be done in genuine independence of science and philosophy, although, he allows, we should have an eye for the deliverances of each. But, as we have seen, Santmire reaches theological conclusions which could not possibly have been obtained on the basis of Scripture alone. Some of the deliverances of science and of scientifically informed philosophies are manifest in his thinking in a way that he eschews. Since Santmire's slippage here is of the sort that he has identified and deplored in his mentor, Karl Barth, the question arises as to whether the theology of nature can be done in the purist fashion which the Neo-Orthodox stance would suggest. The Neo-Orthodox thinker can elaborate a theology of *creation*; but since *nature* is a category which cannot be separated from the disciplines which study it, the theology of nature may not, strictly speaking, be possible on Neo-Orthodox grounds.

Cobb and Teilhard do not have this particular problem, since they both recognize and affirm the relevancy of science and philosophy to theology. Moreover, both allow, either forthrightly (Cobb) or implicitly (Teilhard), the legitimacy of some sort of "natural theology." Thus, each recognizes that science and philosophy have an appropriate contribution to make to both "theology proper," as Cobb calls it, and the propaedeutic to theology proper, whether the propaedeutic be Whiteheadian, Thomistic, or Teilhardian in character. The problem for both Cobb and Teilhard is the failure, and apparent difficulty (if not impossibility), of specifying with precision the exact relationship that pertains between a natural theology and a theology of nature.

Related to all this is another methodological issue which is, at bottom, a metaphysical problem. The failure of all our theologians of nature to specify the character of their enterprise is rooted, in part at least, in the difficulty involved in specifying exactly what it is that they are theologizing about when attending to "nature." None of the theologians of nature taken for our examination and few, if any, other significant contributors to the literature falling under the rubric of the theology of nature engage in a sustained critical treatment of the concept of nature. Surely the methodological confusion can be only imperfectly eradicated, at best, if this underlying source of the difficulty is not confronted early on. We conclude, therefore, that one of the immediate duties of the theologian of nature is to engage in a critical examination of the concept of nature.

CONCLUSIONS METAPHYSICAL AND THEOLOGICAL

The Nature of "Nature". What the theologians we have examined do tell us about the primary object of their inquiries and constructions is this:

"Nature" is "the material-vital aspect of creation" (Santmire); it is all that occurs (Cobb); it is the entirety of the creaturely order (Teilhard). This plurality of definitions of the meaning of nature illustrates some of the difficulty ingredient to employment of the concept. On the one hand, "nature" is a term utilized to refer to that which stands over against "culture" or human artifice; "nature" constitutes the context and provides the resources for human (thus, historical) activity. On the other hand, "nature" is defined as a term referring to the totality of structures, processes, and powers that constitute the universe. Generally speaking, Santmire employs the term "nature" in the former, more restricted sense, while Cobb and Teilhard utilize "nature" and "natural" in the latter, all-inclusive sense. But even here there is divergence. God, too, is included in "nature" in its most inclusive Whiteheadian usage, whereas the Teil-hardian pattern follows Thomas in distinguishing the "natural" from the "supernatural." Thus, for Teilhard, in its inclusive sense, "nature" and its cognates refer to the totality of finite or creaturely reality. Culture, then, and history, are part of the natural order—the whole of which is being elevated towards a "supernatural" end, so that "nothing any longer appears as merely natural." We should say, that at best the usage of all our authors, like usage generally, is shifting and elusive: "nature" means now this and now that.

Nature as Complexifying Temporal Process. In spite of the ambiguity of their usage, certain significant characteristics of the system of nature do stand out in the analysis of the authors to whom we have been attending. Santmire, Cobb, and Teilhard all replace the traditional static under-standing of "nature" (whether understood as the material-vital dimension of the universe or as the whole) with a view of nature as complexifying temporal process. But whereas the evolutionary perspective is determina-tive in salient respects for Cobb and Teilhard, it is incidental to the thinking of Santmire.

Cobb and Teilhard both replace the categories of substance and being by categories of activity and becoming. For each the world—"nature"—is something that is being born rather than a reality which simply is. They reflect the modern revolution in the understanding of time. Time is no longer perceived as a neutral container in which are located self-sufficient objects unaffected by their temporalistic medium; rather time, duration, is perceived as indispensably constitutive of the very nature of things. The world is made up of events and processes, for both Cobb and Teilhard.

This means that there is an important eschatological bearing to the thinking of both these theologians of nature. Santmire's theology, too, has an eschatological thrust; but, as we have seen, in his Neo-

Reformation theology this element is biblically derived and not vitally related to the perception of the nature of nature. Cobb and Teilhard, on the other hand, are driven to include an eschatological element in their respective theologies of nature because of the confluence of biblical and scientific-philosophical considerations. In them, the eschatological motif derived from Scripture is taken up, reflected in, and translated by evolutionary categories of becoming. The reality and the value of the entities that collectively constitute nature, and the reality and value of the whole itself, are a function, in part, of the end(s) towards which all things move. To be sure, Teilhard goes much further than Cobb in postulating a single final telos as being in some sense the appropriate destiny of all natural entities; but the eschatological element is prominent even in the more pluralistic ontology of John Cobb. And this is not unexpected; for in a processive perspective, an entity cannot be defined apart from what it is becoming—and contributing to.

Nor in process perspective can an entity be defined apart from that which it is receiving from. This is to say that both Cobb and Teilhard emphasize the organic interdependence of all things. Entities are constituted not only by the temporal aspect of their "concrescence" but by their relationships as well. Cobb and Teilhard alike develop a doctrine of internal relations in which relationships are viewed as organically constitutive of every entity whatsoever. Even if Cobb gives (a la Whitehead and Hartshorne) somewhat fuller articulation of the "social vision of reality," each thinker regards the world as consisting of a community of interacting temporal events.

Moreover, Cobb, Teilhard, and Santmire all emphasize the reality of both continuity and discontinuity within the world of nature. Of the three authors, Santmire accents the element of discontinuity most heavily, while Cobb and Teilhard tend to stress the principle of continuity. But the latter two authors want to affirm the element of discontinuity within an evolutionary process characterized, overall, by continuity. In regard to nature, Cobb and Teilhard alike deny that there are any sharp gaps between the various levels or dimensions of the natural order. The inanimate and the animate, the living and the thinking, exist on a continuum. Each dimension of nature is rooted in previous and simpler levels and represents the fuller flowering of potentials that were intrinsic to the prior dimensions. Only by postulating the presence—in rudimentary form—of such realities as mind and freedom in even the simplest phenomena, Cobb and Teilhard agree, can we account for their appearance in grand form in the human phenomenon. Nevertheless, the fuller flowerings of the various potentials of nature represent, according to both Cobb and Teilhard, threshold-crossings.[1] Precisely because of their emphasis upon developmental continuities, the two process thinkers are led to recognize, at least in retrospect, critical turning points at which genuine novelties emerge: preeminently, life, thought, and society. Thus, the evolutionary process which is marked by continuity and the emergence of novelty is, intrinsically, also marked by a relative but real element of discontinuity.

In spite of the emphasis on organic interdependence and continuity, the thinking of neither Cobb nor Teilhard results in a simple monism in which the reality of the parts of the organic process is denied or even downplayed. Conversely, in spite of the emphasis upon the plurality of the structural components of nature, neither Cobb nor Teilhard arrives at a simple pluralism in which the unity of the whole and the continuity of its parts, are denied. But the one thinker, Cobb, does place a relatively greater stress on the plurality of nature, while the other, Teilhard, emphasizes somewhat more the unitary character of the world process.[2]

For both Cobb and Teilhard, every existent is a center of spontaneity and self-creativity which both inherits important elements from the past and contributes distinctively to the future. But in Cobb the emphasis on pluralism is developed more fully. Following Whitehead, Cobb begins with a multiplicity of entities whose individuality and integrity are forever preserved. Each actual entity represents a unique synthesis of past influences and "vocational" self-determinations: it is a novel unity arising out of a prior diversity and itself becoming part of a new plurality which in turn contributes to the constituting of still further novel occasions, and so on ad infinitum. Thus, like his philosophical mentor, Cobb views nature as an interconnected series of discrete events; and he accounts for the continuity in nature by this doctrine of the unending successiveness of individual units of process. There is, accordingly, in Cobb's view, no agency other than that of the multiplicity of actual entities (and groupings of actual entities), including God. With the possible exception of the divine being (whom Cobb treats, in a departure from Whitehead, as a route of occasions marked by personal order[3]), Cobb does not trace, or allow for, Teilhard's "temporal threads running back to infinity"; rather,

---

[1] Again, our representative of the Neo-Orthodox approach to the theology of nature tacitly agrees with Cobb and Teilhard on these points; but unlike the other authors, Santmire does nothing important with them.

[2] Cf. Barbour, "Teilhard's Process Metaphysics," 326ff.

[3] Whitehead regards God as the one everlasting actual entity. Cobb reinterprets this aspect of the Whiteheadian philosophy by attempting "to assimilate God more closely to the conception of a living person than to that of an actual entity." See *A Christian Natural Theology*, 188ff.

Cobb emphasizes a complex plurality of "threads" tying together every event with its immediate predecessors.[4] This relatively greater pluralism of Cobb's schema affects a variety of his conclusions.

Unlike Cobb, Teilhard combines an appreciation of the plurality of nature with a relatively greater emphasis upon the unitary character of the total system. "Everything forms a single whole," he says;[5] the world is an integral cosmic process. While, according to Teilhard, the world does not exist apart from the multiple, in an important sense the world process consists precisely of the overcoming of multiplicity. But put more exactly, what Teilhard speaks of as the nisus of the evolutionary process is not the obliteration of plurality as such; it is rather the organization of the many into more complex and unified wholes. And within this Teilhardian holism, the many are "fulfilled" precisely in and through, and not apart from, the wholes in which they participate. This in itself is not dissimilar to the vision of things which we find in Cobb. But in contradistinction to Cobb, Teilhard at times speaks of the entirety of cosmic history as if it is marked by "a unified structure not unlike that of a single Whiteheadian concrescence."[6] Thus, Teilhard projects "the convergence" and "involutive centration" of the universe. Whereas Cobb, following Whitehead, tends to set forth an account of the pattern of the development of all particular entities, Teilhard aims at the discovery and disclosure of the patterns ingredient to the whole history of the world. While there is a notable degree of overlap between the two efforts, they tend to result in distinguishable emphases.

Among the results of Teilhard's greater stress on the unitary character of nature and the world process is the fact that he is sometimes led to speak of the cosmos as a single agency. This is a tendency that bears importantly on the issue of the freedom of the individual components of the process, including especially the human "molecules," and on the question concerning the possibilities for the success and failure of the evolutionary process. Teilhard can speak of "evolution" and "the world" as possessed of the capacities of an agent, as in the following statement:

> To bring us into existence it [the world] has from the beginning juggled miraculously with too many improbabilities for there to be any risk whatever in committing ourselves further and following it right to the end. If it undertook the task, it is because it can finish it, following the same methods and with the same infallibility with which it began.[7]

---

[4]Cf. Barbour, "Teilhard's Process Metaphysics," 327.

[5]*The Divine Milieu*, 30.

[6]Barbour, "Teilhard's Process Metaphysics," 327.

[7]*The Phenomenon of Man*, 232.

The implications of Teilhard's position are many. One possible and highly significant implication is that, finally, the unitary agent operative in the cosmic process is not "the world" as such, or "evolution," but God. Teilhard's suggestions that the cosmos functions as a single agency may be a euphemistic affirmation of the agential character of the divine reality—whose intention for the world, expressed in the entirety of the cosmic process, constitutes its unity.

Two final points. Ingredient to the motifs indicated in summary fashion above is the perception of the world, or nature, as a complexifying process. Cobb and Teilhard agree that nature is possessed of a nisus towards increasing complexity and centricity. It is a nisus resultant from two factors. One is the way in which entities constitute themselves, or are constituted; this is the "structural" factor. In other words, there is within the entities collectively making up the world a tendency to move towards greater complexity and "centreity"—or at least, an openness to be drawn towards such a telos. This suggests the second factor: the action of God-Omega, the One Who Calls.

The complexifying character of the world is then, in turn, dependent upon the presence of a psychic component within each dimension. The capacity of the "natural" to be an "order" in which novelty occurs is, for both Cobb and Teilhard, explicable only if the various components of nature have the capacity to constitute themselves in response to the "vocational" lure proffered by another. Accordingly, Cobb and Teilhard agree that "nature" includes the psychical as well as the physical, the spiritual as well as the material.

Humankind's Place in Nature. Is human existence to be defined, then, over against or as participating in nature? Santmire's characteristically restrictive employment of the term "nature" allows him to affirm at once humankind's participation in and transcendence of the natural. But he purchases this advantage at the price of a somewhat impoverished understanding of "the natural order" as that is being disclosed to us by our best science and scientifically informed philosophies of nature. Cobb and Teilhard, in contrast, reflect what are perhaps the dominant currents in contemporary science and culture by giving priority to the comprehensive employment of the term "nature" as the name of the total system of (finite, creaturely?) reality. This results in Cobb's inclusion of humankind fully and, as we have suggested, rather undialectically within nature. The price of this move is to call in question the possibility of dealing adequately with the uniqueness and superiority of the human dimension as witnessed by humankind's capacity for reflection and self-reflexivity. Teilhard, however, stresses more heavily than Cobb the priority of the personal. As a result, he escapes some of the harsher consequences of Cobb's position.

Not only do Cobb and Teilhard include humankind within nature; they employ human existence as the key to the nature of nature. In this, they are characteristic of the pattern found in the newer forms of naturalism.[8] The reasons for this move seem to be several. Since humankind is an aspect of nature, it is at this one point—namely, our own existence—that we know nature best. Logically, then, human experience is the proper starting point for our attempt to know extra-human nature. With this starting point, the task becomes that of specifying how other entities and dimensions compare and contrast with that aspect of nature which we know best—and from within. Hence, starting with human experience enables us, second, to formulate some idea of the "within" of things. If we accept the continuity of all dimensions of nature, then we have a basis for postulating, and attempting to specify the nature of, the interiority of all entities. Such a move enables us to account, third, for the evolutionary emergence within nature of high orders of interiority and its related capacities. Thought and freedom cease to be anomalies within nature and become instead the key to that which is perceived to exist universally in rudimentary form. Precisely because all entities have interiority or a "within"—a postulate that arises out of the adoption of humankind as the key to the rest—the universal nisus towards greater complexity becomes intelligible. Fourth, then, the adoption of human experience as the key to nature makes possible the development of a coherent set of interpretive categories. This reminds us, fifth, that both Cobb and Teilhard want to overcome the last vestiges of dualism and that they attempt to do this by the development of a unitary ontology based on human existence. Cobb and Teilhard seek a way beyond the Cartesian bifurcation of mind and body; Teilhard rejects as well the dichotomy of spirit and matter. Neither the Neo-Naturalistic nor the Neo-Catholic thinker is content to reduce the one to the other. Rather, both find mind and body, spirit and matter, inseparably interwoven in human experience; and on the basis of this perception both develop a doctrine of the dipolar character of all existents.

God and Nature. Cobb and Teilhard extend their doctrines of dipolarity to the divine reality itself, the one explicitly and systematically, the other (we have argued) implicitly and brokenly. Like Cobb, Teilhard maintains that there is some type of reciprocal interaction between God and the

---

[8]See, e.g. C. F. Delaney, *Mind and Nature: A Study of the Naturalistic Philosophies of Cohen, Woodbridge and Sellars* (Notre Dame: University of Notre Dame Press, 1969).

world. Both thinkers regard traditional Christian theology, including the type represented by Santmire, as having rendered creation too arbitrary and the world somewhat "ontologically superfluous" to God. Accordingly, both call for the development of an understanding of God and an understanding of the world in which each—God and the world—finds completion in the other.

In order to achieve this, both Cobb and Teilhard are led to affirm that creation is a continuing activity of God, and, as such, that creation involves the production of new, more centered and complex realities out of a prior, simpler, multiplicity. Each man develops a metaphysics of "creative union" in which "creation" consists preeminently of the unification of the multiple. Moreover, in order to achieve a more intimate conjunction of the Creator and the created, both thinkers are involved in a redefinition, and restriction, of the power of the former, accompanied by a corresponding redefinition, and exaltation, of the (self-shaping) powers of the latter. This is to say that the view of creation—as ongoing complexifying unitive event—developed by both the Whiteheadian and the Catholic process theologians involves a modification of traditional ways of specifying the power of God and the powers of the world, and the relationship between the two. The modification consists in a reduction of the divine power (sheer omnipotence is denied, although less vigorously and thoroughly by Teilhard than by Cobb) and a redefinition of the same. (God creates and governs by persuasion and, for Teilhard, by sacramental enactment.) The modification consists, further, of an increase in the power(s) of creatures relative to the power of the Creator; for all creaturely existents are posited and shaped by the environing others—of which God is but one—and by themselves.[9]

Teilhard and Cobb appear to differ as to whether their understanding of creation as continuing unitive event, and the correlative understanding of God, entails the denial of the notion of "creation out of nothing." Cobb believes that the logic of his views of God and creation leads away from the idea of an initial act of origination. God has ontological priority in that neither order nor novelty exists apart from him, but the divine reality has no temporal priority. Teilhard, however, appears to affirm the traditional notion of *creatio ex nihilo*; but he identifies the primordial multiplicity (called into existence by an initial act of origination?) as little more than potential-for-being. In any case, his interest and his emphasis focus

---

[9]For Whitehead and Cobb, entities, both microscopic occasions and human beings, come into existence only in the process of experiencing, rather than existing first as subjects who then experience. This implies that entities are, in an important sense, self-positing as well as self-shaping.

upon the process of creative union rather than on the notion of primordial origination; and he leaves the issue of origination incompletely
worked out. As Alpha, God initiates; as Omega, God consummates. And
Teilhard's interests are in endings rather than in beginnings, for it is only
by realizing its telos that a thing becomes fully actual.

Whether or not Cobb and Teilhard allow for a primordial origination
"out of nothing"—an issue many, like Gilkey, have given over to the
scientific community, or have otherwise relegated to the barrel of
unanswerable questions—both process thinkers appear to affirm salient
features of what we have called "the religious intent" of the doctrine of
creation out of nothing. That is, both affirm (along with our Neo-
Reformation theologian of nature) that God is the ultimate source of the
order and novelty found in the world. Both affirm the ontological and
axiological priority of the divine reality, a distinction between the Creator
and the created, a relatedness of the Creator and the creation, the goodness of creation, and the like. Some of these motifs are, in fact, as we have
seen in Part One, affirmed more successfully and powerfully by the
process theologians than by those following different paths. Yet, other
aspects of "the religious intent" of the classical doctrine of creation are
handled less successfully. Some of these issues we shall look at in more
detail in the next chapter as we examine models of the God—world
relationship. But for now we should note that the transcendence of God
as well as his "personal" character, including his freedom, are only
imperfectly affirmed by process theologians. Moreover, as we have seen,
process theology, especially in its Whiteheadian mode, has difficulty
affirming the creaturely transcendence and uniqueness of humankind.
The process perspective has, in short, for all its emphasis upon human
existence, difficulty with the category of the personal. This is a difficulty,
which derives from what is a source of several of its strengths: its preference for the organic and the "natural." But it is a difficulty that is in
tension with significant aspects of the classical doctrine of creation as well
as other of the best insights of Christian thinkers through the ages.

John Cobb's denial of the notion of an initial origination raises certain
problems. The problems are, it would seem, somewhat more pressing for
a thinker whose orientation is, by his own designation, a form of ontological realism. In brief, Cobb leaves us with the issue that William Temple
identified early on as the crux of the problems ingredient to the Whiteheadian philosophy.[10] Like his chief mentor, Cobb explains the reality and
character of the world by reference to God; and he explains the reality and

---

[10]Temple, *Nature, Man and God*, 260.

character of God by reference to the world. But he leaves the whole—God and the world, both marked by eternality—unexplained.

Teilhard's tacit acknowledgment of the notion of an initial originating act on the part of God allows him to escape Cobb's problem, but he thereby makes himself responsible for the issues ingredient to the notion of origination "out of nothing" that have plagued theologies of creation from Augustine onwards.[11] Teilhard is at the same time implicated in the difficulties, as well as the benefits, of a redefinition of creation as a continuing process. And he aggravates his problems by failing to clarify quite fully how God acts in the order of nature. Teilhard claims that God "makes things make themselves." In a creation of an evolutionary type "the only rational ways in which we can conceive the Creator's action on his works are those which oblige us to regard the introduction into things of the divine energy as *being* (from the experiential point of view) *imperceptible.*"[12] This means that

> Where God is operating it is always possible for us (by remaining at a certain level) to see only the *work of nature.* . . . The First Cause is not involved in effects; it acts upon individual *natures* and on the movement of *the whole.* Properly speaking, God *does not make*: He *makes things make themselves.* That is why there is no breach or cleavage at the point at which he enters. The network of determinisms remains intact—the harmony of organic developments continues without discord. And yet the Master has entered into his own.[13]

Such statements as these suggest that, for Teilhard, the evolutionary process is in principle explicable in terms of natural causes alone and that God's role consists of establishing and preserving the conditions and parameters of natural evolution. In one sense, these passages suggest that Teilhard tends towards the scholastic doctrine that God as First Cause operates through the lawful workings of secondary causes.

But Teilhard goes further.

> Without any doubt, there lies hidden beneath the ascending movement of life, the continuous action of a being who raises up the universe from within. Beneath the uninterruted operation of secondary causes, there is produced (in many miracles) an exceptional expansion of natures, much greater than could result from the normal functioning of created factors and stimuli.

---

[11]See, e.g., the conversation between Antony Flew and D. M. MacKinnon entitled "Creation" in *New Essays in Philosophical Theology*, ed. Antony Flew and Alasdair MacIntyre (New York: Macmillan Company, 1964; first published 1955), 170ff.

[12]"Note on the Modes of Divine Action in the Universe" (1920), *Christianity and Evolution*, 25-26.

[13]Ibid., 27-28.

Considered objectively, material facts *have in them something of the Divine.*[14]

Teilhard speaks of the divine involvement in nature as including the animating, vivifying, controlling, and leading of the world to fulfillment.[15] He invokes God to explain phenomena which are otherwise mysterious: "In Omega we have in the first place the principle we needed to explain both the persistent march of things toward greater consciousness, and the paradoxical solidity of what is most fragile."[16] The divine action, thus, appears to involve more than that which is attributable to its working through secondary causative factors alone. As Barbour notes:

God's action is not simply that of an Aristotelian "final cause" which is built into the functioning of all beings as they follow their inherent natures. Teilhard seems to believe that the "within" is a more effective vehicle of divine influence than the "without," *but he does not clarify the modes of causality involved.*[17]

We are confronted here with difficulties in the Teilhardian vision which suggest that the Jesuit may have been "groping" for an alternative beyond both classical Thomism and his own professed process perspective. Taken together, his affirmations, and silences, concerning the mode(s) of the divine action in the world and his claims about the cosmic agency of "evolution" give evidence that he was concerned to identify a conception of agency which was not clarified along either Thomistic or processive lines. He may, in other words, have been working with an inchoately developed conception of God as Agent, a conception that properly focuses not upon the issue of causality but upon the category of intentionality. If this is allowed, certain of the otherwise puzzling aspects of Teilhard's treatment of the divine action in the world become somewhat clearer.

We have noted repeatedly that, like other Neo-Orthodox theologians, Santmire makes claims about the divine workings in nature/creation. But Santmire, again like others who travel his theological path, makes essentially no effort to clarify the modes of the divine action in the world, thereby leaving his claims about the divine operations in the limbo of unintelligibility. Teilhard does make an effort to render thinkable his claims; but the result is an unclear and somewhat unstable amalgam of classical Thomistic, contemporary processive insights, and "gropings"

---

[14]Ibid., 29.

[15]Cf. Barbour, "Teilhard's Process Metaphysics," 340.

[16]*The Phenomenon of Man*, 271.

[17]Barbour, "Teilhard's Process Metaphysics," 340. Emphasis added.

after a new conception of agency. Cobb alone, of the theologians we have examined, proffers a fully developed and coherent explanation of the mode of God's actions in the world of nature, including (for Cobb) humankind. It is a conceptuality borrowed from Whitehead, and it turns on the postulate of the psychic character of all reality. We have examined it at length in chapter 3, and we shall return to it in chapter 6. Ian Barbour sums it up succinctly:

> Whitehead . . . does assign to his equivalent of the "within" the crucial role in God's action of the world. He gives a detailed analysis of causation which includes the influence of past causes, present initiative, and divine purpose in the coming-to-be of each event. Briefly stated, every new event is in part the product of the *efficient causation* of previous events, which in large measure—though never completely—determine it. There is always an element of *self-causation* or self-creation as an entity appropriates and responds to its past in its own way. In the creative selection from among alternatives in terms of goals and aims, there is *final causation.* By structuring these potentialities, God is the ground of both order and novelty, but the final decision is always made by the entity itself; at the human level this means that man is free to reject the ideals which God holds up to him. Whitehead [and through him, Cobb] thus works out in much greater detail than Teilhard a set of categories which allow for lawfulness, spontaneity, and divine influence in the "continuous creation" of the world.[18]

The reconsideration, which we find going on in Cobb and Teilhard, of the nature of the divine power and of the modes of the divine action has resulted in some fresh insights into the problems of evil and theodicy. Herein lie some of the happier results of the theological explorations of process thinkers, Whiteheadian and otherwise. Such theologians have shown that a world in evolution and a world without certain forms of evil (especially disorder) are contradictory concepts. Accordingly, they have been able to maintain at one and the same time that evil is real and extensive but the world is good, that God is responsible for the world as it is but he is not culpable for the evil found therein. Our Neo-Reformation pathfinder has caught glimpses of some of these same conclusions; but, we have argued, he and others who travel his path lack the warranting conceptuality to substantiate their claims about what they have seen from afar.

We began this section by claiming that both Teilhard and Cobb have a doctrine of the divine dipolarity. In concluding our summary of conclusions regarding God and nature, we return to a brief further consideration of this claim.

We have seen, in chapter 4, that Teilhard speaks of both "trinitization" and "pleromization." While claiming that creation adds nothing

---

[18]Ibid., 340-41.

essential to God, he contends also that God completes himself in some sense by the unification of the multiple. Such contentions would seem to entail a revision of the classical Catholic perception of the relationship between divine eternality and worldly temporality.

Cobb works out the revision of the understanding of God implied by the processive understanding of creation much more fully and systematically than Teilhard. But the rudiments of the Whiteheadian/Hartshornean/Cobbian solution are present in the Catholic thinker. Teilhard's Alpha and his notion of trinitization parallel the Cobbian doctrine of the Primordial Nature of God. Teilhard's Omega and his notion of pleromization parallel the Cobbian doctrine of the Consequent Nature of God: they refer to his "concrete actuality," what he is in consequence of that which happens in the complexifying temporal process, or "nature." Both thinkers agree, in contrast to the Neo-Reformation alternative, that taking seriously the nature of nature (as that is disclosed by recent science) and the biblical perception of God as agape leads to a reconsideration, and a modification, of the classical understanding of God. This revisioning has profound axiological consequences.

Christ and the Cosmos. While the three representatives of the theological paths we have followed are all ultimately theocentric, their understandings of God are shaped importantly by Jesus Christ. All our pathfinders attempt either explicitly (Santmire and Teilhard) or implicitly (Cobb) to tie together creation and redemption. Two (Cobb implicitly; Teilhard explicitly) treat Christ as the agent of creation as well as the agent of redemption. All agree, however, that redemption represents the completion of creation.

Taking Christ as "the key to the new theological horizon," our Neo-Reformation pathfinder treats Christ and his work with respect to the material-vital aspect of creation in terms of the themes of "restoration" and "foretaste." Christ is the mediator "who restores the disrupted present creation" and "who represents and realizes the coming of the new creation in the midst of the present creation."[19] Rejecting the notion of the "cosmic fall" as extra-biblical, Santmire interprets the restorative work of Christ as that of making possible the development of a proper (wondering, caretaking, et cetera, rather than exploitatively manipulative) relationship between humankind and otherkind, as well as among human beings themselves. Since "the disruption lies in man's relation to nature, not in nature itself," the coming of Christ is to be interpreted as "affecting the man-nature relationship, *not* the whole of nature directly." "This," we

---

[19]*Brother Earth*, 163.

are told, "is the proper scope for a biblically oriented 'cosmic christology.'
"[20] On the basis of the new relationship with nature made possible by the
appearance of "the creative rule of God" in "the rule of Christ,"[21] creation
(including "nature," the material-vital aspect of creation) is being completed through the agency of responsive and responsible men and women:
creation is being made into "something richer than it [has] ever been
before."[22]

For John Cobb, Christ is the fullest incarnation of the Logos or
Primordial Nature of God (Cobb identifies the two); and the Logos is
depicted as working universally for the "creative transformation" of all
creatures.[23] Moreover, although Cobb does not talk revelation language
very extensively, Christ provides him with the chief clue to the nature of
God.[24] Following his chief philosophical mentor, Cobb takes his theological starting point from the Galilean origin of Christianity: love, the love
"revealed" in the man of Galilee is the key to the divine nature. Furthermore, in him the Christian "vision of reality" is disclosed—the precognitive vision which underlies, shapes, and finds expression in Cobb's
theology of nature.

Now, in saying these things we are going beyond what Cobb makes
explicit. He does not himself closely relate his Christology and his theology of nature. This omission is related, clearly, to his failure to clarify the
relationship between his natural theology and his "theology proper." But
Cobb's Christology does have important bearing for his theology of
nature, the kind of bearing that we have indicated. And it is regrettable
that Cobb has not himself related the two more forthrightly.

---

[20]Ibid., 171.

[21]Ibid., 172.

[22]Ibid., 174.

[23]This term, the key term in Cobb's soteriological theory, is evidently derived primarily
from Wieman. The notion of "creative transformation" does not have the explicit Christological bearing in Wieman that it does in Cobb, but it is crucial to the thinking of the older
as well as the younger process theologian. See Henry N. Wieman, *The Source of Human
Good* (Carbondale IL: Southern Illinois University Press, 1946).

[24]The term "revelation" appears only very occasionally in the writings of Cobb
himself. His student and colleague, David Griffin, has, however, dealt extensively with the
problem of revelation in his book, *A Process Christology* (Philadelphia: Westminster
Press, 1973). Because of the close association between the two process thinkers and the
heavy employment of Cobbian ideas and categories by Griffin, we may safely assume that
Griffin's book represents the gist of Cobb's thinking regarding revelation. If so, the chief
revelatory significance of Jesus Christ, as Cobb sees it, lies in the fact that in Jesus a unique
"vision of reality" was disclosed and became efficacious. This (precognitive) vision
provides the foundations, the context, and the inspiration for subsequent Christian
theologizing.

For the other process pathfinder, however, the theology of nature is preeminently a Christological problem. We do not have to search hard for the lines that tie the two together in Teilhard's thinking, as we do in Cobb's; for in the perspective of the Catholic seer, Christ and the cosmos are inseparable. Each presupposes and completes the other. An interpretation of the person and work of Christ and a theology of nature require each the other.

Teilhard's "cosmic Christology" is rooted in his theory of a "cosmic fall." Unlike Santmire, Teilhard argues that Christ's restorative and completive work involve immediately the whole of creation, human and extra-human alike. Teilhard's universalizing of Christ and his universalizing of "the fall" are coimplicating theological trends.

Teilhard's understanding of the "cosmic Christ" involves the coalescence of his "hyperphysical" vision of the world—as marked by organic interdependence, especially—and his biblical vision of Christ as central, in some sense, to creation. Salvation consists of the fulfilling of the potentialities of the world, and God in Christ does what must be done to make the dream of a fulfilled world a reality. He meets and conquers evil in all its aspects; thereby, he directs the world in its human and extra-human dimensions alike along the ascensional path towards the summit of the personal or spirit—that is, towards Omega. In this fashion, the corporate salvation of the cosmos is integrated, by Teilhard, with the activity of continuing creation. Creation, incarnation, and redemption are tied together by a metaphysical theory (of creative union) that is Christologically centered and biblically grounded. The relationship between Christ and the cosmos, then, is "organic" and internal rather than merely "juridical" and extrinsic. Through the incarnation God participates in matter and universal cosmic history. And by the extension of the incarnation in the Church and the Eucharist—and through them into the whole world of men and matter—God works for the sacramental transformation, or "Christification," of all creation.

CONCLUSIONS AXIOLOGICAL AND ETHICAL

Each of the paths we have followed leads to a fresh valuational perspective on nature; and the theories of value found along each path have, in turn, ethical implications. Each of our pathfinders enlarges our perceptions and enriches our valuations and, as a result, places upon us imperatives for action. But as the perceptions vary, so do the modes of valuing, although from this diversity there follows a great deal of consensus about what is incumbent upon us in our relations with the subhuman order of creation.

Santmire's theory of value derives from his enlargement of the socio-political imagery of the Kingdom of God. Others have noted that the idea of the divine Kingdom entails realm as well as rule.[25] But Santmire explores, more fully than anyone else has done, the consequences of emphasizing the divine realm equally with the divine rule. This results in his claims that nature and man are "fellow citizens," even "brothers," within the divine Kingdom and that God has a history of interaction with and concern for both the human and extra human dimensions of creation. This perspective provides the foundations by which human delight in, and concern for, the subhuman order is theologically legitimated. The divine delight in nature establishes the worth of nature (Santmire improperly identifies this as intrinsic value) and warrants human delight in the extra human object of the divine valuing. From this perspective follows an ethic of responsible stewardship: man is called to exercise a care-taking role with respect to nature, our fellow citizen within the Kingdom of God.

Cobb's theory of value results from his "ecological" vision of reality. It is rooted directly in his processive-organic imagery. The world process is a complex concatenation of experiencing entities, each of which is valuable—intrinsically—to the degree that it feels. Moreover, each entity is valuable because it contributes to larger entities (the organism, the entire biotic community) and to the whole system of the world-in-the-making, the totality of which is, as it were, of supreme value. Diversity, therefore, is inherently valuable, because an assortment of mutually enriching enjoyments is greater or "richer" than a single strand of experience, taken alone, could possibly be. Thus, ultimately the various experiencing entities, human and subhuman alike, that constitute the world process/organism are valuable because they all—individually and collectively—contribute to the enrichment of the divine life, the one non-perishing instance of enjoyment.

From this perspective, too, human responsibility is accented. But in the Cobbian context something other than, and beyond, responsible stewardship is called for. We are called to be responsible participants in the divine creative process. It is the peculiar prerogative of the human components of nature willingly to join with God in the promotion of rich experience or enjoyment, both creaturely and divine. Thus, we are under an imperative to care not only for our own kind but for all kind, since the

---

[25]Cf. Tillich, *Systematic Theology*, 3:358.

total value realized (both creaturely and divine) is greater in a system marked by a high degree of diversity than in a more uniform system.

We have seen that, as engaging as this vision is, it entails certain problems. Two in particular stand out. One issue concerns whether Cobb has so thoroughly immersed human existence in nature as to undercut the possibility of the responsible (moral) mode of participation in the creative process for which he calls. The other issue concerns the question of whether the Cobbian attribution of intrinsic value to the subhuman order is so deeply dependent upon the peculiarities of the Whiteheadian conceptuality that, apart from some of the more problematical aspects of that conceptuality, the notion of intrinsic value simply collapses.

Teilhard's theory of value results from his ecological vision of reality combined with his sacramental theory of the relationship between God and the world. Much of the Cobbian vision is paralleled in the Teilhardian. But Teilhard adds the notion that God is expressing himself—sacramentally—in the entities and processes of the world, human and extra-human alike, in a way not really allowed for by either Santmire or Cobb. Teilhard's perspective suggests the possibility of an alternative theory of the value of worldly actualities that was not expressly developed by Teilhard himself. In this view, the world and the various aspects thereof could be reckoned valuable because through it/them the divine intention is realizing itself. The world process, in its various facets, would thus be valuable in much the same fashion that the body of a person shares in the value actualized through the actions of a finite agent.

In any case, Teilhard parallels Cobb in treating human beings as the evolutionary emergents who have been called to responsible participation in the evolutionary process. But Teilhard's more dialectical mode of placing humanity in, and above, the rest of nature allows him to ground the human vocation of "building the earth" more adequately than Cobb. Moreover, by means of his high Christology and his sacramental theory, Teilhard (re-)invests both human and subhuman existence with sacredness; he suggests that through the agency of Christ (ultimately) and of humankind, especially the faithful (proximately), all creation is being raised to participation in the final divine fulfillment. To be sure, a host of issues surround both Teilhard's cosmic Christology and his sacramental theory. But it is possible to find in his elaborate process of remythologizing an expression of the insight that all creation participates in the actualizing of the divine intentions, and that human agency, informed by Christ, plays a pivotal role in the realization of the divine purposes for both human and subhuman participants in the cosmic adventure.

CHAPTER 6

"METATHEOLOGY" AND THE THEOLOGY OF NATURE

The "new way forward" for which we seek-the alternative path, or paths,-must be rooted in our contemporary cultural and theological situation. Each of the pathfinders we have followed, each of the trails we have traveled, leads us to a vision of something vital if we are to recover the capacity to view nature as the theater of divine grace and glory. On one path we are led to perceive nature as a fellow citizen within the Kingdom of God. On the second path we are led to perceive our fellow citizen as genuinely lovable and truly loved. What is more, on this path we are led to see nature as an arena of divine actions. On the third path we are led to see those actions in nature as actions which express— sacramentally—who God is. None of these visions can be lost if we are to perceive nature as the theater of God's glory. But all must become elements of a larger vision. How is this to occur?

As we examined the various paths we have traveled, we have had occasion to note that each has been hewn around a major mountain, as it were, or series of mountains. That is, each path is tied to a particular feature of the landscape: a particular "model," or set of models, of the God-world relationship.[1] The advantages as well as the limitations of each path are the function of the model to which it is bound. If we move away from the distinguishing model(s) we get onto a different trail with different advantages and limitations. This suggests that the immediate way forward lies in a critical scrutiny of the various models available to and/or operative within the theology of nature. And it is to this task—

---

[1] As shall be shown in the pages that follow, this is the case even though the theologians we have analyzed in detail were not all equally self-consciously engaged in "model-building." In fact, John Cobb alone of those we have discussed can be said to have executed his theological program in something approaching full awareness that he was developing a theological thought experiment anchored in a particular model of the God-world relationship, the consequences and ramifications of which he was determined to explore fully.

which we may denominate the "metatheological" task—that we now turn.

METAPHORS, MODELS, AND PARADIGMS

In the preceding pages we have spoken often of images and metaphors and occasionally of models and myths. Now we must seek to distinguish the functions of the three types of imagery—metaphor, model, and myth—and to inquire about the relationship of diverse models within a particular paradigm tradition.

Metaphors, models, and myths are all forms of analogy; or perhaps better, they are rooted in analogies. Metaphors and models involve both the familiar and the novel. They propose analogies between the ordinary context of a word or idea and the new context(s) into which it is introduced. Some, but only some, of the usual connotations of the term or idea are transferred. The transferred associations function as a "screen" through which the new subject is perceived; certain of its features are highlighted while others are selected out or deemphasized. Thus the subject is viewed in a novel fashion, and fresh attitudes towards it are evoked. Metaphors, accordingly, alter perceptions even while they help us order them.[2]

For this reason, metaphors are not literally true. Yet they are not mere fictions: they suggest meaningful analogies between the subjects they compare. They further tend to be open-ended, inviting the discovery of additional similarities. They are dynamic, both expressing and evoking attitudes and perceptions. Embodied within them is at least "a shy ontological claim."[3]

A great many religious symbols are metaphors based on analogies drawn from a variety of types of experience. The symbolism of height and ascent suggests achievement and excellence; it is rooted in the experienced difficulty of physical movement upwards as well as in the association with power (the elevated thrones of kings). Accordingly, symbols of height are employed to suggest or specify the preeminence of deity: Yahweh is the Most High. The Lord is like an exalted King; and those who would draw nigh unto him must ascend the holy mountain, or its moral equivalent.

---

[2]Max Black, *Models and Metaphors* (Ithaca NY: Cornell University Press, 1962), chs. 3 and 13.

[3]Barbour, *Myths, Models and Paradigms*, 14, citing Philip Wheelwright, *Metaphor and Reality* (Bloomington: Indiana University Press, 1962), 162.

Now metaphors sometimes "pass over" into models.[4] Like metaphors, models are analogical forms which attempt to explicate the character of the unfamiliar in terms of the character of the familiar. Like metaphors, too, models are selective; they highlight certain features and deemphasize others. They suggest ways of seeing, that is, they alter and direct perception. They express and evoke attitudes, reflect and shape behavior, interpret experience, and open up fresh possibilities for experience and understanding. Like metaphors, models make ontological claims—usually less "shy" than those made by metaphors.

The difference between metaphors and models lies in the character and scope of their employment—and in the intention that informs their development. "Metaphors are employed only momentarily and . . . only in a limited range of contexts, but models are more fully elaborated and serve as wider interpretive schemes in many contexts."[5] That is, unlike metaphors, models are designed to fit a wider range of circumstances (data) than metaphors; and models are employed in a more sustained and systematic fashion. Moreover, as this suggests, models are generally developed with a great deal more self-conscious intent than metaphors; this is reflected in such phrases as "model-building." We "construct" models—more or less deliberately—and employ them to express, illuminate, and expand our attitudes, experiences, and perceptions as fully as possible.

Models represent only one facet of that matrix of experience we call "religious." But since religion involves both thought and action, as well as attitudes, models are important in religion; for they arise out of, and shape, all dimensions of religious life.

Models are met in religion, however, not directly and as such—except in treatises in systematic theology or the sociology of religion and the like. In concrete religious life models are embedded in and borne by myths and their correlative rituals. Or, to put the point in a fashion that allows for the element of conscious intent in the development of models, models are suggested by the modes of perception embodied in and transmitted by myth(s). Says Barbour:

---

[4]Max Black has suggested that scientific models are systematically developed metaphors. See *Models and Metaphors*, 237.

[5]Barbour, *Myths, Models and Paradigms*, 16. For a fuller discussion of the character and status of models, both scientific and religious, see Barbour; also the following works: Black, *Models and Metaphors*, Kaufman, *An Essay on Theological Method*, Stephen C. Pepper, *World Hypotheses*, (Berkeley: University of California Press, 1966; first published, 1942), and Ian Ramsey, *Models and Mystery* (London: Oxford University Press, 1964).

> A model represents the enduring structural components which myths drama-
> tize in narrative form. One model may be common to many myths. A model
> is relatively static and lacks the imaginative richness and dramatic power
> which make a myth memorable; men will always express their understanding
> of the meaning of life by telling stories and enacting them in rituals. Models
> result from reflection on the living myths which communities transmit.[6]

Models, then, are distinctive results of the communities that produce
them. They reflect the peculiar ways of interpreting and valuing that
constitute the very essence of particular communities. This is the case for
both scientific and religious/theological models. They arise within and
inform particular "paradigm traditions" (Kuhn), that is, traditions that
involve distinctive ways of perceiving and, in religion, of valuing. A
variety of models, each directed towards the same object (human existence, the world, divine reality), may exist alongside of one another—
competing with and/or complementing each the other. But each model
will express, to a greater or lesser extent, perceptions and valuations
ingredient to, or compatible with, the paradigm tradition.

MAJOR MODELS OF GOD AND THE GOD-WORLD RELATIONSHIP

Models that originate within and express the Christian paradigm are
predominantly personal. They are, thus, also dynamic in character. For
the One with whom we have to do is One who is active in the processes of
creation and redemption.

Several models of the God-world relationship have been developed
and employed within the Christian tradition. Some of them are highly
anthropomorphic; others, more abstract. We shall attend to five: the
deistic, the dialogic, the monarchical, the processive-organic, and the
agential.[7]

---

[6]*Myths, Models and Paradigms*, 27. Some, e.g., Robert P. Scharlemann, maintain
that the construction and employment of models represent "a counterpart in critical
consciousness to myth-telling in mythical consciousness." See Scharlemann's essay
"Models in a Theology of Nature" in David Griffin ed., *Philosophy of Religion and
Theology: 1971* (Chambersburg PA: American Academy of Religion, 1971), 151.

[7]Barbour also discusses these five models (*Myths, Models and Paradigms*, ch. 8). But,
while my treatment is informed by his, my discussion goes beyond and departs from
Barbour's in numerous particulars.

Several other models can appropriately be considered sub-models of these five. The
notion of First Cause, for example, is part and parcel of the deistic model. The understanding of God as the One is ingredient to the monarchical and the agential models, and
possibly others. The idea of Lord is common to several. These all deserve attention in their
own terms; but the five selected for especial attention in this chapter are broad or
"inclusive" models, all of which function importantly in contemporary theological
discussion.

The Deistic Model. The deistic model of the relationship obtaining between God and the world seems to be that presupposed to a greater or lesser extent by several theologians of the last generation. Oftentimes the deistic model is combined, not altogether consistently, with another of a very different character, the dialogic model. In the deistic model, which is the product of early modern science and scientifically informed philosophies, the relation between God and the world is seen as analogous to the relationship between a clockmaker and his clock. The world is reckoned to be a complex machine whose workings are governed by laws built into it. The world—machine is, once created, autonomous and self-sufficient. God is understood, on this model, as essentially a cosmic inventor-mechanic who expresses his benovolence in the making of a world-machine whose workings are reliably efficient. God's providential concern and care are expressed by the overall design and efficiency of his handiwork. God is thus understood as relatively inactive after an initial burst of creative insight and action.

This model has the advantage of sharply defining the character of both natural and divine reality and the relation obtaining between them. But the gain is purchased at the price of a simplistic understanding of both "nature" (here, the world) and God. Post-Newtonian science suggests, as do Scripture and the Christian paradigm tradition, that nature is far more wonder-ful than the mechanistic view of nature characteristic of deism allows. Moreover, the inventor-mechanic is hardly an adequate object of worship or a fitting companion to persons engaged in the human historical drama; that is, the clockmaker God is not really religiously available. He stands at considerable distance from the dominant understanding of God found in the Bible and the Christian tradition.

Thus, the model of God and the God-world relationship characteristic of deism is not really compatible with the distinctive ways of perceiving and valuing found within the (Judeo-)Christian paradigm. Although the model arose within this tradition, its failure to deal adequately with the element of the personal in divine and human being, and its reductionistic treatment of the subhuman created order, relegate it to the fringes of that which is allowable within its parenting paradigm tradition. It appears as a prodigal for which there can be permanent homecoming.

The Dialogic Model. Even those theologians, such as Bultmann, who have attempted to define a place for the deistic model within the Christian orb, have recognized—implicitly—its alien character; for they have often wedded it to another, very different model of God and the world, as if to compensate. With certain exceptions, the dialogic model tends to be strong, and weak, at precisely the opposite points as the deistic.

In the dialogic model the relation between God and the "world" (here, human beings) is analogous to the relation between one person and another person. It is an "I-Thou" relationship. In contrast to the basically impersonal character of the deistic model, the dialogic model is interpersonal. As such, it is more faithful to both Scripture and tradition; and the widespread employment of it in recent times represents, in part (as in Bultmann), an attempt to provide a corrective to the omissions and distortions of deism. Whereas the deistic model demotes the elements of personal relations—love, forgiveness, reciprocity, freedom, responsibility, and the like—to a subordinate status at best, the dialogic model vigorously asserts the priority of the personal. This model is particularly apt at expressing the Christian sense of the covenantal character of divine-human and human-human relations. It provides a means of articulating profound insights into the experience of sin, guilt, forgiveness, and reconciliation—insights that lie at the heart of the Christian paradigm. The strengths, in short, of the dialogic model consist of its capacity to depict God and humanity in relation and to accent the uniqueness of human being as being-in-relation.

But ingredient to its strengths are its major liabilities. The dialogic model involves a separation of human and subhuman "nature." Insofar as nature is something other than a machine (for thinkers like Bultmann who wed the deistic and dialogic models), it is merely a stage for the human historical drama. Nature and humanity are set over against each other. This thoroughgoing separation is in tension with the best insights of science, Scripture, and Christian tradition. Moreover, the existentialists' exclusive emphasis upon interiority and interpersonal relations leaves extra-human nature unrelated to God and deprived of enduring significance. Again, then, the dialogical model is in tension with the Christian paradigm, which it reflects so faithfully in other respects; for, in Scripture and the tradition at its best, God's cause is perceived as the cause of being as such rather than simply, or exclusively, human being. Nature is understood to be involved in the drama of creation-redemption and valued more highly by God than the imagery of the stage allows.

Thus, the first two models of God and the God-world relationship which have claimed our attention deal with the relationship in a one-sided fashion. The deistic model focuses on God and "nature," ambiguously placing human existence within the "world." If human existence is defined as part of nature while the latter is understood as a machine, human existence is radically distorted: freedom is subordinated to the lawfulness of the world-machine. If the peculiarities of human existence are affirmed (as they are, for example, in Galileo), humankind, like God, radically transcends the extra-human aspects of the world; and the relations between human and extra-human finite existents are left poorly defined. The dialogic model focuses on God and human existence, ambiguously placing "nature" within the world. In both models an aspect of the world of finite existents (collectively, either "nature" or humanity), is dealt with reductionistically. The one model really needs to be supplemented, as in Bultmann, by the other.

The remaining models to which we shall attend attempt to specify the relationship obtaining between God and the world, with the "world" being understood in each case inclusively. That is, the monarchical, the processive—organic, and the agential models are all designed to deal with the relationship between God and nature-humanity, rather than specifying simply the relations obtaining between God and one aspect of the polar elements of the "world" taken separately. We shall suggest, accordingly, that that which is valid in the first models examined can be subsumed within one or more of the other three. That is, the deistic and, especially, the dialogic models are really better considered "sub-models" within the monarchical, processive-organic, and agential models.

The Monarchical Model. In the monarchical model the relation between God and the world is seen as analogous to the relationship obtaining between a king and his subjects. Within the Christian paradigm tradition, including the Scriptures, a variety of personalistic images have been employed to express the perception that, as Niebuhr puts it, "the one God who is Being is an 'I,' or like an 'I,' who is faithful as only selves are faithful."[8] The metaphors of father (parent), judge, shepherd, husband, and the like are all employed to depict the personal character of the divine reality. But the image which has been most elaborately developed is the socio-political metaphor of the king. This metaphor, in fact, has been developed with sufficient deliberateness, precision, and comprehensiveness to merit the recognition that it has "passed over" to the status of a model. As Barbour notes:

> The *monarchial model* of God as King was developed systematically, both in Jewish thought (God as Lord and King of the Universe), in medieval Christian thought (with its emphasis on divine omnipotence) and in the Reformation (especially in Calvin's insistence of God's sovereignty). In the portrayal of God's relation to the world, the dominant western historical model has been that of the absolute monarch ruling over his kingdom.[9]

During the history of Christian reflection, the biblical notion of the mighty "acts of God" was expressed and elaborated in the classical

---

[8] *Radical Monotheism and Western Culture*, 45.

[9] *Myths, Models, and Paradigms*, 156.

doctrine of the divine omnipotence or sovereignty. The mighty Suzerain was perceived as governing all things in accordance with his unconditioned freedom and incomparable wisdom. His sovereignty was interpreted as including his "foreknowing" and "predestining" activities. The divine King was understood as controlling *all* events either directly (primary causality) or indirectly (through "secondary" or "natural" causality).

This classical perception has important religious/theological consequences, both positive and negative. The "Godness of God" is affirmed in vigorous terms. God is the Most High, the All-Ruler, the King of kings and Lord of lords. As such, he is eminently worthful. He is the appropriate object of worship. The religious experiences of awe, reverence, holiness, and the like are both evoked and expressed by this way of perceiving the divine reality. Moreover, life is appropriately interpreted as eminently meaningful. The citizen of the Kingdom of God is at once the object of the divine valuing and called to meaningful vocation; membership in the divine Kingdom entails service to the cosmic Suzerain. Meaningful life is defined by covenantal relations with the King and his subjects. Reality can be trusted, for it is under the aegis of all-controlling power which is benevolent in character. The King is perceived as compassionate Father; thus the monarchical imagery is modified by employment of parental and other types of iconography, such as the notion of the shepherd.

The liabilities of the monarchical model are associated with the failure thus to refine it. The emphasis upon the majesty, holiness, and power of the divine King and Legislator, when unqualified by the sensibilities expressed in parental or pastoral imagery, leads to a sense of the divine reality as the "alien other," as in the young Luther. The monarchical model of God functions as the perceptual ground of moral heteronomy, with the observance of the stipulations of the Suzerain becoming the all-consuming concern. Such a way of perceiving leads to the inhibiting of human growth and makes God, as King, religiously unavailable. It is, as Luther saw, impossible to love such a Monarch-Legislator. Thus, if the monarchical model is not qualified by another, the liberating sense of divine preeminence and worthfulness passes into an oppressive sense of the divine reality as something inimical and alien (heteronomy), and it is appropriately opposed in the name of human worth (autonomy).

This valuation problem is closely linked to other consequences often entailed in the employment of the monarchical model. The understanding of God as all-controlling power makes an affirmation of creaturely freedom difficult. Moreover, it aggravates the problem of accounting for the realities of evil and suffering in the world ruled by the divine King.

And, finally, it stands in tension with the notion of the lawfulness, and the spontaneity, of nature which recent science has clarified for us.

Now, the monarchical model is central to the Neo-Reformation theology of nature elaborated by Paul Santmire. While Santmire has not defined his project as that of model-building, he has explored the implications of kingdom imagery with sufficient deliberateness and detail to warrant the recognition that the *model* of a king and his subjects is central to his theological enterprise. As we have seen, Santmire associates familial imagery with the monarchical in a loosely defined fashion. Beyond that, we should now note that he employs the dialogic model within the framework of the overarching monarchical model: the discussion of I-Thou and I-Ens relations provides a sub-model that fills out and extends the dominant model. Moreover, Santmire flirts with, but does not develop, insights which are ingredient to the processive-organic model; and, in a similar fashion, he hints at, but does not systematically explore, the necessity of the agential model. For him, the monarchical model provides the foundation and framework for the theology of nature required for us to transcend our "dilemma with nature."

Santmire is heir to both the strengths and limitations of the monarchical model. To his credit, he has managed to develop the model in such a fashion as to avoid some of the less fortunate consequences of this type of imagery. He avoids, for example, any suggestion that God is the alien other and thus not religiously available to those who value their humanness. In fact, Santmire has adopted, refined, and extended the monarchical model in a very sensitive fashion. As we have seen, he has brought out significant but neglected valuational implications of the kingdom imagery for the divine "realm," the subhuman order of nature.

What Santmire has not succeeded in is the provision of a meaningful affirmation of how, and to what extent, God exercises his power in "ruling" and shaping his realm. That, is Santmire has not specified very clearly how God, the divine King, *acts* on and in his created realm. Santmire's results suggest that the monarchical model, for all its merits, is finally inadequate when taken alone.

That which theologies based on the monarchical model fail to accomplish is that which theologies which center in the processive-organic and agential models are designed to supply: namely, some clarification of the meaning of the action of God.

The Processive-Organic Model. The process or, more accurately, processive-organic model, suggests that the relation obtaining between God and the world is analogous to the relationship between an individual and a community, with "community" being understood as marked by intense or "organic" interrelatedness. On this model, reality is "social" in character: it consists of a society of interacting beings, one of which is preeminent but not "absolute," except in certain carefully defined senses. Moreover, within this model selfhood ("the percipient event") is taken as the key to reality as a whole. Even "organism" is defined in terms of it. Within the context for thought provided by the agential model, the relation between God and the world is perceived to be analogous to the relationship between an agent and his actions. Hence, for both the organic and the agential models human selfhood is taken as, in some sense, the key to the nature of God and of the God-world relationship. Consequently, a comparison and evaluation of the process and agential models of the God-world relationship must center in an examination of the understanding of self which is operative in each.

Of the theologians we have examined, John Cobb can be said to be most deliberately engaged in model-building. His Whiteheadian theology of nature is grounded in, and elaborates, a processive-organic model of reality. Teilhard de Chardin also develops a theology of nature on the basis of a basically processive-organic model. Accordingly, our discussion of the process model presupposes the fuller analyses found in Chapters Three and Four.

In process perspective reality is dynamic and social, involving a plurality of units of becoming. It is ecological, for the units of process are involved in a complex and creative network of relations. Humanity and divinity alike are involved in, contribute to, and receive from the complexifying dynamic, social, relational system which is the world process. This means that God is not unchangeable in all respects, although he is everlastingly the same in regard to his essential character and overarching purposes. He seeks to actualize his purposes through persuasion rather than coercion. Thus the mode of divine action in the world is perceived, on the process model, in such a way as to protect and preserve creaturely freedom and integrity. All entities are at least partially self-shaping. This doctrine entails the insight that, while God is ultimately responsible for the kind of world we inhabit, he is not indictable for its ills; for some forms of evil are the inescapable concomitant of process as such, and other forms of evil originate in the creaturely failure to conform to the divine intentions. The process perspective entails also the insight that all entities are of intrinsic as well as instrumental value.

Now, all this is very powerful and satisfying in numerous respects. Process theology—in both its Whiteheadian and Teilhardian forms— represents a grand contemporary form of theonomy. God is clearly affirmed by process thinkers to be a promoter rather than (as is sometimes the case in theologies rooted in the monarchical model) the inhibitor of humanization. Moreover, worldly integrity is respected and finite existence highly valued. The implicit (and blasphemous) devaluation of the world ingredient to the frequent denial that God receives anything from that which he makes is decisively abolished within this perspective.

But these fruits of process theologizing are associated with some liabilities as regrettable as the achievements are worthy of celebration. We have examined some of the problems ingredient to Cobb's and Teilhard's processive theologies of nature. Now we need to carry our evaluation further by attending to the shape and adequacy of the understanding of selfhood on which the process-organic model is based. We shall center on the Cobbian form of process thinking, for Teilhard appears to depart in various particulars from the process-organic model in his understanding of selfhood, human and divine.[10]

To do this we must look again at Whitehead. Whitehead's fundamental "intuition," like that of Heraclitus, is that "all things flow." His problem is that of finding a philosophical model that can embrace at once the flowingness of reality and such abidingness of form as actually appears. He rejects the dominant Western tendency to account for stability of structure by a doctrine of substance that implicitly denies both change and the essential relatedness of entities. He seeks, then, a perception of a totality that is internally constituted by a unity of becoming marked by the interrelatedness of all the elements of the whole. This he finds in the conceptual model provided by the organism. An organism is a dynamic unit composed of dynamic entities whose existence and character are dependent on the whole to which they contribute. Thus, each "organism" or actual entity "repeats in microcosm what the universe is in macrocosm."[11]

The concept of the actual entity represents Whitehead's transformation of the Aristotelian-Cartesian category of substance into dynamic terms. One result of his denial of the reality of substance (understood as some type of substrate that perdures through various changes) in favor of the concept of society (understood as a series of momentary actual entities) is the denial of the existence of the entitative self. Selves, or subjects, are themselves processes. They are serially ordered routes of occasions involving significant degrees of continuity between earlier and later moments of the series, but they are not "subjects" that undergo process. Entities, whether microscopic or macroscopic, consist, that is to

---

[10]The Teilhardian perspective is examined, in regard to these unique features, in the next section.

[11]*Process and Reality*, 327.

say, of the process of undergoingness or concrescence. "The actualities of the Universe are processes of experience, each process an individual fact. The whole Universe is the advancing assemblage of these processes."[12] Thus, for Whitehead (and Cobb), the "subject" comes to be only in the process of the concrescence of feelings, both physical and conceptual. The "subject" is really, therefore, a "superject" which acquires determinateness only at the very "end" of concrescence.

> The philosophies of substance presuppose a subject which then encounters a datum, and then reacts to the datum. The philosophy of organism presupposes a datum which is met with feelings, and progressively attains the unity of a subject. But with this doctrine, "superject" would be a better term than "subject."[13]

This view of selfhood entails certain difficulties that are pertinent to an evaluation of the processive-organic model of God and the God-world relationship. Frank Kirkpatrick identifies the problems succinctly:

> The first is that the unity of the self is only achieved at the end of the process which produces the self (the satisfaction) and the second is that up to that moment of unity it becomes extremely problematic to talk of the self *doing* anything since the self as a unity does not yet exist. The result of these two difficulties is two-fold. The self cannot relate to others until it is dead and it cannot act on others until it is dead.[14]

An additional difficulty is that Whitehead finds himself in the peculiar position of attributing agency to "feelings" rather than to "subjects." "The feelings are inseparable from the end at which they aim; and this end is the feeler. The feelings aim at the feeler, as their final cause."[15] Again, "a feeling is the appropriation of some elements in the universe to be components in the real internal constitution of its subject. . . . *A feeling is the agency* by which other things are built into the constitution of its one subject in process of concrescence."[16]

In brief, Whitehead (and Cobb essentially follows him in this) presents us with a denial of the reality of an entitative self, on the one hand, and, on the other, he attributes capacities to the self-in-the-making (feeling, self-causality or election of a "subjective aim," hence freedom)

---

[12]*Adventures of Ideas*, 253.

[13]*Process and Reality*, 234.

[14]Frank G. Kirkpatrick, "Process or Agent: Two Models for Self and God" in Griffin, *Philosophy of Religion and Theology: 1971*, p. 79. My treatment of the process model is indebted to Kirkpatrick and to Richard T. Lee, "Whitehead's Theory of the Self" (Ph. D. dissertation, Yale University, 1962).

[15]*Process and Reality*, 339.

[16]Ibid., 354. Emphasis added.

which seem to require an experiencing subject. To be sure, part of the problem is linguistic, as Whitehead contends. Our language is the language of subject and predicate; that is, it has arisen with, and presupposes, a philosophy of the entitative or substantive self. It is not clear, however, that the problems are purely linguistic; for talk about an "aim" in the absence of an aimer or decision and freedom in the absence of a decider is likely to be problematical within any language system. Moreover, it is difficult if not impossible to make a distinction between a spontaneous (and novel) occurrence, or the outcome of an arbitrary conjunction of feelings, and a freely chosen unitative outcome woven from a variety of physical and conceptual prehensions—*if* there is no identifiable subject, or agent, doing the choosing.[17] Novel occurrences are real; but there is no way of determining, in Whitehead's terms, whether the novel occurrence is the result of the acceptance or modification of an initial aim or simply the product of a chance conjunction of factors. Furthermore, Whitehead and his followers are in the awkward position of claiming that a subject is genuinely a subject and has agency only in and by virtue of its perishing. The "self" becomes self, and functions as such in relation to other members of the community, only in the process of "passing away" into objective immortality. A corollary of this doctrine is that actual entities can influence only their successors, not their contemporaries. Thus, notwithstanding all the emphasis upon (inter)relatedness within the processive conceptuality, there is a certain dismal and problematical character to the relations of actual entities. Although relations are perceived as internal to and hence constitutive of subjects, the subjects so constituted are "dead" at the moment of their constitution and present themselves as dead datum for the constituting of succeeding generations of entities, which themselves "die" even as they emerge.

Thus, the process model of the self involves some serious difficulties. It does not readily recommend itself nor make easy contact with our primary intuitions, which, it is worth remembering, Whitehead took quite seriously. Rather, the process model of the self requires quite a leap of perception before it can become persuasive: we must "deny ourselves" in a way never intended by the biblical admonition. Moreover, for all its concern about "living" processes, there is a—strangely incongruent—sense in which the process perspective, as elaborated by the Whiteheadians, represents a philosophy of death more than an affirmation of life.

---

[17]W.S. John Macmurray, *The Self as Agent* (London: Faber and Faber, 1969; first published, 1957), 219. Says Macmurray, if the world is understood in terms of process alone, "it must be a world in which nothing is ever done; in which everything simply happens. . . ."

The process model of the self is the foundation of the process model of God. And the latter, notwithstanding certain exceptions, partakes of some of the same difficulties as the former. In fact, the process doctrine of God, as developed by Whitehead and his followers, is saved from seriously floundering on the problems ingredient to the processive understanding of selfhood only by the tendency to make God the great exception to, rather than (as Whitehead wished) the chief exemplification of, the general metaphysical principles.

Unlike other actual entities, God does not perish; he is everlasting. Since God is not susceptible to perishing, the divine "satisfaction" must be defined along different lines than creaturely satisfaction, which occurs only in the moment of passing away.[18] Apart from some modification of the general doctrine at this point, God would have to be denied self-identity; for his "satisfaction" is never temporally complete. Moreover, as a concrescing actual entity himself, God cannot be conceived as affecting other entities without being made an exception to the general principles — since all other entities become efficacious only in becoming objectively immortal. This includes the notion that God cannot influence his contemporaries, unless he is an exception to the general principles; for, according to Whiteheadians, relations obtain only between the objectified, the "dead," and the concrescing, or "living." The crucial issue, however, is whether the concept of God — after all the qualifications are made — can be said to have genuine unity. That it can is doubtful. "As long as the idea of God is fit coherently and consistently into any model of an actual entity, no matter how revised, his subjecthood and self-unity are problematic."[19]

The Agential Model. The final model of God and the God-world relationship to which we shall attend involves the suggestion that the relationship is analogous to that obtaining between a self and the actions of a self. As in the processive-organic model, the divine reality is understood on the analogy of human selfhood. But the understanding of selfhood operative within this framework is rather different from that found in the organic framework.

The concept of agency has been clarified and the agential model has been developed through the contributions of recent philosophers of

---

[18]For an attempt to solve this problem see William A. Christian, *An Interpretation of Whitehead's Metaphysics* (New Haven: Yale University Press, 1959), 294ff.

[19]Kirkpatrick, "Process or Agent: Two Models for Self and God," p. 84. For a fuller discussion of some of the issues I have raised, see Kirkpatrick's essay and Richard T. Lee, "Whitehead's Theory of the Self".

language.[20] The starting point involves an analysis of our language about human agents and their actions. Examination of an action reveals it to be something done in order to achieve an end. That is, an action consists of an activity or series of activities directed towards the realization of some intention. Thus, intention or purpose is ingredient to the notion of action. The unity of actions involving a plurality of activities consists of the intent that motivates and finds expression in the action(s). The unity is a unity of intentionality.

An action thus differs from an event, although it may include a succession of events. Conversely, a particular event or series of events may represent a variety of actions. The movement of a human arm is such a succession of events linked causally, from the scientific point of view, by human bodily processes and structures. These events are susceptible to detailed causal analysis in terms of physics, physiology, and the like; yet, from the point of view of the agent who raises, lowers, extends, and contracts the arms, the movement is more than a series of causally related events. It is *an action*, informed by an intention. The arm is moved *in order to* mail a letter, pick up a pipe, caress a child, or threaten an intruder. An action, accordingly, can be specified only by reference to the purpose or intent which informs it, not by reference to bodily movements and natural causality alone. This definition carries a corollary: actions are subject to appraisal, whereas events simply are what they are. An action may be wise or unwise, cautious or risky, justified or unjustified; but such judgments do not apply to sheer events.

The notion of an action is inseparable from the concept of an actor. Agency implies agent, a point denied at one level at least (with problematical consequences) by the Whiteheadians. The woman moves her arm. Someone mails a letter, caresses a child, threatens the intruder. The reality of the actor or agent seems to be a datum of self-consciousness. As agents we are aware of a distinction between that which simply occurs and that which we make happen. The agent (I, you) has (have) an immediate

---

[20]The literature, both philosophical and theological, is extensive. The present discussion, and my continuation of it in Chapter 8, is informed by the following, especially: Barbour, *Myths, Models and Paradigms*, 158ff; Norman Care and Charles Landesman, *Readings in the Theory of Action* (Bloomington: Indiana University Press, 1968); John J. Compton, "Science and God's Action in Nature," in Barbour, ed., *Earth Might Be Fair* (Englewood Cliffs NJ: Prentice-Hall, 1972), 33-47; Robert H. King, *The Meaning of God* (Philadelphia: Fortress Press, 1973); Kirkpatrick, "Process or Agent: Two Models for Self and God"; Macmurray, *The Self as Agent*; Michael McLain, "On Theological Models," *Harvard Theological Review* 62 (1969): 155-87; Alan R. White, ed., *The Philosophy of Action* (London: Oxford University Press, 1968); and various works by Gordon Kaufman, including particularly certain of the essays contained in *God the Problem* (Cambridge: Harvard University Press, 1972).

knowledge of the self as agent. Moreover, the agent knows herself, with perhaps somewhat less immediacy, as a *continuing* agent, as one who performed that act yesterday and is doing this act today.

The agent knows herself, furthermore, as an embodied subject. The self as agent is the living body in action. The agent of an action acts through, not on, her body. Action *on* the body is, of course, one type of action performed by agents: she combs her hair. But agency is a function of embodied selfhood; it is not something effected by the "soul" as subject on the "body" as object. The soul-body, the "I," is the agent; the self is the intending subject of action.

Yet the self as agent is not identifiable exhaustively with any action or set of actions. This is to say that the self transcends each action and ensemble of actions performed by the self. Our actions do not fully express our selfhood. Thus, who we are remains always partially hidden, even from those to whom we reveal ourselves—through our activities, including our words—most fully. We are even hidden in part from ourselves; some of our intentions are too complex or inchoate, et cetera, for us to discern.

Action implies a field of action. The understanding of the self as agent carries with it the affirmation of the reality of a "world" within which the agency of the self is actualized. This, too, is a datum of self-consciousness, as it were. We know ourselves as agents capable of acting upon that which is other. Accordingly, interrelatedness is given with the concept of agency. The self as agent is related to the world upon and within which it acts. Moreover, in acting, the self meets resistance; the self thus finds itself the receiver as well as the agent of power. Action involves interrelationship, including *interaction*. For a significant aspect of the agent's arena of action is other agents. We act upon the world, including other selves; other agents act upon us. Thus, interrelatedness is experienced immediately through our actions. Moreover, we experience ourselves as agential units or entities involved in (inter—)relations with other agents that extend over a period of time. "That is," as Kirkpatrick says, "our experience of ourselves as agents is an inclusive experience of being both unified and abiding, *and* of being in relation to (affecting and being affected by) that which is other than us [*sic*]."[21] This perception opens up a way of affirming the reality of relations that are internally constitutive of (contemporaneous) entities without denying, with the Whiteheadians, the reality of the abiding "subject."

---

[21]Kirkpatrick, "Process or Agent: Two Models for Self and God," 86.

Action, then, is the modality of relationship amongt agents. It is not the only modality of relationship (trees, for example, "stand" side by side without acting), but action is the mode of relating peculiar to agents. To act is to express the self *and* to affect the "world": the pipe is picked up, the child caressed, the intruder struck, the tree cut down. Action, thus, is the means by which an agent intentionally effects the dynamics of interrelationship.[22]

In the light of this description of the results of recent attempts to clarify the experience of personal action, we turn now to a consideration of the way in which human agency may function as a model of divine reality and activity. By interpreting the actions of God in terms of his intentions, the cosmic drama can be interpreted as the field of the divine action. God is the agent who expresses himself, or acts, in and through the structures and movements of nature and history—as the human agent expresses her/himself in and through the structures and movements of the body. The cosmic drama (including but not limited to the human historical drama) is, then, an expression of the divine purpose. Gordon Kaufman maintains that the entire, or cosmic, course of evolutionary development can properly be considered as a single all-encompassing divine action unified by the divine intentions: "to conceive the entire movement of nature and history as the expression of one overarching act of God is consistent both with the meaning of the term "act" and with the modern understanding of the cosmos as in evolutionary development."[23] Within this "overarching" or "master act" are various "subacts."

> The creation of the solar system, the emergence of life on earth, the evolution of higher forms of life and finally man—each of these (as well as many other natural processes and events) represents an indispensable step toward the realization of God's ultimate objectives for creation. Furthermore, the crucial phases of the actual movement of human history, and the emergence of *Heilsgeschichte* within that history, can be regarded as further subordinate acts of God . . . . Within this sequence, the ministry and death of Jesus Christ can quite properly be understood as the supreme act through which God at once made himself known to man and began a radical transformation of man according to his ultimate purposes for man. Events in other cultural histories and the more recent events in Western history may all be seen in this way as governed or guided by the activity through which God is moving the whole of creation toward the eschaton, as subordinate acts within God's master act. Thus, the whole course of history (including the history of nature and the

---

[22]These reflections are picked up and continued in the final chapter of this study. In that chapter, I try to show the way in which the notions of "process" and the "continuant" (Macmurray) are appropriate to the notion of agency, as I extend, albeit briefly, the discussion of God's action in nature.

[23]Kaufman, "On the Meaning of 'Act of God,' " *God the Problem*, 140.

evolution of life) can be apprehended once again as under God's providential control.[24]

Treating cosmic history as an expression of the divine intentions in no way impinges upon the scientific account of things. Just as the movements of a human actor can be accounted for in terms of natural causality *and* the intentionality of the agent without conflict or tension, so the scientific causal account of evolutionary events is in no tension with the treatment of those events in terms of divine action. Nor does a "gap" in the natural causal sequence need to be found in order for the events of cosmic history to be interpreted as actions of God, any more than a similar interstice need be found in the scientific account of arm movement in order for such movement to be seen as a human action.

> Each story has a complete cast of characters, without the need for interaction with the other story, but quite compatible with it. What happens is that the evolution of things is *seen* or *read*, in religious life—as my arm's movement is read in individual life—as a part of an action, as an expression of divine purpose, in addition to its being viewed as a naturalistic process.[25]

This view entails an affirmation of the reality of divine immanence and transcendence analogous to the immanence and transcendence of a human agent and her body/action. John Compton has expressed the relation succinctly:

> . . . the agent is not alongside his actions. God is not alongside the world, inserting himself into it at special moments, any more than I am behind or alongside my bodily life. He lives *through* the history of nature as I live through my body. He *is* that history, just as I *am* my body, and yet he is not exhausted in it. He is that history without being identical with any individual part or event in it. As with human agents, he too transcends the particular behavioral expressions we see, with hidden, complex, and inclusive purposes of his own. The central point is that the sense of God's personal transcendence, if we model it on the personal transcendence of the embodied, finite, and personal agent, does *not* require a radical dualism between God and the physical world.[26]

Several implications follow from this view/model. One is that the divine intentions are going to be more fully disclosed in certain "subacts" than in others, just as a human agent reveals herself more clearly through some actions (the hugging of the child) than others (the choice of a bank). While the divine intentions are expressed throughout the cosmic drama,

---

[24]Ibid., 143-44. For a fuller elaboration of these points see Kaufman's *Systematic Theology*, especially Parts 2 and 3, and *God the Problem*, chs. 7 and 8.

[25]Compton, "Science and God's Action in Nature," *Earth Might Be Fair*, 39.

[26]Ibid., 39-40. Cf. Kaufman, especially "Transcendence without Mythology" and "Two Models of Transcendence," chs. 3 and 4 in *God the Problem*.

those intentions require identification, as it were, if they are to become effective in the ordering of human life. Hence, history, the arena of human personal life, is likely to be the locus of the particularly revelatory actions. And this is the Christian claim: that within human history, and especially the history of one people and one human, divine actions have occurred that make transparent the intentionality informing the overarching "master act." Moreover, the perceptions into who God is and what God is up to in creation and redemption—perceptions which are resultant upon the divine initiative in revelation—find embodiment in particular (paradigm) traditions. A pattern of human perceiving, valuing, and acting emerges in response to divine actions expressive of the ultimate intentionality behind all things, natural and historical. That pattern is borne by the historic community receiving it, and the community becomes the locus within which identification of the divine intentionality is refined and life ordered accordingly.

Another implication of the agential model is that God is an agent, or subject, who endures.[27] The divine reality, as enduring subject, relates to and with other subjects through his action—and theirs. His action involves affecting the world and creaturely agents; he modifies the world and its agents in accordance with his intention(s). And this modification is effective for his contemporaries. However, God, as agent, is affected by the actions of other agents.

> If agents need "the Other" then God needs something over-against Him as the field of His action. If He acts in this field then He makes Himself available to be recipient of the acts of other agents in the same field. This would mean God's dependence, in some sense, on others. This would be particularly true if God is attempting to realize an intention which includes the freedom and

---

[27]Such "ontological realism" need not necessarily accompany the employment of the agential model, although it appears to me to be entailed. In recent writings, however, Gordon Kaufman has argued that clarification of the notion of "God" (as agent and otherwise) can, and should, be done independently of the question of the referential content of God-talk. More precisely, Professor Kaufman has urged that we distinguish between the real referent of the term "God" and the *available* referent. According to Kaufman, the overarching criterion of the adequacy of our conceptions (or "imaginative constructs") of "God" has to do with the effectiveness of our constructs in the promotion of the process of humanization. (See especially *An Essay on Theological Method.*)

David Griffin has argued that Kaufman's work is marked by an unresolved tension between two tendencies in his treatment of "God the problem." On the one hand, is found the tendency (clearly evidenced in *Systematic Theology*) towards ontological realism; on the other, is found the tendency (most clearly affirmed in the essay on method) towards what, for want of a better term, we might regard as "instrumentalism." (See Griffin, "Gordon Kaufman's Theology: Some Questions," *Journal of the American Academy of Religion* 41:4 [December 1973]:554-72.) In any case, Kaufman's recent intent seems to be to explore the logic of the agential model independently of a commitment to ontological realism.

humanity of men. Such an intention would have to be realized only with the active, intentional participation of men.[28]

Still another implication of the agential model is that God is an agent, not agency itself. Recognition of this is vital to the protection of human freedom and agency, the reality of which is affirmed by both the process and agential models but less clearly maintained by theologies based on the monarchical model.

Now we have in this pattern of thinking about God and the God-world relationship an approach that is clearly consonant with the major thrusts of Scripture and the Christian paradigm tradition. The emphasis upon history, the priority of the personal, and other motifs are all vigorously affirmed. Moreover, the reality and significance of the subhuman aspect(s) of the world are affirmed and related vitally to the intentionality of both divine and human agency.

We have had to outline this alternative rather independently of the analyses of the approaches considered in Part One of our study. That is because no major theologian of nature has done his work by forthrightly giving the agential model central place. The notion of agency is present in Cobb, but it is vitiated by the denial of the reality of "subjects" who can, as such, function as agents.[29] The notion of agency is present in Santmire, but it is subordinated in his theology to the monarchical model with which it has some affinities but also significant tensions. At best, the agential model is inchoately developed by Santmire.[30] Teilhard de Chardin comes the closest, of those whose thinking we explored in Part One, to developing a theology of nature rooted in the agential model.[31]

Teilhard's emphasis upon the priority of the personal—affirmed finally but awkwardly in his concept of the "hyperpersonal"—suggests his appreciation of the unique kind of existence, human and divine, that is presupposed by the agential model. Like Cobb, Teilhard posits the interiority of subhuman entities. Unlike Cobb, however, Teilhard treats the notion of interiority, and accounts for evolutionary development, in

---

[28]Kirkpatrick, "Process or Agent: Two Models for Self and God," 88.

[29]Thus, Barbour's treatment (*Myths, Models and Paradigms*, 161ff.) of the process model as allowing for the actions of "a multiplicity of agents" is at best misleading. His characterization rests on a failure to attend to the meaning of the concept of agency.

[30]However, many of the finer insights of both Cobb and Santmire could, as our discussion has suggested, be appropriated to a theology of nature based on the agential model.

[31]Bonifazi, Sittler, and Elder all appear to point, to some degree, in the direction of the agential model also; but none of these "pioneering" theologians of nature really develops the model systematically.

such a fashion as to allow him to affirm that self-reflexivity appears only with "hominization." Like Cobb, Teilhard does place human personal existence within nature; but he does this much more dialectically than Cobb. Man is for both thinkers the finest flowering of evolutionary development, but Teilhard appears to preserve a greater sense of the radical character of the threshold-crossing that led to the appearance of evolution's finest emergent. As a consequence, Teilhard is able to affirm the reality and the responsible character of human agency without the same degree of tension that is found in Cobb.

In similar fashion, Teilhard affirms more adequately than Cobb the notion of divine agency. Teilhard rather clearly understands the evolutionary process as a cosmic drama expressive of the divine intention(s). Cosmic evolution represents the field of the divine action. For Teilhard, God is, in effect, the Agent who expresses himself, or acts, in and through the structures and movements of nature and history. Moreover, the many-faceted evolutionary process finds its unity in the divine intention: God wills to bring all creation to fulfillment and the joy of union with himself (Omega).

Teilhard's perception of the divine agency finds expression in the language of incarnation and sacrament. God expresses himself, and accomplishes his purposes for the universe, through the agency of the "cosmic Christ," the Evolver; and this action is completed in the "eucharistic transformation" accomplished by Christ through his body, the Church. Teilhard works out the details of his vision of the cosmic agency of Christ-God-Omega by modifying and extending traditional Catholic motifs through the employment of processive-organic categories.

Thus, the processive-organic and the agential models are interwoven throughout Teilhard's theology. Since evolution is the overarching category for Teilhard, the former model probably dominates the latter; but this judgment must be qualified by the recognition that Teilhard takes man (human agency?) as the key to his understanding of evolution. In any case, Teilhard provides clues but no clear guidance as to the specific shape a theology of nature based on the agential model might assume. For he was not forthrightly developing a theology based on the model of agency in the fullest sense of the word, although elements of his thinking suggest this model more clearly than is the case with any of the other thinkers we have examined. Furthermore, Teilhard left inchoately defined the relationship between his (implicit) development of the agential model and his (more explicit) development of the processive-organic model. But elements of his vision would be quite congenial to a theology of nature intentionally rooted in the agential model. Before proceeding to explore in more detail the direction such an alternative approach might take, however, we need to look, summarily, at the results of the "metatheological" approach to the theology of nature.

COMPLEMENTARITY AND SYNTHESIS IN THEOLOGICAL MODELS

The choice of models within a paradigm tradition is influenced by the basic assumptions of the community. Since models serve a variety of functions, both cognitive and non-cognitive, and since every model has limits as well as advantages, it is not surprising that each paradigm tradition finds expression in a plurality of basic models. Since Christian (religious) experience is variegated (involving numinous, mystical, psychological, historical, moral and interpersonal elements) and since the ultimate Subject of Christian interest transcends all forms of human experience, it is to be expected that a multiplicity of models would have arisen within the Christian paradigm tradition. Not all of these models are equally consonant with the basic assumptions of the Christian faith, or paradigm, community; but all which function compellingly, and survive for long, give expression to at least some of the constitutive perceptions and valuations of the tradition within which they have arisen.

It is now widely recognized that such considerations should lead us to take seriously diverse models and theological formulations, even while we appreciate the limits of all models and formulations. This is to say that a distinctive characteristic of the contemporary theological situation is the appreciation of the value, and necessity, of theological (and, more generally, religious) pluralism.[32] This attitude suggests that we should seek to identify the possibility of a "metatheological" stance in which the effort is made to "rise above" the theological fray—even if only temporarily and as a penultimate step in our theologizing—in order to appropriate and affirm the truth content of a variety of models and theological orientations that are, on the "ordinary level," competitors. This "metatheological" option is reflected in Robert Bellah's "symbolic realism."

> For the religiously orthodox, religious belief systems were felt to represent "objective" reality as it really is, and thus if one of them is true the others must be false, either absolutely or in some degree. For the secular orthodox, all religion is merely "subjective," based on emotion, wish or faulty inference, and therefore false. For the third group, who take symbolism seriously, religion is seen as a system of symbols which is neither simply objective nor simply subjective, but which links subject and object in a way that transfigures reality or even, in a sense, creates reality. For people with this point of view the idea of finding more than one religion valid, even in a deeply

---

[32]Cf., e.g., Kaufman, *Systematic Theology*, 79.

personal sense, is not only possible but normal. This means neither syncre-
tism nor relativism, since it is possible within any social or personal context
to develop criteria for the evaluation of religious phenomena and a consequent hierarchy of choice.[33]

That which Bellah maintains about "religion" is even more obviously
possible and appropriate regarding diverse models and theological orientations within a particular paradigm or religious tradition. A variety of
models and orientations can be regarded as "valid," within limits, "even in
a deeply personal sense."

Now, to perceive diverse, and competing, models within a paradigm
tradition as valid is to regard them as, to a greater or lesser degree,
"complementary." The notion of the complementarity of theological
models and orientations has been suggested by the emergence of the
tendency to think in terms of the principle of complementarity in the
natural sciences, especially microphysics. Theoretical physicists, such as
Niels Bohr, have defended the necessity of regarding electrons in terms of
both the wave model and the particle model.[34] Under particular experi-
mental conditions the electron exhibits the behavior of each type of
phenomenon, the wave and the particle. Neither model is adequate for the
understanding of the electron; but at the present state of our investigative
arts, neither model can be dispensed with if we are to take into account the
whole range of data regarding electron behavior. Bohr and other theorists
suggest that the principle of complementarity is properly applied within
other dimensions as well: mechanical and organic models in biology
function in a complementary fashion, as do behavioristic and introspec-
tive models in psychology.

If we extend the principle of complementarity to theology, we may
consider, for example, the possibility that personal and impersonal models of the divine reality function as complementary representations of that
which, like the electron in another fashion, transcends our experience and
conceptual categories. Moreover, we may view a variety of personalistic
models as themselves complementary of one another, each expressing
and clarifying particular perceptions and valuations.[35]

---

[33]Bellah, "Religion in the University: Changing Consciousness, Changing Structures,"
in Claude Welch, ed., *Religion in the Undergraduate Curriculum* (Association of American Colleges, 1972), 14; cited in Barbour, *Myths, Models and Paradigms*, 173. For a
sustained examination of the shape of the "metatheological" task see Charles-James N.
Bailey, *Groundwork for Comparative Metatheology* (Ann Arbor MI: University Microfilms, 1965).

[34]Niels Bohr, *Atomic Theory and the Description of Nature* (Cambridge: Cambridge
University Press, 1934.)

[35]The notion of complementarity in science or theology should not, any more than the
notion of "paradox," be taken as an excuse for lethargy or a refusal of the search for unity.

In the three major models of God and the God-world relationship that we have examined—the monarchical, the processive, and the agential—we have to do with modes of understanding which do in fact complement one another in the intended sense. Each model specifies an understanding of God and a correlative understanding of the world; and, although there is considerable overlapping, each of the models bears distinctive perceptions and valuations that are not, with equal adequacy, borne by the others. That is, each major model entails certain meanings and emphases that are distinctive of it and that ought not be lost. This claim can be illustrated by several examples.

The monarchical model appears to affirm most forcefully both the divine majesty and the human sense of the numinous. When God is perceived as the mighty King, robed in splendor, the experiences of awe, wonder, and the sense of the holy find full release. God, as Ruler of all, is perceived as eminently worthful; and humankind is called by this perception to worship and faithful (covenantal) action. Theologies rooted primarily in the monarchical model are able to depict the divine reality in ways which express most fully and unambiguously the perceptions and valuations to which our sense of the holy and our experiences of awe and wonder give rise.

By the same token, the monarchical—*and the agential*—models involve a clearer affirmation of the divine transcendence than does the processive-organic model. In both of the more personalistic models, the otherness of God is rather clearly maintained. (He is the All-Ruling, the cosmic Agent, the Holy One, whereas we are limited agents, finite, and distorted.) Conversely, the processive-organic—*and the agential*—models affirm more clearly and powerfully the reality of the divine immanence than does the monarchical model. On the process and agential models God is implicated in the world at every turn even while (within the context of the agential model especially) he is the One who stands beyond the many.

Related to the greater stress upon the divine immanence is the tendency towards the clarification of the mode(s) of the divine action in the world, a tendency characteristic of theologies rooted in the processive and agential models. In the process model God functions as the One Who

---

Ian Barbour has proposed (*Myths, Models and Paradigms*, 77-78) three conditions for applying the principle of complementarity: (1) it should not be employed to justify the "uncritical acceptance of dichotomies"; (2) models ought to be regarded as complementary "only if they refer to *the same entity* and are of *the same logical type*"; and (3) it should be recognized that "the use of one model limits the use of the other; they are not simply 'alternative models' having different domains or functions."

Calls the world—calls largely, as it were, from within—from stage to novel stage.[36] In the agential model God is the One beyond the world who expresses his intention(s) within the world in a way analogous to a finite agent's expression of his intentions in and through his body. In both the processive and the agential models, accordingly, the claim that God is not only present to but active within the world is rendered intelligible. This is the case even though there are limits to the degree of clarification that is possible, limits that are ingredient to the mode of action under investigation.[37] The contrary tendency within the framework of the monarchical model, as that model has tended to be developed by Neo-Reformation thinkers, is to assert the divine sovereignty while leaving relatively unclarified the way in which the cosmic King's power is exercised.

These tendencies are related to another. The affirmation of sovereign divine power, accompanied by a relative lack of clarification of the modes of the exercise of God's power, leaves creaturely freedom imperiled in theologies based on the monarchical model. In the context of the processive and agential models, however, divine activity is intelligibly affirmed in a way that protects and even enhances creaturely freedom.

In spite of the difficulty of relating creaturely freedom to divine power, the monarchical model preserves, along with the agential, the sense of the uniqueness of human existence, both personal and historical. This perception tends to be qualified within the context of thought provided by the processive-organic model. By the implicit attribution of self-reflexivity to the subhuman order and by the general emphasis upon the lines of continuity between the human and prehuman, theologies rooted in the process model imperil the uniqueness and superiority of the human within the created order. Theologies anchored in the monarchical and agential models, however, are able to affirm human transcendence of the rest of creation in a way that is paralleled by their affirmation of the divine transcendence of all creation. Such theologies are, accordingly, generally able to develop more adequate conceptions of human personal and historical existence—the modes of existence from which, indeed, the "root-metaphors" of kingship and agency are derived.

---

[36]Teilhard's greater emphasis upon the transcendence of God involves his stressing, more than Cobb, the idea that God calls the world from "ahead" as well as from within. This tendency on Teilhard's part probably reflects the influence of patterns of thought more appropriate to the agential model (one strand of his thought) than to the processive-organic model (the other strand).

[37]These limits, it is worth noting, are generally acknowledged more forthrightly by theologies rooted in the agential model, with its greater emphasis upon the divine transcendence, than by those that center in the processive-organic model.

But the losses and gains are complexly interrelated. And the processive model provides the clearest option developed to date—perhaps the only option—for affirming the genuinely intrinsic value of the subhuman order. While this affirmation is associated with the highly problematical tendency to impute self-reflexivity to the subhuman order, the affirmation is sufficiently important, and interesting, to merit our (at least provisional) retention of this kind of approach to the understanding of God and the world. It may be, however, that the agential model provides a means of affirming that which needs to be affirmed. This possibility is linked to the fact that it is the agential model, more than either the monarchical or processive, which underlies the perception of the world as a sacramental arena.

Finally, we should note that both the processive and agential models allow for reciprocity between God and the world, whereas within the context of the monarchical model God tends to become the Wholly (as well as the Holy) Other, who remains basically unaffected by that which he has made. This motif of reciprocity is rooted in the fact that, in the context for thought provided by both the processive and agential models, the "new view of nature" indicated by the special sciences is taken very seriously and allowed to become a constitutive element in our theologizing. But beyond that, the motif is anchored in the perceptions of the divine reality that follow from the two root-metaphors of process and agency. These concepts are constitutively open to the concept of reciprocity; they, in fact, require it.

Thus, we conclude that each major model of God and the God-world relationship performs valuable functions; and theologies of nature that are rooted in, and seek to elaborate the consequences of, the various models enrich our perceptions and valuations. Penultimately at least, then, we need to hold the three models and the theologies anchored in them together, allowing the insights of the one type of model/theology to qualify—by enriching and correcting—the insights of the others.[38]

But another conclusion emerges. Our comparison of the logic and consequences of the various models suggests that the agential model

---

[38]Interestingly, at least one recent theologian has, rather self-consciously, employed all three models. The theology of William Temple suggests the complementarity—and even, to some extent, the coinherence—of the monarchical, the processive-organic, and the agential models. These models are reflected in, respectively, Temple's notion of the universal commonwealth of value, his modified Whiteheadian metaphysic, and his sacramental vision. But the tracing of the contours of Temple's synthetic vision, and the evaluation of his proposals, would constitute a major task in itself, and cannot be pursued here. I must acknowledge, however, that Temple's work has suggested several of the lines of thought pursued in this study.

performs more of the functions requisite to an adequate theology of nature, with fewer of the liabilities, than any of the other models of the God-world relationship. "Surveying the horizons" via the "metatheological" approach has thus disclosed to us a path awaiting further exploration. Consequently, we need, in concluding this study, to examine the possibility that the most promising path—the best way forward—lies in the development of a theology of nature rooted in the agential model.

CHAPTER 7

CONCLUSION: NATURE AND DIVINE INTENTIONALITY

We have now already seen many of the features of the kind of theology of nature that would follow from giving the agential model priority. Our characterization of the concept of agency in the previous chapter has defined the contours of the basic vision available along this path. Our analysis of other approaches to the theology of nature in Part One has provided insight into many of the more detailed features of the theological landscape that would be visible along this path also; but everything would—from the better vantage afforded by the agential model—be seen in fresh perspective.

How this is so deserves to be spelled out in detail. We can, however, in concluding this study, only try to review and sketch something of the rich possibilities that come into view along our alternative path. Perhaps our explorations can be resumed after an appropriate period of refreshment and replenishment of our resources. But for now we must content ourselves with suggesting, summarily, something of the unactualized potential of the agential model for the constructive development of a fresh theology of nature. And we shall do this, first, by reviewing the nature of the concept of nature, including its distinguishing contemporary features. Second, we shall briefly explore the way in which the processive understanding of nature might be appropriated to a theology based on the concept of action. And we shall conclude, third, by (reviewing and) making explicit some of the valuational implications of the model of agency.

THE NATURE OF "NATURE" RECONSIDERED

With the emergence of the modern scientific view of nature, the "God hypothesis" became less and less necessary. Events within the phenomenal world could be accounted for quite independently of God-talk. As a result, theology was put on the defensive; and believers retreated to modes of conceptualization which ostensibly relieved their faith affirmations of any conflict with the scientifically indicated mode of perceiving the world. God became Wholly Other (the deistic model) and/or exclusively concerned with and known in interpersonal relationships (the dialogic model). Except, perhaps, for an initial act of origination that ostensibly lay beyond the parameters of scientific inquiry, God was relieved of any responsibility for and involvement in "nature." As the gaps in the scientific mode of explanation became progressively fewer, God went into eclipse in modern consciousness.

But the apparent loss has proven more salutary than tragic. For the new understanding of nature has, both negatively and positively, opened up the possibility of viewing the divine reality and God's mode of relation to, and action in, nature quite differently—and more adequately. Negatively, the triumph of the scientific view of things has precipitated a reconceptualizing of the divine reality and the nature of the God-world relation. Process theology, in its variegated modes, is a dramatic example of the rich fruits of this adjustment of theological perceptions. Positively, the scientific perspective has, in its various refinements (via Darwin, Einstein et al.) shown "nature" to be a much more marvelous arena than previous ages suspected. And faith finds this arena, not exclusive of, but eminently compatible with an affirmation of the divine reality, appropriately reconceived.

The refinements of the scientific perception of nature, which have occurred over the past century or so, reveal nature to be quite different from that which it appeared to be during the early modern period. The general concept of nature that recent science discloses is marked by several features. Nature is enormously complex rather than basically simple in structure. It includes many levels and patterns of order, and the various components of nature are complexly interrelated. Second, the new view of nature suggests that it is a complex of events characterized by statistical as well as causal uniformity; it is a field of "chance" as well as "determinism." Third, nature is dynamic in character, not static; thus it is "open." The new concept of nature centers in a perception of nature as a field of evolving forms possessed of a remarkable potential for (patterned) change. And this dynamic openness is characteristic of nature in all its dimensions, although the tempo of change varies greatly between, say, the inorganic and the organic dimensions.

Now this characterization of the new view of nature, in contrast to the old, suggests something about "nature" itself. Nature is a construct, a concept. It is not simply a "thing," to be readily identified, although the concept of nature is inclusive of things of various kinds. In point of fact, the concept of nature is logically quite similar to the concept of world. Both are notions constructed by the imagination as heuristic devices that enable the ordering of our experiences and our other concepts of things and events. That is, world and nature are "regulative ideas," as Kant suggested. Both concepts can and do specify the "whole." They may specify the totality of that which is other than God. Or they may (as they do for Hegel and Whitehead, and their followers) specify the totality inclusive of deity.

But the concepts world and nature differ too. For "nature" possesses a concreteness that is lacking to "world." Nature can be both conceived and experienced, whereas the world can only be conceived. That is, "world" refers to the totality alone (either inclusive or exclusive of God); "world" does not specify anything that can be empirically and directly encountered. "Nature," however, refers to the totality (either inclusive or exclusive of some understanding of "ultimate reality") *and* to particular aspects (events, structures, qualities, dimensions) of the totality that can be empirically encountered and known. Gordon Kaufman illustrates the contrast this way:

> We would never say a tree is "worldly," but there are no problems at all in regarding it as "natural"; whereas to speak of "laws of the world" (i.e., of the cosmos) sounds exceedingly abstract and obscure, by "laws of nature" we designate everyday experienceable regularities in, for example, light, sound, and gravitation; for one to wish to immerse himself in nature seems comprehensible enough, but what would it be to immerse oneself in the world?[1]

Nature, then, as the concept is used today, tends to refer both to "the totality of all powers and processes conceived as a systematic whole"[2] and to that which exists apart from human artifice—to the extra-cultural aspect(s) of creation. But in both the wider and the narrower usages, "nature" is marked by complex interrelatedness and by plasticity. It is, viewed holistically, a complex, interrelational, novelty-producing process; and its various, concretely experienceable, aspects (trees, dogs, mountains) are products of this process.

Clearly, the concept of nature is "given" to a significant degree by scientific and cultural consensus. Our concept of nature is a part of our "intellectus" (Richardson), our "climate of opinion" (Whitehead), or our "vision of reality" (Cobb). But the Christian thinker is not merely a

---

[1]"A Problem for Theology: The Concept of Nature," 334-45. See Kaufman's essay for a fuller discussion of the concepts of world and nature and their relationship; also, *An Essay on Theological Method* by Kaufman.

[2]"A Problem for Theology: The Concept of Nature," 345.

participant in a general type of culture, nor are his perceptions conditioned purely by his sensitivity to the dominant scientific consensus. The theologian is a participant in a paradigm community with its peculiar ways of perceiving and valuing; and these, as well as those perceptions and valuations derived from the general culture and special subcultures (such as the natural sciences), must function constructively in the shaping of his basic concepts. Hence, "nature," like other concepts, is a complex construct, shaped, for the Christian thinker, from the confluence of a variety of modes of perception: scientific, cultural, philosophical, and theological-religious. Not every concept of nature present and operative in a pluralistic culture is equally available to those whose basic perceptions and valuations are the product of a particular religious paradigm tradition. Some concepts, in fact, are singularly incompatible with the constitutive perceptions/valuations of the Christian paradigm.[3]

But the basic features of the new view of nature—nature understood as a complex, relational, novelty-producing process—is eminently compatible with and even, it could be argued, required by salient features of the distinctive way of perceiving and valuing that is denominated "Christian."[4] The concept of nature as a complexly interrelated dynamic process represents one way of specifying the character of part of that which Christians have intended by "creation." The difficulties set in when nature is construed as the whole system of reality—the totality inclusive of the high order of being/becoming suggested by such terms as "personality," "self-reflexivity," and the like. It is not clear that a concept of nature can be expanded to include such unique forms of being, human or divine, without nature thereby ceasing to be "natural." It may be, however, that the natural can be included in some fashion in the higher order of being/becoming—history—while remaining itself a rich reality. And it is just this possibility that we must explore.

PROCESS AND ACTION

The new understanding of nature centers in the category of process. It is, thus, this category which is given preeminence in theologies, such as

---

[3] The tendency to make nature the ultimate clearly conflicts with the Christian perception that "the one God who is Being is an 'I', or like an 'I,' who is faithful as only selves are faithful" (Niebuhr). For a discussion of the distinctive character of the Christian paradigm see the Appendix to this study.

[4] This is particularly true for a Christian vision anchored in the agential model. (And Teilhard illustrates this, to an extent.) The emergence of the understandfng of nature as a

those based on the philosophy of Whitehead, which attempt to conceive the world as one natural evolutionary happening. This attempt involves, as we have seen, the attribution of at least incipient self-reflexivity to the subhuman orders of being/becoming and, paradoxically, the denial of genuine agency at every level. This results in the concepts of both nature and history being blasted.

We are proposing that another category, that of action, be given priority and that the meaning of nature be rethought in the light of the notion of agency. We are maintaining, moreover, that that which is valid in the notion of process can be affirmed, and even enhanced, by the adoption of this alternative, and more inclusive, stance. We are seeking a way of appropriating the main features of the new view of nature without suffering the reductionistic consequences that have afflicted the so-called process theologies. The logic of our alternative proposal has been explored by John Macmurray.[5]

Assuming Whitehead's own notion of process, we can define process as that which occurs without being effected by an agent or agents. "Process," that is, really refers to bare occurrence or happening. Process is constituted by events; it is not the product of agents or subjects or effectors.[6] "Action," however, refers to that which is done by an agent—intentionally. Like process, action is something that occurs or happens; but unlike process, action is effected by an intentional agent. The ordinary blinking of our eyes is mere occurrence; winking is an act.

---

complex, interrelational, novelty-producing process is precisely the prerequisite of the full elaboration of a Christian theology based on the model of human agency.

It is important to note, however, that the agential model is not new but is, it appears, the model indicated by the biblical perception of God as a God who acts. It is also indicated by much of the classical theological tradition. What is new is the *clarification* of this model and the systematic elaboration of that which is entailed in it—an elaboration that is occurring under the impact of recent developments in intellectual/cultural history, including the deliverances of the natural sciences.

[5]See especially *The Self as Agent*; also *Interpreting the Universe* (London: Faber and Faber, 1936) and *Persons in Relation* (London: Faber and Faber, 1961). The latter work is the second volume of Macmurray's Gifford lectures entitled *The Form of the Personal*. My references are to the 1969 paperback edition of his lectures.

My discussion in this section is informed by Kirkpatrick's essay "Process or Agent: Two Models for Self and God," especially 86-88. I do not attempt to give here a comprehensive characterization of Macmurray's thinking, but only try to suggest a direction of thought whose constructive possibilities for the theology of nature deserve fuller exploration.

[6]Whitehead and Macmurray concur in this understanding of the nature of process; but Macmurray appears to see the implications of the notion of process-as-event more clearly than Whitehead.

Thus, we are able to abstract from our experience of occurrences those which are mere happenings and those which are intentionally produced by human agency. We are able to observe a "world" of events— some unusual and surprising and some more or less regular, patterned, and predictable. The former we refer to "chance" and the latter to "laws of nature," that is, to perceived regularities. This world of occurrences, of process undisturbed by intentional acts, is the world of the "continuant," in Macmurray's language. There is no need to locate agents or subjects within this world, except perhaps metaphorically and for convenience.[7] The world of the continuant, or process, is a causal world; but causal explanation involves a description of the "how" of occurrences. Explanation by causes does not involve specifying the "why" of events. It involves, rather, the specifying of "what is going on." Evolutionary development itself exhibits continuance. Says Macmurray:

> Here we clearly find a pattern of change which *prima facie* repeats itself without change. The theory of an evolution of species requires no modification in principle. If it is spontaneous, then the repetition with variation is itself the pattern which repeats, and the principle of the successive variations is itself determinable. But it seems more likely that the larger variations, and perhaps all variations from type, have their ground in some interference, or in some change in environmental conditions. The belief that organic development is also determined in accordance with natural law; or—which is in the end the same thing—that for a particular organism the pattern of response to stimulus is determinate, is not merely based upon observation. It is a necessity for thought. For the only spontaneous initiation of change which we can conceive is the act of an agent; and whatever is non-agent, that is to say, non-personal, must be conceived as a continuant.[8]

Agent language is introduced in order to discuss "why" something is happening. As long as the intention of an agent is not introduced in the explanation of an occurrence, the reason for the occurrence is not provided; all that is offered is a description of how the continuants operated in a given set of circumstances. And this causal, or descriptive, mode of explanation, involves in principle an infinite regress. As long as intentions are omitted from our efforts to explain, we must try to depict the whole concourse of occurrences in order to provide a complete description of one of them. Whitehead discerned this. He affirmed that all events are interrelated and that no actual entity can be fully accounted for without taking into account the entire world process. Thus, Whitehead's notion of

---

[7] I might say, for example, that my eyes watered without intending to attribute agency to my eyes in the proper sense of the word. "My eyes watered" is shorthand for something like "the tear ducts in my eyes began to function due to the stimulus of excessive smoke in the air."

[8] *The Self as Agent*, 161.

organic process and Macmurray's concept of the continuant overlap considerably: for both Whitehead and Macmurray the world is a processive actuality, involving interrelatedness, but devoid of agents. The world of process and the continuant is a world in which there are no actions, only occurrences. "The only 'subjects' in this world of the continuant are those entities which can be singled out as transmitters of effects and those entities which are the recipients of effects. There are no effectors, no self-initiating agents, except in a metaphorical sense."[9]

So the world of process, that is, the world of nature, is a world without agents in the proper sense of the word. Yet we know ourselves intuitively—as agents. We are forced, then, finally to choose: "The alternatives," as Macmurray says, "are that we should think reality either as a unity of events or as a unity of actions; that is to say, either as one *process* or as one *action*."[10] The price of the first choice is the denial of genuinely human—and divine—reality. But *if action is taken as our unifying category, then our "world" is inclusive of process*. The continuant, process, nature is real but is not exhaustive of the real. Trees, dogs, and the movements of the human body are explicable in processive terms. What is omitted is agency, hence intentionality. But if we are agents—if God is an Agent—then the full "vision of reality" must include process *and* action.

Macmurray's summation is compelling:

> Contemporary thought, under the dominant influence of science, does, at least implicitly, conceive the world as a single process; either biologically as an evolutionary process, or mathematically as a material process of events obeying physical laws. But we are in a position to reject this alternative decisively. For we have seen that the conception of a unity of events, whether conceived physically or organically, is the conception of the continuant, and that the continuant is an ideal abstraction from our experience as agents. It is constituted by the exclusion of action. This concept of process cannot therefore include action as an element in the unity it seeks to express. If the world is a unitary process, it must be a world in which nothing is ever done; in which everything simply happens; a world, then, in which everything is matter of fact and nothing is ever intended. We should have to assert, in that case, that there are no actions. . . .
>
> On the other hand, we have seen that the concept of action includes the concept of the continuant process as its own negative. Any action, in its

---

[9] Kirkpatrick, "Process or Agent: Two Models for Self and God," 87. This position does not entail a denial that subhuman creatures possess some "interiority." That they do must, in fact, be affirmed. But no subhuman existents possess the rich degree or, better, kind of interiority that involves "intending," in the full sense of the word. This is indicated *per definitionem* as well as by observation; for any embodied *creatures* capable of formulating and pursuing purposes are, by definition, "human" (*in potentia*, at least)— whether or not they be upright, featherless, endotherms marked by bilateral symmetry.

[10] *The Self as Agent*, 219.

actuality, if we abstract from its intentionality, and so from the knowledge which directs it, presents itself as a process of events. In reflection, once it is done, it can be described exhaustively as matter of fact, without reference to the intention which determined it. It follows from this that what appears to us to be a process of events which happen in a necessary succession may always be a part or an aspect of an action. Granted that in our empirical experience we must recognize occurrences which we cannot refer to the intention of an agent, and which we must treat as mere happenings, it still does not follow that they are not so referable. If we cannot prove intention from premises that are matter of observed fact, neither can we disprove it. It is therefore *possible* to think the world as one action. It is *not possible* to think it as a unitary process.

It is then logically impossible that the world should be a single process; it is logically possible that it should be one action.[11]

NATURE IN GRACE

To think the world—including but not reduced to "nature"—as a unitary action is to posit an Agent whose act the world is. This is the "metaphysic of action."[12]

This means, as has been suggested, that the complexifying process that we denominate "nature" and the complex drama that we call "history" find their unity in the divine intention that informs the entire sweep of creation-redemption-consummation. The divine intending is the "master act" that ties everything together: the formation of a cosmos from a primordial chaos, the emergence of life, the efflorescence of the personal. In a multitude of "subacts," effected in appropriate fashion within both the prehuman and the human dimensions of the world drama, the cosmic Agent actualizes the divine overarching purpose.

It is in the worldly arena of action—that is, history—that the divine intention expresses itself most fully and clearly; but the long ages of prehistory, cosmic and biological, are not unrelated to the divine purposive activity. Quite the contrary; they are resultant from it and expressive of it. Nature is itself an indispensable aspect of the working out of the divine purpose. The processes of nature are rooted in and expressive of the divine Agent as the processes of bodily movement are rooted in and expressive of human agency. Through the dynamic structures of the (non-intending) continuant, as well as through the (intentional) actions of human historical agents, the divine Agent achieves self-actualization: creative *and* responsive love "communicates" itself. That is, through the

---

11 Ibid., 219-20.

12 Ibid., 214.

intending that entails the positing, the shaping, and the completing of a world other than himself, the divine Agent "is eternally that which eternally He is."

This is to say that, notwithstanding the negativities that mar prehuman and human existence alike, the structures and processes of nature, as well as the drama of history, are sacramental in character. Through both nature and history, albeit in different ways, the divine intending is realized. Nature, then, has its existence in and of grace. For nature is the product, and vehicle of expression, of the divine good-favor. It is one form taken by the actualization of the divine love. Nature thus exists in a nexus of meaning—meaning resultant upon the only meaning-constituting reality there is, the purposing of an agent.

From the vantage at which we have arrived we are in a position to appropriate many of the finer features of the visions found along the Neo-Reformation, the Whiteheadian, and the Neo-Catholic paths. Santmire employs the Kingdom imagery to bring an affirmation of the divine concern for and governance of nature into an affirmation of the divine concern for and governance of history. Systematically linking the monarchical to the agential model provides a way of warranting Santmire's claims, claims that are left relatively unsubstantiated by Santmire's own development of them. Moreover, it is within the context for thought provided by the notion of agency that Santmire's Edwardsean-Niebuhrian value theory finds its proper grounding and fulfillment. Santmire's theory of value requires a model of transcendence that can integrate the interests of nature and history, on the one hand, and the individual and the universal community, on the other. The monarchical model achieves this to a significant degree. But if Santmire's basic model is correlated with—or, better, developed in the context of—the model of agency, Santmire's valuational results are reinforced, as it were. For nature and history, the individual and the totality of history-nature, are unified by virtue of the enactment of the divine intention(s) in and through each and all creaturely entities, structures, and processes.

We have already seen that much of the Whiteheadian vision can be appropriated to—and corrected by—the model of agency. The theological understanding of nature elaborated by Cobb is positively contributory to an understanding of nature as part of the arena of the enactment of the divine intention. But the Whiteheadian-Cobbian vision must be altered—to a great extent by enlargement—in order to allow for *action* in a world characterized by *process*.

Much the same can be said of Teilhard, although he has done more than Cobb to correct his own tendencies towards organic reductionism. In the thinking of Teilhard, we find a groping after a more comprehensive understanding of nature-history, an understanding which neither separates nature from history nor dissolves the one into the other. For Teilhard, nature and history alike constitute a sacramental arena. Grace does not simply complete or perfect nature; grace is expressed in and through nature, and nature exists in grace. Like Joseph Sittler, Teilhard tends to suggest that, in an important sense, nature and grace coinhere.

We conclude that the vision of the world, including nature, as the theater of divine glory is a vision that can be renewed in our time. But the renewed vision of the world as the theater of divine splendor and grace will consist not of a simple return to the vision of Calvin or anyone else. It will, rather, if it occurs, be a far more complex and richly variegated vision than any held historically. If nothing else, our new knowledge of nature necessitates that. With the help of resourceful theological pathfinders like Santmire, Cobb, Teilhard, Sittler, Niebuhr, and others, we can confidently hope to give expression again to our conviction that nature is the theater of the divine glory and grace. For the heavens are still telling the glory of God. The whole earth remains full of his glory.

THE CHRISTIAN PARADIGM: ITS DISTINCTIVE CHARACTER

During the course of this study we have referred on occasion to "the Christian paradigm," suggesting thereby that there is something genuinely distinctive about that which is denominated "Christian." We have suggested, moreover, that a viable contemporary theology of nature must preserve and protect that which is "distinctively Christian," even as it attempts to do greater justice to the category of "nature" than has been the case in much classical, and recent, theology. We have concluded that a theology of nature developed within the framework of the agential model holds the greatest promise of meeting these challenges: affirming afresh the reality and value of nature while affirming fully and vigorously the motifs constitutive of the Christian paradigm tradition. We have faulted certain recent experiments in the theology of nature precisely for their failure to preserve the distinctively Christian in their laudable eagerness to reexamine nature and to appropriate more fully the category and concerns of nature to Christian conceptualizing and sensibilities. Accordingly, we would do well to indicate our understanding of the distinctive shape of the Christian paradigm—the understanding of the Christian phenomenon that would inform the development of the kind of theology of nature that we have called for in chapters six and seven of this study.

To identify the distinctively Christian ways of perceiving and valuing we shall need to attend to one or more of the exemplars of the Christian paradigm. The determinative exemplar is, or course, Jesus of Nazareth; but he is accessible to us only through the mediations of subsequent exemplars. And it is expedient to examine one who is, like us, shaped by his influence, as well as a contributing participant in the tradition that is defined by reference to him. The choice of any such secondary exemplars involves some element of arbitrariness. Moreover, almost anyone chosen will be, in terms of someone's orthodoxy, denied to be a faithful representative of the Christian paradigm. Still, by consensus of the informed judgment of the Christian community certain figures stand out as peculiarly powerful embodiments of the Christian mode of perceiving and valuing. Our choice of exemplar is conditioned, in part, by the needs of our inquiry. It is helpful, for our purposes, to focus on a recent exemplar of the Christian tradition, one whose language has contemporary relevancy. It is helpful, further, to attend to a theologian, especially one whose thinking has significant ecological bearing. In the light of these criteria, we shall examine the character of the Christian paradigm as it is reflected in the theology of H. Richard Niebuhr.[1]

Niebuhr is congenial for our purposes also because the understanding of Christianity as a paradigm community (which we have arrived at by way of Barbour) is not alien to him. Niebuhr refrained from defining a Christian as a "follower of" or "believer in" Jesus Christ. He suggested rather that the Christian "might more adequately be described as one who counts himself as *belonging to that community of men for whom Jesus Christ*—his life, words, deeds, and destiny—*is of supreme importance as the key* [determinative exemplar] to the understanding of themselves and their world, the main source of the knowledge of God and man, good and evil, the constant companion of the conscience, and the expected deliverer from evil."[2] The Christian, in other words, is one who participates in the tradition of perceiving and valuing (and hence acting) that derives from the man Jesus. The Church is that historical community of men and women whose perceptions and valuations are being shaped and reshaped under the influence of their determinative exemplar and who are themselves thereby constituted as the bearers of his pattern of perceiving and valuing.

Niebuhr begins his theological reflections with the observation that men and women are valuing beings who determine themselves (plan, decide, act) in accordance with what they value. This is true of all people in all ages. Humans are fiducial beings; we trust in, and serve the cause of, some beloved center of our valuing. That is to say, that all human beings, as fiducial or valuing beings, have some god or gods. Human valuing and the reality of the gods are correlative.

> Now to have faith and to have a god is one and the same thing, as it is one and the same thing to have knowledge and an object of knowledge. When we believe that life is worth living by the same act we refer to some being which makes our life worth living. We never merely believe that life is worth living,

---

[1] For an examination of the presence and character of the concept of divine agency in the theology of Niebuhr, see Fowler, *To See the Kingdom*, especially chs. 2 and 3.

[2] H. Richard Niebuhr, *Christ and Culture* (New York: Harper & Brothers; Harper Torchbooks, 1956) 11. Emphasis added. Cf. Niebuhr's *Radical Monotheism and Western Culture*, 60.

but always think of it as made worth living by something on which we rely.
And this being, whatever it be, is properly termed our god.[3]

The objects of human valuing are diverse: there are gods many and lords many. In fact, suggests Niebuhr, the two "universal" forms of the faith of human beings are "polytheism" and "henotheism." We orient ourselves in the world by reference to multiple centers of value or by reference to one center drawn from the realm of "the many" and invested with ultimacy. The inevitable result is conflict and frustration, both personally and corporately. For the multiple centers of valuation compete with one another for our energies and service. Polytheism fails as a form of faith because the individual experiences the fragmentation and disintegration of his selfhood as he seeks to serve many "gods." Similarly, henotheism fails because various individuals and societies find their causes limiting of one another, with conflict between the worshipers of the various partial gods (such as science and religion, or nature or humanity, taken as objects of ultimate trust and loyalty) being the inevitable result. "The pluralism of the gods has its counterpart in the pluralism of self and society."[4] Moreover, the finite deities—those centers of value drawn from the realm of the many—fail to sustain through the limiting experiences of life. If the death of the nationalist is penultimately swallowed up in victory by the triumph of the national cause, ultimately the meaning of his life is threatened, or lost, in the perishing of the nation, or the race. The gods many—all those centers of value on whom the self has depended for its meaning—promise integration and fulfillment but deliver instead disintegration and futility. The universal forms of faith, polytheism and henotheism, are alike the harbingers of nihilism and death.

Now, Niebuhr suggests, there is a third form of faith, an alternative way of valuing, which appears historically "more as hope than as datum, more perhaps as a possibility than as an actuality, yet also as an actuality that has modified at certain emergent periods our natural social faith and our polytheism."[5] This third form of faith involves trust in and loyalty to no relative existent, but the One beyond the many from whom the many derive their being. It involves adopting as the center of human valuing that which is the source of all being. In contradistinction to "henotheism" (idolatrous monotheism), Niebuhr calls this pattern of faith "radical monotheism."

---

[3] *Radical Monotheism and Western Culture*, 119.

[4] Ibid., 30.

[5] Ibid., 31.

> For radical monotheism the value-center is neither closed society nor the principle of such a society but the principle of being itself; its reference is to no one reality among the many but to One beyond all the many, whence all the many derive their being, and by participation in which they exist. As faith, it is reliance on the source of all being for the significance of the self and of all that exists. . . . It is the confidence that whatever is, is good, because it exists as one thing among the many which all have their origin and their being, in the One—the principle of being which is also the principle of value. In Him we live and move and have our being not only as existent but as worthy of existence and worthy in existence. It is not a relation to any finite, natural or supernatural, value—center that confers value on self and some of its companions in being, but it is value relation to the One to whom all being is related.[6]

Radical monotheism involves then the perception that the principle of unity, the principle of being, and the principle of value are identical. This means that wholeness and fulfillment, personal and social, become possible. The salvation that the gods from among the many promise but cannot deliver becomes actual as trust and loyalty are directed towards the One beyond the many. Fragmentation is transcended. For when the principle of being becomes the center of value, the self is—consensually—implicated in the cause of universal being. Its cause is the inclusive cause of the Maker of heaven and earth. The neighbor becomes every "companion in being."

> Hence universal loyalty expresses itself as loyalty to each particular existent in the community of being and to the universal community. . . . Love of the neighbor is required in every morality formed by a faith; but in polytheistic faith the neighbor is defined as the one who is near me in my interest group, *when* he is near me in that passing association. In henotheistic social faith my neighbor is my fellow in the closed society. Hence in both instances the counterpart of the law of neighbor-love is the requirement to hate the enemy. But in radical monotheism my neighbor is my companion in being; though he is my enemy in some less than universal context the requirement is to love him.[7]

Radical monotheism is, in this way, an uncompromising form of theocentric faith that expresses itself in trust in and loyalty to the One whose cause is the realm of being as such. Within this pattern of faith/valuing, every lesser loyalty is transcended and every form of fragmentation is, in principle, overcome. Even humanism and naturalism are transcended as the self adopts as its cause not the promotion of human good alone, or the good of the living alone (Schweitzer), or even creaturely (natural) good alone, but universal good.

---

[6]Ibid., 32.

[7]Ibid., 34.

> Radical monotheism dethrones all absolutes short of the principle of being itself. At the same time it reverences every relative existent. Its two great mottoes are: "I am the Lord thy God; thou shalt have no other gods before me" and "Whatever is, is good."[8]

Now, the Christian "paradigm" is defined by precisely this "radically monotheistic" perception: that the source of being should be the center of valuation and that positive valuation should be extended to all being(s). The Christian paradigm is distinguished, moreover, by the claim that this pattern of perceiving and valuing has become "incarnate"—uniquely incarnate in one people and in one human and, because of them potentially incarnate in all peoples and every human. "We may," says Niebuhr, "use the theological word 'incaration' in speaking of the coming of radically monotheistic faith into our history, meaning by it the concrete expression in a total human life of radical trust in the One and of universal loyalty to the realm of being."[9] Radical faith appeared in the people of Israel, for whom life became defined in covenantal terms. "Promise-making and promise-keeping were the essential elements in every connection between persons. . . . Faith as confidence in the One and as loyalty to the universe of being was ingredient in every action and relation."[10] Often, to be sure, the covenant was broken; but distrust and disloyalty stood under the judgment provided by the prophetic norm: "Thou shalt have no other gods . . ." and "Whatever is, is good." Moreover, within the history of Israel, marked by a struggle unique (in intensity and quality) amongst the peoples of earth between radical faith and partial faiths, the radically monotheistic pattern of perceiving and valuing found its full flowering:

> Jesus Christ represents the incarnation of radical faith to an even greater extent than Israel. The greatness of his confidence in the Lord of heaven and earth as fatherly in goodness toward all creatures, the consistency of his loyalty to the realm of being, seem unqualified by distrust or by competing loyalty. The faith is expressed in acts of healing as well as in teaching, in his interpretation of the historic moment in which he lives and in the leadership he seeks to give to his people, in his relations to national enemies and to the morally rejected. His confidence and his fidelity are those of a son of God. . . . The word of God as God's oath of fidelity became flesh in him in this sense that he was a man who single-mindedly accepted the assurance that the Lord of heaven and earth was wholly faithful to him and to all creatures, and who in response gave wholehearted loyalty to the realm of being.[11]

---

[8]Ibid., 37.

[9]Ibid., 40.

[10]Ibid., 41.

[11]Ibid., 42.

"Christianity" is defined by reference to Christ, and "Christ" is the name of the definitive occasion of the right ordering of human life. In Jesus, the Christ, love of God and love of companion find full and proper actualization. In him, absolute love is directed towards the Absolute and a relative love towards the relative; and life is organized accordingly. Hence, Jesus is the paradigmatic instance of the right ordering of human loyalties—and life. He is thus the paradigm of the "responsible" human;[12] he responds appropriately to all that impinges upon him and serves the cause of the One by promoting the good of the many. Moreover, as the incarnation of radical faith and as the paradigmatic instance of responsible selfhood, Jesus becomes the preeminent agent of reconciliation. For the authentically human way of perceiving, valuing, and acting that finds expression in him becomes the occasion of a perpetual revolution (*metanoia*) in the lives of those who come under his influence.

Jesus is the revealer as well as the reconciler. Since "revelation specifies those events in which radical faith was elicited,"[13] as the incarnation of radical faith Jesus is the historical moment in which the character of divine and creaturely reality alike is most fully disclosed.

> When Christians refer to Jesus Christ as the revelation of God they do not or ought not have less than the three notes of faith in mind, the note that the valuing, saving power in the world is the principle of being itself; that the ultimate principle of being gives and maintains and re-establishes worth; that they have been called upon to make the cause of that God their cause.[14]

Niebuhr goes further. That which is given in revelation is not only the disclosure of a unique way of perceiving and valuing. The disclosure of a salvific perceptual-valuational pattern is grounded in the disclosure of divine personhood. In Israel the principle of being is identified as "the First Person": "if the cornerstone of Christian philosophy is the conviction that 'there is but one God and this God is Being,' the cornerstone of Christian as of Jewish and all radical monotheist confidence and loyalty is that the one God who is Being is an 'I,' or like an 'I,' who is faithful as only selves are faithful."[15]

> To say that God makes himself known as First Person is to say that revelation means less the disclosure of the essence of objective being to minds than the demonstration to selves of faithful, truthful being. What we try to point to with the aid of conceptual terms as principle of being or as the One beyond the many is acknowledged by selves as "Thou." The integrity that is before

---

[12]See, especially, *The Responsible Self* (New York: Harper & Row, 1963).

[13]*Radical Monotheism and Western Culture*, 42.

[14]Ibid., 43.

[15]Ibid., 45.

them here is the oneness of a self; it is the faithfulness that keeps promises, is indefectibly loyal, is truthful in freedom. God is steadfast self, keeping his word, "faithful in all his doings and just in all his ways." This principle of personlike integrity is fundamental in a revelation that is an event which elicits the confidence of selves in their ultimate environment and calls upon them as free selves to decide for the universal cause.[16]

This, too, is a distinctive aspect of the Christian paradigm: the priority of the personal. The Judeo-Christian understanding of being is relational: God and hunankind are bound together with each other and with otherkind in a nexus of relationships. And the relations are self-involving relations, relations marked by the personal functions of trust and fidelity. Promise-making and promise-keeping are not epiphenomenal but constitutive of—central to—being. For Israel, covenant is indissolubly involved with Being. This means that "there is something in our human existence, in our world, with our companions and in ourselves that cannot be denied yet cannot be understood with the aid of impersonal categories."[17] And that something—the personal—has a certain priority. Reality, ultimately, is "personlike" and devoted to the summoning forth of persons. "As revelation . . . means the event in which the ultimate unity is disclosed as personal or faithful, so the human response to such revelation is the development of integrated [and responsible] selfhood."[18] Such development involves perpetual revolution, or *metanoia*, in which every partial loyalty is transcended as the self embraces the universal cause of the One beyond, but present to and with, the many. "So faith in God involves us in a permanent revolution of the mind and heart, a continuous life which opens out infinitely into ever new possibilities."[19]

Let us now sum up certain of the salient elements that give the Christian paradigm its distinctive character. By looking at the Christian paradigm and its "determinative exemplar" through the eyes of our secondary exemplar, Niebuhr, we have found several distinguishing features, either directly or by implication.

The Christian perspective is radically theocentric. It provides a particular way of perceiving and valuing. The world of the many is perceived as derivative from the One. This vision of the world as creation carries with it the conviction that the Creator is to be loved preeminently but the created is to be loved too—and loved relatively. Second, this way of perceiving and valuing has found expression in history in Jesus of Naza-

---

[16]Ibid., 46-47.

[17]Ibid., 45.

[18]Ibid., 47.

[19]Ibid., 126.

reth. Third, through his agency, and the agency of the community that submits itself to his influence, the radically monotheistic pattern of perceiving and valuing continues to be incarnated in human life. Fourth, as this implies, history is the most significant medium through which the divine reality expresses and communicates itself. The determinative exemplar for the Christian relation to God is a historical personage. Fifth, the divine reality discloses itself as personal and as devoted to the project of person-formation within the overall project of world-making and world-fulfilling. Hence, the personal has a certain priority in being. Sixth, reality is "communal" or relational in character; each existent "has been called into membership in the society of universal being."[20] Seventh, all members of the universal community, personal and extra-personal alike, are valuable; and their value is grounded above all, in their common Source.

---

[20]Ibid., 60.

BIBLIOGRAPHY

Alexander, Samuel. *Space, Time, and Deity.* 2 vols. London: Macmillan and Company, 1920.

Alpers, Kenneth P. "Starting Points for an Ecological Theology: A Bibliographical Survey." *Dialog* 9 (Summer 1970): 226-35. Reprinted in *New Theology No. 8.* Edited by Martin E. Marty and Dean G. Peerman. New York: Macmillan Company, 1971.

Anderson, Bernard W. "Human Dominion Over Nature." In *Biblical Studies in Contemporary Thought*, pp. 27-45. Edited by Miriam Ward. Somerville MA: Greeno, Hadden & Company, 1975.

——————. "The Earth is the Lord's: An Essay in the Biblical Doctrine of Creation." *Interpretation* 9:1 (January 1955): 3-20.

Armstrong, Edward A. *Saint Francis: Nature Mystic.* Berkeley: University of California Press, 1973.

Atkins, Anselm. "Neville's Dialectical Argument for an Indeterminate Creator." *Theological Studies* 30:1 (March 1969): 90-107.

Atkinson, Brooks, ed. *"Walden" and Other Writings of Henry David Thoreau.* New York: Random House, 1937.

Bailey, Charles-James N. *Groundwork for Comparative Metatheology.* Ann Arbor MI: University Microfilms, 1965.

Baillie, John, ed. *Natural Theology.* Translated by Peter Fraenkel. London: Geoffrey Bles; Centary Press, 1946.

Baltazar, Eulalio R. *Teilhard and the Supernatural.* Baltimore: Helicon Press, 1966.

Barbour, Ian G. "An Ecological Ethic." *Christian Century* 87:40 (7 October 1970): 1180-84.

——————. "Five Ways of Reading Teilhard." *Soundings* 51:2 (Summer 1968):115-45. Reprinted in *The Teilhard Review* 3:1 (Summer 1968):3-20.

——————. *Issues in Science and Religion.* Englewood Cliffs NJ: Prentice-Hall, 1966.

——————. *Myths, Models and Paradigms: A Comparative Study in Science and Religion.* New York: Harper & Row, 1974.

——————. "Teilhard's Process Metaphysics." *Process Theology: Basic Writings*, 323-50. Edited by Ewert H. Cousins. New York: Newman Press, 1971. Reprinted from *The Journal of Religion* 49 (1969):136-59.

Barbour, Ian G., ed. *Earth Might Be Fair: Reflections on Ethics, Religion, and Ecology.* Englewood Cliffs NJ: Prentice-Hall, 1972.

——————, ed. *Finite Resources and the Human Future.* Minneapolis: Augsburg Publishing House, 1976.

_____, ed. *Science and Religion: New Perspectives on the Dialogue*. New York: Harper & Row; Harper Forum Books, 1968.

_____, ed. *Western Man and Environmental Ethics: Attitudes Toward Nature and Technology*. Reading MA: Addison-Wesley Publishing Company, 1973.

Barnette, Henlee H. *The Church and the Ecological Crisis*. Grand Rapids: Eerdmans, 1972.

Barth, Karl. *Church Dogmatics*. 4 vols. Translated and edited by G. W. Bromiley, et al. Edinburgh: T & T Clark, 1936-1969.

_____. *Dogmatics in Outline*. Translated by G. I. Thomson. New York: Harper & Row, 1959.

_____. *The Epistle to the Romans*. Translated by Edwyn C. Hoskyns. London: Oxford University Press, 1933.

Bellah, Robert N. *Beyond Belief*. New York: Harper and Row, 1970.

_____. "Religion in the University: Changing Consciousness, Changing Structures." In *Religion in the Undergraduate Curriculum*, pp. 13-18. Edited by Claude Welch. Washington DC: Association of American Colleges, 1972.

Bennett, John B. "Nature—God's Body?" *Philosophy Today* 18:3/4 (Fall 1974):248-54.

_____. "On Responding to Lynn White: Ecology and Christianity." *Ohio Journal of Religious Studies* 5:1 (April 1977):71-77.

Benz, Ernst. *Evolution and Christian Hope: Man's Concept of the Future, from the Early Fathers to Teilhard de Chardin*. Translated by Heinz G. Frank. Garden City NY: Doubleday & Company, 1966.

Bergson, Henri. *Creative Evolution*. Translated by Arthur Mitchell. New York: Modern Library, 1944.

Birch, L. Charles. *Nature and God*. Philadelphia: Westminster Press, 1965.

_____. "What Does God Do in the World?" *Union Seminary Quarterly Review* 30 (1975):80-81.

Black, Max. *Models and Metaphors*. Ithaca: Cornell University Press, 1962.

Bloch, Ernst. *Man on His Own*. Translated by E. B. Ashton. New York: Herder and Herder, 1970.

Bohr, Niels. *Atomic Theory and the Description of Nature*. Cambridge: Cambridge University Press, 1934.

Bonifazi, Conrad. *A Theology of Things: A Study of Man in His Physical Environment*. Philadelphia: J. B. Lippincott Company, 1967.

Bowman, Archibald Allan. *A Sacramental Universe*. Princeton: Princeton University Press, 1939.

Brauer, Jerald C. "In Appreciation of Joseph Sittler." *Journal of Religion* 54:2 (April 1974):97-101.

Bravo, Francisco. *Christ in the Thought of Teilhard de Chardin*. Translated by Cathryn B. Larme. Notre Dame: University of Notre Dame Press, 1967.

Bright, John. *The Kingdom of God*. Nashville: Abingdon Press, 1953.

Brown, Delwin, et al., eds. *Process Philosophy and Christian Thought*. Indianapolis: Bobbs-Merrill Company, 1971.

Brunner, Emil. *Dogmatics*. 3 vols. Translated by Olive Wyon. Philadelphia: Westminster Press, 1950-1962.

Buber, Martin. "Brother Body." In *Pointing the Way: Collected Essays*, 20-24. Translated by Maurice Friedman. New York: Harper & Brothers, 1957.

——————. *I and Thou*. Translated by Ronald G. Smith. 2nd ed. New York: Charles Scribner's Sons, 1958.

——————. *Mamre: Essays in Religion*. Translated by Greta Hort. Melbourne: Melbourne University Press, 1946.

Bugbee, Henry H. "Wilderness in America." *Journal of the American Academy of Religion* 42:4 (December 1974):614-20.

Bultmann, Rudolf. *Faith and Understanding*. Translated by Louise Pettibone Smith. London: SCM Press, 1969.

——————. *Jesus Christ and Mythology*. New York: Charles Scribner's Sons, 1958.

Buren, Paul van. *The Secular Meaning of the Gospel*. New York: Macmillan Company, 1963.

Burtt, Edwin A. *The Metaphysical Foundations of Modern Science*. New York: Doubleday and Company; Anchor Books, 1954.

Calvin, John. *Commentary on the Epistles of Paul the Apostle to the Corinthians*. Translated by John Pringle. Edinburgh, 1849.

——————. *Institutes of the Christian Religion*. 2 vols. Edited by John T. McNeill. Philadelphia: Westminster Press, 1960.

Care, Norman, and Landesman, Charles. *Readings in the Theory of Action*. Bloomington: Indiana University Press, 1968.

Carson, Rachel. *Silent Spring*. Greenwich CT: Fawcett Publications, 1970. First published, 1962.

Cassirer, Ernst. *The Philosophy of the Enlightenment*. Translated by Fritz C. A. Koelln and James P. Pettegrove. Boston: Beacon Press, 1966. First published, 1932.

Cauthen, Kenneth. *Christian Biopolitics: A Credo and Strategy for the Future*. Nashville: Abingdon Press, 1971.

——————. *Science, Secularization, and God: Toward a Theology of the Future*. Nashville: Abingdon Press, 1969.

Chauchard, Paul. *Science and Religion*. Translated by S. J. Tester. New York: Hawthorn Books, 1962.

Cherry, Conrad. *Nature and Religious Imagination: From Edwards to Bushnell*. Philadelphia: Fortress Press, 1980.

Christian, C. W., and Wittig, Glen R., eds. *Radical Theology: Phase Two*. Philadelphia: J. B. Lippincott Company, 1967.

Christian, William A. *An Interpretation of Whitehead's Metaphysics*. New Haven: Yale University Press, 1959.

Clark, John Rustan. "The Great Living System: The World as the Body of God." *Zygon* 9 (1974):57-93.

Cobb, John B., Jr. *A Christian Natural Theology: Based on the Thought of Alfred North Whitehead*. Philadelphia: Westminster Press, 1965.

——————. *Christ in a Pluralistic Age*. Philadelphia: Westminster Press, 1975.

——————. *God and the World*. Philadelphia: Westminster Press, 1969.

——————. *Is It Too Late? A Theology of Ecology*. Beverly Hills CA: Bruce, 1972.

_____. *Living Options in Protestant Theology: A Survey of Methods*. Philadelphia: Westminster Press, 1962.

_____. *The Structure of Christian Existence*. Philadelphia: Westminster Press, 1967.

Cobb, John B., Jr., ed. *The Theology of Altizer: Critique and Response*. Philadelphia: Westminster Press, 1970.

Cobb, John B., Jr., and Griffin, David Ray. *Mind in Nature: Essays on the Interface of Science and Philosophy*. Washington DC: University Press of America, 1977.

_____ *Process Theology: An Introductory Exposition*. Philadelphia: Westminster Press, 1976.

Cobb, John B., Jr. "A New Christian Existence." In *Neues Testament und Christliche Existenz*, pp. 59-94. Edited by Hans Dieter Betz and Louise Schottroff. Tübingen: J. C. B. Mohr, 1973.

_____ "Christian Natural Theology and Christian Existence." In *Frontline Theology*, pp. 39-45. Edited by Dean G. Peerman. Richmond VA: John Knox Press, 1967.

_____ "Christian Theism and the Ecological Crisis." *Religious Education* 66 (January-February 1971):31-35.

_____ "Ecological Disaster and the Church." *The Christian Century* 87 (7 October 1970):1185-87. Also as "Out of the Ashes of Disaster." *Resource* 12 (March 1971): 20-23.

_____ "Ecology, Ethics and Theology." In *Toward a Steady-State Economy*, pp. 303-20. Edited by Herman E. Daly. San Francisco: W. H. Freeman and Company, 1973.

_____ "Men and Animals." *The Christian Science Monitor*, 6 May 1974.

_____ "Natural Causality and Divine Action." *Idealistic Studies* 3 (September 1973):207-22.

_____ "Nihilism, Existentialism, and Whitehead. " *Religion in Life* 30 (Autumn 1961):521-33.

_____ "The Christian Concern for the Non-Human World." *Anticipation* 16 (March 1974):32-34.

_____ "The Christian, the Future, and Paolo Soleri." *The Christian Century* 91 (30 October 1974):1008-11.

_____ "The Local Church and the Environmental Crisis." *The Christian Ministry* 4 (September 1973):3-7. Also in *Foundations* 17 (April-June 1974):164-72.

_____ "The Population Explosion and the Rights of the Subhuman World." *IDOC-International: North American Edition* (12 September 1970):40-62. Abridged in *Dimensions of the Environmental Crisis*, 19-32. Edited by John A. Day, F. F. Fost, and P. Rose. New York: John Wiley & Sons, 1971.

Collingwood, R. G. *The Idea of Nature*. New York: Oxford University Press, 1972. First published, 1945.

Commoner, Barry. *The Closing Circle: Nature, Man and Technology*. New York: Bantam Books, 1972.

Compton, John J. "Science and God's Action in Nature." In *Earth Might Be Fair*, 33-47. Edited by Ian G. Barbour. Englewood Cliffs: Prentice-Hall, 1972.

Cousins, Ewert H., ed. *Hope and the Future of Man*. Philadelphia: Fortress Press, 1972.

——————— *Process Theology: Basic Writings*. New York: Newman Press, 1971.

Cox, Harvey. *On Not Leaving It to the Snake*. New York: Macmillan Company, 1967.

——————— *The Feast of Fools: A Theological Essay on Festivity and Fantasy*. Cambridge: Harvard University Press, 1969.

——————— *The Secular City*. New York: Macmillan Company, 1965.

Crespy, Georges. *From Science to Theology: An Essay on Teilhard de Chardin*. Translated by George H. Shriver. Nashville: Abingdon Press, 1968.

Cuénot, Claude. *Teilhard de Chardin: A Biographical Study*. Translated by Vincent Colimore. London: Burns & Oates, 1965.

Csikszentmihalyi, Mihaly. "Sociological Implications in the Thought of Teilhard de Chardin." *Zygon* 5:2 (June 1970):130-47.

Dahl, N. A. "The Parables of Growth." *Studia Theologica* 5:2 (1951):132-66.

Darwin, Francis, ed. *The Autobiography of Charles Darwin and Selected Letters*. New York: Dover Publications, 1958. First published, 1892.

De Bell, Garrett, ed. *The Environmental Handbook*. New York: Ballantine Books, 1970.

Delaney, C. F. *Mind and Nature: A Study of the Naturalistic Philosophies of Cohen, Woodbridge and Sellars* Notre Dame: University of Notre Dame Press, 1969.

Deer, Thomas Seiger. *Ecology and Human Need*. Philadelphia: Westminster Press, 1975.

Dillenberger, John. *Protestant Thought and Natural Science: A Historical Interpretation*. Nashville: Abingdon Press, 1960.

Dilley, Frank B. "Does the 'God Who Acts' Really Act?" *Anglican Theological Review* 47:1 (January 1965):66-88.

Ditmanson, Harold H. "The Call for a Theology of Creation." *Dialog* 3 (August 1964): 264-73.

Dobzhansky, Theodosius G. *Heredity and the Nature of Man*. New York: New American Library; Sequet Books, 1966.

Dubos, René. *A God Within*. New York: Charles Scribner's Sons, 1972.

Dyson, Anthony, and Towers, Bernard, eds. *Evolution, Marxism and Christianity*. London: Granstone Press, 1967.

Ebeling, Gerhard. *God and Word*. Translated by James W. Leitch. Philadelphia: Fortress Press, 1967.

Edwards, Jonathan. *A Dissertation Concerning the Chief End for Which God Created the World*. In *The Works of President Edwards*, vol. 3. New York: S. Converse, 1829.

——————— *The Nature of True Virtue*. Ann Arbor: University of Michigan Press, 1960.

Eiseley, Loren. *The Firmament of Time*. New York: Atheneum, 1966.

——————— *The Immense Journey*. New York: Random House, 1957.

Elder, Frederick. *Crisis in Eden: A Religious Study of Man and Environment*. Nashville: Abingdon Press, 1970.

Elwood, Douglas J. *The Philosophical Theology of Jonathan Edwards*. New York: Columbia University Press, 1960.

Emmet, Dorothy. *The Nature of Metaphysical Thinking*. London: Macmillan and Company, 1949.

Engel, David E. "Elements in a Theology of Environment." *Zygon* 5:3 (September 1970): 216-27.

Farmer, H. H. *The World and God: A Study of Prayer, Providence and Miracle in Christian Experience.* London: Nisbet and Company, 1936.

Ferkiss, Victor C. *Technological Man: The Myth and the Reality.* New York: New American Library; Mentor Books, 1970.

Ferré, Frederick. *Language, Logic and God.* New York: Harper & Row, 1961.

_____ "Metaphors, Models, and Religion." *Soundings* 51 (1968):327-45.

Fisher, Joseph L. et al. Papers of the 1970 Conference on Ethics and Ecology of the Institute on Religion in an Age of Science. *Zygon* 5:4 (December 1970).

Flew, Antony, and MacIntyre, Alasdair, eds. *New Essays in Philosophical Theology.* New York: Macmillan Company, 1964. First published, 1955.

Foster, M. B. "The Christian Doctrine of Creation and the Rise of Modern Science." *Mind* 43 (1934).

Fowler, James W. *To See the Kingdom: The Theological Vision of H. Richard Niebuhr.* Nashville: Abingdon Press, 1974.

Francoeur, Robert T., ed. *The World of Teilhard.* Baltimore: Helicon Press, 1961.

Gay, John H. "Four Medieval Views of Creation." *The Harvard Theological Review* 56:4 (October 1963):243-73.

Gilkey, Langdon. "Cosmology, Ontology, and the Travail of Biblical Language." *The Journal of Religion* 41:3 (July 1961):194-205.

_____ *Maker of Heaven and Earth: A Study of the Christian Doctrine of Creation.* Garden City NJ: Doubleday and Company, 1959; Anchor Books edition, 1965.

_____ *Naming the Whirlwind: The Renewal of God-Language.* Indianapolis: Bobbs-Merrill Company, 1969.

_____ *Reaping the Whirlwind: A Christian Interpretation of History.* New York: Seabury Press, 1976.

_____ *Religion and the Scientific Future: Reflections on Myth, Science and Theology.* New York: Harper & Row, 1970; Macon GA: Mercer University Press (Rose),   1981.

_____ Review of *A Christian Natural Theology*, by John B. Cobb, Jr. *Theology Today* 22:4 (January 1966):530-45.

Glacken, Clarence J. *Traces on the Rhodian Shore: Nature and Culture in Western Thought from Ancient Times to the End of the Eighteenth Century.* Berkeley: University of California Press, 1967.

Godsey, John D. "Thinking the Faith Historically: The Legacy of Carl Michalson." *The Drew Gateway* 36:3 (Spring-Summer 1966):76-88.

Graham, Frank, Jr. *Since Silent Spring.* Boston: Houghton Mifflin Company, 1970.

Greene, John C. *Darwin and the Modern World View.* New York: New American Library; Mentor Books, 1963.

_____ *The Death of Adam: Evolution and Its Impact on Western Thought.* New York: New American Library; Mentor Books, 1961.

Griffin, David Ray. *A Process Christology.* Philadelphia: Westminster Press, 1973.

_____ *God, Power, and Evil: A Process Theodicy.* Philadelphia: Westminster Press, 1976.

_____ "Gordon Kaufman's Theology: Some Questions." *Journal of the American Academy of Religion* 41:4 (December 1973):554-72.

Griffin, David, ed. *Philosophy of Religion and Theology: 1971.* Chambersburg PA: American Academy of Religion, 1971.

Griffin, David Ray and Altizer, Thomas J. J., eds. *John Cobb's Theology in Process.* Philadelphia: Westminster Press, 1977.

Hamilton, Michael, ed. *This Little Planet.* New York: Charles Scribner's Sons, 1970.

Hanley, Wayne. *Natural History in America: From Mark Catesby to Rachel Carson.* New York: New York Times Book Company, 1977.

Hartshorne, Charles. *The Divine Relativity: A Social Conception of God.* New Haven: Yale University Press, 1948.

——————— *The Logic of Perfection.* Lasalle IL: Open Court Publishing Company, 1962.

Haselden, Kyle, and Hefner, Philip, eds. *Changing Man; The Threat and the Promise.* Garden City NY: Doubleday & Company; Anchor Books edition, 1969.

Hefner, Philip. "The Politics and the Ontology of Nature and Grace." *Journal of Religion* 54:2 (April 1974):138-50.

——————— *The Promise of Teilhard.* Philadelphia: J. B. Lippincott Company, 1970.

——————— "The Relocation of the God-Question." *Zygon* 5:1 (March 1970):5-17.

Hegel, G. W. F. *The Phenomenology of Mind.* Translated by J. B. Baillie. London: George Allen & Unwin, 1931.

——————— *Philosophy of Nature.* Translated by A. V. Miller. Oxford: Clarendon Press, 1970.

Heim, Karl. *Christian Faith and Natural Science.* Translated by N. Horton Smith. New York: Harper & Row; Harper Torchbooks, 1957.

——————— *The World: Its Creation and Consummation.* Translated by Robert Smith. Philadelphia: Muhlenberg Press, 1962.

High, Dallas M. *Language, Persons, and Belief.* New York: Oxford University Press, 1967.

Inbody, Tyron. "Paul Tillich and Process Theology." *Theological Studies* 36:3 (September 1975):472-92.

James, Ralph E. *The Concrete God: A New Beginning for Theology—The Thought of Charles Hartshorne.* New York: Bobbs-Merrill Company, 1967.

Jaspers, Karl. *The Origin and Goal of History.* Translated by Michael Bullock. London: Routledge and Kegan Paul, 1953.

Johnson, S. E. "Matthew." In *The Interpreter's Bible*, vol. 7. Edited by George A. Buttrick. New York: Abingdon-Cokesbury Press, 1951.

Jonas, Hans. *The Phenomenon of Life: Toward a Philosophical Biology.* New York: Harper & Row, 1966.

Kaufman, Gordon D. *An Essay on Theological Method.* Missoula MT: Scholars Press, 1975.

——————— "A Problem for Theology: The Concept of Nature." *Harvard Theological Review* 65 (1972):337-66.

——————— *God the Problem.* Cambridge: Harvard University Press, 1972.

——————— "Metaphysics and Theology." *Cross Currents* 28:3 (Summer 1978):325-41.

——————— *Relativism, Knowledge and Faith.* Chicago: University of Chicago Press, 1960.

_____. *Systematic Theology: A Historicist Perspective*. New York: Charles Scribner's Sons, 1968.

Kazantzakis, Nikos. *Report to Greco*. Translated by P. A. Bien. New York: Simon and Schuster, 1960.

_____. *The Last Temptation of Christ*. Translated by P. A. Bien. New York: Simon and Schuster, 1960.

Keen, Sam. *Apology for Wonder*. New York: Harper & Row, 1969.

Kenney, W. Henry. *A Path through Teilhard's Phenomenon*. Dayton OH: Pflaum Press, 1970.

King, Robert H. "The 'Ecological Motif' in the Theology of H. Richard Niebuhr." *Journal of the American Academy of Religion* 42:2 (June 1974):339-43.

_____. *The Meaning of God*. Philadelphia: Fortress Press, 1973.

Kirkpatrick, Frank G. "Process or Agent: Two Models for Self and God." *Philosophy of Religion and Theology: 1971*, pp. 74-94. Edited by David Griffin. Chambersburg PA: American Academy of Religion, 1971.

Kuhn, Thomas S. *The Structure of Scientific Revolutions*. 2nd ed. Chicago: University of Chicago Press, 1970.

Lee, Richard T. "Whitehead's Theory of the Self." Ph. D. dissertation, Yale University, 1962.

Leiss, William. *The Dominion of Nature*. New York: George Braziler, 1972.

Leopold, Aldo. *A Sand County Almanac*. New York: Ballantine Books, 1970. First published, 1949.

Ligneul, André. *Teilhard and Personalism*. Translated by Paul Joseph Oligny and Michael D. Meilach. New York: Paulist Press, 1968.

Löwith, Karl. *Nature, History and Existentialism*. Edited by Arnold Levison. Evanston: Northwestern University Press, 1966.

de Lubac, Henri, *Teilhard de Chardin: The Man and His Meaning*. Translated by René Hague. New York: Hawthorn Books, 1965.

Lukas, Mary, and Lukas, Ellen. *Teilhard*. Garden City NY: Doubleday and Company, 1977.

Macmurray, John. *Interpreting the Universe*. 2nd ed. London: Faber and Faber, 1936. First published, 1933.

_____. *The Form of the Personal*. 2 vols. Vol. 1: *The Self as Agent*. Vol. 2: *Persons in Relation*. London: Faber and Faber, 1969. First published, 1957 and 1961.

Macquarrie, John. *God-Talk: An Examination of the Language and Logic of Theology*. New York: Harper & Row, 1967.

_____. "The Idea of a Theology of Nature." *Union Seminary Quarterly Review* 30:2-4 (Winter-Summer 1975):69-75.

Malinowski, Bronislaw. *Magic, Science, and Religion*. Garden City: Doubleday & Company; Anchor Books, 1954.

Maloney, George. *The Cosmic Christ, from Paul to Teilhard*. New York: Sheed & Ward, 1968.

Maly, Eugene H. "Creation in the New Testament." In *Biblical Studies in Contemporary Thought*, 104-12. Edited by Miriam Ward. Somerville MA: Greeno, Hadden & Company, 1975.

Marsh, George Perkins. *Man and Nature*. Edited by David Lowenthal. Cambridge: Harvard University Press, Belknap Press, 1965. First published, 1864.

Marx, Leo. *The Machine in the Garden: Technology and the Pastoral Ideal in America*. New York: Oxford University Press, 1964.

McHarg, Ian L. *Design with Nature*. Garden City NJ: Natural History Press, 1969.

McLain, Michael. "On Theological Models." *Harvard Theological Review* 62 (1969): 155-87.

Medawar, P. B. Review of *The Phenomenon of Man*. *Mind* 70 (1961):99-106.

Meland, Bernard E. "Grace: A Dimension within Nature?" *Journal of Religion* 54:2 (April 1974):128-37.

———————— "New Perspectives on Nature and Grace." In *The Scope of Grace: Essays on Nature and Grace in Honor of Joseph Sittler*, 141-61. Edited by Philip Hefner. Philadelphia: Fortress Press, 1964.

Michalson, Carl. *The Hinge of History: An Existential Approach to the Christian Faith*. New York: Charles Scribner's Sons, 1959.

———————— *The Rationality of Faith: An Historical Critique of the Theological Reason*. New York: Charles Scribner's Sons, 1963.

———————— *Worldly Theology: The Hermeneutical Focus of an Historical Faith*. New York: Charles Scribner's Sons, 1967.

Miller, Perry. *Errand Into the Wilderness*. Cambridge: Harvard University Press, Belknap Press, 1956.

———————— *Jonathan Edwards*. New York: World Publishing Company, 1959. Meridian Books.

———————— *Nature's Nation*. Cambridge: Belknap Press, 1967.

Mitchell, John G., and Stallings, Constance F., eds. *Ecotactics: The Sierra Club Handbook for Environmental Activists*. New York: Simon & Schuster; Pocket Books, 1970.

Mooney, Christopher F. *Teilhard de Chardin and the Mystery of Christ*. New York: Harper & Row, 1964.

Moule, C. F. D. *Man and Nature in the New Testament: Some Reflections on Biblical Ecology*. Philadelphia: Fortress Facet Books, 1967.

Mumford, Lewis. *The Myth of the Machine*. 2 vols. New York: Harcourt, Brace and World, 1967 and 1970.

———————— *Technics and Civilization*. New York: Harcourt, Brace and Company, 1943.

———————— *The Transformations of Man*. New York: Harper & Brothers, 1956.

Murdy, W. H. "Anthropocentrism: A Modern Version." *Science* 187 (28 March 1975): 1168-72.

Murray, George B. "Teilhard and Orthogenetic Evolution." *Harvard Theological Review* 60 (1967):281-95.

Murray, Michael H. *The Thought of Teilhard de Chardin*. New York: Seabury Press, 1966.

Neville, Robert C. "Creation and the Trinity." *Theological Studies* 30:1 (March 1969):3-26.

———————— *God the Creator: On the Transcendence and Presence of God*. Chicago: University of Chicago Press, 1968.

Niebuhr, H. Richard. *Christ and Culture*. New York: Harper & Brothers; Harper Torch-
    books, 1956. First published, 1951.

_____ *Radical Monotheism and Western Culture*. New York: Harper & Row;
    Harper Torchbooks, 1970. First published, 1943.

_____ *The Responsible Self*. New York: Harper & Row, 1963.

Niebuhr, Reinhold. *Moral Man and Immoral Society*. New York: Charles Scribner's
    Sons, 1960.

_____ *The Nature and Destiny of Man: A Christian Interpretation*. New York:
    Charles Scribner's Sons, 1955. First published 1941-43.

Niebuhr, Richard R. *Resurrection and Historical Reason*. New York: Charles Scrib-
    ner's Sons, 1957.

_____ *Schleiermacher On Christ and Religion*. Charles Scribner's Sons, 1964.

Nygren, Anders. *Agape and Eros*. Philadelphia: Westminster Press, 1935.

O'Connor, Daniel, and Oakley, Francis, eds. *Creation: The Impact of an Idea*. New York:
    Charles Scribner's Sons, 1969.

Ogden, Schubert M. "Prolegomena to a Christian Theology of Nature." In *A Rational
    Faith: Essays in Honor of Levi A. Olan*. Edited by Jack Bemporad. New York: Ktav
    Publishing House, 1977.

_____ *The Reality of God*. New York: Harper & Row, 1966.

Overman, Richard. *Evolution and the Christian Doctrine of Creation*. Philadelphia:
    Westminster Press, 1967.

Padgett, Jack F. *The Christian Philosophy of William Temple*. The Hague: Martinus
    Nijhoff, 1974.

Pannenberg, Wolfhart. "The Doctrine of the Spirit and the Task of a Theology of
    Nature." *Theology* 25 (1972):8-21. Reprinted in *New Theology No. 10*. Edited by
    Martin E. Marty and Dean G. Peerman. New York: Macmillan Company, 1973.

_____ *Theology and the Kingdom of God*. Philadelphia: Westminster Press, 1969.

_____ *Theology and the Philosophy of Science*. Translated by Francis
    McDonagh. Philadelphia: Westminster Press, 1976.

Pannenberg, Wolfhart, and Muller, A. M. Klaus. *Erwägungen zu einer Theologie der
    Natur*. Gütersloh: Gütersloher Verlagshaus Gerd Mohn, 1970.

Patterson, Robert E., ed. *Science, Faith, and Revelation*. Nashville: Broadman Press,
    1979.

Pepper, Stephen C. *World Hypotheses: A Study in Evidence*. Berkeley: University of
    California Press, 1966. First published, 1942.

Perrin, Norman. *The Kingdom of God in the Teaching of Jesus*. Philadelphia: West-
    minster Press, 1963.

Peters, Eugene H. *Hartshorne and Neoclassical Metaphysics*. Lincoln: University of
    Nebraska Press, 1970.

Pollard, William G. *Chance and Providence: God's Action in a World Governed by
    Scientific Law*. New York: Charles Scribner's Sons, 1958.

Prenter, Regin. *Creation and Redemption*. Translated by Theodore I. Jensen. Phila-
    delphia: Fortress Press, 1967.

von Rad, Gerhard. *Genesis: A Commentary*. Translated by John H. Marks. Philadelphia:
    Westminster Press, 1961.

von Rad, Gerhard, et al. "Basileia." In *Bible Key Works,* vol. 2. Translated and edited by J. R. Coates and H. P Kingdon. New York: Harmper & Brothers, 1958.

Ramsey, Ian T. *Models and Mystery.* London: Oxford University Press, 1964.

——————— *Religious Language.* New York: Macmillan Company, 1963.

Raven, Charles E. *Natural Religion and Christian Theology.* 2 vols. Cambridge: Cambridge University Press, 1953.

Raven, Charles E. *Teilhard de Chardin: Scientist and Seer.* London: Collins, 1962.

Rauschenbusch, Walter. *A Theology for the Social Gospel.* New York: Abingdon Press, 1945. First published, 1919.

Reumann, John. *Creation and New Creation: The Past, Present, and Future of God's Creative Activity.* Minneapolis: Augsburg Publishing House, 1973.

Richardson, Herbert Warren. "The Glory of God in the Theology of Jonathan Edwards." Ph. D. dissertation, Harvard University, 1962.

Rideau, Emile. *The Thought of Teilhard de Chardin.* Translated by René Hague. New York: Harper & Row, 1967.

Robinson, James M., and Cobb, John B., Jr., eds. *The Later Heidegger and Theology.* Vol. 1 in *New Frontiers in Theology.* New York: Harper & Row, 1963.

Rupp, George. *Christologies and Cultures.* The Hague: Mouton & Co., 1974.

Rust, Eric C. *Evolutionary Philosophies and Contemporary Theology.* Philadelphia: Westminster Press, 1969.

——————— *Nature and Man in Biblical Thought.* London: Lutterworth Press, 1953.

——————— *Nature—Garden or Desert? An Essay in Environmental Theology.* Waco TX: Word Books, 1971.

——————— *Science and Faith: Towards a Theological Understanding of Nature.* New York: Oxford University Press, 1967.

——————— "The Holy Spirit, Nature, and Man." *Review and Expositor* 43:2 (Spring 1966):157-76.

——————— *Towards a Theological Understanding of History.* New York: Oxford University Press, 1963.

Santmire, H. Paul. *Brother Earth: Nature, God and Ecology in Time of Crisis.* New York: Thomas Nelson, 1970.

——————— "Creation and Nature: A Study of the Doctrine of Nature with Special Attention to Karl Barth's Doctrine of Creation." Th. D. dissertation, Harvard University, 1966.

Santmire, H. Paul, and Lutz, Paul E. *Ecological Renewal.* Philadelphia: Fortress Press, 1972.

Santmire, H. Paul. "Ecology and Ethical Ecumenics." *Anglican Theological Review* 59:1 (January 1977):98-102.

——————— "Ecology and Schizophrenia: Historical Dimensions of the American Crisis." *Dialog* 9 (Summer 1970):175-92.

——————— "Ecology, Justice and Theology: Beyond the Preliminary Skirmishes." *Christian Century* 93:17 (12 May 1976):460-64.

——————— "The Integrity of Nature." In *Christians and the Good Earth.* Edited by Alfred Stefferud. Alexandria VA: The Faith-Man-Nature Group, 1969.

——————— "Is Dogmatic Theology Dead?" *Dialog* 8 (Winter 1969):48-50.

_____ "I-Thou, I-It, and I-Ens." *Journal of Religion* 48:3 (July 1968):260-73.

_____ "It's His World We're Spoiling." *Resource* 11 (May 1970):2-5.

_____ "A New Theology of Nature?" *Lutheran Quarterly* 20:3 (August 1968):290-308.

_____ "On the Mission of the Church: Reflections Along the Way." *Lutheran Quarterly* 23:4 (November 1971):366-87.

_____ "Reflections on the Alleged Ecological Bankruptcy of Western Theology." *Anglical Theological Review* 57:2 (April 1975):131-52.

_____ "The Reformation Problematic and the Ecological Crisis." *Metanoia* 2 (June 1970), Special Supplement.

_____ "The Struggle for an Ecological Theology: A Case in Point." *Christian Century* 87:9 (4 March 1970):275-77.

_____ "World Hunger (I): A Global 'Final Solution'?" *Dialog* 14 (Winter 1975): 6-10.

_____ "World Hunger (II): A 'Confessing Church' in the U.S.?" *Dialog* 14 (Spring 1975):87-89.

Schaeffer, Francis A. *Pollution and the Death of Man: The Christian View of Ecology.* London: Hodder and Stroughton, 1970.

Scharlemann, Robert P. "Models in a Theology of Nature." In *Philosophy of Religion and Theology: 1971*, pp. 150-165. Edited by David Griffin. Chambersburg PA: American Academy of Religion, 1971.

_____ "Theological Models and Their Construction." *The Journal of Religion* 53:1 (January 1973):65-82.

Scheffczyk, Leo. *Creation and Providence.* Translated by Richard Strachan. New York: Herder and Herder, 1970.

Scheler, Max. *Man's Place in Nature.* Translated Hans Meyerhoff. New York: Noonday Press, 1962.

Schilling, Harold K. *Science and Religion: An Interpretation of Two Communities.* New York: Charles Scribner's Sons, 1962.

Schoonenberg, Piet. *Covenant and Creation.* Notre Dame: University of Notre Dame Press, 1969.

Scott, Nathan A., Jr. "The Poetry and Theology of Earth: Reflections on the Testimony of Joseph Sittler and Gerard Manley Hopkins." *Journal of Religion* 54:2 (April 1974): 102-20.

Seidenberg, Roderick. *Posthistoric Man.* Chapel Hill: University of North Carolina Press, 1950.

Shepherd, Paul. *Man in the Landscape.* New York: Alfred A. Knopf, 1967.

Shepherd, Paul and McKinley, Daniel, eds. *The Subversive Science: Essays Toward an Ecology of Man.* Boston: Houghton Mifflin Company, 1969.

Sherrell, Richard E., ed. *Ecology: Crisis and New Vision.* Richmond VA: John Knox Press, 1971.

Simpson, George Gaylord. *The Meaning of Evolution.* New Haven: Yale University Press, 1967.

_____ *This View of Life.* Harcourt, Brace and World, 1964.

Sittler, Joseph A., Jr. "A Theology for Earth." *The Christian Scholar* 37:3 (September 1954):367-74.

_____ "Called to Unity." *The Ecumenical Review* 14 (1961-62):177-87.

_____ "Ecological Commitment as Theological Responsibility." *Zygon* 5 (June 1970):172-81.

_____ *Essays on Nature and Grace.* Philadelphia: Fortress Press, 1972.

_____ "Nature and Grace: Reflections on an Old Rubric." *Dialog* 3 (August 1964): 252-56.

_____ "The Care of the Earth." *Sermons to Intellectuals.* Edited by Franklin H. Littell. New York: Macmillan Company, 1963.

_____ *The Ecology of Faith.* Philadelphia: Muhlenberg Press, 1961.

_____ "The Presence and Acts of the Triune God in Creation and History." In *The Gospel and Human Destiny.* Edited by Vilmos Vajta. Minneapolis: Augsburg Publishing House, 1971.

_____ Untitled essay. *Criterion* 6 (Winter 1967):21-23.

Slusser, C. and D. M. *Technology: The God that Failed.* Philadelphia: Westminster Press, 1971.

Smulders, Piet. *The Design of Teilhard de Chardin.* Translated by Arthur Gibson. Westminster MD: Newman Press, 1967.

Smuts, Jan Christiaan. *Holism and Evolution.* New York: Viking Press, 1961. First published, 1926.

Snook, Lee E. "Ecology and Ecclesiology: An American View." In *The Church Emerging: A U.S. Lutheran Case Study*, pp. 37-84. Edited by John Reumann. Philadelphia: Fortress Press, 1977.

Speaight, Robert. *Teilhard de Chardin: A Biography.* New York: Harper & Row, 1967.

Speaight, Robert; Casserly, J. V. Langmead; and Wilshire, Robert V. *Teilhard de Chardin: Re-Mythologization.* Waco TX: Word Books, 1970.

Stefferud, Alfred, ed. *Christians and the Good Earth: Address and Discussions at the Third National Conference of The Faith-Man-Nature Group.* Faith/Man/Nature Papers, no. 1. Alexandria VA: The Faith-Man-Nature Group, 1969.

Stewart, Claude Y., Jr. "Process Theology and the Protestant Principle." *Foundations* 21:4 (October-December 1978):356-64.

_____ Review of *Crisis in Eden*, by Frederick Elder. *Foundations* 14:2 (April-June 1971):189-92.

Stone, Glen C., ed. *A New Ethic for a New Earth.* Faith/Man/Nature Papers, no. 2. New York: Friendship Press, 1971.

Strawson, P. F. *Individuals: An Essay in Descriptive Metaphysics.* Garden City NY: Doubleday & Company; Anchor Books, 1963.

Strawson, P. F., ed. *Studies in the Philosophy of Thought and Action.* London: Oxford University Press, 1968.

Teilhard de Chardin, Pierre. *Building the Earth.* Translated by Noel Lindsay. New York: Avon Books; Discus Edition, 1969.

_____ *Christianity and Evolution.* Translated by René Hague. New York: Harcourt Brace Jovanovich, 1971.

_____ *The Divine Milieu.* Translated by Bernard Wall. New York: Harper & Row, 1960.

_____ *The Future of Man.* Translated by Norman Denny. New York: Harper & Row, 1964.

_____ *The Heart of Matter*. Translated by René Hague. New York: Harcourt Brace Jovanovich, 1978.

_____ *Human Energy*. Translated by J. M. Cohen. New York: Harcourt Brace Jovanovich, 1969.

_____ *Hymns of the Universe*. Translated by Gerald Vann. New York: Harper & Row; Perennial Library Edition, 1972.

_____ *Letters from a Traveler*. Translated by René Hague et al. New York: Harper & Row; Torchbooks Edition, 1961.

_____ *The Making of a Mind*. Translated by René Hague. New York: Harper & Row, 1965.

_____ *Man's Place in Nature*. London: William Collins Sons & Company, 1966.

_____ *The Phenomenon of Man*. Translated by Bernard Wall. New York: Harper & Row; Torchbooks Edition, 1961.

_____ *Science and Christ. (Translated by René)* Hague. New York: Harper & Row, 1968.

_____ *Toward the Future*. Translated by René Hague. New York: Harcourt Brace Jovanovich, 1975.

_____ *The Vision of the Past*. Translated by J. M. Cohen. New York: Harper & Row, 1966.

_____ *Writings in Time of War*. Translated by René Hague. New York: Harper & Row, 1968.

Temple, William. *Christus Veritas: An Essay*. London: Macmillan & Company, 1962. First published, 1924.

_____ *Mens Creatrix*. London: Macmillan & Company, 1961. First published, 1917.

_____ *Nature, Man and God*. London: Macmillan & Company, 1964. First published, 1934.

Tillich, Paul. *Biblical Religion and the Search for Ultimate Reality*. Chicago: University of Chicago Press, 1955.

_____ *Dynamics of Faith*. New York: Harper & Row; Harper Torchbooks, 1958.

_____ *Systematic Theology*. 3 vols. Chicago: University of Chicago Press, 1951-1963.

_____ *The Protestant Era*. Translated by James Luther Adams. Chicago: University of Chicago Press; Phoenix Books, 1957.

_____ *Theology of Culture*. Edited by Robert C. Kimball. New York: Oxford University Press, 1959.

Toulmin, Stephen. "Contemporary Scientific Mythology." In *Metaphysical Beliefs*. Edited by Alasdair MacIntyre. London: SCM Press, 1957.

Townsend, H. G. *The Philosophy of Jonathan Edwards, from his Private Notebooks*. Eugene: University of Oregon Press, 1955.

Tracy, David. *Blessed Rage for Order*. New York: Seabury Press, 1975.

Wargelin, R. Alvar. "Metaphor Versus Symbol in Man's Relationship to Nature." *The Lutheran Quarterly* 23:4 (November 1971):356-65.

Weber, Max. *The Protestant Ethic and the Spirit of Capitalism*. Translated by Talcott Parsons. New York: Charles Scribner's Sons, 1958.

Weisberg, Barry. *Beyond Repair: The Ecology of Capitalism*. Boston: Beacon Press, 1971.

von Weizsacker, C. F. *The History of Nature*. Translated by Fred D. Wieck. Chicago: University of Chicago Press, 1949; Phoenix Books, 1966.

Westerman, Claus. *Creation*. Translated by John J. Scullion. Philadelphia: Fortress Press, 1974.

——————— *The Genesis Accounts of Creation*. Translated by Norman E. Wagner. Philadelphia: Fortress Press, 1964.

White, Alan R., ed. *The Philosophy of Action*. London: Oxford University Press, 1968.

Whitehead, Alfred North. *Adventures of Ideas*. New York: Macmillan Company, 1933.

——————— *Modes of Thought*. New York: Macmillan Company, 1938.

——————— *Science and the Modern World*. New York: Macmillan Company, 1926.

——————— *Process and Reality*. New York: Macmillan Company, 1929.

——————— *Religion in the Making*. New York: Macmillan Company, 1926.

Whitehouse, W. A. "Towards a Theology of Nature." *Scottish Journal of Theology* 17 (1964):129-45.

Whitla, William. "Sin and Redemption in Whitehead and Teilhard de Chardin." *Anglican Theological Review* 47:1 (January 1965):81-95.

Whitney, Barry L. "Process Theism: Does a Persuasive God Coerce?" *The Southern Journal of Philosophy* 17 (Spring 1979):133-43.

Wilman, Henry Nelson. *The Source of Human Good*. Carbondale: Southern Illinois University Press, 1946.

Wildiers, N. M. *An Introduction to Teilhard de Chardin*. Translated by Hubert Hoskins. New York: Harper & Row, 1968.

Williams, Daniel Day. *The Spirit and the Forms of Love*. New York: Harper & Row, 1968.

Williams, George H. *Wilderness and Paradise in Christian Thought*. New York: Harper & Brothers, 1962.

Wittgenstein, Ludwig. *Philosophical Investigations*. Translated by C. E. M. Anscombe. Oxford: Basil Blackwell, 1953.

Worster, Donald. *Nature's Economy: The Roots of Ecology*. San Francisco: Sierra Club Books, 1977.

Wright, G. Ernest, and Fuller, Reginald H. *The Book of the Acts of God*. Garden City NY: Doubleday & Company; Anchor Books, 1960.

Young, Norman. *Creator, Creation and Faith*. Philadelphia: Westminster Press, 1976.

INDEX

Actual entities, 117-22, 132n, 133, 134, 135, 140, 149n, 151, 152, 153n, 156, 240, 241, 242, 245n, 249, 253
Aquinas, Thomas, 166, 181, 239

Barbour, Ian, 5, 147n, 162-67, 248, 249, 261
Barth, Karl, 48-49, 52-55, 58, 61, 63, 67, 70-71, 74, 86, 106-107, 108, 109n, 131, 238
Benedict of Nursia, 16, 21-23
Bonifazi, Conrad, 24-26, 31, 274n
Buber, Martin, 74, 75, 77, 78n

Call forward, 126-27, 243
Calvin, John, 1, 9-10, 39, 54, 58-59, 61, 65, 153, 292
Christ: person and work, 14, 96, 110, 112-13, 131, 148-49, 182-222, 226-27, 250-52, 298
Church, 45-50, 210-15
Cobb, John B., Jr., 6, 53, 89-160, 194, 198-99, 218, 227, 231, 233, 237-47, 249-54, 255n, 264, 274-75, 291-92
Complexification, 119, 168-82, 239-43, 245, 250
Concrescence, 118, 119, 132, 240, 242
Cox, Harvey, 31, 46-48
Creation, doctrine of, 6-15, 99, 135, 139, 146, 215-22, 229, 244-50, 292,
Creative transformation, 101, 113, 141-48, 149n, 251

Dipolar theism, 128-29, 244
Dubos, Rene, 16, 21-23

Edwards, Jonathan, 71-73
Elder, Frederick, 30-34, 204-205
Enduring objects, 114n, 120-22, 135-36
Enjoyment, 119-20, 122-24, 132-36, 138
Eternal objects, 118, 132
Ethics, 3, 15, 42, 79-82, 105, 116-17, 123-25, 142, 148-51, 152, 158, 246, 250, 252-54

Eucharist, 30, 185-86, 191-93, 280
Evil, 68-71, 138-39, 194-203. *See also* theodicy
Existence: axial, 93, 94, 95, 143-44; Christian, 93-97, 99, 100, 109n, 113, 125n, 141-51; structures of, 91-102, 111, 141-49, 157-58
Existentialism, 91-92, 97-98, 101, 103, 104, 117, 154

Feeling (prehension), 117-21, 132, 156
Francis of Assisi, 16-23, 86-87, 146

Gilkey, Langdon, 7n, 8, 246
God: consequent nature of, 129-30, 250; creative-responsive love, 125-33, 136, 151, 159, 251; primordial nature of, 131-32, 149n, 250, 251. *See also* Models of the God-world relationship
Griffin, David Ray, 90, 251n

Hartshorne, Charles, 116, 126, 127, 128-29, 130, 137, 153, 240, 250
Hegel, G. W. F., 103, 156

Image of God, 11-13, 75, 145, 146
Initial aim, 132, 149n

Kant, Immanuel, 2, 51, 58, 103, 108, 123
Kaufman, Gordon, 13n, 156n, 157n, 271, 273, 285
Kirkpatrick, Frank, 266, 268-70, 273-74, 289

Luther, Martin, 58-59, 65, 153

Macmurray, John, 24, 271n, 287-90
Models of the God-world relationship, 255-58, 276-77; agential, 268-76, 278-81, 286-92; deistic, 259; dialogical, 259-61; familial, 19-21, 86-87; mechanical-utilitarian, 2-4, 259-61; monnarchical, 20, 84-88, 261-63, 278-81; processive-organic, 263-68, 278-81; theatrical, 1-2, 4, 292

Natural theology and the theology of
    nature, 34-35, 50-56, 91, 106, 108-15,
    162-67, 237-38, 251
Nature, definition of, 50-51, 114-15, 154,
    155, 156, 238-50, 283-86
Niebuhr, H. Richard, 57, 71-72, 80, 83,
    261, 292, 294-300
Novelty, 121-22, 127, 135, 136, 149n,
    241, 245, 246, 249

Omega Point, 181-84, 252

Paradigm, 226, 256-58, 276-77, 293-300
Persuasion, 131-34, 137, 140, 153, 245
Pleromization (Pleroma), 209-22, 249-50

Rauschenbusch, Walter, 57, 87
Reality, 117, 123, 124, 156, 246, 249

Santmire, H. Paul, 6, 39-88, 109n, 112,
    119, 125, 131, 151-53, 204-205, 237-40,
    241n, 243, 245, 248, 250, 252-54, 263,
    274, 291-92
Satisfaction, 118, 133
Self-conscious self-transcendence, 96,
    100, 101, 148
Sittler, Joseph, 27-30, 31, 292

Society, 120, 121, 122
Subjective aim, 118, 132

Teilhard, de Chardin, Pierre, 6, 30, 31,
    62, 81-82, 119, 161-234, 237-50, 252,
    254, 274-75, 291-92
Temple, William, 193, 219, 225, 246
Theodicy, 68-71, 116, 136-40, 249
Tillich, Paul, 24, 58, 82, 106-108, 113,
    128
Tracy, David, 110-11
Trinitization, 249-50

Value theory, 1-6, 35, 40-50, 56-60,
    71-78, 119, 121-24, 125, 134-36, 139,
    147, 152, 153, 156, 157, 252-54, 278-81
Vision of reality, 91, 92, 97-102,
    102-108, 110, 111, 113, 115-40, 141,
    142, 145, 148-51, 240, 251, 253

White, Lynn, 16-23, 31, 40
Whitehead, A. N., 28, 89, 98, 103, 111-15,
    115-16, 117-22, 124, 125-33, 135,
    137-39, 143, 152-54, 156, 159n, 166,
    225, 230, 239, 240, 241, 242, 246, 250,
    254, 264-68, 287-89

DATE DUE

~~MAR 26 1991~~			
MAY 2 0 1992			
MAY 1 0 1994			